ELECTRONICS SERVICING VOL. 2
(Analogue and Digital Core Studies
and Science Background)

D1438232

ELECTRONICS SERVICING VOL. 2 (Analogue and Digital Core Studies and Science Background)

K. J. Bohlman
I.Eng., F.I.E.I.E.

Dickson Price Publishers Ltd
Hawthorn House
Bowdell Lane
Brookland
Romney Marsh
Kent TN29 9RW

Dickson Price Publishers Ltd
Hawthorn House
Bowdell Lane
Brookland
Romney Marsh
Kent TN29 9RW

First published 1993
© K. J. Bohlman 1993

British Library Cataloguing in Publication Data
A catalogue record for this book is
available from the British Library

ISBN 0-85380-177-0

Photoset by
R. H. Services, Welwyn, Hertfordshire
Printed and bound in Great Britain by
The Bath Press, Avon.

CONTENTS

Contents

PREFACE

THIS VOLUME FULLY covers the Core Studies (Analogue and Digital Electronics Technology) and Science background sections for Part 2 of the City and Guilds 224 Course in Electronics Servicing.

Presented in the new format of Volume 1, which has proved so popular with students and lecturers, the style of the previous editions has been retained to provide the student with essential background reading and to link many of the syllabus topics together in an interesting and enlightening manner.

The qualified electronics servicing technician in today's rapidly expanding world of electronics technology has to take on board many new concepts and readily apply diagnostic skills to advanced electronic and communications systems. The technician will be better equipped to do so if initial training stems from a good understanding of basic electronic principles.

K. J. Bohlman
Lincoln, 1993

Other Books of Interest

Part 1
Electronics Servicing Vol 1 (Electronic Systems and Science Background)
Electronics Servicing 500 Q & A (Revision)

Part 2
Electronics Servicing Vol 2 (Analogue and Digital Core Studies and Science Background)
Electronics Servicing Vol 3 (Control Systems Technology)
Electronics Servicing Vol 4 (Radio and Television)
Electronics Servicing 500 Q & A (Revision)
Fault Location in Electronic Equipment

Part 3
Digital Techniques
Colour and Mono Television Vol 2
Colour and Mono Television Vol 3
Principles of Domestic Video Recording and Playback Systems
Video Recording and Playback Systems 500 Q & A (Revision)

Inspection Copies

Lecturers wishing to examine any of these books should write to the publishers requesting an inspection copy.

Complete Catalogue available on request.

CHAPTER ONE

BASIC THEORY OF SEMICONDUCTORS

Objectives

1 To outline the properties of semiconductor materials.
2 To explain conduction in pure semiconductors.
3 To explain how current flows in P-type and N-type materials.

MOST MATERIALS USED in electronic engineering fall clearly into the class of conductor or insulator. There are a number of materials in between these classes called semiconductors which have become vitally important and form the basis of the whole semiconductor industry.

PROPERTIES OF SEMICONDUCTOR MATERIALS

Resistivity

The name 'semiconductor' suggests that it has a conductivity lying somewhere between that of an insulator and that of a conductor. A good insulator such as polystyrene has a resistivity of the order of 10^{16}ohm-metre whereas the resistivity of a good conductor, e.g. copper, is approximately 10^{-8}ohm-metre. Semiconductor materials have intermediate resistivity values as shown in Fig. 1.1. For example, the semiconductor silicon of the type used in the manufacture of transistors may have a resistivity of about 1 ohm-metre at 20°C. Thus one property of a semiconductor lies in its resistivity value, typically in the range of 0·01 ohm-metre to 1 ohm-metre.

Effect of Temperature

It would be wrong to assume that any

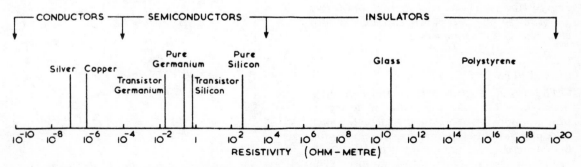

Fig. 1.1 Comparison of resistivity values.

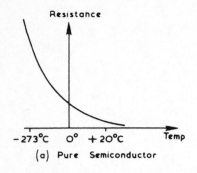
(a) Pure Semiconductor

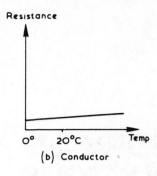
(b) Conductor

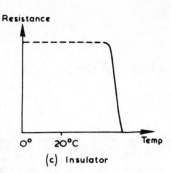
(c) Insulator

Fig. 1.2 Effect of temperature on resistance.

material with a resistivity of this order is a semiconductor (this value could be fabricated by mixing materials with high and low resistivities in suitable proportions). The semiconductor has other characteristics one of which is that it has a negative temperature coefficient of resistance, i.e. its resistance decreases with an increase in temperature. This is shown in Fig. 1.2(a), the resistance decreasing in a non-linear (exponential) manner as the temperature is raised. In contrast the resistance of a metallic conductor increases in direct proportion to the temperature, Fig. 1.2(b). This positive temperature coefficient of resistance is typical of all good conductors. The high insulation resistance of a good insulator does not appreciably change with temperature until a comparatively high temperature is reached at which point the resistance falls rapidly and the material becomes conductive (i.e. the insulator 'breaks down'). Like the semiconductor, the insulator exhibits a negative temperature coefficient of resistance, see Fig. 1.2(c). The difference between the insulator and semiconductor is therefore one of degree: the semiconductor being conductive at normal room temperature and the insulator at some higher temperature.

Crystal Form

The crystal structure of the materials used in the manufacture of semiconductor devices is rather important. When industrial metals such as copper solidify they produce a polycrystalline structure, i.e. many small crystals grow each of different size and orientation. The small crystals or grains fail to fit exactly where

they meet causing areas between the grains called 'grain boundaries'. Such a crystal structure would be unsuitable for use in semiconductor devices since the grain boundaries would interfere with the motion of current through the material. Also, the electrical properties of apparently identical manufactured devices would most probably be quite different. Thus in the preparation of the materials used in practical devices the aim is to produce a perfect crystal, as then the more predictable will be its electrical properties.

The atoms in a perfect crystal arrange themselves into a regular geometric pattern which is repeated throughout the dimensions of the crystal. When the semiconductors germanium and silicon crystallise, the atoms arrange themselves into a regular cubic pattern or lattice as in Fig. 1.3.

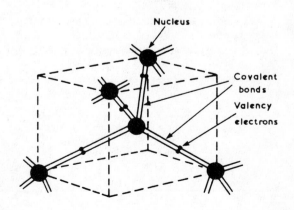

Fig. 1.3 Cubic crystal structure of germanium and silicon.

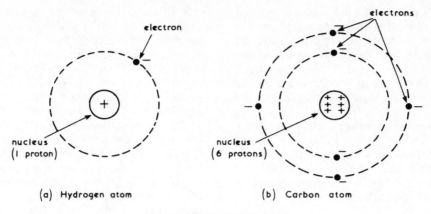

Fig. 1.4 Simple atomic structure.

ATOMS

All materials are built up from molecules. A molecule is the smallest particle of material that can exist and still retain its original properties. In general, each molecule of a material is composed of smaller particles known as **atoms**. Materials formed by one type of atom only are called **elements**; there are approximately 100 elements known to science today. Some elements such as oxygen, hydrogen and carbon exist in large quantities and others are relatively rare, e.g. gold, plutonium and radium. In nature, one element rarely occurs separately from other elements. More often, elements exist in mixtures and in chemical combinations to form compounds. Water is a compound comprising two atoms of hydrogen and one atom of oxygen for each molecule.

Although different, atoms of all types of element have a common characteristic. They all consist of a **positively-charged central nucleus** around which rotate at a very high velocity one or more minute **negatively-charged** particles called **electrons**. The central nucleus contains two types of particles: **protons** exhibiting positive charges; and **neutrons** (except for the hydrogen atom) which are of zero electrical charge. The rotating electrons may all be in one orbit or a number of orbits. The number of protons and electrons in a normal atom are equal to one another and since their charges are equal in magnitude but opposite in sign they cancel out. Thus a normal atom is electrically neutral.

Examples of the structures of hydrogen and carbon atoms are shown in Fig. 1.4. The electrostatic attraction of the unlike charges of the electrons and protons provides the force required to maintain the electrons in their orbits. This force prevents the electrons from escaping from the atom, whilst the electron motion prevents them from plunging into the nucleus. With more complex atoms other orbits or 'shells' are used by the rotating electrons. The **maximum** number of electrons that can exist in any shell is the same for all elements, see Table 1. The first (inner) shell is

TABLE 1

Shell	Maximum number electrons for all atoms	Germanium atom (electrons per shell)	Silicon atom (electrons per shell)
1st	2	2	2
2nd	8	8	8
3rd	18	18	4 (outer shell)
4th	8	4 (outer shell)	–

full with 2 electrons, the second with 8 electrons, the third with 18 electrons and the fourth with 8 electrons. Electrons having the least energy occupy the inner shell and are tightly bound to the atom. On the other hand, electrons with the greatest energy occupy the outer shell and are loosely attached to the atom.

The electrons in the outer shell or orbit of an atom are called the 'valency electrons'. Since electrons in the outer shell are more easily detached from the atom it is the valency electrons that take part in chemical reaction and electrical conduction.

COVALENT BONDS

In the category of 'semiconductor' there are many materials. The most common devices – semiconductor diodes and transistors – are made from silicon and germanium and we will confine our attention to these particular materials.

In a germanium atom there are 32 electrons which are therefore grouped into four shells, see Table 1. The silicon atom has 14 electrons arranged in three shells. It will be noted from the table that germanium has an incomplete fourth shell (maximum number is 8 electrons) whilst silicon has an incomplete third shell (maximum number is 18 electrons) When a shell is incomplete it will try to make up the number from outside. One way of doing this is to form a 'covalent bond' with a neighbouring atom. The idea of covalent bonds is shown in Fig. 1.5 which is a two-dimensional representation of the crystal lattice structure of Fig. 1.3.

The silicon atoms (Si) used in the diagram are shown only with their valency electrons; the inner shell electrons do not interest us. Each atom shares its valency electrons with neighbouring Si atoms thus in some respects the atoms behave as if they had 8 electrons in their outer shells. The third shell is stable when either 8 or 18 electrons are present. It is the sharing of valency electrons by neighbouring atoms that provides the covalent bonds within the crystal and keeps the atoms stable. In the diagram all the electrons are engaged in forming covalent bonds thus there are no current carriers available, i.e. the material is acting like an insulator. This condition is true only at absolute zero ($-273°C$).

CONDUCTION IN PURE SEMICONDUCTORS

When energy is supplied to the crystal either in the form of heat or light, the atoms vibrate

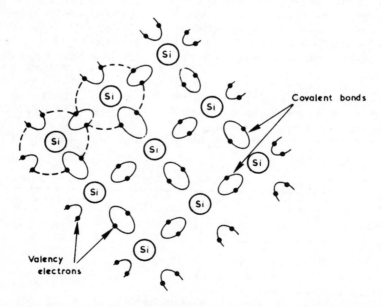

Fig. 1.5 Lattice of silicon atoms showing idea of covalent bonds (electron sharing) at $-273°C$.

and some of the covalent bonds are broken. Thus the condition illustrated in Fig. 1.5. cannot be realised in practice since heat is everywhere.

At normal room temperature (+20°C) the occasional bond is broken and the situation may be expressed diagrammatically as in Fig. 1.6. The thermal energy given to the crystal causes an electron to break away from its orbit and drift in a random manner in the spaces between atoms. Every electron that breaks away from its parent atom leaves behind it a vacancy called a 'hole'. This vacancy or hole which behaves with a unit positive charge equal to one electron can then be filled (due to the attraction of opposite charges) by another drifting electron leaving behind it a vacancy which thus becomes filled again, and so on. We may therefore think of a movement of positively-charged holes in the opposite direction to the movement of the negatively-charged drifting electrons. Holes move more slowly than electrons and so under the application of a p.d. would carry less than 50% of the current.

Thermally generated holes and electrons are produced in pairs and the higher the temperature the greater their production. Thus the conduction in a pure semiconductor, called 'intrinsic conduction', increases with temperature. In particular, the intrinsic conduction of silicon is very much less than that of germanium at a given temperature. This is because more energy is required to break the covalent bonds of silicon atoms than germanium atoms.

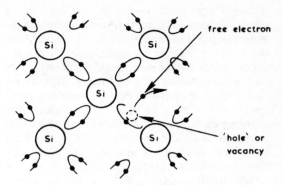

Fig. 1.6 Conduction in pure semiconductor (breaking of covalent bonds at 20°C).

CONDUCTION IN DOPED SEMICONDUCTORS

The materials in the state so far described are seldom used in practical devices since the conductivity at normal temperatures is not high, the conduction is very sensitive to temperature changes and is composed partly of electrons and partly of holes. By the controlled addition of minute traces of impurity to the intrinsic material these disadvantages may be overcome.

N-type Material

If an impurity with atomic dimensions similar to those of the intrinsic material are introduced into the pure material, the impurity atoms can take up a position without seriously disturbing the crystal lattice. The idea is shown in Fig. 1.7(a) where an impurity

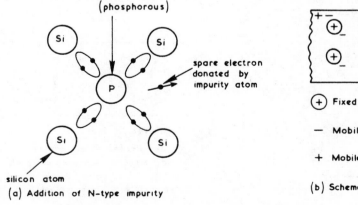

(a) Addition of N-type impurity

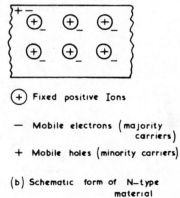

(b) Schematic form of N-type material

Fig. 1.7 N-type material.

atom of phosphorous (P) is 'sitting' in the crystal lattice of silicon atoms. Now, phosphorous has five electrons in its outer shell, thus four of its valency electrons will readily form bonds with neighbouring silicon atoms but the fifth electron is left spare. It is found that very little energy is required to detach the spare electron from its parent atom. The thermal energy at room temperature is sufficient to part most of the spare electrons from their impurity atoms and the electrons can then be used as current carriers.

The amount of impurity added is of the order of 1 impurity atom to every 10^8 intrinsic atoms. Even this minute trace of impurity is sufficient to increase the conductivity by a factor of about 15. The process of adding controlled levels of impurity is called 'doping'. In this case the doping has bestowed N-type conductivity since the charge carriers are negatively-charged electrons. The impurity atoms are sometimes called 'donor atoms' as they give electrons to the lattice. Other examples of N-type impurities (those with five valency electrons) are arsenic and antimony.

When an impurity atom loses an electron its electrical neutrality is upset. Having lost an electron the impurity atom exerts a positive charge and becomes what is called a 'positive ion'. The ion does not move as it is held immobile by the covalent bonds; only the donated electrons are free to move. In diagrams, N-type material is often represented as shown in Fig. 1.7(b). It should be remembered that there will also be electrons

and holes produced by the breaking of bonds of the intrinsic atoms as previously explained. However, in N-type material at normal temperatures the density of the donated electrons is greater than the thermally generated holes. Thus in N-type material the electrons are referred to as the **majority carriers** and the holes the **minority carriers**.

P-type Material

The opposite type of conductivity can be obtained by adding minute quantities of impurities that have only three electrons in their outer shells. The idea is shown in Fig. 1.8(a) using a boron (B) impurity atom. The three valency electrons of the boron atom will readily form covalent bonds with the valency electrons of three neighbouring silicon atoms. However, the fourth lattice valency is short of an electron and this vacancy behaves like a hole, i.e. with a positive charge influence. Very little energy is required to attract a nearby valency electron (from a silicon atom) to the hole which thus becomes filled and the hole moves away from the impurity atom (to a silicon atom). At room temperature the thermal energy given to the crystal is sufficient to fill nearly all the holes created by the addition of the impurity.

In this case the doping has given P-type conductivity to the pure material since the carriers are positively-charged holes. The impurity atoms are called 'acceptors' because the holes created accept electrons from the

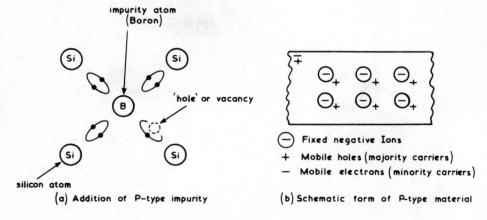

(a) Addition of P-type impurity

(b) Schematic form of P-type material

Fig. 1.8 P-type material.

crystal lattice. Other P-type impurities are gallium and indium.

When the impurity atom gains an electron its electrical neutrality is upset. Having gained an electron the impurity atom exerts a negative charge and becomes a 'negative ion'. Again, the ion does not move as it is held immobile by the covalent bonds; only the holes are free to move. In diagrams, P-type material is often represented as in Fig. 1.8(b). As for the N-type material there will also be electrons and holes produced by the breaking of bonds in the intrinsic material. However, in P-type material at normal temperatures the density of the holes is greater than that of the thermally generated electrons. Thus in P-type material the holes are referred to as the **majority carriers** and the electrons as the **minority carriers**.

The special conductivity of both N-type and P-type materials is called 'extrinsic conduction' since it is due to the addition of impurities to the pure semiconductor. In their separate forms both P-type and N-type materials are electrically neutral since the charge of the fixed ion is balanced by the opposite charge of the mobile carrier.

Current Flow

If a p.d. is applied to an extrinsic semiconductor there will be a drift of charge carriers from one end of the material to the other.

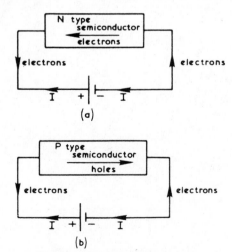

Fig. 1.9 Current flow in N-type and P-type semiconductors.

With N-type material and an external battery arranged as in Fig. 1.9(a) there will be a drift of electrons from right to left within the material. In the wires of the external circuit, current is supported by the movement of electrons in an anticlockwise direction moving into the material at the right-hand side and leaving the material at the left-hand side. The current (I) by convention moves clockwise around the circuit. With P-type material, Fig. 1.9(b), holes move from left to right within the material. In the external circuit however, current can only be supported by electron movement and for every hole arriving at the right-hand side of the material an electron is received from the external circuit. It will be noted that conventional current (I) is in the same direction as hole movement.

QUESTIONS ON CHAPTER ONE

(1) The resistivity of semiconductors is typically:
 (a) 10^{-6} to 10^{-8} ohm-metre
 (b) 10^{6} to 10^{8} ohm-metre
 (c) 10^{12} to 10^{14} ohm-metre
 (d) 0·01 to 1 ohm-metre.

(2) A positive temperature coefficient of resistance is typified by:
 (a) Insulators
 (b) Conductors
 (c) Semiconductors
 (d) Silicon.

(3) An atom consists of:
 (a) A negatively-charged nucleus and orbiting positive charges
 (b) A positively-charged nucleus and orbiting negative charges
 (c) A positively-charged nucleus and orbiting neutrons
 (d) Electrons and holes in equal numbers.

(4) The semiconductor silicon atom has:
 (a) 3 valency electrons
 (b) 4 valency electrons
 (c) 8 valency electrons
 (d) No valency electrons.

(5) Intrinsic conduction occurs only in:
    (a) Pure and doped semiconductors
    (b) Doped semiconductors
    (c) Pure semiconductors
    (d) Silicon.

(6) Extrinsic conduction occurs only in:
    (a) Pure and doped semiconductors
    (b) Doped semiconductors
    (c) Pure semiconductors
    (d) Silicon.

(7) The majority charge carriers in N-type material are:
    (a) Electrons
    (b) Holes
    (c) Positive ions
    (d) Negative ions.

(8) The addition of an impurity atom having five valency electrons to pure germanium will cause the material to become:
    (a) Non-conductive
    (b) P-type
    (c) N-type
    (d) More thermally sensitive.

(Answers on page 369)

CHAPTER TWO

SEMICONDUCTOR DIODES

Objectives
1 To explain the action of a p-n junction under forward and reverse bias.
2 To study the characteristics and construction of p-n diodes.
3 To explain the action of a p-n diode rectifier.
4 To outline the characteristics and uses of varactor, zener and point-contact diodes.

A SEMICONDUCTOR OR p-n diode device is obtained from the junction formed by separate areas of extrinsic germanium or silicon one of which has P-type conductivity and the other N-type, Fig. 2.1. Nearly all the important effects that occur in semiconductor devices take place in the region of the junction between different materials. The most important of these is the low resistance offered by the junction to the flow of current in one direction and high resistance in the other direction, a characteristic that is always present.

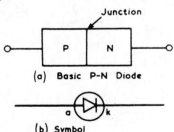

(a) Basic P-N Diode

(b) Symbol

Fig. 2.1 Semiconductor diode.

THE P-N JUNCTION

There are a number of methods used in the fabrication of p-n junctions and some will be described later. Current techniques use a single crystal to form the junction with suitable 'doping' applied to provide a change in the semiconductor from N-type to P-type. This change may be abrupt as in Fig. 2.2 or may occupy many lattice spacings of the crystal. A junction cannot properly be formed by taking a piece of N-type material and joining it to a section of P-type.

Figure 2.2 shows a small section of a p-n diode in the vicinity of the junction but at this point no external connections are made. When the junction is first formed, larger numbers of electrons wander from left to right across the junction than in the opposite direction since the N-region contains many electrons but the P-region only a few. Similarly, more holes wander across the junction from right to left rather than in the opposite direction as the P-region contains many more holes than the N-region. This initial exchange of carriers across the junction is due to 'diffusion', a process whereby electrons and holes spread out from their respective concentrations to try to occupy the space uniformly. Another example of diffusion is the mixing of a dye (e.g. ink) in an unstirred glass of water. This initial diffusion process in the p-n junction is not electronically based.

The two separate areas to start with were of the same potential (zero). However as the

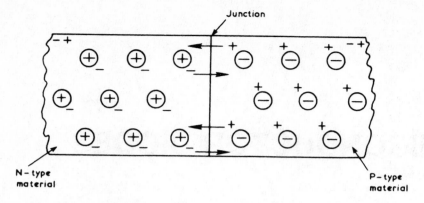

Fig. 2.2 Small section of p-n junction (showing initial diffusion of majority carriers).

diffusion process progresses the N-side gains holes and loses electrons and the P-side gains electrons and loses holes. The N-region having lost electrons and gained holes acquires a positive charge whereas the P-region having lost holes and gained electrons assumes a negative charge. Thus a potential difference is established across the junction with the P-region negative with respect to the N-region, see Fig. 2.3(a). This p.d. is called the 'diffusion p.d.' or 'barrier p.d.' Majority electrons and holes from either side now crossing the junction have to work **against** a rising p.d. Some of these carriers will have greater energy than others, overcoming the p.d. and so cross the junction thereby causing the p.d. to rise. This will reduce the numbers of majority carriers subsequently crossing and the action will become self-limiting. Pictorially, the diffusion p.d. may be represented by a fictitious battery as in Fig. 2.3(b). The diffusion p.d. cannot be measured with a voltmeter; when connections are made to the N and P sides, two p.d.s will appear at the

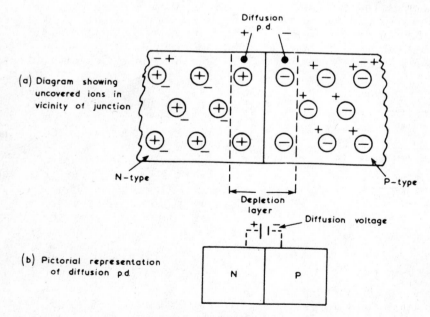

Fig. 2.3 Diffusion p.d. and depletion layer.

connections. These will have a net value that will exactly balance the diffusion p.d. This must be so otherwise the diffusion voltage would be a perpetual source of energy.

Depletion Layer

When the majority carriers diffuse across the junction they recombine thereby neutralising one another. This causes a lack of charge carriers in the immediate vicinity of the junction and the immobile ions are 'uncovered', see Fig. 2.3(a). This area of uncovered ions (positive ions on the N-side and negative ions on the P-side) is called the 'depletion layer' because it is depleted of mobile charge carriers. Typically the width of the depletion layer is about 0·0001 cm, or 1μm.

Junction Under Bias Conditions

Figure 2.4(a) represents a p-n diode in schematic form with **ohmic** connections made to the separate areas. An ohmic connection is a non-rectifying one.

Reverse Bias

When an external supply (V_r) is connected with polarity as indicated in Fig. 2.4(b), the junction is said to be 'reverse biased'. Under this condition the external voltage subjects the majority carriers of each region to an electric field which draws them away from the junction. This action causes more immobile ions to be uncovered thereby increasing the width of the depletion layer and so increasing the diffusion p.d. Due to the rise in the diffusion p.d., majority carriers (electrons from the N-region and holes from the P-region) find it more difficult to cross the junction and in consequence the actual numbers of majority carriers crossing decrease. The rise in diffusion p.d. will however aid the passing of minority carriers (holes from the N-region and electrons from the P-region). The net current crossing the junction is composed of a small number of minority carriers as indicated by the arrow heads in the diagram. This condition corresponds to the 'non-conducting' or 'cut-off' state of the p-n diode when it may be regarded as almost an open circuit. When the reverse voltage is large, the rise in diffusion p.d. reaches a point where no majority carriers cross the junction. In this case only minority carriers make the crossing, but they are small in numbers.

In the external connecting wires, current can only be supported by electron movement. Thus when minority electrons crossing from right to left arrive at the left-hand ohmic connection they will pass into the connecting wire and move towards the positive terminal of the supply. When minority holes moving from left to right reach the right-hand ohmic connection they will receive electrons from the negative terminal of the supply and become neutralised.

Forward Bias

If the polarity of the external voltage is changed to that shown in Fig. 2.4(c), the junction is said to be 'forward biased'. In this condition the external voltage (V_f) exerts a force on the majority carriers urging them closer to the junction thereby reducing the number of 'uncovered' ions. In consequence, the width of the depletion layer is reduced which causes the diffusion p.d. to fall. As a result large numbers of majority carriers are able to cross the junction since majority electrons and holes of lower energy will find the diffusion p.d. surmountable. A large current now flows across the junction and this condition corresponds to the 'conducting' or 'on' state when the junction is of low resistance.

Majority carriers crossing the junction are indicated by the arrow heads in Fig. 2.4(c). The majority electrons crossing from the left will recombine with holes in the P-material almost immediately they have crossed the junction. For every recombination that occurs an electron is given up from an area close to the right-hand ohmic connection to the positive terminal of the supply. For every electron 'sucked-off' in this way by the supply, a hole is created which moves towards the junction. Majority holes crossing the junction from the right will recombine with electrons in the N-material. For each recombination that takes place, an electron is given up by the negative terminal of the supply, enters the crystal by way of the left-hand ohmic connection and subsequently moves towards the

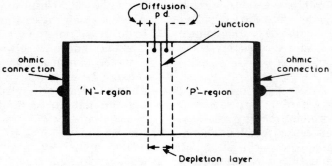

(a) Junction without external connections showing
width of depletion layer

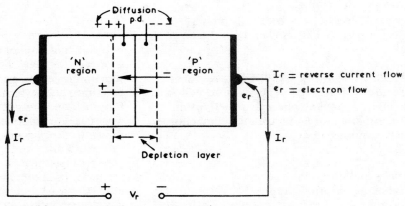

I_r = reverse current flow

e_r = electron flow

(b) Junction under Reverse Bias (small numbers
of minority carriers cross junction)

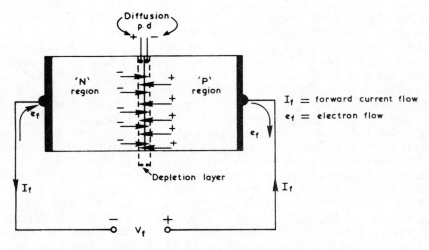

I_f = forward current flow

e_f = electron flow

(c) Junction under Forward Bias (large numbers
of majority carriers cross junction)

Fig. 2.4 Diode-like property of p-n junction.

junction. Thus again in the external circuit, current is supported by electron movement only. Note however that the large forward current (I_f) is in the opposite direction to the small reverse current (I_r).

The term 'diode' in p-n diode means two electrodes which are called 'anode' and 'cathode' (as used in the thermionic diode valve). To place a p-n diode in the forward bias condition or low resistance state, the anode terminal *a* of Fig. 2.1(b) must be made positive with respect to the cathode terminal *k*. The arrow in the symbol points the direction of conventional current flow.

Typical Characteristic of P-N Diode

The graph of Fig. 2.5 shows the relationship between the current in a p-n diode and the voltage drop across it. As the voltage is increased from zero in the forward direction, the diffusion p.d. of the junction is reduced and majority carriers cross the junction in increasing numbers. Further increases in forward voltage increases not only the number of carriers crossing but also their speed of travel. Thus, as the diffusion p.d. is overcome by the applied voltage and it falls almost to zero, the forward current rises rapidly in exponential form.

When the polarity of the applied voltage is

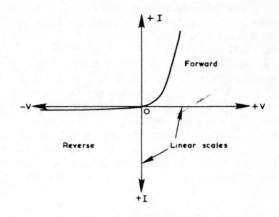

Fig. 2.5 Voltage–current characteristic of p-n diode.

reversed and gradually increased, the current rises a little at first and then settles down to a constant but very small value. At this steady level, the current passing across the junction is due entirely to minority carriers. The characteristic illustrates the almost perfect rectifier action of the p-n diode.

For practical purposes the scales of Fig. 2.5 are adjusted so that we can see more clearly the usual high-current, low-voltage operation in the forward direction and the high-voltage, low-current operation in the reverse direction. In Fig. 2.6 the scales have been adjusted. The

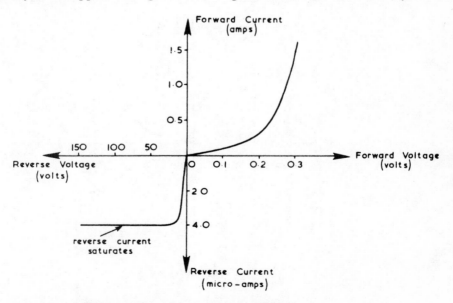

Fig. 2.6 Voltage and current scales adjusted.

forward current commences its steep upward swing at a very low forward voltage of somewhere between 0·2V and 0·3V for a germanium device and 0·6V to 0·8V for a silicon diode. At these low forward voltages a significantly large current can be sustained. In the reverse bias state the reverse current saturates in this example at about 4μA. If this value is compared with a forward current of say 1A, the forward current is $2·5 \times 10^5$ greater than the reverse flow. Here, we are using a Ge diode as an example; in a silicon type the reverse current is very much smaller.

Effect of Temperature

The effect of a rise in temperature on the characteristics of a p-n diode (Ge type assumed) is illustrated by Fig. 2.7. Raising the temperature increases the number of minority carriers generated and as these carriers are responsible for the reverse current the reverse saturation level will increase. Roughly, for each increase of 5°C for silicon and 8°C for germanium the reverse current is doubled. Although the rate of increase is greater for silicon, the absolute numbers of minority carriers are very much less than for germanium. Therefore, silicon is chosen for semiconductor junctions which have to work at

high temperature (150°C max. for silicon and 85°C max. for germanium).

In the forward direction, the thermal energy given to the device during a temperature rise increases the energy of the carriers and there is a rise in the forward current. When maintaining a given current the **voltage drop** across the diode decreases by approximately 2mV for every degree C rise in temperature for germanium and silicon. In the example, with a given current of 0·7A and a temperature rise of 8°C the voltage drop across the diode decreases by 16mV.

The temperature of a junction may rise due to an increase in the surrounding air temperature (ambient temperature) or as a direct result of power dissipated within the device under forward or reverse bias conditions. In both cases the rise of current that follows modifies the voltage–current characteristic. An increase in reverse current causes a rise in the power dissipated and hence an increase in junction temperature. This creates more minority carriers causing an increase in reverse current, the power dissipated rises producing a further increase in the junction temperature, and so on. The current continues to rise as the temperature of the junction grows, creating a cumulative effect known as 'thermal runaway', which may eventually

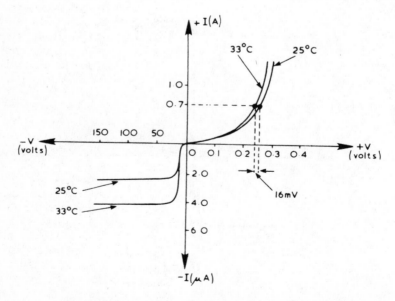

Fig. 2.7 Effect of temperature rise on characteristic.

destroy the diode unless the current can be limited. This is a condition most likely to arise under high ambient temperature or when the heat transfer (heat sink) is inadequate.

A.C. or Slope Resistance

The **d.c. resistance** of a diode is simply the ratio of the voltage drop (V) across the device to the current (I) passing through it and is measured in ohms. Since the characteristic of the p-n diode is not linear, the d.c. resistance will vary with the point of measurement. Generally, we are interested in the value of resistance offered by active devices such as the p-n diode to **changes in voltage**, i.e. **a.c. resistance**. The a.c. resistance (r_a) of a diode at a particular d.c. voltage is defined as

$$r_a = \frac{\delta V}{\delta I} \text{ ohm}$$

where δ (the Greek letter delta) means a 'small change of'.

The actual value may be ascertained from the characteristics as shown in Fig. 2.8. Clearly, the value will vary with the particular d.c. voltage around which the small change of voltage is taken. As shown, if the same 'small change of voltage' is taken further up the characteristic the resultant 'small change of current' will be greater. As a result the a.c. resistance is less when the slope of the characteristic is large. In the forward direction

its value may vary from tens of ohms to a fraction of an ohm. In the reverse direction, where the slope of the characteristic is extremely small, the a.c. resistance is of the order of thousands of ohms.

Construction of Junction Diodes

There are two main techniques used one of which is shown in Fig 2.9. A small pellet of indium is placed on a thin wafer of N-type germanium and then heated to a temperature above the melting point of indium but below that of germanium. This causes the indium (a P-type impurity) to alloy with the germanium producing on cooling an area in the wafer having P-type conductivity. Thus we now have a germanium wafer that is part P-type and part N-type. The wafer is soldered to a copper or brass base (to provide good heat transfer)

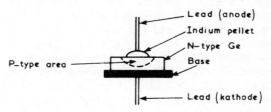

Fig. 2.9 Alloy junction diode.

using a solder rich in antimony. The antimony being an N-type impurity prevents the formation of another junction during the process of soldering, i.e. an ohmic contact is created. Leads are then attached to the indium pellet and base. The device is then hermetically sealed in a case of metal and glass or metal and ceramic to exclude moisture and impurities which can cause deterioration. This method is known as the 'alloying process'. Silicon alloy juction diodes can be made in the same way using a wafer of N-type silicon and a pellet of aluminium (a P-type impurity).

The other technique is known as the 'diffusion process' and the basic idea is shown in Fig. 2.10 for a germanium juction. P-type germanium is heated to a high temperature (just below the melting point of germanium) and at the same time exposed to an N-type impurity in gaseous form (the element antimony may be used), see Fig. 2.10(a). The gaseous antimony diffuses into the germanium

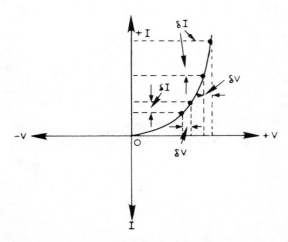

Fig. 2.8 A.C resistance of diode.

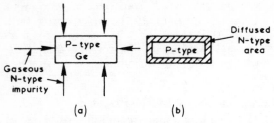

Fig. 2.10 The diffusion method of producing a p-n junction.

to produce an N-type area as shown in Fig. 2.10(b). If a silicon device is required, phosphorous in gaseous form is allowed to diffuse into a section of P-type silicon. The rate at which the impurity gas diffuses depends upon the temperature and may take up to 1–2 hours. This process is more easily controlled than the alloying method.

Silicon junction rectifiers are commonly manufactured using the diffusion process and they are used almost exclusively in the power section of radio and television receivers and other electronic equipment. A typical characteristic of a silicon junction rectifier is given in Fig. 2.11. It is similar to a germanium juction diode (see Fig 2.6) but there are important differences. The forward characteristic is more non-linear and commences its abrupt upward swing at about 0·6 to 0·8V. For a small diode passing about 10mA the forward voltage drop may be about 0·6V, whereas for a larger type passing say 1A the voltage drop may be about 1·0V. In the reverse direction the

current is extremely small and for most practical purposes it is negligible; note that the reverse current scale is nA (10^{-9}A). With any junction diode, if the applied reverse voltage is too high is may cause the junction to break down causing a large reverse current to flow (shown dotted). There is, therefore, a maximum voltage that may be applied in the reverse direction. For a silicon rectifier this may be as high as 2000V as opposed to about 500V for a germanium rectifier. Silicon rectifiers are made to pass currents in the forward direction of up to 1000A. When large currents are required rectifiers may be placed in parallel, and in series when higher voltage ratings are required.

THE P-N DIODE AS A RECTIFIER

In Volume 1 of this series a rectifying unit was shown as a block forming part of a power supply. It is in power supplies that p-n diode(s) may be used as the rectifying unit to convert a.c. to d.c. A simple rectifier circuit (half-wave) is shown in Fig. 2.12 using a p-n diode and a load (represented by a resistor) fed with an alternating voltage at its input.

When terminal A is positive to terminal B during the first half-cycle of the input, the diode is placed in its 'forward' or low resistance state. Thus a current will flow from terminal A through the diode and load and back to the supply at B. During the following half-cycle when the input is negative, terminal

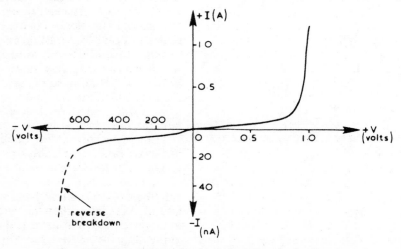

Fig. 2.11 Typical characteristic of silicon junction rectifier.

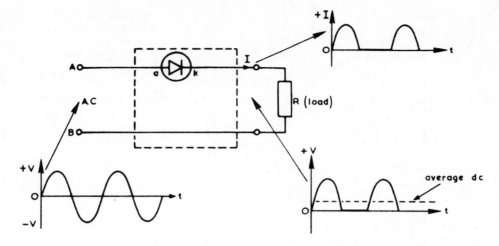

Fig. 2.12 Use of p-n diode in half-wave rectifier circuit.

A is negative to terminal B and the diode is placed in its 'reverse' or high resistance state. If we ignore the small reverse current that flows, no current flows during the negative half-cycle. On the second positive half-cycle of the input, the diode is again placed in the 'forward' state and current flows in the rectifier and load once more. During the second negative half-cycle the diode is placed in the 'reverse' state and again no current flows. Thus the current in the load and hence the voltage across it consist of half-cycles as shown. This is d.c. since the half-cycles are acting in one direction only (positive); they would be in the opposite direction (negative) if the connections of the diode were reversed. The d.c. as it stands would not be smooth enough to provide a d.c. supply for electronic equipment so a smoothing circuit would be required. Further details of complete rectifier circuits including smoothing components are given in Chapter 11.

Current in Rectifier and Resistive Load

The voltage drop across a semiconductor rectifier may be quite small compared with that across the load in some power supplies, in which case it may be neglected. However, it is useful to consider how the value of the peak current flowing in the rectifier and resistive load may be obtained when the voltage drop of the rectifier cannot be neglected.

One method is shown in Fig. 2.13 where the *V–I* characteristic of the rectifier is plotted in the normal way. A straight line or 'load line' representing the resistance of the load is drawn commencing at A and is joined to point B. Point A represents the peak value of the supply voltage (V_{supply}) on the voltage axis. Point B is calculated from

$$\frac{V_{supply}}{\text{load resistance}}$$

and is marked on the current axis. Since the rectifier and load are in series, the current through both must be the same and the sum of rectifier and load voltage drops must equal the supply voltage. The only point that satisfies these conditions is X where the load line cuts the rectifier characteristic. The peak current through each device is now I_p, the voltage across the rectifier OC and that across the load CA.

Choice of Rectifier

When choosing a semiconductor rectifier for a particular application there are a number of points to be considered.

(a) Reverse Voltage Rating. The maximum voltage that a rectifier will withstand in the reverse direction is known as the 'peak inverse voltage' (p.i.v.). The actual voltage across the rectifier in the reverse direction depends , of

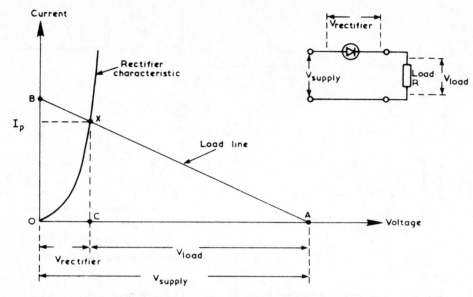

Fig. 2.13 One method of finding the peak current in a rectifier circuit.

course, upon the peak value of the input voltage but also on the type of rectifier circuit used (which is considered in Chapter 11). For the simple circuit of Fig. 2.12 the rectifier must withstand the peak value of the input voltage in the reverse direction. With, say, 240V r.m.s. applied this would be $1 \cdot 414 \times 240 = 339V$. Thus a rectifier with a p.i.v. rating of 500V would be suitable for this circuit.

OK UNTIL CAPACITOR IS ADDED.

(b) Forward Current Rating. When a semiconductor rectifier is passing current there is a small voltage drop in the forward direction, thus dissipating power that appears as heat in the rectifier. Because of the allowable temperature rise of semiconductor devices there is a limit to the power dissipated. There is, therefore, a limit on the mean forward current passing through the rectifier and also a limit to the permissible maximum peak current. For example, the maximum mean or average (d.c.) current may be 160mA for a silicon diode with a maximum peak current rating of 250mA at an ambient temperature of 25°C. At an ambient temperature of 125°C, these absolute maximum current ratings would be reduced to about 50mA and 125mA respectively. In some rectifier circuits, the peak current passing through the rectifier may be very much larger than the steady current delivered to the load.

(c) Rectifier Capacitance. All semiconductor diodes exhibit capacitance between two terminals, the value depending upon the construction of the diode. This capacitance becomes important at high frequencies in diodes selected for signal detection in receivers and high speed switching applications. Although the capacitance of semiconductor diodes may be quite high considering their small size, it is not normally important in rectifiers chosen to convert power frequencies from a.c. to d.c.

In addition to observing the above parameters it is often necessary to ensure that excess voltage even of only a few microseconds duration, is not applied to the rectifier. Short duration voltage spikes or transients of considerable magnitude are present in the mains supply and may be generated inside the electronic equipment in which the rectifier is fitted. Protection against these voltage spikes is provided by a capacitor connected in the circuit, usually across the rectifier.

VARACTOR DIODE

When discussing the action of the p-n junction under reverse and forward bias conditions it was noted that the width of the depletion layer varied with the applied voltage. In particular we saw that when the bias

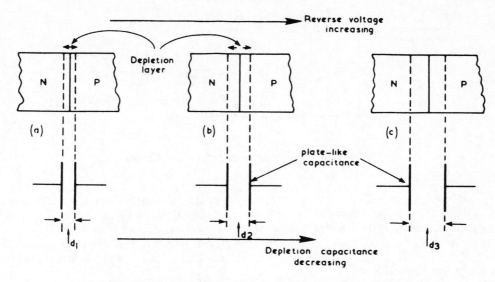

Fig. 2.14 Plate-like capacitance (depletion capacitance) of p-n diode.

was applied in the reverse direction the width of the depletion layer increased causing a rise in the diffusion p.d. The same sort of thing occurs when a voltage is applied to a capacitor. Charges build up on the plates creating a 'back voltage' which opposes the applied voltage. Thus a p-n junction must have a capacitance associated with it.

A p-n junction has a capacitance similar to that of a parallel plate capacitor and the basic idea is shown in Fig. 2.14 where the depletion layer acts as a dielectric and the conductive P and N areas serve as the plates. Fig. 2.14(a) represents the junction in the unbiased state where the distance between the plates is shown as $d1$. As the bias is increased in the reverse direction, the width of the depletion layer is extended and the plate separation increased to $d2$ and $d3$ in Fig. 2.14(b) and (c). Since capacitance is inversely proportional to plate separation, the capacitance of the junction will decrease. Unlike a conventional capacitor, the depletion capacitance varies with the applied voltage and use of this effect is made in Varactor or Variable Capacitance (Vari-Cap) diodes. Although all p-n junctions exhibit this variable capacitance effect it is enhanced in varactor diodes by varying the doping levels of the P and N areas. By heavily doping the P-region and lightly doping the N-region, the depletion capacitance lies mainly in the lightly doped side of the junction.

A typical characteristic is given in Fig. 2.15 where the capacitance varies between a maximum of about 23pF to a minimum of 3pF over a reverse voltage range of say, 5–20V. Other varactor diodes may give a capacitance range of 80pF to 25pF or 12pF to 2·5pF to suit different applications.

The relationship between the capacitance (C) and the reverse voltage (V) is given by

$$C = \frac{k}{\sqrt{V}} \text{ where } k \text{ is a constant}$$

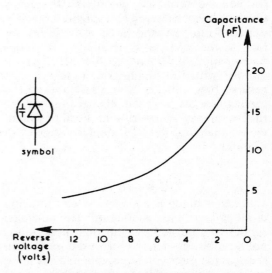

Fig. 2.15 Typical capacitance–voltage characteristic of varactor diode.

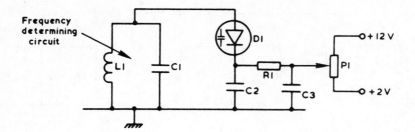

Fig. 2.16 Use of varactor diode for electronic tuning.

Example: A varactor diode has a capacitance of 78pF at a reverse voltage of 2V. What will be its capacitance if the reverse voltage is increased to 10V?

From the above $78 = \dfrac{k}{\sqrt{2}}$

or $k = \sqrt{2} \times 78 = 110 \cdot 3$.

Therefore at 10V

$C = \dfrac{110 \cdot 3}{\sqrt{10}} \text{ pF} = 34 \cdot 88 \text{ pF}.$

Typical applications for varactor diodes include electronic tuning of radio and television receivers and automatic frequency control. A basic circuit showing how a varactor diode may be used to provide electronic tuning is given in Fig. 2.16. Here $L1$, $C1$ form the frequency-determining circuit the frequency of which may be altered by applying a variable voltage from $P1$ to the varactor diode $D1$. As far as the a.c. is concerned, the series combination of $D1$ and $C2$ are effectively in parallel with the tuning circuit, thus as the reverse bias voltage from $P1$ is altered the capacitance of $D1$ will change so varying the frequency of operation. Further circuit details including varactor diodes are given in Chapter 14.

ZENER DIODE

A zener diode is a special silicon junction diode which has a forward characteristic similar to a normal p-n junction diode but is not normally used in the forward direction. In the reverse direction negligible current flows until a certain voltage (called the 'zener voltage') is reached, when the current rises rapidly with little change of voltage across the diode. Operation in this breakdown region does not damage the diode provided the maximum power dissipation for the device is not exceeded. A typical characteristic is given in Fig. 2.17.

The zener or breakdown voltage (which may be altered by varying the impurity levels to set the width of the depletion layer during manufacture) is commonly 2 to 50V, but higher voltage devices are available. Typical zener voltages are $3 \cdot 3$, $5 \cdot 6$, $6 \cdot 2$, $7 \cdot 5$, $10 \cdot 6$, $12 \cdot 6$, $15 \cdot 6$V, etc. The knee of the reverse characteristic is generally more abrupt in the case of the higher-voltage diodes. When selecting a zener diode for a particular application, one must ensure that its power rating is adequate. Devices are available with power dissipations from 100mW to 50W, the larger power diodes requiring heat sinks. Diodes with breakdown voltages above about 5V are also known as 'avalanche' diodes and an alternative name for the family of diodes where use is made of the breakdown effect is 'voltage regulator diodes'. Below about 5V, the effect (zener) causing the large flow of current is the electric field across the junction which is powerful enough to 'pull' electrons away from the valency bonds of the silicon atoms on the P-side which cross the junction to the N-side These carriers then add to the normal reverse current. Above about 5V, breakdown is due to the 'avalanche effect'. The stronger electric field increases the velocity of the electrons 'pulled' away from the silicon covalent bonds and these electrons collide with atoms, causing ionisation. Extra electrons generated in this way add to the number of carriers crossing the junction and subsequently collide with further atoms producing a cumulative process.

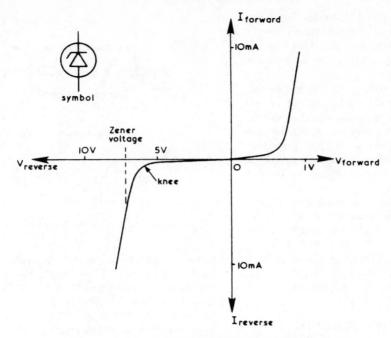

Fig. 2.17 *Typical characteristic of zener diode.*

Zener diodes are commonly used to provide constant voltage sources in stabilised power supplies and a basic circuit is shown in Fig. 2.18. The polarity of the d.c. voltage (V_s) to be stabilised is applied so that the diode is in the reverse bias state and a series resistor (R) is used to ensure that the power rating of the diode is not exceeded. For good stabilisation the power rating of the zener diode should be such that it will carry a current of about four times the expected load current. The value of

the series resistor required may be found from

$$R = \frac{V_s - V_z}{I_d + I_L} \text{ ohm}$$

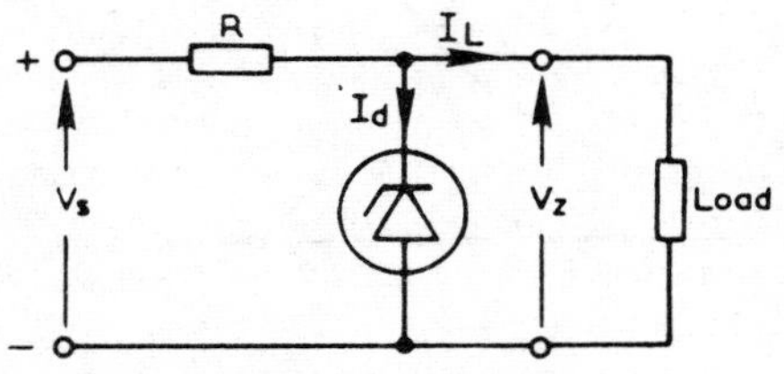

Example:

A 10V zener diode is used to provide a stabilised voltage supply to feed an amplifier demanding a constant current of 20mA. Determine the value of the series resistor required and the power dissipated in the diode if fed from a 20V supply.

$$I_d = 4 \times I_L = 80\text{mA}$$

$$\text{Therefore } R = \frac{V_s - V_z}{I_d + I_L} = \frac{20 - 10}{100 \times 10^{-3}}$$

$$= 100\Omega$$

Power (P) dissipated in diode $= V_z \times I_d$ watts
$= 10 \times 80 \times 10^{-3} = 0{\cdot}8\text{W}.$

The following points should be noted in connection with the operation of the basic circuit of Fig. 2.18.

(a) If the load current increases, the diode current will fall in order to maintain a constant voltage drop across R and hence a constant output voltage.

$V_s =$ unstabilised supply voltage

$V_z =$ zener voltage

$I_d =$ zener diode current

$I_L =$ load current

Fig. 2.18 *Basic stabilizer using zener diode.*

(b) On the other hand if the load current decreases, the diode will pass a larger current to maintain a constant voltage drop across R and hence a constant output voltage.

(c) If the supply voltage (V) is increased, the diode will take a larger current so that extra voltage is dropped across R. Reducing the supply voltage will cause the diode to pass a smaller current so that less voltage is dropped across R thus maintaining a constant output voltage.

Another application for a zener diode is the clipping of various waveforms at a constant voltage level. This use can provide, for example, a waveform of constant amplitude for calibration purposes with the Y-amplifiers of a c.r.o. Further details of circuits using zener diodes are given in Chapter 11.

POINT-CONTACT DIODE

A typical construction for a germanium point-contact diode is given in Fig. 2.19. The diode consists of a small pellet of N-type germanium (about 1mm square) attached to one of the connecting leads and a tungsten wire (or whisker) attached to the other connecting lead. The tip of the tungsten wire is made to press against the germanium pellet to form a 'point contact'. During manufacture, a

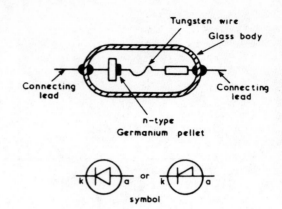

Fig. 2.19 Germanium point-contact diode.

pulse of current is passed through the diode forming an area of P-type material adjacent to the tungsten wire tip. The diode is then sealed in a small glass bulb for protection against moisture and chemicals.

Apart from its small size this diode has the advantage of a low value of capacitance resulting from the small area of p-n junction that is formed. Due to it small capacitance (0·2 to 1pF) it is commonly used as a signal demodulator in radio and television receivers and may also be used for switching in computer applications.

A typical characteristic is given in Fig. 2.20. In the forward (conducting) direction the

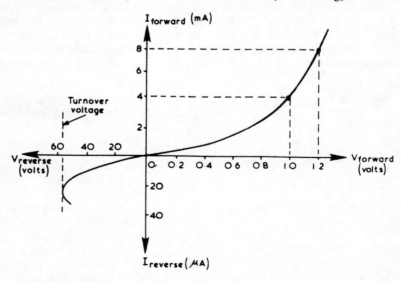

Fig. 2.20 Characteristic of point-contact diode.

voltage drop is small and may be about 1·0V at a current of, say, 4mA rising to about 1·2V at a current of 8mA. In the reverse direction a small reverse current of about 5μA flows with a reverse voltage of 10V rising to 10μA at 40V. At larger reverse voltages the current rises rapidly and a sudden increase occurs if the voltage is increased to a point known as the 'turnover voltage' which varies between about 45V and 150V for the average diode. The maximum reverse voltage applied must be kept well below the turnover voltage.

Because of the very small area of contact between the whisker and germanium pellet, the heat that can be dissipated without excessive temperature rise is severely limited. Thus the rating of the point contact diode is small: a peak current rating of 100mA and a maximum power dissipation of 100mW is typical.

QUESTIONS ON CHAPTER TWO

(1) A p-n junction is normally made by:
   (a) Forming separate areas of P and N material in a single crystal
   (b) Mixing P and N impurities in a single crystal
   (c) Taking a section of P-type material and joining it to a section of N-type
   (d) Joining a germanium crystal to a silicon one.

(2) The diffusion p.d. is:
   (a) The voltage applied to a p-n junction in the reverse direction
   (b) The voltage applied to a p-n junction in the forward direction
   (c) The p-d established across a p-n junction with the P-side positive and the N-side negative
   (d) The p.d. established across a p-n junction with the N-side positive and the P-side negative.

(3) The depletion layer of a p-n junction:
   (a) Is of constant width
   (b) Acts like an insulating zone under reverse bias
   (c) Has a width that increases with an increase in forward bias
   (d) Is depleted of ions.

(4) Under forward bias conditions the current flowing in the supply leads connected to a p-n diode consists of:
   (a) Holes moving from the negative terminal to the positive terminal of the supply
   (b) Electrons moving from the negative terminal to the positive terminal of the supply
   (c) Holes and electrons moving in opposite directions
   (d) Majority carriers only.

(5) The voltage drop across a silicon junction diode with appreciable forward current flow would be about:
   (a) 0·2V
   (b) 3–4V
   (c) 2mV
   (d) 800mV.

(6) When maintaining a given forward current in a p-n diode, the voltage drop across the diode will fall for every degree C rise in temperature by:
   (a) 0·8V
   (b) 40mV
   (c) 2mV
   (d) 5V.

(7) The maximum voltage that a p-n diode rectifier will withstand in the reverse direction is called the:
   (a) Peak-to-peak value
   (b) Mean reverse voltage
   (c) Zener voltage
   (d) Peak inverse voltage.

(8) A point contact diode is normally used for:
   (a) Electronic tuning
   (b) Power rectification
   (c) Signal demodulation
   (d) Voltage stabilisation.

(9) A varactor diode may be used for:
   (a) Automatic frequency control in receivers
   (b) Signal demodulation in receivers
   (c) Voltage stabilisation
   (d) Waveform clipping.

(10) A zener diode is normally operated:
    (a) Above its zener voltage
    (b) Below its zener voltage
    (c) In the 'forward' direction only
    (d) In both the 'forward' and 'reverse'
        directions.

(Answers on page 369)

CHAPTER THREE

THE BIPOLAR TRANSISTOR

Objectives
1 To explain the fundamental action of a bipolar transistor.
2 To show the three basic modes of connection.
3 To study the construction and characteristics.
4 To explain how the current gain varies with collector current.

THE TERM 'TRANSISTOR' is derived from 'transfer-resistor' and is a device transferring the current in a low-resistance circuit to approximately the same current in a high-resistance circuit. Bipolar means that both holes and electrons are involved in the action of the transistor (as in the p-n diode). A bipolar transistor consists of three separate areas of semiconductor as shown in Fig. 3.1. With two outer P-regions and a central N-region we have a P-N-P transistor as in Fig. 3.1(a); if the areas are given opposite type conductivity as in Fig. 3.1(b) an N-P-N transistor is formed. The two outer regions are called the 'emitter e' and 'collector c' and the central region the 'base b'. Although in this

type of diagram emitter and collector regions are shown having the same size this is not so in practice; the collector region is made physically larger as it will normally dissipate the greater power. Both silicon and germanium may be used in the fabrication of the transistor but silicon is more common. The corresponding circuit symbols are given which are similar except for the emitter arrow head. This points in the direction of conventional current flow (or hole movement) through the transistor.

BASIC ACTION

The bipolar transistor consists of two p-n diodes arranged back-to-back thus forming two junctions $J1$ and $J2$, see Fig. 3.2. In normal use the emitter–base junction ($J1$) is forward biased and the base–collector junction ($J2$) is reverse biased. $B1$ provides the forward bias for $J1$ and $B2$ the reverse bias for $J2$.

Suppose that the bias supply for the emitter–base junction is disconnected as in Fig. 3.3. As the base–collector junction is reverse biased, only a small leakage current will flow between base and collector. This current comprises (in the transistor) minority carriers only; holes moving from base to collector and electrons moving from collector to base regions. If a high resistance load were

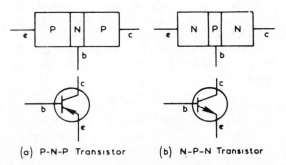

(a) P-N-P Transistor   (b) N-P-N Transistor

Fig. 3.1 P-N-P and N-P-N bipolar transistors.

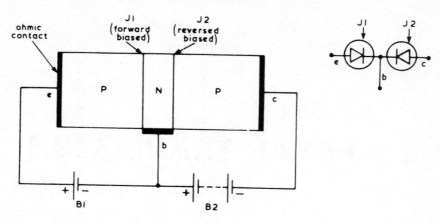

Fig. 3.2 Principle of operation of bipolar transistor (P-N-P).

included in series with the collector lead, the power developed would be quite small since the current is very small. Quite high powers could be obtained if extra current carriers could be made available from some other source; this is the purpose of the forward biased emitter–base junction. If the source of the extra carriers is of low power, the device becomes an amplifier, i.e. the output power exceeds the input power. *+ Supply Power*

Consider now Fig. 3.4, where the forward bias supply for the base–emitter junction has been reconnected. With the emitter–base junction in the forward bias state a large current will flow between the emitter and base regions. This current is composed of holes moving from emitter to base and electrons moving from base to emitter. Both are good current carriers, but the only carriers that have a chance of reaching the collector regions are the holes. Thus to ensure that most of the emitter current reaches the collector, the emitter P-region is more heavily doped than the base N-region.

Having got a large number of holes into the base region, the problem is to ensure that most of them reach the collector region. Once holes enter the base region they slowly diffuse in all directions. They must not spend too long in the base otherwise they will recombine with electrons and produce base current which is undesirable. Thus the base region must be thin thereby increasing the speed of diffusion through the base. When the diffusing holes reach the base–collector junction they are quickly swept into the collector region by the diffusion p.d. Note that this p.d. across the base–collector junction will aid the passing of holes from the base to collector region, i.e. the injected holes from the emitter appear as minority carriers as far as the base–collector junction is concerned. Most of the emitter current thus reaches the collector and only a small amount arrives at the base. In a well-designed transistor, 0·995 of the emitter current reaches the collector, the remaining 0·005 flowing in the base.

The total current flowing into the transistor must be equal to the total current flowing out, thus

$$I_e = I_c + I_b.$$

It should be noted that the collector current is in two parts: the portion of the emitter current reaching the collector, plus the base–collector leakage current which forms only a small proportion of the total collector current

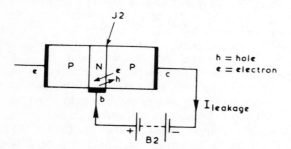

Fig. 3.3 Collector leakage current (emitter–base junction unbiased).

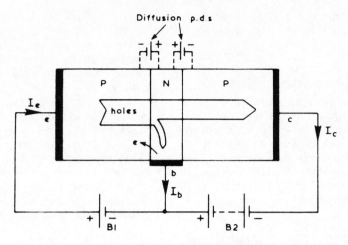

Fig. 3.4 Emitter–base junction forward biased.

provided the temperature of the device is not excessive.

The action of an N-P-N transistor is just the same as the P-N-P, see Fig. 3.5. Here large numbers of electrons are injected into the base region from the emitter, most of which arrive at the collector. Note that the polarities of *B*1 and *B*2 are reversed and the circuit currents are in the opposite direction.

Controlling the Collector Current

When a transistor is used as an amplifier it is necessary to be able to vary the collector current, which may be done by altering the emitter current. We have seen that the amount of current flowing across a p-n junction may be altered by varying the forward bias. Thus, in a transistor if the emitter–base forward bias should be increased there will be a larger emitter current and in consequence a larger collector current (also a larger base current). If it is reduced there will be a smaller emitter current and hence a smaller collector current (and smaller base current). This variation in the forward bias of the emitter–base junction is performed by the signal to be amplified as will be seen later. At this stage it should be noted that when the forward bias is altered all three currents are affected – emitter, base and

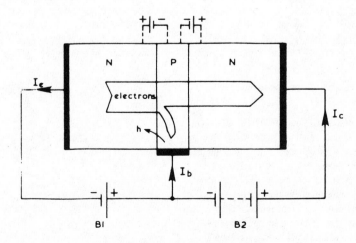

Fig. 3.5 N-P-N transistor action.

collector. This is important as in some circuits the emitter current is used as the output current.

MODES OF CONNECTION

There are three ways of connecting a bipolar transistor in a circuit. In each, one of the electrodes is common to both the input and output circuits. Although the physical action of the transistor is exactly the same in all of the connections, viewed from the circuit terminals it appears different.

Common Base

In the arrangement shown in Fig. 3.6, the base is common to input and output circuits and is similar to the diagram of Fig. 3.5. Here we are using an N-P-N transistor with $B2$ reverse biasing the base–collector junction and $B1$ forward biasing the emitter–base junction. E_i represents a sine wave signal source having negligible internal resistance. The currents I_e, I_b and I_c represent the steady or d.c. currents flowing in the emitter, base and collector leads corresponding to the particular forward bias applied from $B1$. In the common-base connection, the **emitter is the input electrode** and the **collector the output electrode**.

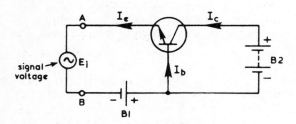

Fig. 3.6 Common-base connection.

Since the signal source is in series with $B1$, any variations of E_i will either add to or subtract from $B1$. Suppose that the signal source is on a positive half-cycle making point A positive with respect to point B. This will reduce the effective emitter–base bias causing the emitter current to decrease and the collector current to decrease. Conversely, when the input signal is on a negative half-cycle making point A negative to point B,

the effective emitter–base bias will be increased. This will cause a larger emitter current to flow and hence a larger collector current. In this manner the collector current is made to vary in accordance with the signal voltage E_i.

In a similar way to quoting the resistance value of a resistor or the capacitance value of a capacitor we may quote a figure or figures to indicate particular properties of a transistor. These figures or properties are called 'parameters' and we have already met one for the p-n diode, the a.c. resistance. One important parameter for the common-base circuit is a.c. current gain (h_{fb}) and is defined as:

$$h_{fb} = \frac{\delta I_c}{\delta I_e}$$

with the collector–base voltage held constant (where δ means 'small change of').

This is sometimes called the 'short-circuit forward-current gain' since, with no load in the output circuit, the collector is short-circuited to a.c. by the negligible internal resistance of $B2$. The value of h_{fb} normally lies in the range 0·9 to 0·99 and the closer it is to unity the better.

Common Emitter

The arrangement shown in Fig. 3.7 is that most frequently found in practical circuits and here the emitter is common to input and output circuits. The currents indicated on the diagram are again steady or d.c. components. The base–emitter junction is forward biased by $B1$ and the base–collector junction is reverse biased by the difference in voltage between $B2$ and $B1$. Since $B2$ voltage may be

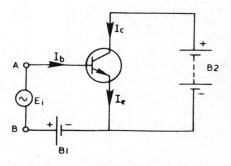

Fig. 3.7 Common-emitter connection.

typically 9V and $B1$ voltage small, say, 0·8V for a silicon transistor, the difference is large. In the common-emitter connection the **base is the input electrode** and the **collector the output electrode**.

As before, the signal source E_i is in series with the forward bias supply for the base–emitter junction. Thus when terminal A goes positive with respect to B on the positive half-cycle of the input signal, the forward bias is increased causing the emitter and hence base and collector currents to increase. Conversely, on the negative half-cycle when A goes negative with respect to B the forward bias is reduced causing the emitter and hence base and collector currents to decrease. In this manner the collector current, which is the output current, varies in accordance with the signal voltage E_i. It should be carefully noted, however, that the input current is the base current and not the emitter current as with the common-base connection. This input current, when a signal is applied, must be supplied from the signal voltage source, i.e. a.c. power is required from the signal source.

The a.c. current gain h_{fe} in the common-emitter mode of operation is defined as:

$$h_{fe} = \frac{\delta I_c}{\delta I_b}$$

with the collector–emitter voltage held constant There is a relationship between h_{fe} and h_{fb} which may be seen from the following.

Suppose that the emitter current is made to change by a small amount δI_e causing corresponding small changes in collector current δI_c and base current δI_b. Since the basic current equation holds good we may express this as:

$$\delta I_e = \delta I_c + \delta I_b$$

or when rearranged

$$\delta I_b = \delta I_e - \delta I_c$$

Now $h_{fe} = \dfrac{\delta I_c}{\delta I_b}$

or substituting for δI_b

$$h_{fe} = \frac{\delta I_c}{\delta I_e - \delta I_c}$$

Dividing numerator and denominator by δI_e gives

$$h_{fe} = \frac{\dfrac{\delta I_c}{\delta I_e}}{1 - \dfrac{\delta I_c}{\delta I_e}}$$

but $\dfrac{\delta I_c}{\delta I_e} = h_{fb}$

$$\therefore h_{fe} = \frac{h_{fb}}{1 - h_{fb}}$$

Suppose, for example, that h_{fb} is 0·995

then $h_{fe} = \dfrac{0·995}{1 - 0·995}$

$$= \frac{0·995}{0·005} = 199.$$

Thus the a.c. current gain in the common emitter can be quite large and may lie in the range 50 to 250.

Common Collector

The third form of connection is shown in Fig. 3.8. Here the collector is common to input and output circuits. The base–collector junction is reverse biased by $B1$ and the base–emitter junction is forward biased by the difference between $B2$ and $B1$ voltages. For example, if $B2$ is, say, 9·0V and $B1$ 8·2V, the difference is 0·8V and is of the correct polarity to forward bias the base–emitter junction of an N-P-N silicon transistor. In practice, a resistor would be used in place of $B1$ as will be seen later. In the common-collector connection the **base is the input electrode** and the **emitter the output electrode**.

As with the other connections, the signal voltage E_i will cause variations in the forward bias of the base–emitter junction. On one half-cycle of the input signal when point B

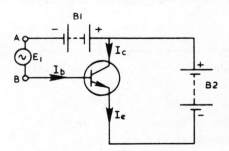

Fig. 3.8 Common-collector connection.

goes positive with respect to point A, the forward bias will be increased thus causing an increase in emitter current. On the other half-cycle when B is negative with respect to A, the bias is reduced and the emitter current will decrease. In this manner the emitter output current varies in accordance with the input signal voltage. As with the common-emitter connection the input current is the base current.

The a.c. current gain h_{fc} in the common-collector configuration is defined as:

$$h_{fc} = \frac{\delta I_e}{\delta I_b}$$

with the collector–emitter voltage held constant.

Now $\dfrac{\delta I_e}{\delta I_b} = \dfrac{\delta I_e}{\delta I_e - \delta I_c}$

or $\dfrac{\delta I_e}{\delta I_b} = \dfrac{\dfrac{\delta I_e}{\delta I_e}}{\dfrac{\delta I_e}{\delta I_e} - \dfrac{\delta I_c}{\delta I_e}}$

(dividing numerator and denominator by δI_e)

$$= \frac{1}{1 - \dfrac{\delta I_c}{\delta I_e}}$$

But $\dfrac{\delta I_c}{\delta I_e} = h_{fb}$

$$\therefore h_{fc} = \frac{1}{1 - h_{fb}} = h_{fe} + 1$$

If the a.c. current gain in common emitter is, say, in the range 50–250, it will be in the range 51–251 in common collector. Thus there is considerable current gain in this mode of connection.

Table 2 gives a summary of the important characteristics mentioned so far for the three modes of connection

CONSTRUCTION OF BIPOLAR TRANSISTORS

There are several methods of manufacturing bipolar transistors but only two will be considered here. One method, used also in the manufacture of junction rectifiers, is shown in Fig. 3.9. Two pellets of indium are alloyed to a thin wafer of N-type germanium, resulting in two areas of the germanium slice being converted to P-type. Sandwiched between these areas is a thin region having N-type conductivity which becomes the base layer. It will be noted that the larger P-area forms the collector of the transistor, so emitter and collector connections are not interchangeable as might be suggested by a simple type of schematic diagram such as Fig. 3.2.

An important method of construction is the 'silicon planar' and the various stages in manufacture are given in Fig. 3.10. The starting point is a slice of N-type silicon about 50mm in diameter and 0·3mm thick which is oxidised to a depth of about 1·0μm, see Fig. 3.10(a). A large number of transistors are produced from this slice (about 5000), but only one transistor is considered in the diagram.

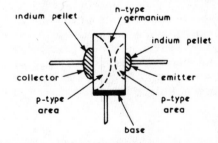

Fig. 3.9 Alloy method of manufacture for p-n-p transistor.

TABLE 2

Mode	Input Electrode	Output Electrode	A.C. Current Gain
Common Base	Emitter	Collector	h_{fb} (0·9 to 0·99)
Common Emitter	Base	Collector	h_{fe} (50 to 250)
Common Collector	Base	Emitter	h_{fc} (50 to 250) approx. same as h_{fe}

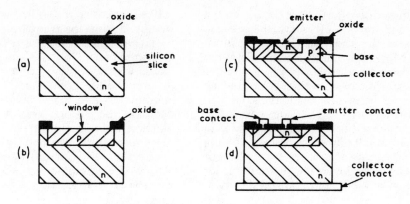

Fig. 3.10 Planar construction of silicon p-n-p transistors.

The next step is to make a 'window' or hole in the oxide layer which is done by photo-etching. A P-type impurity is then allowed to diffuse through the 'window' using a suitable mask to produce the result shown in Fig. 3.10(b). The surface of the wafer is then reoxidised and a smaller window is made through which an N-type impurity is allowed to diffuse to a predetermined depth. This produces the result shown in Fig. 3.10(c). The slice now consists of a P-region sandwiched between two N-regions. Finally, after the surface has been reoxidised and small openings made to take the base and emitter contacts (aluminium), the result is as given in Fig. 3.10(d) with the collector contact, also aluminium.

The slice is then cut to produce the individual transistors and leads are attached to the base, emitter and collector metal contacts. Each transistor is then encapsulated to keep out moisture and impurities. This type of transistor has the advantage that the top surface (containing the junctions) is protected by the oxide layer.

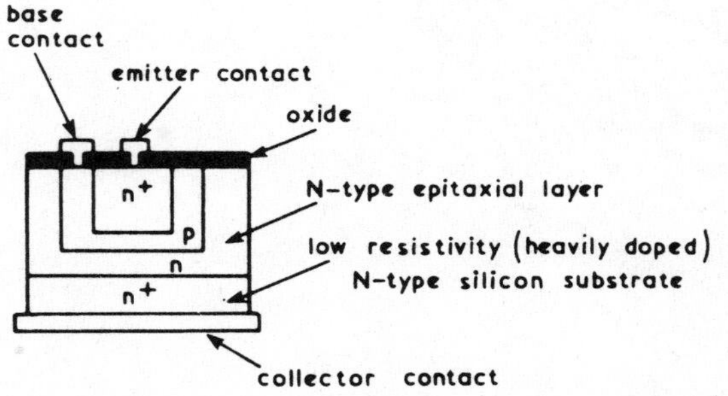

For some applications the resistance of the collector region in the silicon planar transistor is too large. This may be adjusted without introducing undesirable effects (such as an increase in the capacitance or reduction in breakdown voltage) by using an 'epitaxial layer' in the collector. The epitaxial layer is a thin layer of high resistivity material which is formed on a slice of low resistivity silicon (called the 'substrate'). The transistor is then constructed on the epitaxial layer as previously described to produce a **silicon planar epitaxial transistor**, Fig. 3.11.

Ratings

Bipolar transistors are made with maximum collector voltage ratings from about 10V to 1kV, which corresponds to the maximum breakdown of the collector–base junction. This voltage should not be exceeded for even short periods or the transistor may be permanently damaged. Maximum current ratings vary from about 10mA to 10A or more and are mainly settled by the maximum power dissipation. When a transistor is operating it has a voltage across it and a current through it, thus there will be a power dissipated equal to $I_c \times V_{ce}$ (assuming only steady current and voltage). This power is converted into heat causing the temperature of the transistor to rise. The maximum temperature is limited to about 150°C for silicon and 85°C for germanium.

Fig. 3.11 The silicon planar expitaxial transistor (basic structure).

The amount of power that can be dissipated depends mainly on how efficiently the heat can be removed so that the temperature rise is not excessive. Most of the heat generated is at the collector–base junction since V_{cb} is greater than V_{be} across the base–emitter junction (the current in each being practically the same). In many constructions the collector–base junction is in contact with the case and so assists in cooling. With small power transistors, cooling is simply by convection due to the air surrounding it. The lower the surrounding air temperature (ambient temperature) the lower will be the case temperature and the more heat removed from the transistor.

To assist in cooling, large power transistors are fitted to a heat sink which is a large mass of metal with a large surface area. The heat sink should be a good heat conductor, e.g. aluminium, and is usually fitted with fins to increase the surface area. Convection, conduction and radiation all play a part in cooling the transistor. If the heat sink is painted matt black the radiation efficiency is increased. Three types of common heat sink construction are shown in Fig. 3.12.

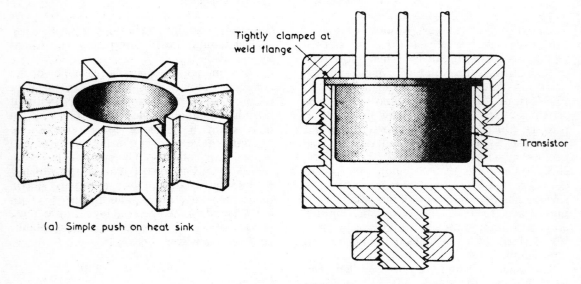

(a) Simple push on heat sink

(b) Positive contact type heat sink

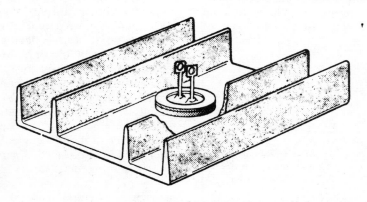

(c) Power heat sink

Fig. 3.12 Heat sinks.

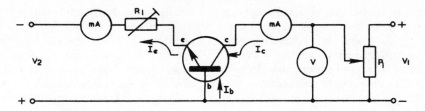

Fig. 3.13 *Circuit for measuring common-base characteristics.*

STATIC CHARACTERISTICS

Of the important static characteristic curves for the bipolar transistor only those relating to the common-base and common-emitter connections will be described.

Output Characteristics

These may be obtained using a test circuit and a suitable one for obtaining the common-base characteristics is given in Fig. 3.13. The circuit is so arranged that the emitter current can be varied by means of $R1$ and the collector-to-base voltage by $P1$. The polarity of the voltage supplies $V1$ and $V2$ are connected so that the collector–base junction is reverse biased and the emitter–base junction is forward biased, as for normal operation of the transistor. Current meters are used to measure the emitter and collector currents and a voltmeter to indicate the collector–base voltage. The method of obtaining the characteristics is as follows.

$R1$ is set to give a convenient emitter current of, say, 1mA and the collector–base voltage is increased in steps of, say, 0·5V from 0V up to 9V with the aid of $P1$. At each setting of $P1$ the corresponding value of collector current is noted. This procedure is repeated with the emitter current set at 2mA, 3mA, 4mA, etc. In this way a family of curves may be obtained as shown in Fig. 3.14.

The output characteristics of Fig. 3.14 are fairly typical for a small power transistor in common base. It will be noted that the collector–base voltage has negligible effect on collector current, the characteristic being practically horizontal. Another feature is that collector current continues to flow when the collector–base voltage is reduced to zero. This is because the collector–base diffusion p.d. aids the passing of carriers injected from the

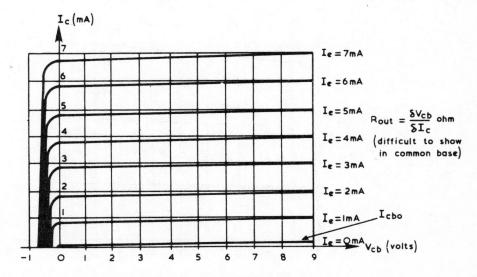

Fig. 3.14 *Common-base output characteristics.*

emitter. Thus, to reduce the collector current to zero, the diffusion p.d. must be reduced to zero. This is achieved by reversing the collector–base voltage to a few tenths of a volt. These characteristics and others that follow are called 'static characteristics' because the collector voltage is held steady when the collector current changes, (unlike a normal amplifier when a load is included in the collector circuit).

Another important parameter of the transistor is the a.c. output resistance (R_{OUT}). This is defined as:

$$R_{OUT} = \frac{\delta V_{cb}}{\delta I_c} \text{ ohm (with } I_e \text{ constant).}$$

Since the characteristics are nearly horizontal (small slope), the output resistance is high and of the order of $100k\Omega$ to $1M\Omega$.

Common-emitter output characteristics are given in Fig. 3.15. These may be obtained using a type of test circuit similar to Fig. 3.13. This time, however, the base current is set to a convenient level, say $25\mu A$ and the collector–emitter voltage increased in discrete steps. At each step the corresponding value of collector current is noted. This is repeated for various values of base current so building up a family of characteristics.

Although in a general way the common-emitter output characteristics are similar to those in common base there are a number of differences. First, the collector–emitter voltage has a greater influence on the collector current, i.e. the characteristics are not so horizontal as in Fig. 3.14. This is because the common-emitter d.c. current gain increases by a greater amount with an increase in collector–emitter voltage than the d.c. current gain in common base. Secondly, the characteristics are not as parallel which again is due to the larger change in common-emitter d.c. current gain than common-base d.c. current gain at the higher currents. Thirdly, when V_{ce} is zero then the collector current has fallen to zero irrespective of the value of base current. This is because once the collector–emitter voltage has fallen below the base–emitter voltage (say 0·6V for a silicon transistor), the **collector–base** junction becomes **forward biased** and not reverse biased. The collector current remains at full level until the collector–emitter voltage falls to about 0·3V below that of the base–emitter voltage at which point the collector current falls abruptly (the forward bias of the collector–base junction prevents charges injected from the emitter reaching the collector). This minimum value of collector–emitter voltage when maintaining full collector current is called the 'bottoming voltage' and will

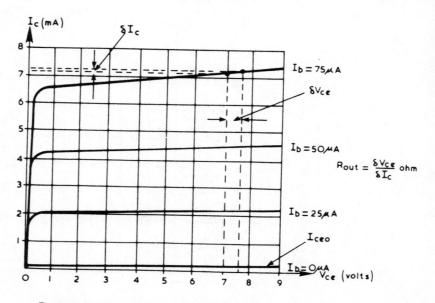

Fig 3.15 Common-emitter output characteristics.

be considered again in Chapter 5. Finally, with zero base current there is still some collector current flowing.

This is the common-emitter leakage current I_{CEO} and is greater than the leakage current I_{CBO} in common base (see Fig. 3.14). The leakage currents are related by the expression:

$$I_{CEO} = I_{CBO} (1 + h_{fe}).$$

Assuming a leakage current of, say, $2\mu A$ in common base, it will be in common emitter (with an h_{fe} of 100)

$$2(1 + 100) \ \mu A = 202 \mu A.$$

The above calculation is for a germanium transistor and emphasises the need for preventing excessive temperature rise which will increase the leakage current. For a silicon transistor I_{CBO} may be only 25nA, thus under the same conditions I_{CEO} would be only $2 \cdot 525 \mu A$.

In common emitter, the a.c. output resistance (R_{OUT}) is defined as

$$R_{OUT} = \frac{\delta V_{ce}}{\delta I_c} \text{ ohm (with } I_b \text{ constant)}$$

Its value may be obtained from the output characteristic as shown for a specified steady V_{ce}. As the slope of the lines is greater than in common base, the value of R_{OUT} will be lower and commonly lies in the range of 10kΩ to 50kΩ for small transistors.

The common-emitter output characteristics

of a high-power transistor capable of providing up to 100W for industrial electronics applications is given in Fig. 3.16 for comparison with Fig. 3.15. Note that I_c is in amperes and I_b correspondingly larger in milliamperes The a.c. output resistance for a transistor of this type will be of the order of 5–10 ohms. Power transistors with ratings somewhat lower, about 30W, are used in colour television receivers and audio equipment.

Input Characteristics

Another useful characteristic is the input characteristic which shows how the input current varies with the voltage applied between base and emitter. A typical input characteristic for the common-base connection is shown in Fig. 3.17. As the forward bias is increased from zero there is practically no emitter current until V_{cb} exceeds about $0 \cdot 5V$ for the silicon transistor shown, or about $0 \cdot 1V$ for a germanium type. Thereafter, the current increases abruptly in a non-linear manner. The non-linearity of the characteristic will give rise to distortion when the transistor is used as an amplifier but this may be reduced as explained later.

A typical input characteristic for the common-emitter connection is given in Fig. 3.18. This is similar to the common-base characteristic except that in common-emitter the input current is the base current. Again, the input

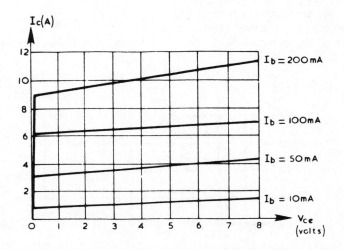

Fig. 3.16 Common-emitter output characteristic for large power transistor.

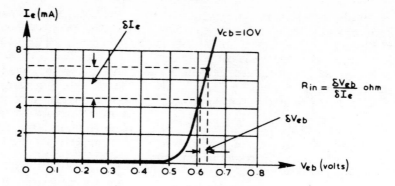

Fig. 3.17 Common-base input characteristic.

current rises abruptly when the forward bias reaches about 0·6V for a silicon transistor.

A further important parameter is the a.c. input resistance (R_{IN}). This is defined as:

For common base

$$R_{IN} = \frac{\delta V_{eb}}{\delta I_e} \text{ ohm } (V_{cb} \text{ constant})$$

and for common emitter

$$R_{IN} = \frac{\delta V_{be}}{\delta I_b} \text{ ohm } (V_{ce} \text{ constant})$$

The values may be obtained from the input characteristics by considering small changes as shown. The value will depend upon the point of measurement since the curve is non-linear. In common base, R_{IN} lies in the range of about 30Ω–100Ω whereas in common emitter it is higher, lying in the range of about 750Ω–5kΩ. These values are for small power transistors. A high-power transistor operating in common emitter may have an R_{IN} of only 0·5Ω to 10Ω.

Transfer Characteristics

These characteristics show how the **output current** of the transistor varies with the **input current**. Typical examples for small power transistors when operating in common base and common emitter are given in Figs. 3.19 and 3.20 respectively.

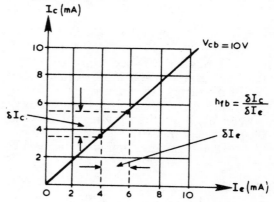

Fig. 3.19 Common-base transfer characteristic.

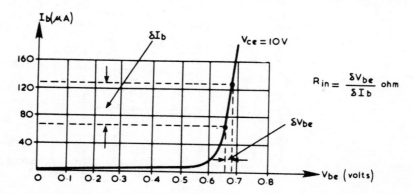

Fig. 3.18 Common-emitter input characteristic.

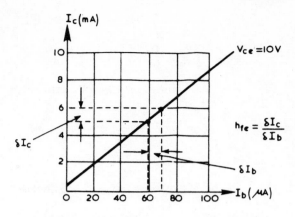

Fig. 3.20 *Common-emitter transfer characteristic.*

The transfer characteristic may be used to determine the value of h_{fb} or h_{fe} by considering small changes as illustrated. Departure from the linear characteristic shown often occurs at low and high values for input current.

Frequency and Gain Characteristics

The current gain h_{fb} or h_{fe} does not remain constant at all frequencies, as time is required for carriers injected from the emitter to diffuse through the base region, which is a relatively slow process. Thus the output is slightly delayed on the input which causes a reduction in gain at high frequencies. There is, therefore, an upper limit on the useful frequency range of any transistor. This upper frequency is called the 'cut-off frequency' (f_β) and is defined as the frequency where the gain of the transistor has fallen to 0·707 of its low-frequency value, see Fig. 3.21. For a transistor used in the audio output stage of a radio

receiver, f_β should be at least 20kHz whereas in the video stage of a t.v. receiver an f_β of 6MHz would be suitable.

The manner in which the current gain varies with collector current is important and for many transistors the relation is similar to that shown in Fig. 3.22. Generally, as the collector current (or emitter current) is increased the value of h_{fe} increases as shown. Use of this effect is made in receivers fitted with automatic gain control (a.g.c.). By reducing the forward bias, thereby decreasing the collector current, the gain of the transistor may be reduced. This method of reducing gain is known as 'reverse a.g.c.'.

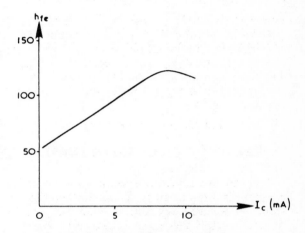

Fig. 3.22 *Variation of current gain with collector current (found in transistors used with reverse a.g.c.).*

Some transistors are specially designed to exhibit a collapse in current gain when the collector current rises above a high value, say 5mA. Fig. 3.23 shows the characteristic of

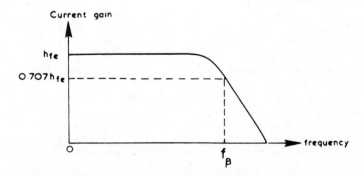

Fig 3.21 *Variation of current gain with frequency.*

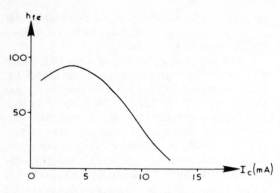

Fig. 3.23 Collapse of current gain at high collector currents (found in some transistors used with forward a.g.c.).

such a transistor. This type is used in high-frequency receivers, e.g. f.m. radios and t.v. receivers, for a.g.c. purposes. By increasing the forward bias the collector current increases causing a reduction in gain. This method of reducing transistor gain is called 'forward a.g.c.'

QUESTIONS ON CHAPTER THREE

(1)   In a bipolar transistor:
    (a) The collector–base junction is forward biased and the emitter–base junction reverse biased
    (b) The collector–base junction is reverse biased and the emitter–base junction forward biased
    (c) The emitter–base junction and the collector–base junction are both reverse biased
    (d) The emitter–base junction and the collector–base junction are both forward biased.

(2)   With an N-P-N transistor:
    (a) Emitter and collector are normally positive to the base
    (b) Emitter and base are normally positive to the collector
    (c) Collector and base are normally negative to the emitter
    (d) Collector and base are normally positive to the emitter.

(3)   The relation between the collector, base and emitter currrents is given by:

(a) $I_c = I_e + I_b$
(b) $I_e = I_b + I_c$
(c) $I_b = I_c - I_e$
(d) $I_e = I_c - I_b$.

(4)   A typical value for the h_{fb} of a transistor would be:
    (a) 0·99
    (b) 50kΩ
    (c) 100Ω
    (d) 50.

(5)   The h_{fe} of a transistor may be defined as:

(a) $\dfrac{\delta V_{ce}}{\delta I_c}$

(b) $\dfrac{\delta I_c}{\delta V_{ce}}$

(c) $\dfrac{\delta I_b}{\delta I_c}$

(d) $\dfrac{\delta I_c}{\delta I_b}$.

(6)   The output current in common collector is taken from:
    (a) The collector
    (b) The base
    (c) The emitter
    (d) The signal source.

(7)   The a.c. output resistance of a small power transistor in common emitter is about:
    (a) 10–50Ω
    (b) 10kΩ–50kΩ
    (c) 200Ω–1kΩ
    (d) 200kΩ–2MΩ.

(8)   The a.c. input resistance for a small power transistor connected in common base is about:
    (a) 750Ω–5kΩ
    (b) 7·5kΩ–50kΩ
    (c) 30Ω–100Ω
    (d) 3kΩ–100kΩ.

(9)   The a.c. input resistance of a transistor connected in common base is lower than that in common emitter because:
    (a) The physical action of the transistor is different
    (b) The input current is greater for similar changes in V_{be}

(c) The output current is greater for similar changes in V_{be}

(d) The input current is practically zero.

(10) The transfer characteristic of a bipolar transistor shows the relationship between:
   (a) V_{be} and output current
   (b) V_{be} and input current
   (c) V_{be} and V_{ce}
   (d) Input current and output current.

(11) The input characteristic of a transistor in common base shows the relationship between:
   (a) V_{be} and I_e
   (b) V_{be} and I_b
   (c) I_c and I_b
   (d) V_{cb} and V_{be}.

(12) For most transistors the current gain:
   (a) Is constant with changes in I_c
   (b) Increases with a decrease in I_c
   (c) Decreases with an increase in I_b
   (d) Increases with an increase in I_c.

(Answers on page 369)

CHAPTER FOUR

THE FIELD-EFFECT TRANSISTOR

Objectives

1 To explain the operation of JUGFET and MOSFET devices.
2 To study typical characteristics.
3 To show the three basic modes of connection for an FET.
4 To describe the construction of Dual-gate MOSFET and VMOS devices.

ALTHOUGH THE PRINCIPLE of the field-effect transistor (fet) has been known for quite some time, it is only in recent years that semiconductor technology has made possible its production on a commercial scale.

A fet is a resistive channel of semiconductor material (silicon) whose resistance can be varied by an electric field cutting into the channel and altering its cross-sectional area. The fet is a **unipolar** device, i.e. it conducts by majority carriers only, a feature that makes it less temperature dependent. There are a number of types available which can be either conducting or non-conducting with zero bias applied.

JUNCTION GATE FET (JUGFET)

The basic idea of the junction gate fet is given in Fig. 4.1. It consists of a thin wafer of either N-type or P-type silicon with ohmic contacts at each end called the 'source' (s) and 'drain' (d). On opposite faces there are diffused two heavily doped areas which are connected together. These areas are P-type with an N-channel device and N-type for a P-channel device. The areas form the 'gate' (g) or control electrode. Source, gate and drain electrodes correspond to the emitter, base and collector connections of the bipolar transistor. The arrow in the circuit symbol points in the direction of forward current flow in the p-n

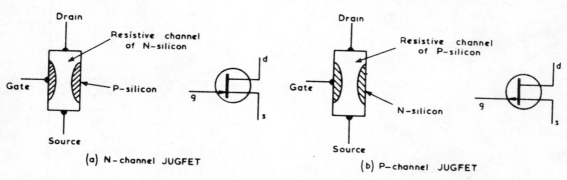

Fig. 4.1 Basic form of construction for junction-gate fet.

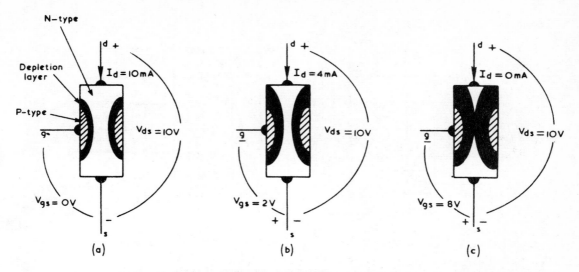

Fig. 4.2 Effect of gate–source voltage on drain current.

junction formed between the gate and the resistive channel.

If we consider an N-channel jugfet as in Fig. 4.2(a) where the drain is held positive with respect to the source, then electrons (majority carriers) will flow in the resistive channel between source and drain. With zero voltage between the gate and source ($V_{gs} = 0V$), i.e. the gate at the same potential as the source, a reverse biased junction is formed between the gate areas and the resistive channel. When a voltage is applied between drain and source there is a voltage drop along the channel. Thus the portion of the N-channel close to the P-area will be positive to the source by an amount depending upon the manufactured dimensions of the P-areas, which are different in practice from the simple idea shown in Fig. 4.2. As with any p-n junction there will be a depletion layer and let us say that under the bias conditions stated it has the area shown. This layer will lie mainly in the lightly doped N-channel and will be wider at the top of the P-area than at the bottom since the reverse bias is greater towards the top of the P-area. Under these conditions maximum current flows in the resistive channel and the drain and source connections, say 10mA. Since the gate–channel junction is reversed biased, only a very small leakage current will flow in the gate lead.

If the gate is made negative with respect to

the source by, say, 2V as in Fig. 4.2(b), the reverse bias on the gate-to-channel junction is increased. Thus the depletion area width is increased which reduces the cross-sectional area of the conductive channel. In consequence, the resistance of the channel is increased causing the drain current to decrease. If V_{gs} is progressively increased the depletion area extends further into the channel and a situation is eventually reached where the cross-sectional area of the N-channel is reduced to zero as in Fig. 4.2(c). The channel is cut-off or is said to be 'pinched-off'. The value of V_{gs} corresponding to zero drain current is called the 'pinch-off voltage'.

A typical transfer characteristic (or mutual characteristics) of an N-channel jugfet is given in Fig. 4.3(a) which shows how the drain current varies with the bias voltage applied between gate and source. The characteristic is not linear but follows an approximate square law. There is a maximum bias voltage that may be applied between gate and source, this being the p-n junction breakdown voltage. If the gate is made positive to the source, the drain current will increase. However, if made too positive the gate-channel diode will become forward biased. The gate is not usually operated with a positive gate voltage above about 0·5V.

A family of output characteristics is given in Fig 4.3(b). With a fixed gate voltage the

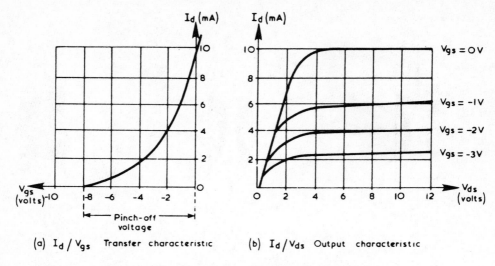

(a) I_d / V_{gs} Transfer characteristic

(b) I_d / V_{ds} Output characteristic

Fig. 4.3 Characteristic of jugfet (common source).

current increases fairly linearly at first with increases in the drain-to-source voltage. Thereafter, the drain current is almost independent of V_{ds}.

Parameters

The fet is a voltage-operated device, unlike the bipolar transistor which is current operated. One important parameter of the fet is the mutual conductance (g_m).

$$\text{This is defined as } g_m = \frac{\delta I_d}{\delta V_{gs}},$$

with V_{ds} maintained constant.

As this is an I/V relationship it is measured in the unit of conductance, the siemens (S). This parameter shows how effective are changes in V_{gs} in producing variations in the drain current. Typical values for g_m lie in the range 1·5mS to 7mS.

Other useful parameters are the a.c. input resistance R_{IN} and the a.c. output resistance R_{OUT}.

$$R_{IN} \text{ may be defined as } \frac{\delta V_{gs}}{\delta I_g} \text{ ohm,}$$

with V_{ds} constant.

Since the input is a reversed biased juction the gate current (I_g) is extremely small, typically of the order of tens of pico-amps. Thus R_{IN} is

very high, about 10^7 ohms at low frequencies.

$$R_{OUT} \text{ may be defined as } \frac{\delta V_{ds}}{\delta I_d} \text{ ohm,}$$

with V_{gs} constant.

The value of R_{OUT} is normally very high, lying in the range 20kΩ to 1MΩ.

METAL OXIDE SEMICONDUCTOR FET (MOSFET)

The mosfet or insulated gate fet (igfet) is available in two different forms known as the 'enhancement' and 'depletion' mode types. Both types can be fabricated with either P or N channels. The major difference between the mosfet and jugfet is that with the mosfet the gate terminal is insulated from its channel by a thin insulating layer.

Enhancement Mosfet

The basic construction is shown in Fig. 4.4(a). The source and drain are heavily doped N regions (indicated by N^+) which are diffused close together on to a P-type silicon section called the substrate. Between the source and drain and extending to the edge of the substrate is a thin layer of silicon dioxide. This layer acts as an insulating zone between the substrate and aluminium gate electrode. A

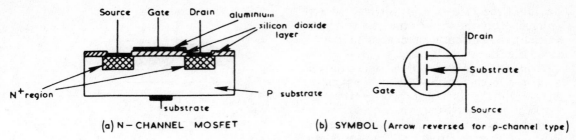

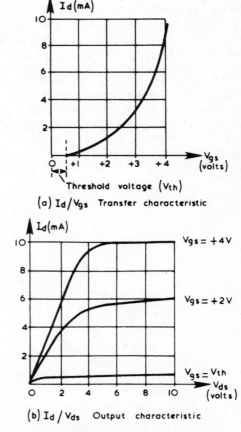

(a) N-CHANNEL MOSFET

(b) SYMBOL (Arrow reversed for p-channel type)

Fig. 4.4 Mosfet (enhancement type).

connection is also made to the substrate and in most transistors it is internally connected to the source terminal but may be brought out as a separate electrode.

With the drain made positive to the source and the gate voltage zero, very little current flows since the two p-n junctions formed are in series opposition. If the gate is made positive to the source, the electric field set up across the silicon dioxide layer attracts electrons out of the substrate. This creates an n-type surface channel between the source and drain through which conduction may take place. Hence the enhancement mosfet has to be forward biased

like the bipolar transistor, but of course is voltage operated.

When the gate-to-source voltage is increased in the positive direction as in Fig. 4.5, the width of the surface enhancement channel is increased. As a result the resistance of the channel is decreased thereby permitting a larger current to flow between source and drain. Typical characteristics are given in Fig. 4.6. Drain current does not commence to

(a) $V_{gs} = 0V$

(b) $V_{gs} = +2V$

(c) $V_{gs} = +4V$

Fig. 4.5 Effect of forward biasing the gate.

(a) I_d/V_{gs} Transfer characteristic

(b) I_d/V_{ds} Output characteristic

Fig. 4.6 Characteristics of enhancement type mosfet.

flow until the gate is made slightly positive with respect to the source; the gate voltage at which drain current commences to flow is called the 'threshold voltage' (V_{th}).

Owing to the presence of the silicon dioxide layer, the input resistance is higher than the jugfet ($10^{10}\Omega$ or more). To prevent the possibility of damage to the gate oxide layer by an electrostatic charge building up on the high resistance gate electrode, the mosfet is normally supplied with a conductive rubber ring fitted round the leads of the device. This ring should not be removed until after the transistor has been mounted in the circuit.

An n-channel device has been considered here but a p-channel mosfet may be formed using an N-type substrate and highly doped P-areas. Conduction through the channel is enhanced by making the gate negative with respect to the source.

Depletion Mosfet

The principle of operation of the depletion mode mosfet is illustrated in Fig. 4.7, using an n-channel device as an example. Between the highly doped source and drain regions a small n-channel is formed during manufacture. This channel has a higher resistivity than the n$^+$ sections. If the drain is held at a positive voltage with respect to the source and V_{gs} is zero, a current will flow between source and drain. When the gate voltage is made negative with respect to the source electrons are

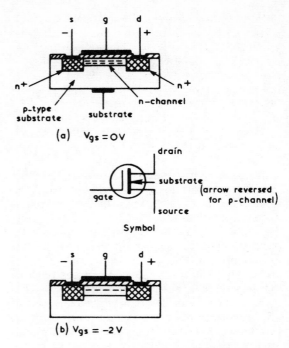

Fig. 4.7 Depletion mode mosfet (n-channel).

repelled from the channel. This increases the resistivity of the channel thereby reducing current flow. The more negative the gate voltage, the more depleted the channel becomes of electrons thus the less the current flow, Fig. 4.7(b). Typical characteristics are given in Fig. 4.8. If the gate is made positive with respect to the source, electrons will be

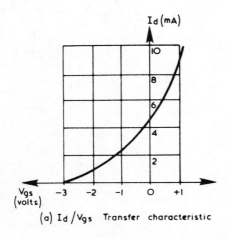

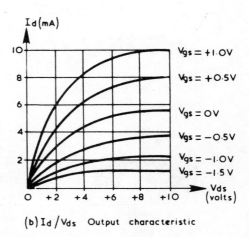

Fig. 4.8 Characteristics of depletion-type mosfet.

attracted into the channel and the source-to-drain current increased. Thus, over the positive range of gate voltage this mosfet behaves as an enhancement type.

It will be seen that the enhancement type of mosfet is normally an 'off' type of transistor whereas the depletion mode type is normally an 'on' type of device. In either case the current flowing between source and drain can be varied by altering the gate-to-source voltage.

The main parameters previously discussed for the junction-gate fet apply also to the mosfet device. The parameter g_m is typically in the range 2–10mS; R_{IN} lies in the range 10^{10}–10^{12} ohms and R_{OUT} typically in the range 10–50kΩ.

Circuit Configurations of the Fet

In the same way that bipolar transistors may be connected in three different configurations (as explained in Chapter 3), fets can be connected in:

(a) The common-source mode (corresponding to common emitter);
(b) The common-drain mode (corresponding to common collector);
(c) The common-gate mode (corresponding to common base).

The basic circuit configurations using a jugfet as an example are shown in Fig. 4.9. A battery *B2* is used to provide the correct biasing of the fet, but in practice the bias would be obtained from a resistor connected in the source circuit which will be described later. All three connections may be used but the common source arrangement is the most usual.

Dual-gate Mosfet

Another type of mosfet is one having two independent gates. The basic construction of an n-channel depletion mosfet with dual gates is shown in Fig. 4.10. It consists of three diffused n^+ areas on a P-type substrate with two channels have N-type conductivity formed during manufacture. The current flowing between drain and source may be controlled by a voltage applied to either gate. If gate 1 or gate 2 is made sufficiently negative the current may be cut off.

With an ordinary mosfet the capacitance between drain and gate is about 0·5pF. Although this is a small capacitance it can cause feedback between the output electrode (drain) and input electrode (gate) at high frequencies, resulting in possible oscillation. The introduction of a second gate reduces the capacitance between drain and gate 1 to about

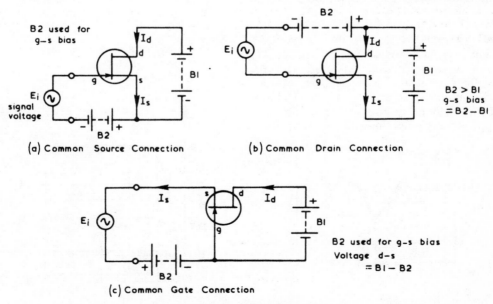

(a) Common Source Connection

(b) Common Drain Connection

(c) Common Gate Connection

Fig. 4.9 Fet circuit configurations.

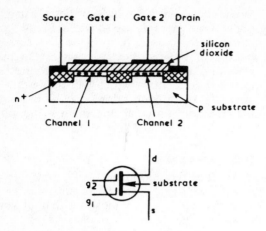

Fig. 4.10 Dual-gate mosfet.

0·02pF provided gate 2 is held at a constant voltage. In effect gate 2 acts as a screen between drain and gate 1.

The gain of the transistor may be altered by varing the steady d.c. voltage on gate 2 with gate 1 used as the signal input electrode. This is useful for automatic gain control in receivers where the a.g.c. voltage is applied to gate 2 and the signal to be amplified is applied to gate 1. The dual-gate mosfet may also be used as a mixer in a receiver with the signal frequency voltage applied to gate 1 and the oscillator frequency voltage applied to gate 2.

VMOS Power Fet

The power capabilities of the mosfets described so far are usually limited to less than 1W. This is because the ordinary mosfet is so constructed that a horizontal surface channel is formed, therefore the current density is low. To produce a power mosfet using the normal method of manufacture would result in a large area device which would be much costlier to fabricate than an ordinary bipolar transistor.

A new fet technology called VMOS (devoloped by Siliconix) allows high current densities and high voltage operation to be achieved. VMOS devices make use of an enhanced channel and vertical current flow, hence the name VMOS (vertical mosfet).

The basic idea of construction for one type is shown in Fig. 4.11. The VMOS fet has a four-layer vertical structure which is formed using a diffusion process. In operating this n-channel enhancement-mode device the gate and drain are both held positive with respect to the source. The voltage applied to the gate induces an n-channel into the p-region on both sides of the V-groove. This allows electrons to flow from the source through the n-channel and N^- area to the N^+ region which is connected to the drain. Current thus flows vertically through the transistor from the source on top to the drain on the bottom of the silicon chip. The higher the gate voltage, the wider is the enhanced channel and the greater the current flow. The N^- region (epitaxial layer) is a lightly doped layer and is used to increase the drain-to-source breakdown voltage and to reduce the feedback capacitance.

A typical family of output characteristics for a VMOS power fet is given in Fig. 4.12. These are similar to the ordinary mosfet except for the following:

(a) The drain current is now in amps rather than milliamps;

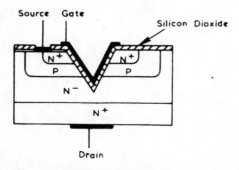

Fig. 4.11 VMOS (enhancement).

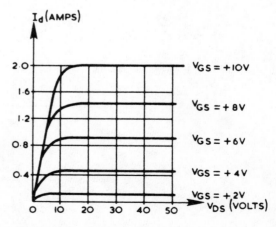

Fig. 4.12 Output characteristic of VMOS power fet.

(b) The output resistance is very high (the curves are practically horizontal);

(c) The spacing between curves is constant above about 0·4A, i.e. the relationship between V_{gs} and I_d is a linear one and not square law.

QUESTIONS ON CHAPTER FOUR

(1) A field-effect transistor is:
   (a) A unipolar device
   (b) A current-operated device
   (c) Very temperature dependent
   (d) A bipolar device.

(2) In an n-channel JUGFET:
   (a) The drain and source are connected to P-type silicon
   (b) The gate is connected to an area of N-type silicon
   (c) The drain is connected to P-silicon and the source to N-silicon
   (d) The gate is connected to an area of P-type silicon.

(3) The g_m of a field-effect transistor is given by:
   (a) $\dfrac{\delta V_{gs}}{\delta I_g}$

   (b) $\dfrac{\delta V_{ds}}{\delta I_d}$

   (c) $\dfrac{\delta I_d}{\delta I_g}$

   (d) $\dfrac{\delta I_d}{\delta V_{gs}}$.

(4) The value of R_{IN} for a JUGFET is of the order of:
   (a) $1\text{k}\Omega$
   (b) 100Ω
   (c) $10^7\Omega$
   (d) $10^{-6}\Omega$.

(5) In an n-channel enhancement mosfet, current flows between drain and source when:
   (a) Drain and source are both positive with respect to the gate
   (b) Drain and gate are both positive with respect to the source
   (c) Drain is positive to the source and the gate voltage is zero
   (d) Drain is negative to the source and the gate voltage is zero.

(6) The common-gate mode for a fet corresponds to the bipolar:
   (a) Common-emitter connection
   (b) Common-base connection
   (c) Common-collector connection
   (d) Emitter-follower connection.

(7) The type of transistor to be found in the output stage of a 20W audio amplifier would be:
   (a) A JUGFET
   (b) A dual-gate fet
   (c) A VMOS fet
   (d) An n-channel MOSFET.

(Answers on page 369)

CHAPTER FIVE

THE TRANSISTOR AS AN AMPLIFIER

Objectives

1 To consider the selection of suitable bias point for transistors.
2 To show methods of providing bias for transistors.
3 To study the operation of simple amplifiers in common base, common emitter and common collector and the corresponding arrangements for the FET.
4 Determine the voltage gain.
5 To explain bottoming and clipping.

IN VOLUME 1 of this series the main characteristics of a.c. and d.c. amplifiers were discussed. It was noted that all amplifiers have the general property of amplifying, i.e. producing an output signal which is greater than the input signal. All amplifiers are power amplifiers where the output signal power exceeds the input signal power. However, they may be divided into voltage amplifiers, current amplifiers or power amplifiers depending upon whether the main concern is a large voltage, current or power gain. In this chapter we shall consider the basic operation of a small signal voltage amplifier which is intended to serve as an introduction to show how bipolar and unipolar transistors may be used as amplifiers.

THE VOLTAGE AMPLIFIER

When dealing with the basic operation of the bipolar transistor it was seen that by altering the base–emitter voltage the collector current could be varied. Similarly with the unipolar transistor the drain current could be altered by varying the gate–source voltage. This property of the two types of transistor is

used to achieve amplification by allowing the input signal to vary the bias of the transitor and hence vary the output current. If voltage amplification is required, the output current must be directed through a resistance load (R_L) connected in the output circuit of the transistor, Fig. 5.1.

Selection of Bias Point

When amplifying a signal we ideally require the output signal to be a faithful but magnified replica of the input signal. If the shape of the output signal voltage from the circuits of Fig. 5.1 is to be an exact replica of the input signal voltage, the output signal current flowing in R_L must be a faithful replica of the input signal voltage. To determine how the input current will vary with the input voltage we may use the dynamic mutual characteristic of the transistor. This characteristic shows how the output current varies with changes in the bias voltage when the transistor is used with a particular value of load resistance and supply voltage.

For the output signal current to be identical

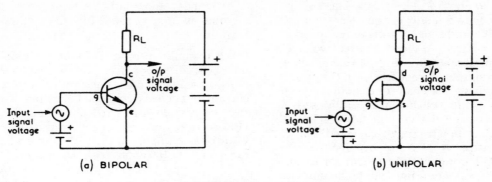

Fig. 5.1 Basic transistor voltage amplifiers.

in shape to the input signal voltage the relationship between the output current and bias voltage should be linear. In practice, there is always some non-linearity which may cause distortion in an amplifier. Thus it is necessary to select a suitable bias point and to

limit the amplitude of the input signal voltage so that operation is confined to a portion of the characteristic where the linearity is good. To achieve maximum signal performance, the bias point is chosen so that it lies in the centre of the linear part of the dynamic characteristic

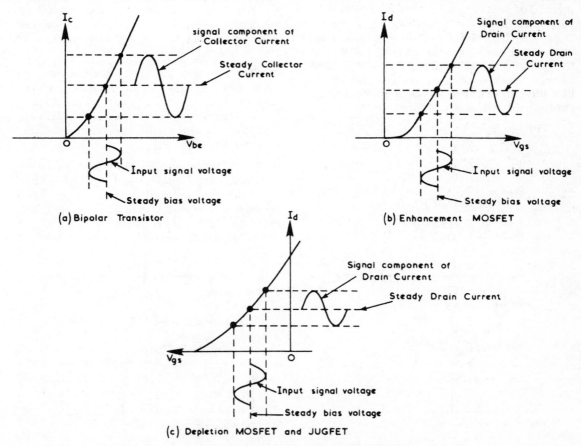

Fig. 5.2 Class-A operation of bipolar and unipolar transistors.

as shown in Fig. 5.2. This steady bias voltage will give rise to a steady (or quiescent) output current. When the signal voltage is applied at the input centred on the steady bias voltage, the output current will swing above and below the steady output current level, i.e. the output current consists of a steady or d.c. current with an a.c. component of current superimposed on it. When the output current flows at every instant of a complete input cycle as in Fig. 5.2, the transistor is said to be operated in 'Class-A'. Throughout the remainder of this section Class-A operation will be assumed.

Obtaining the Bias Voltage

We must now discuss practical methods of obtaining bias voltage for the transistor to set the operating point to Class-A.

(a) **Bipolar Transistor Bias.** The simplest method of providing a forward bias voltage or current for a bipolar transistor is to connect a resistor R_B between the supply line V_L and the base if the transistor as shown in Fig. 5.3(a). If the required bias voltage V_{be} is, say, 0·6V and the magnitude of the base current and supply line voltage is known, the value of R_B may be determined as follows.

Voltage drop across $R_B = V_L - V_{be}$

$$\therefore R_B = \frac{V_L - V_{be}}{I_b} \text{ ohms}$$

With a supply voltage of 10V and a base current of $20\mu A$

$$R = \frac{10 - 0·6}{20 \times 10^{-6}} \ \Omega = 4·7M\Omega$$

Although apparently satisfactory, this method is rarely used for the following reasons.

(1) An amplifier requires a fixed value of quiescent collector current. With a fixed value of R_B we would obtain a constant value of base current and hence a constant collector current for a transistor with a particular value of h_{FE}. However, in mass-produced transistors the value of h_{FE} is liable to vary over quite a large range of, say, 100 to 500 with transistors of the same type number. Thus with a fixed value of base current, the collector current would vary over a large range of 1:5. This would upset the operating conditions of the amplifier and cause severe distortion.

(2) If the supply line voltage to the amplifier were to vary, the base current of the transistor would also vary since the bias current is approximately proportional to the supply voltage. This would cause a large variation in the quiescent collector current and would adversely affect the operating conditions of the amplifier.

(3) The arrangement does not provide any protection against variations in ambient temperature. An increase in working temperature of the transistor will increase the leakage current I_{CEO} which will increase the quiescent collector current.

A far better arrangement and one most commonly used is shown in Fig. 5.3(b). First, a resistor R3 is placed in the emitter circuit which will thus carry the emitter current. The emitter voltage V_e is given by $I_e \times R3$. A potential divider R1, R2 is used to feed an

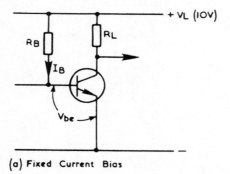

(a) Fixed Current Bias

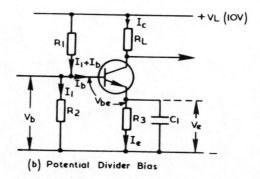

(b) Potential Divider Bias

Fig. 5.3 Methods of providing bias for bipolar transistors.

approximately constant voltage V_b to the base. The required value of V_b (the voltage across $R2$) is V_e plus the base–emitter voltage drop V_{be}.

Assume that the value of $R3$ is chosen to give a V_e of 1·4V and that the forward bias V_{be} is 0·6V. The voltage V_b across $R2$ will be 1·4V + 0·6V = 2·0V. In order that the base voltage does not vary appreciably with the base current, the bleeder current I_1 flowing in $R1$ and $R2$ should be large compared with the base current. Suppose I_1 is made $10 \times I_b$. Thus if the base current is 20μA, I_1 will be 200μA which is the current in $R2$. The value of $R2$ is therefore

$$\frac{2}{200 \times 10^{-6}} = 10\text{k}\Omega$$

The current flowing in $R1$ will be $I_1 + I_b = 220\mu$A, and the voltage across $R1$ will be $V_L - V_b = 10 - 2 = 8$V. The value of $R1$ is therefore

$$\frac{8}{220 \times 10^{-6}} = 36\cdot363\text{k}\Omega, \text{ say } 36\text{k}\Omega.$$

In practice the nearest preferred value of 33kΩ or 39kΩ would be used. If a collector current of 2mA is aimed for, then since the emitter current is practically the same the approximate value of $R3$ would be

$$\frac{1\cdot4}{2 \times 10^{-3}} = 700\Omega$$

(The nearest preferred value of 680Ω would be used.)

The particular feature of this biasing arrangement will now be explained. Suppose that the emitter current increases. Since this current flows in $R3$, the emitter voltage V_e will

rise. Now if I_e increases, I_b must increase but as the bleeder current I_1 is made large compared with I_b the base voltage V_b will remain reasonably constant. In consequence, due to the rise in V_e, the forward bias V_{be} is reduced. This will cause the emitter current to fall thereby practically cancelling the original rise. If the emitter current decreases V_e falls thereby increasing V_{be} (V_b remaining constant) and the emitter current will rise. This rise will oppose the original fall of emitter current.

Thus the action of $R3$ together with the potential divider $R1$, $R2$ supplying constant base voltage V_b, is to stabilise the emitter current and hence the collector current of the transistor. This stabilising action on the collector current will take place if I_c varies as a result of (a) change in h_{FE}; or (b) variation in supply rail voltage; or (c) variation in ambient temperature.

In this description we have been considering only the stabilisation of the d.c. or quiescent conditions of the transistor amplifier. When a signal is applied, the effect of $R3$ (without $C1$) would be to reduce the signal variations of collector current. This is undesirable as the a.c. gain of the amplifier would be reduced. Thus to maintain the a.c. gain, $R3$ is decoupled by the capacitor $C1$ which has such a value that its reactance is very much smaller than the value of $R3$. This is discussed fully in Chapter 14.

An alternative method of biasing which is sometimes used is shown in Fig. 5.4(a). The forward bias current is supplied by $R1$ connected between collector and base. Suppose that R_L is 1kΩ and a collector current of 2mA is to be used. The voltage drop across R_L

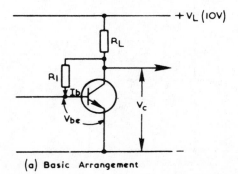

(a) Basic Arrangement

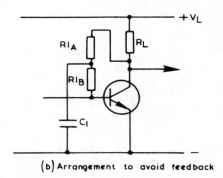

(b) Arrangement to avoid feedback

Fig. 5.4 Alternative biasing arrangement for bipolar transistors.

will be $2 \times 10^{-3} \times 10^3 = 2V$. With a supply rail of 10V, the steady collector voltage V_c will be $10 - 2 = 8V$. Now $V_c = V_{R1} + V_{be}$, thus if $V_{be} = 0.6V$ the voltage drop across $R1$ (V_{R1}) will be $8 - 0.6 = 7.4V$. If the base current is $20\mu A$ as in the previous example, the value of $R1$ will be

$$R1 = \frac{7.4}{20 \times 10^{-6}} = 370\,000\Omega$$

(The nearest preferred value of 390kΩ would be used.)

This method also provides a stabilising action on collector current. If, say, I_c increases for any of the reasons discussed there will be an increase in the volt drop across R_L and the collector–emitter voltage V_c will fall. In consequence the base–emitter voltage V_{be} and I_b will fall thereby reducing the collector current until equilibrium is reached. Since $R1$ is connected between collector and base any signal voltage variations across R_L will also be fed back to the base and reduce the a.c. gain of the amplifier. To avoid a reduction in the a.c. gain the circuit may be modified to that shown in Fig. 5.4(b). $R1_A + R1_B$ is made the same value as previously calculated and the operation as regards d.c. is identical. If, however, $C1$ is included and given a value so that its reactance is small compared with $R1_A$ value, the a.c. feedback will be eliminated.

(b) **Unipolar Transistor Bias.** An n-channel JUGFET is normally operated with its gate negative with respect to its source and a common method of achieving this is shown in

Fig. 5.5(a). Here a resistor R_s is connected between the source and common line such that it carries the source current I_s which will provide a voltage drop (V_s) across R_s with polarity as shown. This voltage drop provides the required value of bias voltage. The gate is connected to the common line via a resistor R_G and since the gate current is minute there will be negligible voltage drop across R_G if it is not made more than 1–2MΩ. Thus the gate potential is the same as that of the common line, i.e. the same as the potential at the lower end of R_s. Therefore the gate is negative to the source by the voltage drop across R_s.

With a source current of, say, 4mA and a required bias of 2·8V the value of R_s would be

$$\frac{2.8}{4 \times 10^{-3}} = 700\Omega$$

(A preferred value of 680Ω may be used.)

The source resistor method of biasing stabilises the operating point of the fet against variations in the source–drain current in the same way as the emitter resistor in Fig. 5.3(b). To prevent a reduction in the a.c. gain of the amplifier the source resistor is decoupled by capacitor C_1.

The biasing arrangement of Fig. 5.5(b) is sometimes used as this is more effective in dealing with wide spreads in the g_m of JUGFETS of the same type. A potential divider $R1$, $R3$ provides a voltage on the gate (V_g) which is positive to the common line. This voltage is made less than the voltage drop (V_s) across the source resistor R_s and the difference between V_s and V_g gives the required bias

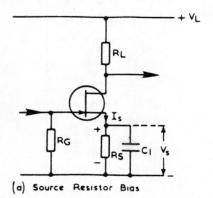

(a) Source Resistor Bias

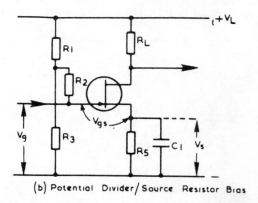

(b) Potential Divider/Source Resistor Bias

Fig. 5.5 Methods of providing bias for jugfets.

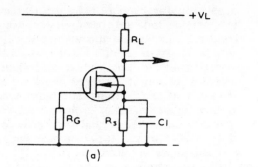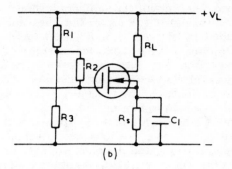

Fig. 5.6 Biasing arrangements for n-channel depletion mosfets.

voltage. For example if V_s is 5V and V_g is 2V the effective bias voltage is 3V with the gate negative to the source. This method allows a larger value of R_s to be used for a given source-to-drain current and gives better stabilisation of the drain current with spreads in g_m. The presence of the potential divider $R1$, $R3$ would tend to lower the input resistance of the amplifier if the junction of these resistors were connected directly to the gate. As regards a.c., $R1$ and $R3$ are effectively in parallel with each other and would shunt the input terminals of the fet. The use of $R2$ effectively increases the input impedance to

$$R2 + \frac{R1 \times R3}{R1 + R3}.$$

With an n-channel depletion mosfet the gate is biased negatively with respect to the source and either of the arrangements shown in Fig. 5.6. may be used. These are directly equivalent to the methods used in Fig. 5.5. for jugfets, the principle of biasing and stabilisation being the same. When an n-channel enhancement mosfet is used the gate must be biased positively to the source and the circuit of Fig. 5.7 may be used. This arrangement is the same as that used in Fig. 5.3(b) for the bipolar transistor except for the 'stand-off' resistor $R2$. $R1$ and $R3$ values are chosen so that the gate is made positive to the source, i.e. there is a greater volts drop across $R3$ than across R_s. The source resistor R_s provides d.c. stabilisation of the drain current by altering the effective gate-to-source voltage. It will be noted that this biasing arrangement can be used for enhancement and depletion type mosfets. However, for the depletion type, as was explained, the values of the bias components are chosen to make the gate negative with respect to the source.

Common-emitter and Common-source Voltage Amplifier

The common-emitter and common-source modes of operation are the connections most frequently used. Basic operation of the

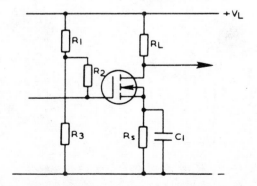

Fig. 5.7 One method of biasing an n-channel enhancement mosfet.

common-emitter voltage amplifier is shown in Fig. 5.8(a). Forward bias for the transistor is provided by R1, R2 with R3 used for d.c. stabilisation of the collector current. C1 prevents the d.c. base bias voltage being shorted out via the input signal source. This capacitor will have a low reactance to the input signal, assumed to be sinusoidal.

The steady forward bias V_{be} applied to the transistor will give rise to a steady value of collector current and a steady voltage drop across the collector load R_L. Thus the voltage between the collector and negative line (V_c) will also be steady and its value is assumed to be half the line supply voltage, see waveform B. When the input signal is applied through C1 it causes the forward bias to alter. On positive half-cycles, the forward bias will be increased thereby increasing the collector current and the voltage developed across R_L. In consequence, V_c will fall below its steady level. During

negative half-cycles of the input, the forward bias will be reduced thereby decreasing the collector current and the voltage developed across R_L. As a result V_c will rise above its steady level. In this way a magnified but **inverted** version of the input signal voltage is obtained at the output. The output signal voltage may be taken from across R_L or between the collector and the negative line since, as regards a.c., the positive and negative rails are short circuited.

The operation of a common source amplifier is similar. With an n-channel depletion mosfet the gate is biased negatively with respect to the source and in Fig. 5.8(b) is obtained by the voltage drop across R2. The input signal is applied to the gate via the low reactance of C1. This capacitor will block any d.c. component present in the signal. The steady bias voltage V_{gs} of waveform A will give rise to a steady drain current thereby produc-

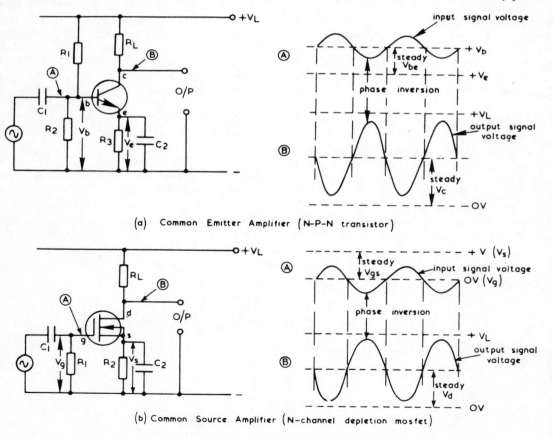

(a)   Common Emitter Amplifier (N-P-N transistor)

(b) Common Source Amplifier (N-channel depletion mosfet)

Fig. 5.8 Common-emitter and common-source amplifiers.

ing a steady voltage drop across the load resistor R_L. Thus the voltage between drain and the common negative line (V_d) will also be steady and is assumed to be half the line supply voltage, see waveform B. On positive half-cycles of the input signal the bias will be reduced causing an increase in the drain current and the voltage drop across R_L, and V_d will fall below its steady level. Conversely, on negative half-cycles of the input the bias is increased causing a decrease in drain current and the voltage drop across R_L. As a result V_d will rise above its steady level. Again, a magnified but **inverted** version of the input signal voltage is obtained at the output. The voltage gain of the common-source amplifier is less than that of the common-emitter amplifier.

Common-base and Common-gate Voltage Amplifier

Circuit arrangements for the common-base and common-gate amplifiers are shown in Fig. 5.9. With the common-base amplifier of Fig. 5.9(a), $R1$ and $R2$ bias the base positively to the emitter in the same way as for the common-emitter amplifier. $R3$ is the emitter stabilising resistor, decoupled by $C2$ to prevent a.c. negative feedback. $C1$ is added to connect the base to the common line as regards a.c. This is essential to prevent the a.c. component of base current flowing in $R2$, i.e. it makes the circuit common-base by connecting the base to the common line.

The input signal is now applied to the emitter and the signal source must provide a path for the d.c. component of emitter current. Waveforms A and B show the basic operation for sinewave input. As for common-emitter operation, the steady V_{be} gives rise to a steady I_c and this produces a steady voltage drop across R_L. In consequence the collector-to-common line voltage V_c is also steady. When the input signal is on a positive half-cycle at the emitter the forward bias is reduced causing I_c to fall and V_c to rise above

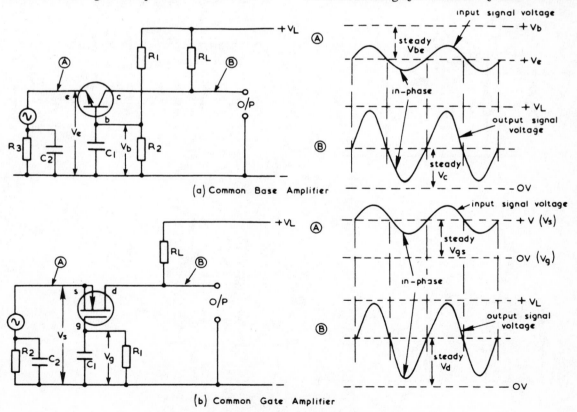

Fig. 5.9 Common-base and common-gate amplifiers.

its steady level. Conversely, on negative half-cycles of the input signal the forward bias is increased causing I_c to increase and V_c to fall below its steady level. Thus at the output a magnified replica of the input signal is obtained which is in phase with the input signal.

In the common-gate amplifier of Fig. 5.9(b), $R2$ provides the required bias and is decoupled by $C2$ to prevent a.c. feedback. Resistor $R1$ provides a d.c. return to the common line for the gate and $C1$ connects the gate to the common line as regards a.c. The input signal is applied to the source electrode and the signal source must provide a d.c. path for the source current.

Positive half-cycles of the input signal increase the bias thereby reducing the drain current and causing the drain-to-common line voltage to rise above its steady level. Con-

versely, on negative half-cycles the bias is reduced, the drain current is increased and the output voltage falls below its steady level. An amplified version of the input signal is obtained at the output and, as for the common-base circuit, input and output signal voltages are in phase. The voltage gain of the common-gate amplifier is less than that of a common-base amplifier.

Common-collector and Common-drain Amplifiers

In the common-collector amplifier of Fig. 5.10(a), the potential divider $R1$, $R2$ forward bias the transistor in the usual way. The output signal voltage is developed across R_L placed in the emitter circuit and this resistor also provides d.c. stabilisation of the operating point.

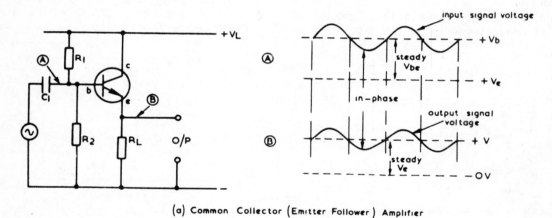

(a) Common Collector (Emitter Follower) Amplifier

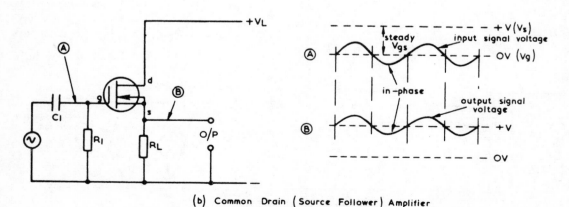

(b) Common Drain (Source Follower) Amplifier

Fig. 5.10 Common-collector and common-drain amplifiers.

The steady forward bias V_{be} will cause a steady emitter current to flow and produce a steady voltage drop V_e across the emitter resistor R_L. When the input signal voltage goes positive the forward bias is increased causing an increase in emitter current and in the voltage drop across R_L. During negative half-cycles of the input the forward bias is reduced causing the emitter current to decrease and less voltage to be developed across R_L. Input and output signal voltages are thus in phase in the common-collector connection but there is however **no voltage gain**. This is because the signal voltage across R_L provides a.c. feedback reducing the effective signal voltage applied between base and emitter. If the output signal voltage were able to rise to an amplitude such that it equalled the input signal voltage (which is impossible) the net signal voltage between base and emitter would be zero and so the output would be zero. Thus the voltage gain is less than unity, permitting a net signal voltage between base and emitter to drive the transistor. Because of the a.c. feedback the input resistance of the common-collector amplifier is higher than the common-emitter amplifier, lying typically in the range 5–500kΩ. The output resistance is low and lies in the range 50–500Ω. The main use of the common-collector or 'emitter-follower' amplifier is as a buffer amplifier connected between a high-impedance source and a low-impedance load.

The equivalent circuit arrangement for the unipolar transistor is given in Fig. 5.10(b). Here the steady voltage drop across R_L biases the gate negative with respect to the source in the normal way. The signal voltage output across R_L has an in-phase relationship with the input signal voltage as for the common-

collector circuit and a voltage gain less than unity.

The table below summarises the features discussed for the three modes of amplifier connection:

Determining the Voltage Gain of a Common-emitter/source Amplifier

The voltage gain (A_v) of an amplifier

$$= \frac{\text{Change of output voltage}}{\text{Change of input voltage}}.$$

If the parameters of the transistor are known the voltage gain may be calculated as follows:

(a) **Common-emitter Amplifier**

For a common-emitter amplifier the voltage gain (A_v) is given approximately by

$$A_v = \frac{h_{fe} \times R_L}{R_{IN}} \text{ (or } A_v = g_m R_L)$$

Example

A common-emitter transistor amplifier has an h_{fe} of 60 and an input resistance of 800Ω. What will be the voltage gain when used with a collector load of 1·5kΩ?

$$A_v = \frac{60 \times 1·5 \times 10^3}{800} = 112·5.$$

(b) **Common-source Amplifier**

For a common-source amplifier the voltage gain (A_v) is given by

$$A_v = \frac{g_m \times R_L \times r_{ds}}{r_{ds} + R_L}$$

where r_{ds} is the drain-to-source a.c. resistance.

Connection	Voltage Gain	Phase relationship between input and output signal voltages
Common Emitter	High	Phase reversal
Common Base	High	In phase
Common Collector	< 1	In phase
Common Source	Medium	Phase reversal
Common Gate	Medium	In phase
Common Drain	< 1	In phase

If r_{ds} is much greater than R_L which is often the case, the expression may be simplified to

$$A_v \approx g_m \times R_L.$$

Example

An fet common-source amplifier has a g_m of 5×10^{-3}S and an r_{ds} of 100kΩ. What will be the voltage gain when used with a drain load of 5kΩ?

Since r_{ds} is much greater than R_L the simplified expression may be used, thus

$$A_v \approx g_m \times R_L$$
$$\approx 5 \times 10^{-3} \times 5 \times 10^3$$
$$\approx 25$$

The voltage gain for a fet amplifier is appreciably smaller than for a bipolar transistor amplifier since the g_m is much lower (3mS for a fet as opposed to 40mS for a bipolar device).

Use of a Load Line

The voltage and current gain of a bipolar transistor may also be determined with the aid of a load line drawn on the output characteristics.

Consider Fig. 5.11 which shows the steady voltages and current that exist in a common-emitter amplifier. Under all operating conditions the supply voltage V_L must be equal to the sum of the voltages between the collector and common line (V_c) and the voltage drop V_{R_L} across the collector load resistor, i.e.

$$V_L = V_{R_L} + V_c$$

Now $V_{R_L} = I_c R_L$

Therefore $V_L = I_c R_L + V_c$ \qquad (1)

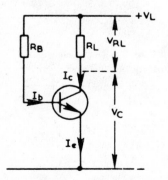

Fig. 5.11 Common-emitter amplifier.

Equation (1) is of the form $y = mx + c$ and is the equation to a straight line. To draw the line it is only necessary to plot two points and connect them.

Point 1

$$\text{Let } I_c = 0$$
$$\therefore \text{ using equation (1),}$$
$$V_L = V_c.$$

Point 2

$$\text{Let } V_c = 0$$
$$\therefore \text{ using equation (1),}$$
$$V_L = I_c R_L$$
$$\text{or } I_c = \frac{V_L}{R_L}$$

Thus if the two points $I_c = 0$, $V_c = V_L$ and $V_c = 0$, $I_c = V_L/R_L$ are plotted on the output characteristics and the points joined, a load line is formed for a particular value of load resistance and supply voltage.

It will be assumed that the output characteristics of Fig. 5.12 are those of the transistor used in the circuit of Fig. 5.11 and that the supply V_L is 10V and R_L is 2kΩ.

Point 1 is given by:

$$I_c = 0, \ V_c = V_L = 10\text{V}.$$

Point 2 is given by;
$$V_c = 0, \ I_c = \frac{V_L}{R_L} = \frac{10}{2 \times 10^3} = 5\text{mA}.$$

These two points are shown on the characteristics with a line drawn between them. This line is the load line for the condition $R_L = 2$kΩ and $V_L = 10$V. If the load is changed or the supply voltage altered a new load line must be constructed.

With the base of the transistor supplied with a steady base current of, say, 30μA via R_B, the interception of the curve of $I_b = 30\mu$A with the load line (marked X) gives the d.c. operating point. Normally, this point is chosen to lie towards the middle of the load line. By projecting down and across from point X the steady V_c and I_c may be found, which in this example are approximately 4·2V and 2·8mA respectively.

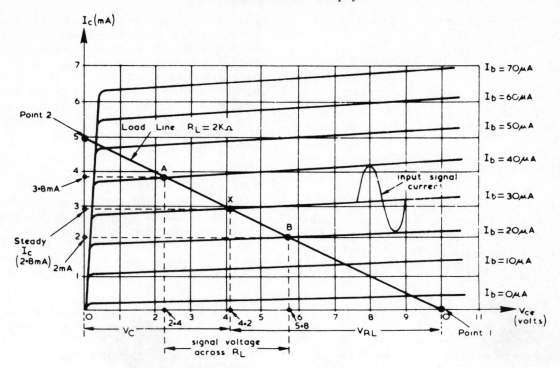

Fig. 5.12 Common-emitter output characteristics and load line.

The product of the supply voltage V_L and the steady I_c gives the d.c. power taken from the supply.

Therefore d.c. power taken from the supply
$$= 10 \times 2{\cdot}8 \times 10^{-3}\text{W} = 28\text{mW}.$$

The d.c. power dissipated in the load R_L is the product of the voltage across R_L and the steady collector current.

Thus d.c. power dissipated in R_L =
$$(10 - 4{\cdot}2) \times 2{\cdot}8 \times 10^{-3}\text{W} = 16{\cdot}24\text{mW}.$$

The d.c. power dissipated at the collector of the transistor is the product of the steady V_c and the steady I_c.

Thus d.c. power dissipated at collector =
$$4{\cdot}2 \times 2{\cdot}8 \times 10^{-3}\text{W} = 11{\cdot}76\text{mW}.$$

Note that the sum of the d.c. powers dissipated at the collector and in R_L is equal to the d.c. power taken from the supply.

If the input signal voltage v_i and the input resistance R_{IN} are known the voltage gain may be determined as follows. Suppose that v_i is 20mV peak-to-peak and R_{IN} is 1kΩ, then the input current (base current) i_i is $v_i/R_{IN} = 20\mu A$ peak-to-peak, see Fig. 5.13. Thus the operating point on the load line moves between points A and B, i.e. $10\mu A$ peak swing either side of the steady base current of $30\mu A$. By projecting down from points A and B to the voltage axis the peak-to-peak signal voltage developed across R_L may be found, which in this example is approximately $5{\cdot}8 - 2{\cdot}4 = 3{\cdot}4V$.

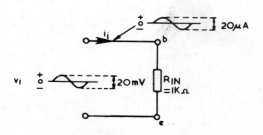

Fig. 5.13 Signal input current.

Since the voltage gain A_v

$$= \frac{\text{Output signal voltage}}{\text{Input signal voltage}}$$

Therefore $A_v = \dfrac{3\cdot4}{20 \times 10^{-3}} = 170$.

The current gain

$$A_i = \frac{\text{Output signal current}}{\text{Input signal current}}$$

and may be obtained directly using the load line. The peak-to-peak output current may be found by projecting across to the current axis from points A and B which in this example is $3\cdot8 - 2 = 1\cdot8\text{mA}$. The peak-to-peak input current is $20\mu\text{A}$.

$$\text{Thus } A_i = \frac{1\cdot8 \times 10^{-3}}{20 \times 10^{-6}} = 90.$$

Additional information that may be obtained from the load line includes an estimation of the amount of distortion that may be present in the output. This may be found by noting whether the increments AX and BX are equal. If these distances are the same then the peak swings either side of the steady operating point will be equal and distortionless output will be obtained. In our example the distance AX is slightly greater than the distance BX, thus there will be some distortion in the output.

Bottoming and Clipping

When a large input signal is applied to a transistor the output may be severely flattened on one or both peaks depending upon the operating conditions. Consider the load line CD of Fig. 5.14. where a steady base current of $40\mu\text{A}$ results in a quiescent operating point X. If the peak base input signal current is $40\mu\text{A}$ the operating point will move up the load line to point A on one half-cycle and down the load line to point B on the other half-cycle.

At point A where the load line cuts the knee

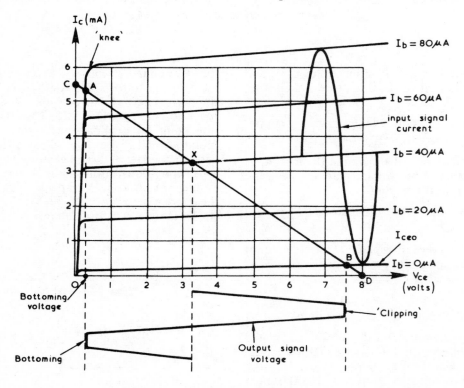

Fig. 5.14 Clipping and bottoming.

of the characteristic for $I_b = 80\mu A$, the collector-to-emitter voltage falls to an extremely small value (a fraction of a volt). If the base current is increased above $80\mu A$ there will be no further reduction in the collector-to-emitter voltage which remains at its minimum level. This condition is known as 'bottoming' and results in a flattening of the negative peak of the output signal voltage.

Similarly, at point B where the collector-to-emitter voltage is practically the same as that of the supply, the positive peak of the output voltage will be flattened when the base current reaches zero or the signal input attempts to reverse bias the transistor. This condition is called 'clipping' and is the supply rail limit in rise of the output voltage. The clipping level of the output signal voltage is slightly less than the supply voltage due to the voltage drop across R_L produced by the leakage current I_{ceo}.

If the quiescent operating point is chosen for maximum output then clipping and bottoming

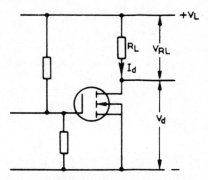

Fig. 5.15 *Common-source amplifier.*

will occur approximately at the same point on both half-cycles. If the operating point is moved up the load line, bottoming will occur before the clipping level is reached or vice versa with point X lower down the load line.

The load line for a field-effect transistor may be constructed in the same way as for the bipolar transistor. Consider Fig. 5.15 and the steady voltages and current in the amplifier. Under all operating conditions

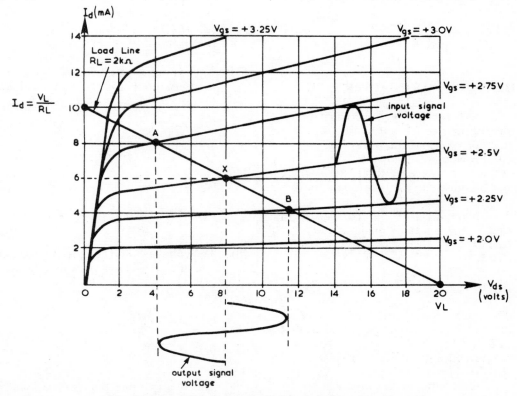

Fig. 5.16 *Common-source output characteristics and load line.*

$$V_L = V_{RL} + V_d$$
$$\text{or } V_L = I_d R_L + V_d.$$

The two points required to construct the load line are:

$$\text{(i) } I_d = 0, \ V_L = V_d$$
$$\text{and (ii) } V_d = 0, \ I_d = \frac{V_L}{R_L}$$

A load line for $R_L = 2k\Omega$ and $V_L = 20V$ is given in Fig. 5.16 superimposed on the output characteristics. With a steady bias voltage of $+2{\cdot}5V$ for an n-channel enhancement mosfet, the steady operating point is at X providing a quiescent V_{ds} of 8V and a quiescent I_d of 6mA. Assuming an input signal voltage of $0{\cdot}5V$ peak-to-peak, the operation moves between the limit points of A and B on the load line. The output signal voltage varies between the limits of approximately 4V and $11{\cdot}5V$, a peak-to-peak variation of about $7{\cdot}5V$.

The voltage gain A_v is thus $\dfrac{7{\cdot}5}{0{\cdot}5} = 15$.

QUESTIONS ON CHAPTER FIVE

(1) With reference to Fig. 5.3(b) on page 50, the purpose of $R3$ is to:
(a) Forward bias the transistor
(b) Provide a.c. feedback
(c) Reverse bias the transistor
(d) Stabilise the d.c. working point.

(2) The magnitude of the current I_1 in Fig. 5.3(b) is usually made about:
(a) $10 \times I_e$
(b) $I_b/10$
(c) $10 \times I_b$
(d) $10 \times I_c$.

(3) The advantage of the biasing arrangement of Fig. 5.5(b) on page 52 over that of Fig. 5.5(a) is that it:
(a) Provides a smaller bias
(b) Provides a larger bias
(c) Deals better with spreads in g_m
(d) Has a higher input resistance.

(4) In a resistive-loaded, common-base amplifier:
(a) There is no phase reversal between input and output signal voltages
(b) The output resistance is low and the input resistance high
(c) The output current is the base current
(d) The input current is the base current.

(5) The voltage gain of a common-drain amplifier would be typically:
(a) 100
(b) 25
(c) 10
(d) 0·99.

(6) The steady voltage between the collector and common line of a common-emitter amplifier is 5V and the steady collector current is 2mA. If the supply rail voltage is 13V the value of the collector load resistance is:
(a) $4k\Omega$
(b) $2k\Omega$
(c) $16k\Omega$
(d) $9k\Omega$

(7) The voltage gain A_v of a common-emitter amplifier is given approximately by:
(a) $A_v = \dfrac{R_L}{h_{fe}}$
(b) $A_v = \dfrac{h_{fe} \times R_L}{R_{IN}}$
(c) $A_v = \dfrac{R_L}{g_m}$
(d) $A_v = \dfrac{R_L}{h_{fe}}.$

(8) The voltage gain A_v of a common-source amplifier is given approximately by:
(a) $A_v = g_m \times R_L$
(b) $A_v = g_m \times R_{IN}$
(c) $A_v = \dfrac{g_m}{R_L}$
(d) $A_v = \dfrac{g_m}{R_{IN}}.$

(9) The two extreme points on a load line drawn on the output characteristics of a

common amplifier are given by Point 1 I_c = 0, V_c = 10V and Point 2 V_c = 0, I_c = 2·0mA. The values of the supply rail voltage and the collector load resistance are respectively:

(a) 15V and 1kΩ
(b) 10V and 5kΩ
(c) 5V and 20kΩ
(d) 10V and 20kΩ.

(10) If the supply rail voltage in Fig. 5.16 is

reduced from 20V to 16V and a load line is drawn for this condition, it will:

(a) Have a greater slope than the original load line
(b) Lie parallel to the original load line
(c) Coincide exactly with the original load line
(d) Have less slope than the original load line.

(Answers on page 369)

OTHER SEMICONDUCTOR DEVICES

Objectives
1 To explain the operation, characteristics and uses of the SCR, Triac, Diac, SCS and Unijunction transistor.
2 To describe the construction of thick-film, thin-film and monolithic integrated circuits.
3 To describe the operation and characteristics of LEDs, Liquid Crystal displays and Hall effect devices.

THYRISTORS

The thyristor family embraces any semiconductor switch whose 'on'/'off' action depends upon a regenerative effect in a p-n-p-n sandwich. These devices can be made to conduct easily in one direction only or in both directions. They are available with two, three or four terminals.

(a) Silicon Controlled Rectifier (SCR)

The most commonly used member of the thyristor family is the SCR or 'reverse blocking triode thyristor'. It has three terminals and is unidirectional. Manufacturing methods include planar and alloy-diffused techniques. Figure 6.1 illustrates the alloy-diffused method. The centre n-type silicon wafer is diffused on both faces with a p-type impurity thus forming a p-n-p structure. A connection to one of the p-regions forms the anode electrode. A pellet of n-type impurity is then alloyed to the other p-region to form the **cathode** electrode. The **gate** terminal is bonded to the lower p-region which constitutes the control layer. This constitutes what is called a 'cathode controlled SCR'. The gate terminal may be brought out from the upper n-region producing an 'anode controlled SCR'. Circuit symbols for both types are given in Fig. 6.2.

Between the anode and cathode leads of the

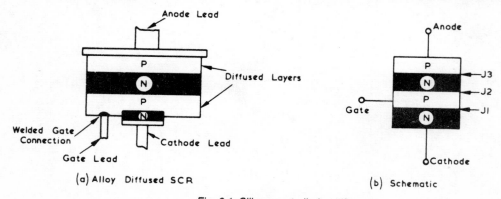

(a) Alloy Diffused SCR (b) Schematic

Fig. 6.1 Silicon controlled rectifier.

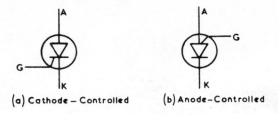

Fig. 6.2 SCR circuit symbols.

device there are thus four layers with 'p' and 'n' material alternately arranged as shown in schematic form in Fig. 6.1(b). At first sight the structure appears to form three separate diode junctions ($J1$, $J2$ and $J3$). Let us first examine this '3-diode' concept and see if we can use it to explain the action of the device. Suppose the anode is made negative to the cathode but no connection is made to the gate. $J1$ and $J3$ would then be reverse biased but $J2$ forward biased. Thus very little current would flow from cathode to anode until the applied voltage was sufficient to break down the junctions $J1$ and $J3$. This is true of the device in that it behaves as a reverse biased diode when the anode is negative to the cathode (see the reverse blocking region of Fig. 6.3). If the supply voltage polarity is now reversed making the anode positive to the cathode, $J1$ and $J3$ will be forward biased and $J2$ reverse biased. Again the current would be small until

the applied voltage was high enough to break down $J2$. This time however when breakdown occurs the characteristic is not like that of a diode. As Fig. 6.3 shows the voltage drop across the device rapidly falls to a very low value. Thus the '3-diode' concept falls down at this point because the three diodes are not isolated from one another.

The p-n-p-n structure is best visualised as consisting of two transistors one of which is a p-n-p and the other a n-p-n, directly coupled as shown in Fig. 6.4(c). The internal feedback loop formed allows the collector current of one transistor to feed the base of the other. Consider now the operation when the anode is made positive to the cathode but the magnitude of the voltage is insufficient to cause breakdown, i.e. the device is in the forward blocking region of Fig. 6.3 and the collector–base junction of both transistors is reverse biased. Now the collector–base leakage current of, say, TR1 will be amplified by TR1 and the resulting collector current fed to TR2 base. This input current will be amplified by TR2, the collector current of which will be fed back to TR1 base for subsequent amplification. The magnitude of the current I flowing between anode and cathode depends upon the current gain around the internal feedback loop. The loop gain is the product of the individual current gains of the two transistors. Provided the loop gain is less than one, the current I is

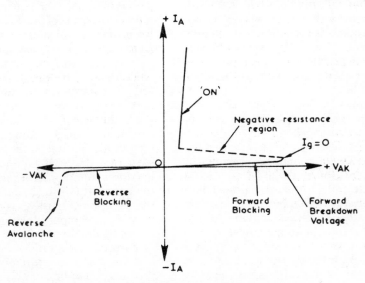

Fig. 6.3 Voltage–current characteristics of SCR.

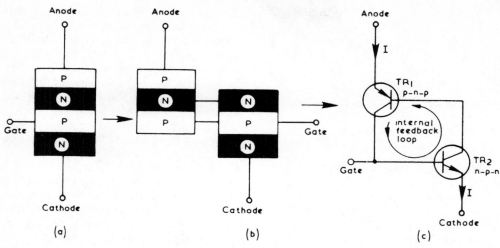

Fig. 6.4 Two-transistor analogy of SCR.

small. If the loop gain is equal to one, the loop becomes regenerative and each transistor drives the other into saturation. At this point all junctions assume a forward bias and the current I rapidly rises to a large value, being limited only by the external circuit resistance.

During manufacturing it is arranged that the loop gain is less than unity at low currents and voltages. To turn the SCR 'on' it is necessary to increase the loop gain. It is a property of transistors that the gain increases with increase in emitter current. There are several mechanisms that will initiate a rise in emitter current and hence a rise in current gain. The important mechanisms are: (a) increasing the collector–emitter voltage; (b) forward biasing the base–emitter junction, i.e. providing base current; and (c) allowing light energy to fall on the centre junction.

Mechanism (a) is that responsible for turning 'on' the SCR with zero gate current (Fig. 6.3). It occurs when the collector–emitter voltage is raised to such a level that the energy of the leakage current carriers is sufficient to cause the removal of additional carriers from the collector–base region. These carriers in their turn dislodge more carriers which add to the numbers arriving at the collector. This results in an avalanche breakdown and the current increases sharply. As a result the gain of both transistors is increased and when the loop gain reaches unity the SCR comes 'on'.

The usual way of switching 'on' an SCR is via mechanism (b) by forward biasing the base–emitter junction of one of the analogous transistors. With a cathode-controlled SCR the gate is made positive to the cathode and will thus forward bias the base–emitter junction of the analogous n-p-n transistor TR2 of Fig. 6.4(a). For an anode-controlled SCR, the gate is made negative to the anode thus forward biasing the base–emitter junction of the p-n-p transistor TR1.

As the forward bias voltage applied to the gate is increased the gate current rises and the effect is to cause the SCR to turn 'on' at a lower forward break-over voltage as illustrated in Fig. 6.5. Once the SCR has 'fired' the gate voltage may be removed and the device will remain in the 'on' state. To switch the SCR 'off' it is necessary to remove or reduce the anode voltage so that the current falls below the 'holding level' I_h. The SCR will then revert to the forward blocking or 'off' state. The magnitude of the gate current required to switch-on the SCR is much smaller than the maximum anode-to-cathode current and since the gate–cathode voltage is small, the power that is supplied to the gate circuit need be only very small compared with the power that can be controlled by the SCR. Only a short pulse of current is required to switch an SCR 'on' and the time of switch-on is a few microseconds depending upon the magnitude of the gate current.

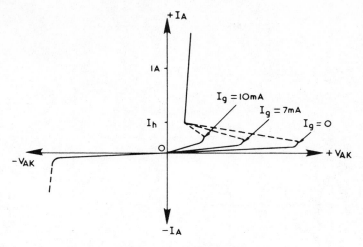

Fig. 6.5 Effect of increasing gate current.

Although light may easily be excluded from the device, mechanism (c) permits an SCR to be switched 'on' by a beam of light. Such a device is called a **Light Activated Silicon Controlled Rectifier (LASCR)** which does not require a gate connection.

Use of the SCR

The main use of an SCR is as a control device, controlling the amount of power fed to a load. Applications include the control of the average power fed to motors, lamps, heaters and d.c. supplies for electronic equipment.

The basic idea of one form of control is shown in Fig. 6.6 using a cathode-controlled SCR. The resistor R represents the load and the SCR is in series with it. The gate electrode is fed with positive pulses, the phase of which, relative to the a.c. supply, are made variable. If the phase of the pulses applied to the gate occur slightly delayed on the start of the positive half-cycles of the input voltage, the SCR will not fire until instants Z. Current will commence to flow in the load at these points and continue until instants X when the anode-to-cathode voltage has been reduced to zero. The magnitude of the current flowing during the 'on' period of the SCR will be determined by the value of R and the amplitude of the applied voltage. No current will flow during the negative half-cycles of the input as the SCR will be in the non-conducting direction. Current thus flows in bursts during each positive half-cycle. By delaying the phase of the gate triggering pulses, the SCR is made to fire at later instants Y in each positive half-cycle. As a result the current in the load flows in much shorter bursts as shown. The average value of the load current is proportional to the shaded area of the current wave form and can be varied from full value (corresponding to flow during a complete half-cycle) down to zero.

This method of controlling the average power fed to a load is known as 'phase control'. It is an efficient method when compared with traditional methods of controlling the power fed to lamps and motors using dropper resistors, gear boxes, clutches and drive belts, etc. If R is a lamp or motor the thermal or mechanical inertia of the load is used to smooth out the effect of the current pulsations.

The voltage drop across the SCR when 'on' is low (about 1V) hence the power loss is small compared with the power it is controlling. SCRs are available with forward and reverse blocking voltages up to 1kV and with current ratings up to several hundred amperes. Although the forward voltage drop is small, there is considerable power developed in the SCR with large-current operation and a heat sink must be used.

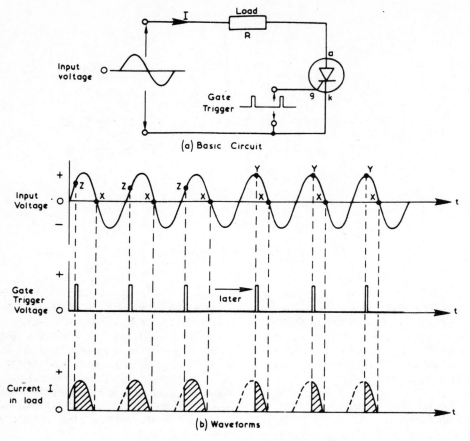

Fig. 6.6 Use of SCR to control current in load.

(b) Triac or Bidirectional SCR

A triac is a bidirectional triode thyristor and a basic construction is shown in Fig. 6.7. It has two main terminals T2 and T1 between which the main 'on' current flows and a gate electrode. The triac differs from the ordinary SCR in that current can be made to flow in either direction between T2 and T1, i.e. when T2 is positive to T1 or T2 negative to T1. In addition, it can be triggered into conduction by a gate pulse having either positive or negative polarity with respect to T1. The device may be regarded as two SCRs connected in inverse parallel with a common gate connection.

A typical characteristic is given in Fig. 6.8. In Quadrant 1, the device may be triggered into conduction when T2 is positive with respect to T1 and the gate trigger voltage is

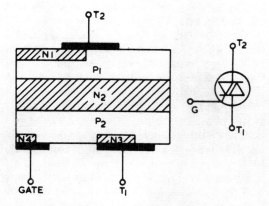

Fig. 6.7 Triac construction and circuit symbol.

positive with respect to T1. In this mode of operation, a four-layer semiconductor sandwich is formed between T2 and T1 by the P1,

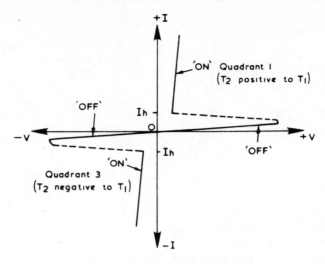

Fig. 6.8 Characteristic of the triac.

N2, P2 and N3 layers with the gate connection formed by the P2 layer. As for the ordinary SCR, increasing the gate current will cause the triac to trigger into the 'on' state at a lower T2-to-T1 voltage.

If the supply polarity is reversed making T2 negative with respect to T1, the device may be triggered 'on' by applying a gate trigger voltage having negative polarity with respect to T1. This is shown by the characteristic in Quadrant 3. Here the four-layer sandwich is formed by the N1, P1, N2 and P2 layers between T2 and T1 with the gate connection formed by the N4 layer. Again, increasing the gate current will cause the triac to fire at a reduced value of voltage between T2 and T1.

To turn 'off' the triac in either of its 'on' states it is necessary to reduce or remove the voltage applied between the two main terminals so that the current falls below the holding level I_h. The advantage of the triac over the SCR is that it can be triggered into conduction with a supply voltage of either polarity applied to the main terminals and can thus be used in relatively simple circuits for the control of current in a.c. systems. In general, the current and voltage ratings of a triac are lower than those of an SCR.

(c) Diac

Diacs are bidirecitonal diode thyristors having two electrodes. A typical characteristic is shown in Fig. 6.9. The device can be made to conduct in either direction (with terminal A positive to terminal B or vice versa) when the applied voltage exceeds the break-over voltage V_{bo}. With the applied voltage level below V_{bo} the diac passes only a small current (less than 100μA) and may be regarded as being in the 'off' state. When V_{bo} is exceeded, the voltage drop across the device falls and the current rises rapidly and this corresponds to the 'on' state.

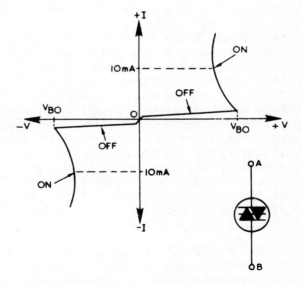

Fig. 6.9 Typical diac characteristic and circuit symbol.

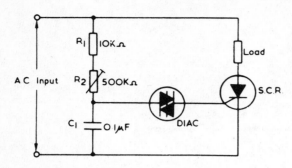

Fig. 6.10 Use of diac in trigger circuit for SCR.

The break-over voltage V_{bo} is of the order of 28–36V and the voltage drop across the diac at a current of 10mA is about 6–10V lower than V_{bo} for a typical device. An average power dissipation is about 150mW.

Diacs are widely used in control circuits to apply trigger pulses to SCRs and triacs and an example is given in Fig. 6.10. Here an SCR is used to control the current in a load fed from an a.c. supply. The diac supplies trigger pulses to the gate of the SCR from a timing circuit consisting of $R1$, $R2$ and $C1$ which is fed from the input supply. During positive half-cycles of the input a voltage builds up across $C1$ at a rate depending upon the time-constant of the timing circuit. When the voltage across $C1$ exceeds the break-over voltage of the diac it is triggered into conduction. $C1$ is then partially discharged by the gate current of the SCR which switches 'on' allowing current to flow in the load. The SCR switches 'off' in the usual way when its anode-to-cathode voltage falls to zero. During negative half-cycles of the input the voltage across $C1$ will reverse its polarity but the SCR will not come 'on' as it will be in its reverse blocking state. If a triac is used in place of the SCR, current will also flow in the load during negative half-cycles of the input when the reversal of voltage across $C1$ once exceeding V_{bo} will cause the diac to conduct in the other direction. Current will then flow in the gate of the triac causing it to go into the 'on' state (Quadrant 3 mode).

(d) Silicon Controlled Switch

A Silicon Controlled Switch (SCS) is a low-power thyristor where connections are brought out from all four semiconductor layers. The circuit symbol is shown in Fig. 6.11.

An SCS may be triggered into conduction by applying positive pulses to the cathode gate or negative pulses to the anode gate. The operation is identical to an SCR but the additional gate improves the versatility of the device. It is used in a wide range of switching applications including memory circuits and field oscillator circuits in television receivers.

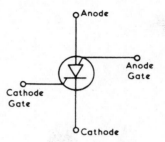

Fig. 6.11 Silicon controlled switch (SCS).

UNIJUNCTION TRANSISTOR

The unijunction transistor (UJT) is another type of trigger device which is often used to control SCRs. The device consists of a small bar of n-type silicon with ohmic (non-rectifying) contacts at either end called the base connections B2 and B1, see Fig. 6.12. A p-n junction is formed between the emitter lead and the bar by alloying an aluminium wire to the bar as shown.

In use, B2 is supplied with a positive voltage with respect to B1 and in the absence of any voltage on the emitter, the resistance between B2 and B1 is high (of the order of 5–10kΩ). It may be considered that the silicon bar acts as a

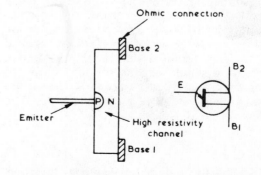

Fig. 6.12 Construction of unijunction transistor.

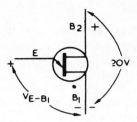

Fig. 6.13 Operation of UJT.

potential divider causing the N-region close to the p-n junction formed to take up a potential between that of B2 and B1. The actual potential depends upon the position of the emitter lead which is usually arranged so that the potential lies in the range of 0·4 to 0·8 of the voltage applied between B2 and B1.

Suppose, for example, the voltage applied between B2 and B1 is 20V as shown in Fig. 6.13 and that the emitter is positioned such that the potential of the N-region close to the p-n junction is 14V (0·7 × the voltage between B2 and B1). Now, if a voltage V_{E-B1} is applied between emitter and B1 with polarity shown and is less than 14V, then the p-n junction will be reverse biased and no emitter current will flow. However, increasing V_{E-B1} so that it exceeds 14V by a small amount (say 0·6V) will cause the p-n junction to become forward biased and emitter current to flow. The flow of current between the emitter and B1 will reduce the resistance

between these electrodes causing more current to flow. Thus the emitter current rises rapidly and the emitter-to-B1 voltage drops, see characteristic of Fig. 6.14. The characteristic shows that emitter current commences to flow when V_{E-B1} is approximately 14·6V but this will vary for a particular device depending upon the position of the emitter lead and the voltage applied between B2 and B1. After passing through a negative resistance region the current rapidly builds up and above a particular emitter current the voltage drop between emitter and B1 rises slightly.

An example of how a UJT may be used to produce trigger pulses for an SCR or timing pulses for an electronic circuit is shown in Fig. 6.15. The UJT is arranged as a relaxation oscillator which generates a sawtooth voltage waveform at the emitter by the slow charging of a capacitor C1 to the supply voltage via R1 and R2 and the rapid discharging of C1 via the UJT.

At switch-on, C1 is uncharged, so the emitter potential is zero and the UJT is 'off'. As C1 slowly charges via R1 and R2, the voltage across C1 rises exponentially. When the voltage across C1 exceeds the potential of the N-region close to the p-n junction, the junction becomes forward biased causing emitter current to flow. C1 will therefore rapidly discharge via the low-value resistor R4. At the end of the discharge period the UJT junction becomes reverse biased and the device goes 'off'. C1 then recommences

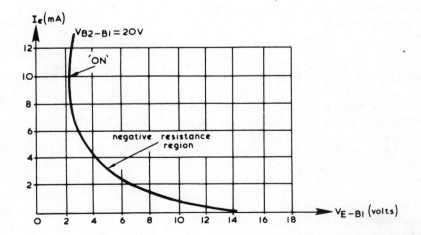

Fig. 6.14 UJT characteristic.

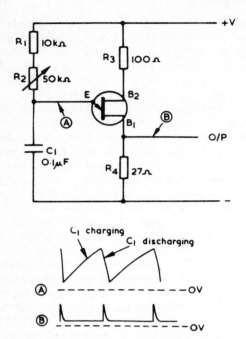

Fig. 6.15 *UJT oscillator for producing timing pulses.*

charging via $R1$ and $R2$ and the cycle is repeated. Each time $C1$ discharges, the current in $R4$ produces a positive-going pulse at the output. These pulses could be used to trigger an SCR or be used as timing pulses for some other purpose. Varying the CR time-constant by altering the value of $R2$ will vary the repetition rate of the output pulses. For the values given, the repetition rate will be in the range 30–200Hz depending upon the characteristics of the UJT. The resistor $R3$ is used to compensate for temperature variations.

MICROMINIATURE ELECTRONIC CIRCUITS

Following the introduction of the bipolar transistor into the electronics industry, efforts were made to make complete electronic circuits very small and more reliable. There are three types of microminature electronic circuits.

(1) Thin-film Circuits

With this type, the passive components, e.g. resistors, capacitors and conductors are built up by the evaporation of metals and insulators through masks to form patterns on a small piece of glass substrate.

The stages in the production of a thin-film circuit may be explained using the simple amplifier circuit of Fig. 6.16(a) and its thin-film version in Fig. 6.16(b). The first step is the evaporation of nichrome through a mask to form the resistors $R1$ and $R2$ on the glass substrate. The next stage is the evaporation of aluminium through a mask to form the lower electrode of the capacitor $C1$. This is followed by the evaporation of an insulator such as silicon monoxide to form the dielectric of $C1$, again applied through a suitable mask. The upper electrode of $C1$ is then produced by forming another thin film of aluminium through a mask on top of the silicon monoxide. Conducting strips are then formed to

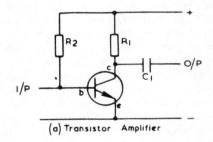

(a) Transistor Amplifier

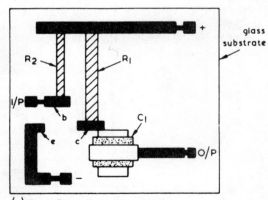

(b) Thin Film version of amplifier

■ Conductors – gold

▨ Resistors – nichrome

▢ Capacitor plates – aluminium

▦ Capacitor dielectric – silicon monoxide

Fig. 6.16 *Evaporated thin-film circuit.*

connect the thin-film components together by evaporating a metal such as gold through a suitable mask. Finally, the transistor is soldered into circuit, its leads being connected to appropriate points on the conducting strips. The complete circuit is then encapsulated in epoxy resin cushioned by silicon rubber.

There are limits to the values of resistors and capacitors that can be formed by this technique and generally inductors cannot be produced. Evaporation of the materials on to the substrate (ceramic may be used in place of glass) is carried out in a high vacuum.

(2) Thick-film Circuits

These are similar to the thin-film circuits but are manufactured using 'screening' techniques. The passive components and conductors are formed by passing the resistive or conductive materials in the form of a glass mixture (frit) through a fine wire mesh to form patterns on a ceramic substrate. After drying, the ceramic substrate is heated in an oven to a high temperature (700–800°C). This causes the glass frit to melt and for the resistive or conductive material contained in the frit to form firm patterns on the substrate. On removal from the oven, hard glassy patterns are formed on the substrate which will withstand rougher handling than the fragile thin film circuits. The process of forming a complete microcircuit is carried out in stages using different frits for the resistors, conductors and capacitor component parts. Active

devices (transistors and diodes) are soldered into circuit at points which have been previously tinned during the manufacturing stages of the substrate.

(3) Monolithic Silicon Integrated Circuits

These are the most important and most widely used type of microcircuit. Here, active and passive components are formed simultaneously on a small slice of a silicon crystal to create complete electronic circuits. Each complete microcircuit is approximately 1mm square and 0·3mm thick and up to one thousand can be made at a time from a thin slice of silicon having a diameter of 50mm, see Fig. 6.17.

In one type of integrated circuit, bipolar transistor technology is used where transistors, diodes, resistors and small-value capacitors are formed by diffusing impurities into the silicon slice using techniques similar to those described for planar transistors in Chapter 3. All of the components are formed on the top surface of the silicon slice as shown in Fig. 6.18, and are interconnected to form the required circuit by evaporating aluminium connections on top of the silicon dioxide. Resistors can be made using a doped portion of the silicon as a resistance, the value depending upon the doping level, the length and cross-sectional area. These are called 'diffused resistors' and can be economically produced in the range 20Ω to $20k\Omega$. Resistor tolerances are about $\pm10\%$ but it is possible to

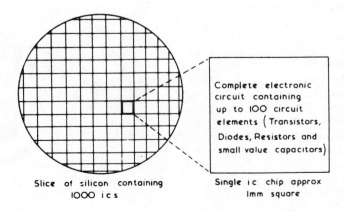

Slice of silicon containing 1000 i c s

Complete electronic circuit containing up to 100 circuit elements (Transistors, Diodes, Resistors and small value capacitors)

Single i c. chip approx 1mm square

Fig. 6.17 An integrated circuit chip.

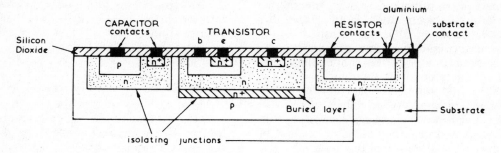

Fig. 6.18 *Components in integrated circuit form (bipolar transistor technology).*

produce a better matching accuracy between two resistors on the same slice of ±2%. Thus accurate potential dividers can be formed using resistance ratio rather than absolute values as the controlling factor.

One way of forming an integrated capacitor is to utilise the capacitance of a reverse biased p-n junction but this will require a suitable reverse bias voltage. Capacitance values up to about 100pF can be obtained by this technique. If larger values are required, discrete capacitors must be connected external to the i.c. In Fig. 6.18 the resistor element is formed by the p-channel between the contacts and the capacitor utilises the capacitance of a p-n junction. The transistor is an n-p-n using a special buried layer (n$^+$) to reduce the collector resistance. As all of the components on an i.c. are formed on the same slice of a conductive substrate, they must be isolated from each other in some way. The most common method is known as 'junction isolation' where each component is isolated from the common substrate by a p-n junction as shown. Each isolating junction is reverse biased by applying a negative voltage to the source contact which is greater than the potential of any element in the circuit. After all of the components have been formed on the silicon slice and the circuit connections deposited, each i.c. is tested by means of probes and the faulty ones noted. The slice is then scribed and broken into individual chips. Wires are then bonded to the good chips which are then encapsulated. Two methods of encapsulation are illustrated in Fig. 6.19. The most common package shown in (a) is the **dual-in-line** (DIL) which normally uses a moulded plastic unit. Dual-in-line types are

available in 8-pin, 14-pin and 16-pin versions. The TO metal package of (b) is similar to that used for a discrete transistor and is available with 8 pins, 10 pins or 12 pins.

The metal-oxide semiconductor technology used in the manufacture of field effect transistors can also be employed to produce complete circuits in integrated circuit form. These i.c.s are called 'MOS integrated circuits'. An integrated circuit MOS transistor has the advantage that it occupies about one-fifth of the area of an integrated bipolar transistor. Also, MOS devices are self-isolating and do not need the additional isolating areas used with bipolar devices. Small MOS capacitors can be produced using a thin layer of silicon dioxide sandwiched between two 'plate-like' surfaces. This type of capacitor does not, of course, require a reverse bias voltage as with the p-n junction capacitor of the bipolar i.c. MOS integrated circuits are

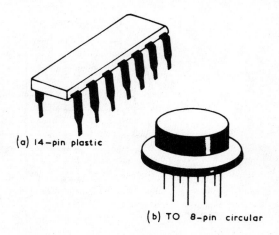

(a) 14-pin plastic

(b) TO 8-pin circular

Fig. 6.19 *Integrated circuit packages.*

now being used more in electronics as an alternative to bipolar integrated circuits in digital applications. For linear applications in radio and television receivers, bipolar transistor i.c. technology is the most common.

HANDLING INTEGRATED CIRCUITS

The following precautions should be observed when handling integrated circuits.

(a) Soldering-iron temperature. An i.c. may be damaged permanently if excess heat is transferred to it during soldering or desoldering operations. With the tip of the soldering iron at a temperature in the range 245°C to 400°C the soldering or desoldering time should be less than 5 secs. At a tip temperature below 245°C the maximum time may be increased to 10 secs. Soldering irons with thermostatically controlled element temperatures are available to meet the special temperature requirements of i.c.s.

(b) Removal of I.C. Where an i.c. is soldered on to a printed circuit board it may be removed by desoldering each pin in turn. To reduce the risk of excess heat being transferred to the i.c. the molten solder may be quickly removed by suction using a desoldering tool. Integrated circuits which plug into a socket must be removed carefully to avoid damage to the pins which are brittle. Uneven grip during extraction may cause the pins to bend, twist or fracture. Removal is best carried out using an extraction tool which has specially designed teeth to grip the i.c. during and after extraction.

(c) Fitting of I.C. Before fitting a new i.c. into circuit it is prudent to check that the d.c. supplies and input signal levels are of normal magnitude, also that the external components are not faulty e.g. short circuit, low or high resistance. Note that excess voltage or faulty components may damage the i.c. Next, check that the i.c. is the right way round; a slot or white spot at one end of the package is normally used as a reference to ensure correct orientation. Prior to insertion the pins of the i.c. should be carefully aligned. An i.c. insertion tool is particularly useful in this respect. Not only does the tool ensure that even pressure is applied when inserting the i.c. but automatically aligns the pins to the correct insertion distance.

(d) Checking of I.C. When checking d.c. voltages or waveforms on the pins of an i.c. ensure that the test probe does not short pins together otherwise permanent damage may occur. It may be rather difficult in some items of electronic equipment to get to the pins on both sides of the i.c. In these circumstances an i.c. test clip should be used. This is clipped over the i.c. to be tested and brings out the pin connections on top where there is less risk of accidental shorting.

(e) Static Charges. MOS integrated circuits, like MOS field effect transistors, can be damaged by electrostatic discharges. Although MOS i.c.s incorporate built-in protection against the effect of static charges, they can nevertheless be damaged by overvoltages. For this reason MOS devices are usually supplied in conductive bags which should not be removed during storing or transporting.

Special precautions should be taken when handling as static may be introduced during normal servicing. Manufacturers recommend that work on MOS devices be carried out on a conductive surface, e.g. a metal top bench and that the person doing the servicing be connected to the conductive surface by a metal bracelet and a conductive cord or chain. Everything connected with the servicing operation should be at the same potential as the conductive surface, e.g. tools, printed board receiving the i.c., the i.c. and the person carrying out the work. It is important, however, that in conforming to recommended procedures, personal safety is not endangered.

MOS devices should not be inserted or removed whilst the equipment is switched 'on', nor signals applied to the i.c. when the power is 'off'.

LIGHT-EMITTING DIODES

All p-n diodes passing current in the forward direction emit radiation. This radiation results from the recombination of minor-

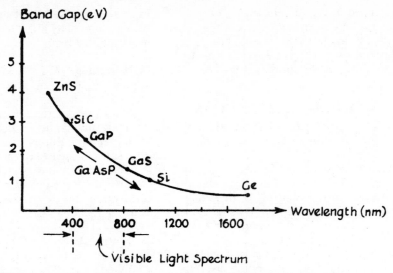

Fig. 6.20 *Wavelength of radiation emitted from forward biased p-n junction.*

ity carriers with majority carriers in the vicinity of the junction and, in simple terms, is due to electrons moving from a high-energy level to a lower-energy level. In moving from a high-energy level to a lower one, electrons give up energy in the form of an e.m. radiation.

The wavelength of the emitted radiation depends upon the size of the 'band gap' of the material used in the construction of the diode, see Fig. 6.20. To obtain emission in the visible light spectrum, band gaps in excess of 1·71eV are required. This rules out the common semiconductor materials of silicon and germanium whose band gaps are 1·1eV and 0·7eV respectively. A suitable crystalline material is gallium arsenide phosphide which can be made to emit light in the red, green, yellow or infra-red parts of the e.m. spectrum.

Not all of the light that is radiated from the vicinity of the junction finds its way out of the surface of the material, see Fig. 6.21(a). Some

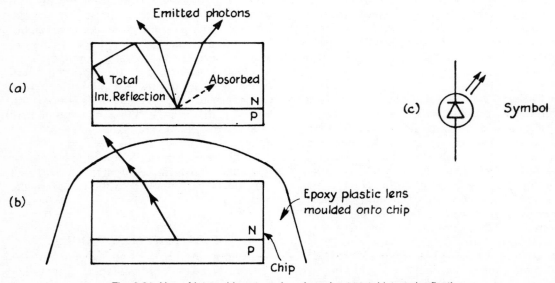

Fig. 6.21 *Use of integral lens to reduce loss due to total internal reflection.*

of the photons are absorbed and some are totally internally reflected. The internal reflection can be reduced by placing the crystal in intimate contact with an epoxy plastic lens of high refractive index, see Fig. 6.21(b).

Voltage–Current Characteristic

Electrically, light-emitting diodes resemble ordinary junction diodes. Those made from gallium arsenide and gallium phosphide have higher forward voltage drops than silicon diodes (1·5V to 2·0V), see Fig. 6.22. They have lower reverse voltages (3V to 10V) but similar temperature coefficients ($-2mV/°C$ at room temperature).

Efficiency of radiation increases with forward current; however, this is more than offset by the consequent rise in junction temperature, when the efficiency falls. By operating an l.e.d. under pulse conditions, the high efficiency can be used to advantage since the rise in temperature is minimised because of the cooling period between pulses.

Applications

Typical applications include:

(a) Alpha-numeric displays where 28 l.e.d.s are used to form a seven-segment read-out, see Fig. 6.23.

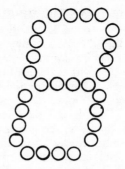

Fig. 6.23 *28 L.E.D.s forming seven-segment read-out.*

(b) Tuning indicators for f.m. receivers, giving an indication of signal strength and stereo signal operation.

(c) Infra-red remote control transmitters where an infra-red beam is modulated by digital pulses, see Fig. 6.24.

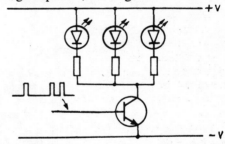

Fig. 6.24 *Part of infra-red transmitter showing pulse operation of l.e.d.s.*

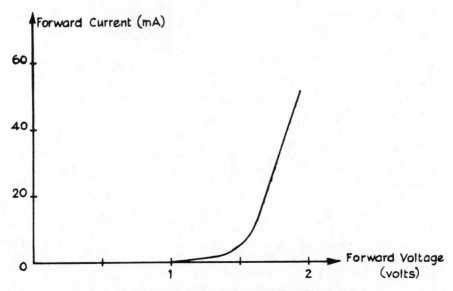

Fig. 6.22 *Forward characteristics of l.e.d.*

LIQUID CRYSTAL DISPLAY

An alternative to an l.e.d. display is one which uses a **liquid crystal**. The basic idea of the common form of liquid-crystal display is given in Fig. 6.25(a) which illustrates the construction of a seven-segment element. Here liquid-crystal material is sandwiched between two sheets of glass which have conductive coatings on their insides. One glass plate has a common electrode etched on it. These very thin conductive coatings (tin oxide) will allow the transmission of light through them.

To produce a particular display digit, a voltage is applied between the appropriate segments and the common electrode. This causes a change in the optical properties of the liquid crystal which appears as the display. The operation is illustrated in Fig. 6.25(b), using additionally two polaroid filters (with their planes of polarisation at right-angles to one another) and a mirror. Without any voltage applied between the electrodes, external light falling on the device is polarised by the first filter and is twisted through 90° by the liquid crystal so that it will pass through the second filter. After reflection by the mirror the light returns by the same path; in this state the cell is 'clear'.

When a voltage is applied between any of the segments and the common electrode the optical properties of the liquid crystal change in those areas. The liquid crystal then no longer produces the 90° twisting of the polarised light as it enters the crystal, thus the light will not pass the second polaroid filter. Hence the parts of the display where the electric field is applied appear black.

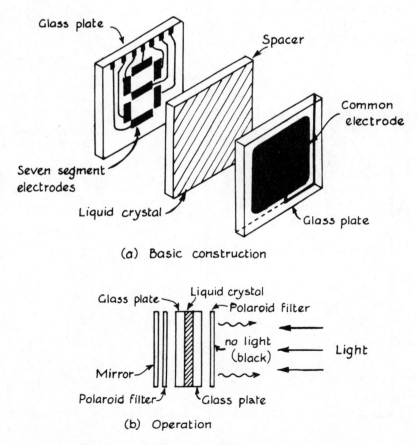

(a) Basic construction

(b) Operation

Fig. 6.25 Liquid crystal seven-segment display.

L.E.D. and liquid-crystal display drivers and decoders are considered in Chapter 20.

HALL-EFFECT DEVICES

If a material is placed in a magnetic field and a current passed through the material at right-angles to the magnetic field, it is found that a voltage is developed between the sides of the material that are at mutual right-angles to the current and flux directions. This voltage (the Hall voltage) occurs in conductors, insulators and semiconductors when the stated conditions prevail, but is more prevalent in semiconductor materials.

The principle is illustrated in Fig. 6.26 where a current is passed through a slab of n-type semiconductor with a magnetic field disposed at right-angles to the direction of current. The action of the magnetic field is to cause the charge carriers (electrons) to drift to one side of the material, resulting in a Hall voltage with polarity as shown between the faces at mutual right-angles to the current and flux directions. The effect is similar to the 'motor principle'; each electron has its own magnetic field which reacts with the external magnetic field to produce a force on the electron causing it to be deflected. If the material were p-type, the charge carriers (holes) would drift to the right and the polarity of the Hall voltage would reverse.

The magnitude of the Hall voltage generated is small (tens of millivolts) and is proportional to the flux density of the magnetic field and the strength of the current that is passed through the material. Also, reversing the direction of the current or the magnetic field will reverse the polarity of the Hall voltage.

Applications

The Hall-effect device (small slab of semiconductor material) is usually mounted in an

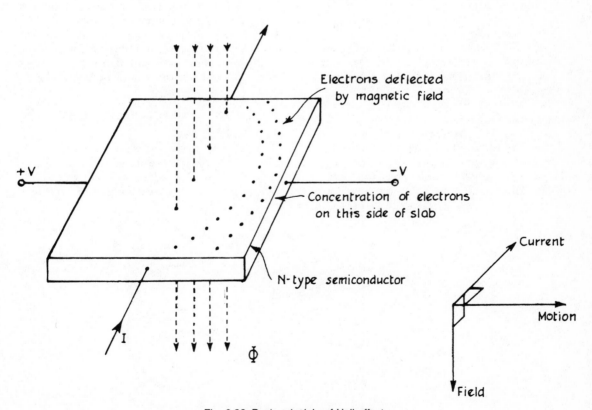

Fig. 6.26 Basic principle of Hall effect.

i.c. together with amplifiers to amplify the small Hall voltage that is generated. Connections are brought out so that an external voltage may be supplied to produce the current to be passed through the semiconductor material, the same voltage normally being used to provide the supply for the i.c. amplifier. The magnetic field is supplied externally. Typical applications include:

(a) Magnetic Field Measurements

The Hall effect device is mounted at the end of a probe which is placed in the centre of the magnetic field to be measured. The Hall voltage that is generated is amplified and used to provide an indication on a meter which may be calibrated in units of magnetic flux density (tesla).

(b) Audio Power Measurements

In this application, the d.c. voltage source is replaced by an audio voltage source. The alternating Hall voltage produced is amplified and used to provide an indication on a meter which may be calibrated in watts.

(c) Proximity Switch

A Hall-effect device may be utilised to give a 'bounce-free' switching action when influenced by a magnetic field and the idea is shown in Fig. 6.27.

When the small permanent magnet is bought close to the magnetic centre of the Hall device i.c. a Hall voltage is generated. On reducing the proximity of the magnet and the i.c. by only a few millimetres the Hall voltage will cease to be generated. Thus the output voltage from the i.c. may be used to provide a switching action and is particularly useful in

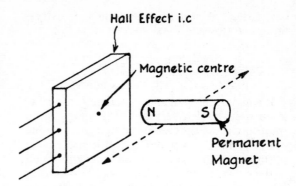

Fig. 6.27 Hall-effect proximity switch.

logic circuits where 'bounce-free' switching is required.

A similar idea is used in the 'vane' switch illustrated in Fig. 6.28, but here the permanent magnet is in a fixed position so that a Hall voltage is generated continually by the i.c. sensor. However, when a ferrous metal vane passes through the gap between the magnet and the sensor the Hall voltage is inhibited thus providing a 'bounce-free' switch action. The device may be used for position or counting applications in industry, particularly in dusty or high ambient lighting situations where optical sensors would be unsuitable.

QUESTIONS ON CHAPTER SIX

(1)   An SCR has:
      (a) An anode and cathode only
      (b) An anode, cathode and two gates
      (c) A source, drain and one gate
      (d) An anode, cathode and a single gate.

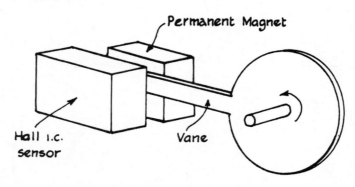

Fig. 6.28 Hall-effect vane switch.

(2) An SCR may be taken from the 'on' to the 'off' condition by:
 (a) Reducing the 'on' current below the 'holding' level
 (b) Increasing the gate current
 (c) Decreasing the gate current
 (d) Reverse biasing the gate.

(3) A triac comprises:
 (a) P-N-P-N and N-P-N-P structures in parallel and a common gate connection
 (b) Two P-N-P-N structures in parallel and two gate connections
 (c) Three N-P-N-P structures in series and a single gate connection
 (d) Three P-N-P-N structures in parallel and a single gate connection.

(4) The circuit symbol for a triac is:

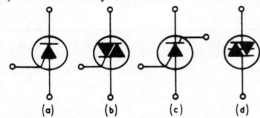

(a)   (b)   (c)   (d)

(5) A bidirectional thyristor having two electrodes only is called:
 (a) A Unijunction Transistor
 (b) A Diac
 (c) A Silicon Controlled Switch
 (d) An SCR.

(6) Microcircuits where complete electronic circuits are formed on a small chip of silicon are called:
 (a) Printed circuits
 (b) Monolithic integrated circuits
 (c) Thick-film circuits
 (d) Thin-film circuits.

(7) There is 24V applied between the B2 and B1 electrodes of a unijunction transistor and the emitter is positioned so that it lies three-quarters of the distance from B1 to B2. The device will be in the 'on' condition when the emitter-to-B1 voltage is approximately:
 (a) 12·4V
 (b) 18·6V
 (c) 6·6V
 (d) 16·6V.

(Answers on page 369)

CHAPTER SEVEN

THE CATHODE RAY TUBE

Objectives

1 To describe the principle of operation and component parts for an oscilloscope c.r.t.
2 To show typical operating voltages for an oscilloscope c.r.t.
3 To explain the principle of magnetic deflection and operation of a monochrome television c.r.t.
4 To show typical supply voltages for a monochrome television c.r.t.
5 To describe the basic principle of an in-line colour c.r.t.

THE CATHODE RAY tube (c.r.t.) forms the basis of the display devices found in monochrome and colour television receivers, oscilloscopes and visual display units used in computers and other systems. In a c.r.t. a fine beam of electrons is directed at high velocity towards a glass screen the inside of which is coated with a layer of electroluminescent material which emits light on being struck by the electrons, see Fig. 7.1. This layer is called the **screen phosphor** and the colour of the light emitted depends upon the chemical composition of the layer. With cathode ray oscilloscopes the c.r.t. phosphor usually emits green or blue light. For a monochrome television tube a mixture of phosphors emitting blue and yellow light is used to create white light, whereas in a colour television tube separate phosphors in the form of small dots or stripes are used to produce light in the primary colours of red, green and blue. The emission of light is due to both fluorescence and phosphorescence. Fluorescence occurs when the screen layer is excited by the electrons whilst phosphorescence occurs after the excitation has ceased and is called the 'afterglow'.

The fine electron beam is produced by an electron gun assembly which is positioned inside a funnel-shape glass envelope that is highly evacuated, i.e. all the air and other gases released from the electrodes during manufacture are pumped out. It is normally arranged for the electron beam to be deflected either horizontally or vertically or in both directions simultaneously. The mechanism producing deflection has not been shown in Fig. 7.1 as the 'deflecting field' may originate from inside the neck of the c.r.t. or outside it depending upon whether electric or magnetic deflection is used. A cathode ray tube can be divided into three basic sections.

(1) The electron gun assembly which produces the electrons and focuses them into a fine beam.

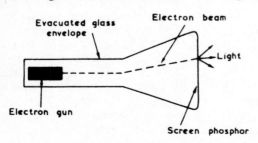

Fig. 7.1 Basic idea of c.r.t.

(2) The deflecting system which deflects the beam over the screen.

(3) The viewing area or screen which emits light on being excited by the arriving electrons.

The basic principle and construction of an oscilloscope tube will be considered under these three headings.

(1) ELECTRON GUN

Before an electron beam can be produced a source of electrons is required. At normal room temperatures the electrons in a metal wander at random through the atomic structure of the material. The electrons have insufficient energy to leave the material owing to the electrostatic forces that restrain them. If, however, sufficient additional energy is supplied to the material, high-energy electrons near the surface overcome the retarding electrostatic forces and escape from the material. One way of providing the additional energy to cause the emission of electrons is by the application of heat. This process is called thermionic emission, see Fig. 7.2, and is the principle used in the cathode ray tube and other thermionic devices such as valves.

In practice three main materials are used as thermionic emitters but the most common and that used in c.r.t.s consits of a mixture of barium and strontium oxides – referred to simply as 'oxide emitters'. These oxides give appreciable emission at a temperature in the range 750°C – 950°C which corresponds to a red heat. Since the oxides are white powders it is necessary to apply them as a coating on a conductor, which can be suitably heated. The oxide coated conductor (usually nickel) is called the **cathode** of the electron gun assembly.

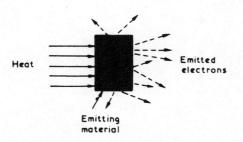

Fig. 7.2 Thermionic emission.

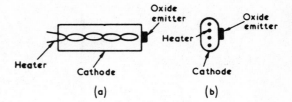

Fig. 7.3 C.R.T. cathode construction.

Two forms of cathode construction for use in a c.r.t. are shown in Fig. 7.3. In diagram (a) the cathode is a nickel tube with an oxide coating at one end. The oxide area is made as small as possible to produce a narrow electron beam source. To heat the oxide to its emitting temperature a tungsten heater wire is placed inside the nickel tube but is electrically insulated from it by coating the heater with aluminium oxide. In diagram (b) the cathode is formed from a short length of flat tube containing the heater wire with again a small area of oxide coating on one side. When the cathode is raised to its emitting temperature by passing a current through the heater wire, electrons are emitted in all directions from the oxide but the velocity of the emitted electrons will not be high. The electrons must be concentrated into a fine beam and accelerated to a high velocity so that a bright enough spot is formed on the screen of the c.r.t.

A simple way of accelerating the emitted electrons to a high velocity and producing a beam is shown in Fig. 7.4(a). Here a plate called the **anode** with a small hole in it is placed between the cathode and the c.r.t. screen. If the anode plate is held positive with respect to the cathode the emitted electrons will be attracted towards it (owing to the attraction of unlike charges). The anode will collect a large number of electrons but some will pass through the hole to form a beam. The arrangement is not very efficient as it stands since only a small proportion of the emitted electrons passes through the hole. A better and more practical arrangement is shown in Fig. 7.4(b). A cylinder which is closed at one end except for a small hole at its centre is placed over the cathode. This cylinder is sometimes known as a 'Wehnelt cylinder' but is often referred to as the **grid**. The cylinder is placed at a negative potential with respect to the cathode so that it tends to repel the

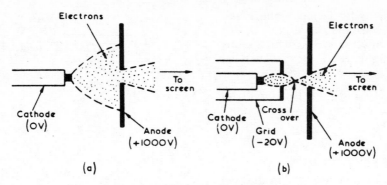

Fig. 7.4 *Producing a beam of electrons.*

negative electrons (like charges repel). Electrons which are emitted from the cathode at an angle are now turned round and cross over as shown before passing through the anode aperture. We now have a more efficient arrangement having provided a more intense beam passing through the anode. The velocity of the electrons leaving the anode will depend upon the anode voltage and the higher the voltage the greater the velocity. With an anode voltage of 1000V the velocity will be approximately 19×10^6 metres per second which is very high. By varying the potential of the grid, the number of electrons in the beam or the beam current may be altered, hence adjusting the brightness of the spot on the screen. As the grid is made more negative to the cathode there is a greater repulsive force acting on the emitted electrons urging them back towards the cathode. The beam current is made smaller and the spot brightness reduced. If the grid is made sufficiently negative no

electrons will pass through the grid aperture, hence the beam current will be zero and the spot of light extinguished.

Focusing the Beam

The divergent beam of electrons emanating from the anode aperture of Fig. 7.4(b) has to travel the length of the tube to the screen. During its travel there will be some additional widening of the beam due to the natural electrical repulsion between electrons in the beam. Thus the spot on the screen would be large and not very useful. It is therefore necessary to focus the beam so that a fine spot of light is produced on the screen. An **electrostatic lens** is used for this purpose which behaves in a way similar to an optical lens on a beam of light. One type of electrostatic lens is shown in Fig. 7.5 consisting of three anodes. The first anode, grid and cathode operate as previously described. The first and third

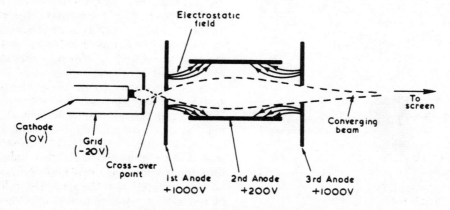

Fig. 7.5 *Electrostatic focusing lens formed by three anodes.*

anodes are in the form of discs whilst the second anode is usually of cylindrical construction. A potential of about one-fifth of the first and third anode voltage is applied to the second anode. In this example the five electrodes constitute the complete 'electron gun' assembly. Since the anodes are at different potentials, electric or electrostatic fields will be set between them as shown. Electrons entering these fields are subjected to forces urging them to travel in paths exactly opposite to the direction of the lines of force. When an electron enters a field at an angle, its direction will therefore be changed. This principle is the basis of the electrostatic lens. Due to the shape of the anodes and their electric field patterns a converging beam of electrons emerges from the third anode to produce a fine spot of light on the c.r.t. screen. While within the electric fields the electons may travel in curved paths but on leaving the fields they travel in straight line paths. In effect the electrostatic lens focuses the crossover point which is the apparent source of electrons or 'object' on to the screen of the c.r.t.

To ensure that the point of focus coincides exactly with the screen of the c.r.t., the voltage fed to the second anode (called the 'focus anode') is made variable. This is equivalent to varying the focal length of an optical lens. Some electrostatic lenses use only two anodes but the principle of operation is the same.

(2) DEFLECTION SYSTEM

Now that the electron beam has been focused to produce a small spot of light on the c.r.t. screen, it is necessary to be able to deflect the beam in two directions at right angles. For cathode ray tubes used in oscilloscopes this is achieved by employing **electrostatic deflection**, the principle of which is shown in Fig. 7.6

The electron beam is passed through a pair of plates as shown in Fig. 7.6(a). If there is no voltage between the plates, the electrons will continue to travel in a straight line along the tube axis and the beam will not be deflected. With a voltage applied between the plates making the upper plate positive to the lower plate as shown, the electrons will be attracted towards the upper plate and repelled by the lower plate. Thus the electron beam will be bent upwards as it passes between the plates.

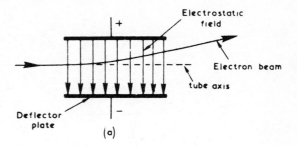

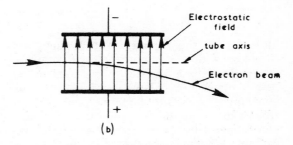

Fig. 7.6 Electrostatic deflection of electron beam.

The force acting on the beam while it is between the plates urges the electrons to travel in the exact opposite direction to the lines of the electrostatic field. This force progressively alters the path of the electrons from the point of entry to the point of exit causing them to follow a curved path in the deflecting field. On leaving the deflecting field, the electrons travel in a straight line path at an angle to the tube axis. The spot on the screen will therefore be deflected in an upward direction. The amount of deflection, and hence the movement of the spot, is proportional to the magnitude of the voltage applied between the plates. The **deflection sensitivity** of the plates is the voltage that must be applied between the plates to produce 1cm deflection of the spot on the c.r.t. screen. If the polarity of the voltage applied between the plates is reversed as in Fig. 7.6(b) the beam and hence the spot on the screen will be deflected in a downward direction.

Since we require deflection of the beam in two directions at right-angles, two sets of deflector plates disposed at right-angles to one another are necessary as shown in Fig. 7.7. In an oscilloscope tube the beam is first deflected in the vertical or Y direction by the **Y-plates** and then deflected in the horizontal or X

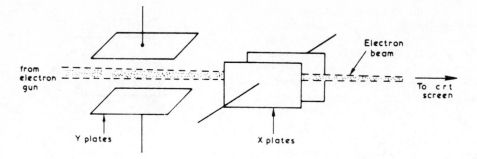

Fig. 7.7 Deflection of electron beam in two directions at right-angles.

direction by the **X-plates**. The X-plates are supplied with a sawtooth voltage from the internal timebase oscillator of the c.r.o. while the Y-plates are fed with the signal to be examined. As quite large voltages (20 to 100V) are required to produce appreciable deflection of the beam, the plates are fed via suitable amplifiers. The plates nearest to the gun assembly produce the greatest deflection sensitivity (all other factors being equal) since the distance to the screen from these plates is longer than for the other set of plates. It is thus advantageous to feed the signal to be examined to the plates having the greatest deflection sensitivity. Usually the deflecting plates are shaped using one of the configurations shown in Fig. 7.8. This enables, for a given length of c.r.t., greater deflection angles to be obtained without significantly reducing the deflection sensitivity.

The use of two sets of plates at right-angles

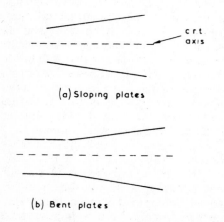

(a) Sloping plates

(b) Bent plates

Fig. 7.8 Use of shaped deflecting plates.

allows the beam to be deflected at any angle to the X or Y axis of the tube thereby permitting the spot of light to take up a position anywhere on the screen. Two examples are shown in Fig. 7.9 to illustrate this effect. In Fig. 7.9(a) equal steady voltages are applied to the two sets of plates (assumed to be of the same sensitivity) with polarities as indicated. Considered individually, the effect of the voltage applied between the X-plates would cause the beam to move to the right whereas the voltage applied between the Y-plates would cause the beam to move upwards. The resultant deflection of the beam with voltages applied simultaneously is as indicated and at 45° since the deflection voltages are the same. The spot on the screen can therefore take up any position along this resultant path by increasing or decreasing the deflection voltages by the same amount. If the polarities of both voltages are reversed, the resultant deflection will be diagonally opposite to that shown. The effect of reducing the voltage applied across the Y-plates and reversing the polarity at the same time is shown in Fig. 7.9(b). Considered individually, the X voltage would cause deflection to the right whereas the Y voltage would cause downward deflection. The resultant deflection due to the simultaneous application of the deflection voltages would be as indicated and at an approximate angle of 27° to the horizontal, since the deflection in the X direction is twice that in the Y direction. Again, by increasing or decreasing the deflection voltages by the same amount, the spot on the screen can take up any position along this resultant. If the polarities of both voltages are reversed the resultant deflection of the beam will be diagonally opposite to that shown.

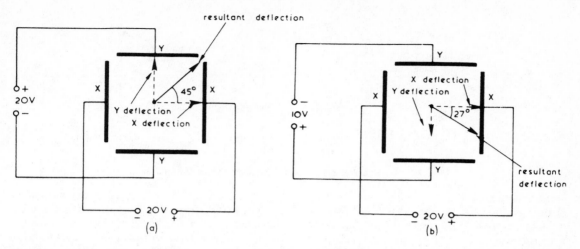

Fig. 7.9 Examples showing simultaneous deflection of beam in two directions at right-angles with steady voltages applied to the plates.

Post-Deflection Acceleration (P.D.A.)

When an oscilloscope tube is used to display high-frequency waveforms or fast transients, the trace has to be brightened otherwise it is difficult to discern some of the detail. The trace brightness may be increased by increasing the beam current, i.e. reducing the grid bias voltage so that more electrons reach the screen phosphor. This, however, increases the spot size and so there is a limit to the maximum beam current in a c.r.t. The only other way is to increase the velocity of the electrons striking the screen by raising the accelerating voltage. If the voltages applied to the first and third anodes of the gun assembly in Fig. 7.5. were increased, the electron velocity would be increased but the deflection sensitivity of the deflector plates would be reduced since the electrons would spend less time in the deflecting fields. Higher deflecting voltages

could be used but this is difficult at high frequencies.

The above problems are solved in a P.D.A. tube by increasing the velocity of the elctrons **after they have been deflected**. The basic idea is that if the final anode of the gun assembly is held at a voltage of about 1kV, the electrons will have relatively low velocity when passing through the deflector plates thus ensuring high deflection sensitivities. If the electrons are accelerated after deflection it will have little or no effect on deflection sensitivity. One method of achieving post deflection acceleration of the electrons is to use a high-resistance coating on the inside of the c.r.t. deposited in the form of a helix as shown in Fig. 7.10. The screen end of the helix coating is connected to a high voltage (5 to 10kV) and the other end is connected to a potential at or near the final anode of the gun assembly. The electrostatic field set up by the helix accelerates the electrons leaving the deflection plates so that they strike the screen phosphor with high velocity. Due to the greater kinetic energy of the arriving electrons a larger light output from the spot is possible.

(3) VIEWING AREA

As mentioned at the beginning of this chapter, the screen is made of an electroluminescent material which fluoresces on being bombarded by the electron beam. The kinetic

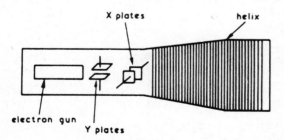

Fig. 7.10 Helix-type P.D.A. cathode ray tube.

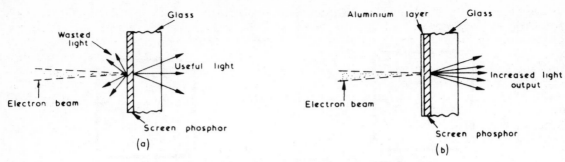

Fig. 7.11 *Use of aluminising to improve light output from screen.*

energy acquired by the electrons during motion is given up to the screen coating on impact causing it to fluoresce. Light is emitted from the screen phosphor in all directions at the point of impact as shown in Fig. 7.11(a). A large proportion of the light output is wasted being emitted backwards into the tube. This loss of light can be reduced by applying a thin layer of aluminium on one side of the screen phosphor as shown in Fig. 7.11(b). The aluminium layer acts as a highly reflective backing for the screen phosphor causing the rearward light to be reflected forwards and increasing the light output from the viewing side. There will be some small loss of electron energy in passing through the inter-atomic spaces of the aluminium and for this reason the coating is made very thin. 'Aluminising' the screen in this way also reduces the chance of screen 'burns'. The screen may be burnt by a stationary spot of light as the larger portion of the kinetic energy of the arriving electron beam causes heating of the screen phosphor; only about 10% is converted into light.

The face of the c.r.t may be circular but a larger proportion of the screen surface can be utilised if it is rectangular. For this reason, dual trace c.r.o.s often use a rectangular shaped tube screen. To enable the amount of deflection to be read in either the X or Y direction a **graticule** is fitted over the face of the screen. This usually consists of an engraved piece of plastic which is illuminated from the edge by one or more bulbs. Since the screen glass is thick and the phosphor coating is on the inside, parallex errors may arise when viewing the display. To avoid these errors the point to be read should be viewed at right angles.

C.R.T. SUPPLY VOLTAGES

Typical supply voltages for a basic oscilloscope tube are given in Fig. 7.12. An important point is that the mean potential of the X- and Y-plates must be approximately the same potential of the final (third) anode of the electron gun. It is therefore most convenient

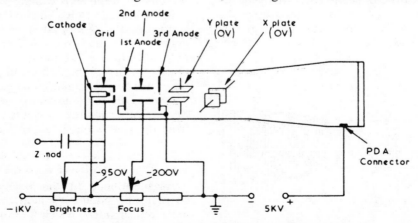

Fig. 7.12 *Typical supply voltages for oscilloscope tube.*

to arrange that the final anode is at earth potential and to place the cathode at a high negative potential of 1–2kV. This does not alter the principle of operation since the first anode (also at earth potential) is positive with respect to the cathode and provides the initial acceleration of the electrons on their way to the screen. The grid is held at a potential more negative than that of the cathode but its potential is made variable by the brightness control to vary the brilliance of the spot. Accurate focusing of the beam is achieved by providing a variable voltage to the second anode from the focus control. The X- and Y-plates are fed from their respective amplifiers in push-pull, i.e. one plate will change in voltage by $+V$ with respect to earth whilst the other changes by $-V$ with respect to earth, the mean voltage being zero as is required. A separate positive supply of 5–10kV is used to provide a post-deflection acceleration voltage for the tube.

TELEVISION DISPLAY TUBES

Cathode ray tubes used in television receivers operate similarly to those found in oscilloscopes. The main differences lie in the method of beam deflection, tube shape and operating voltages. The basic idea of a monochrome television c.r.t. is shown in Fig. 7.13. A large rectangular-faced c.r.t. is used, typical screen sizes being 22 in and 26 in (measured diagonally across the screen area). An electron gun assembly employing electrostatic focusing shoots a well-defined electron beam towards the screen phosphor at high velocity. Magnetic deflection of the beam is utilised as it is impracticable to obtain the large deflection angles required (of 90° or 110°) using electrostatic deflection. To produce white light the screen phosphor is composed of a mixture of zinc sulphide (emitting blue light) and zinc cadmium sulphide (emitting yellow light).

Magnetic Deflection

The basic principle of magnetic deflection is shown in Fig. 7.14. The deflecting magnetic field is represented by the crosses with the direction of the field into the paper. A moving electron beam will have a magnetic field existing around it (the same as a current in a wire) and this will react with the deflecting field causing a force to be exerted on the electron beam. This force acts in a direction at right angles to both the direction of the deflecting field and the direction of the beam current thus deflecting the beam downwards as shown. While in the deflecting field the electrons travel in a curved path along the arc of a circle but on leaving the deflecting field they travel in a straight-line path.

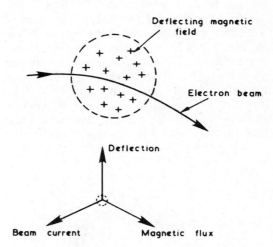

Fig. 7.14 Principle of magnetic deflection.

To deflect the beam in both the horizontal and vertical directions two pairs of deflector coils are employed as shown in Fig. 7.15. Each pair is disposed at right angles to each other and both pairs are situated at the same place along the tube neck. This saves space and

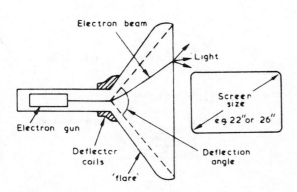

Fig. 7.13 Basic idea of monochrome television tube.

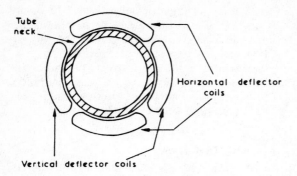

Fig. 7.15 Magnetic deflection in two directions at right-angles.

reduces the length of tube required. With electric deflection one set of plates follows the other, it not being practical to mount both sets of plates in the same position.

Deflection due to each pair of coils is considered separately in Fig. 7.16. The horizontally disposed coils (the field coils) of Fig. 7.16(a) produce deflection of the beam in the vertical direction. The direction of deflection (up or down) may be altered by reversing the direction of the magnetic flux which is achieved by reversing the direction of the current flowing in the coils. Fleming's left-hand rule may be used to find the direction of deflection but remember that electron flow is in the opposite direction to conventional current flow. The vertically disposed coils (the line coils) of Fig. 7.16(b) produce deflection of the beam in the horizontal direction. The direction of deflection (left or right) may be altered by reversing the direction of current flow in the coils. The amount of deflection

produced depends upon the strength of the magnetic field or the current in the deflector coils. To achieve a concentrated magnetic field passing through the tube neck, the coils are usually wound on a ferrite core and often the coils are taken up the flare of the tube to permit wide deflection angles.

Supplies to Monochrome Television C.R.T.

Further details showing the construction of a typical c.r.t. for use in a monochrome t.v. receiver are shown in Fig. 7.17. The electron gun assembly is composed of the heater, cathode, grid and four anodes. The first anode A1 is held at about 600–700V positive with respect to the cathode and provides the initial acceleration of the electrons on their way to the screen. The grid is placed at a negative potential with respect to cathode and by varying the grid voltage the brightness of the trace may be altered. Once the electrons leave the aperture in A1, they are accelerated to a high velocity as A2 is held at a potential of +15 to +20kV depending upon the tube size. Anodes A2, A3, and A4 form an electrostatic focusing lens with the focus of the beam controlled by adjustment of the potential applied to A3. The e.h.t. voltage required for A2 (also A4) is supplied via an e.h.t. connector on the tube flare, an internal conductive coating of graphite (called the 'aquadag') and spring clips as shown. At the back of the screen phosphor there is a thin layer of aluminium which is used to increase the light output and to reduce the possibility of burning the screen coating. The aluminium

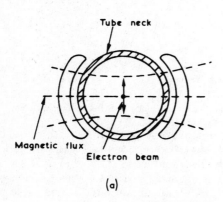

(a)

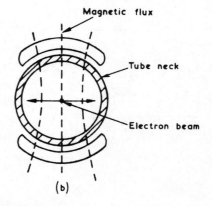

(b)

Fig. 7.16 Vertical and horizontal deflection of beam.

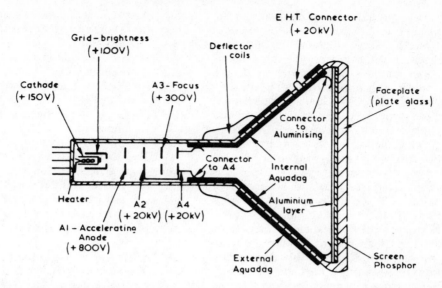

Fig. 7.17 Details of monochrome television tube using electric focusing and magnetic deflection.

layer is held at the final anode potential and thus provides the return path for the electrons striking the screen. A further conductive coating applied over the external surface of the tube flare is also used which is normally connected to the chassis of the receiver via a spring clip. The external and internal coatings together with the interposing glass layer of the tube envelope form a small capacitor (500–1000pF) which is used to provide smoothing of the e.h.t. supply.

The line and field deflector coils are fed with sawtooth currents at 15 625Hz and 50Hz respectively, deflecting the beam over the screen to form the television raster.

To produce the television picture the electron beam is intensity-modulated by applying the video signal output of the receiver to the cathode of the c.r.t. This signal alters the grid-to-cathode bias and hence the intensity of the light output from the screen.

Colour Television C.R.T.

The basic principle of one type of colour display c.r.t. is shown in Fig. 7.18(a). Here three separate electron guns, arranged horizontally in-line, shoot fine electron beams towards the screen. The outer two guns are tilted slightly inwards so that the three beams

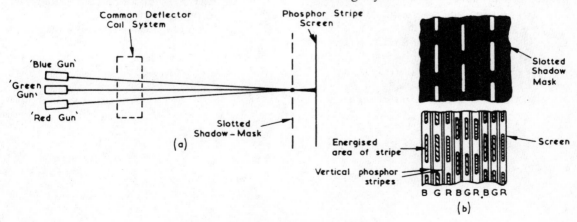

Fig. 7.18 Principle of in-line colour c.r.t.

cross over at a point lying in the plane of the shadow-mask as shown. The shadow-mask is made from thin sheet steel and has slots in it through which electrons from the three beams pass. After passing through the mask the beams fall on phosphor stripes deposited on the inside of the glass faceplate which emit light in the primary colours of red, green and blue. The electron beams are carefully aligned so that each beam falls on its respective colour phosphor stripe, thus energising small areas of the stripes as shown in Fig. 7.18(b). It is because the energised areas are so small that the eye does not see the individual coloured areas but only their additive mixture.

Each beam is electrostatically focused by anodes in its electron gun assembly but all three beams are deflected by a common deflection coil assembly using magnetic deflection. Apart from the need to provide three electron guns inside the neck of the c.r.t. and the special requirement of a shadow-mask, many of the constructional features of a colour c.r.t. are similar to those of a monochrome tube. A higher e.h.t. supply (up to 24kV) is required for the final anode and a higher focus voltage (about 5kV) is supplied to the focusing anode.

QUESTIONS ON CHAPTER SEVEN

(1) The 'emitting' material in a c.r.t. is:
  (a) Tungsten
  (b) Copper
  (c) Nickel
  (d) Barium and strontium oxides.

(2) The grid electrode of a c.r.t. is used to:
  (a) Vary the focus of the electron beam
  (b) Accelerate the electrons
  (c) Vary the brightness of the spot
  (d) Deflect the electron beam.

(3) An oscilloscope tube normally employs:
  (a) Magnetic deflection and electric focusing
  (b) Electric deflection and magnetic focusing
  (c) Electric focusing and electric deflection
  (d) Magnetic deflection and magnetic focusing.

(4) The X-plates of a c.r.t. produce:
  (a) Vertical deflection of the beam
  (b) Horizontal deflection of the beam
  (c) Horizontal and vertical deflection of the beam
  (d) Focusing of the beam.

(5) When 20V is applied between the Y-plates of an oscilloscope tube the spot on the screen is deflected by 4cm. The deflection sensitivity of the plates is:
  (a) 80V per cm
  (b) 5V per cm
  (c) 0·2V per cm
  (d) 2V per cm.

(6) The screen phosphor of a c.r.t. is 'aluminised' to:
  (a) Increase the light output
  (b) Increase the electron velocity
  (c) Provide a graticule
  (d) Reduce the spot size.

(7) A television tube normally employs:
  (a) Magnetic deflection and electric focusing
  (b) Electric deflection and magnetic focusing
  (c) Magnetic deflection and magnetic focusing
  (d) Electric deflection and electric focusing.

(Answers on page 369)

CHAPTER EIGHT

LCR CIRCUITS

Objectives
1 To define and determine CR and LR time-constants.
2 To consider the action of L, C and R in a.c. circuits and to show phasor diagrams.
3 To explain series and parallel resonance and show circuit responses.
4 To explain the action of low-pass and high-pass RC filters.

THIS CHAPTER IS concerned with the effects of inductance, capacitance and resistance in d.c. and a.c. circuits, an understanding of which provides an important basis for the study of the diverse range of circuits used in electronic equipment.

L, C AND R IN D.C. CIRCUITS

CR **Time-Constant**
    Consider the circuit of Fig. 8.1(a) where a capacitor C is to be charged via a resistor R to the d.c. supply of 10V. At the instant the switch is closed, the voltages in the circuit are as shown in Fig. 8.1(b). Initially all of the supply voltage appears across R, there being no voltage drop across C (capacitor uncharged). The initial charging current I that flows is given by Ohm's law,

$$I = \frac{E}{R} = \frac{10}{10} = 1\text{A}$$

As the current commences to flow, the capacitor charges and the voltage across it rises. Suppose that shortly after closing the switch, the voltage across the capacitor has risen to 2V, see Fig. 8.1(c). Since the sum of the voltages across C and R must be equal to the supply voltage at all times, there will be

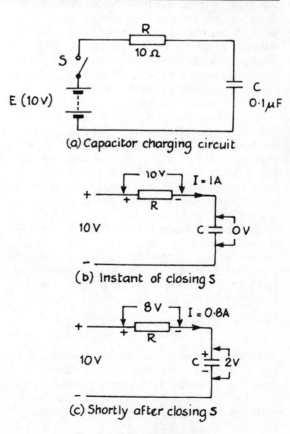

(a) Capacitor charging circuit

(b) Instant of closing S

(c) Shortly after closing S

Fig. 8.1 CR charging circuit.

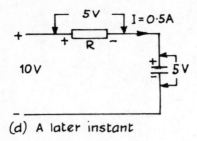

(d) A later instant

only 8V across R. Accordingly, the charging current will now reduce to $8/10 = 0.8$A. The capacitor voltage will continue to rise but due to the reduction in charging current, the rate of rise in voltage will not be so great as it was initially.

At a later instant, when, say, the voltage across the capacitor has risen to 5V, see Fig. 8.1(d), there will be only 5V across R and the charging current will reduce to $5/10 = 0.5$A, reducing further the rate of rise in voltage across C.

This process continues with the voltage across C rising towards 10V and the voltage across R falling towards 0V. Because the charging current reduces as the capacitor voltage rises, the rise of voltage follows a non-linear (exponential) relationship with time, as illustrated in Fig. 8.2(a). The decaying charging current is shown in Fig. 8.2(b). Eventually, when the voltage across C reaches 10V, the voltage across R will be 0V (no current will flow) and the capacitor will be fully charged to the supply voltage.

The **time constant** (or CR time) of the CR circuit is defined as the time (seconds) taken for the voltage across the capacitor to reach 0.63 of the applied voltage and is given by the product of C (farads) and R (ohms). For the values given in Fig. 8.1(a),

Time constant =
$$0.1 \times 10^{-6} \times 10 \text{ seconds} = 1\mu s$$

Time constant may alternatively be defined as the time taken for the voltage across the capacitor to reach the supply voltage if the initial rate of charge had been maintained. It will be seen that the voltage across C gradually approaches the supply voltage once it has exceeded the $0.63 \times$ supply voltage point. For

practical purposes it may be considered that the capacitor is fully charged after an interval corresponding to **5 × time constant**.

Example 1

A capacitor of 10nF is charged via a resistance of 100kΩ to a d.c. supply voltage of 50V. Calculate:
(a) the time constant of the circuit;
(b) the initial charging current at switch-on;
(c) the voltage across the capacitor after a period equal to the time constant;
(d) the approximate time for the voltage across the capacitor to reach 50V.

Solution
(a) Time constant
$$= C \times R \text{ seconds}$$
$$= 10 \times 10^{-9} \times 10^5 \text{ seconds}$$
$$= 10 \times 10^{-9} \times 10^5 \times 10^3 \text{ ms}$$
$$= 1\text{ms}$$

(b) Initial charging current
$$= \frac{E}{R} = \frac{50}{10^5}\text{A} = 0.5\text{mA}$$

(c) After a period equal to 1ms,
Voltage across the capacitor
$$= 0.63 \times 50\text{V}$$
$$= 31.5\text{V}$$

(d) Time taken for capacitor to charge fully
$$= 5 \times \text{times constant}$$
$$= 5\text{ms}$$

Discharging Circuit

Consider now the circuit of Fig. 8.3(a), where the capacitor which was previously charged to 10V is allowed to discharge through R. At the commencement of discharge,

$$\text{Current } I \text{ flowing} = \frac{V}{R} = \frac{10}{10} = 1\text{A}$$

When current flows in R, charge is lost from C, resulting in the voltage across C falling. This fall in voltage will reduce the magnitude of the current flowing, thus the rate at which the capacitor voltage falls is not constant but follows the non-linear (exponential) form shown in Fig. 8.3(b). The decay of current with time will be exactly the same as in Fig. 8.2(b).

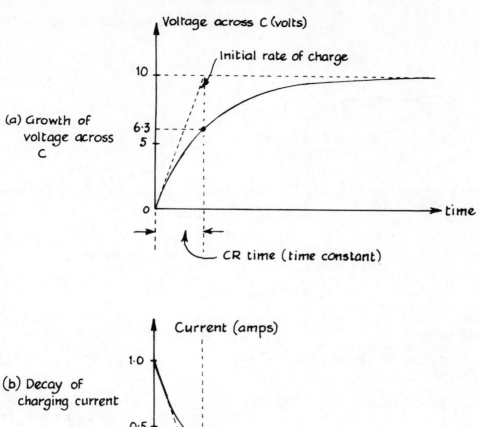

Fig. 8.2 Voltage and current as capacitor charges.

The time constant of the discharge circuit may be defined as the time taken for the capacitor voltage to fall to 0·37 of its initial value. The time constant is, as before, given by C (farads) $\times R$ (ohms) seconds and is precisely the same for the charging circuit since the same value of resistor is used. After a period equal to approximately 5 × time constant, the capacitor may be considered to be completely discharged (0V).

Example 2

A capacitor of value $3\mu F$ previously charged to 80V is discharged through a $1M\Omega$ resistor. Calculate:
(a) the time constant;
(b) the initial discharge current;
(c) the voltage across the capacitor after a period equal to the time constant;
(d) the approximate time for the capacitor to discharge fully.

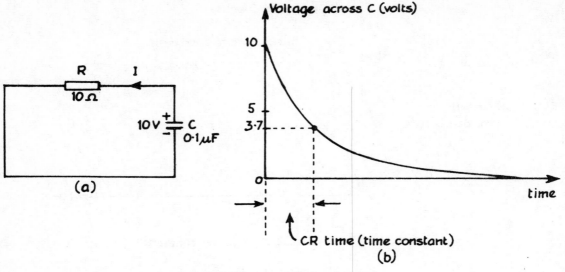

Fig. 8.3 Voltage as capacitor discharges.

Solution

(a) Time constant

$$= C \times R \text{ seconds}$$
$$= 3 \times 10^{-6} \times 10^6 \text{ seconds}$$
$$= 3s$$

(b) Initial discharge current

$$= \frac{V}{R} = \frac{80}{10^6}A = 80\mu A$$

(c) After a period equal to 3s the voltage across the capacitor will be $0.37 \times 80 = 29.6V$

(d) Time taken for capacitor to discharge fully

$$= 5 \times \text{time constant}$$
$$= 15s$$

The diagram of Fig. 8.4 shows the effect of varying the time constant when the capacitor is charging. Clearly, the longer the time constant the longer will be the time required for the capacitor to charge fully or to reach any specified voltage level.

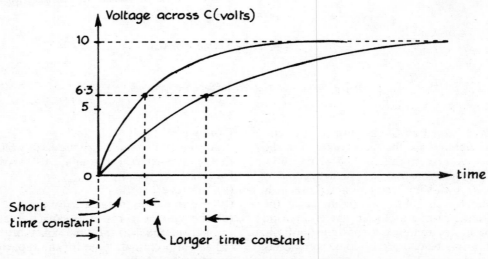

Fig. 8.4 Effect of varying time constant (CR time).

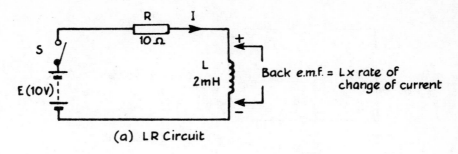

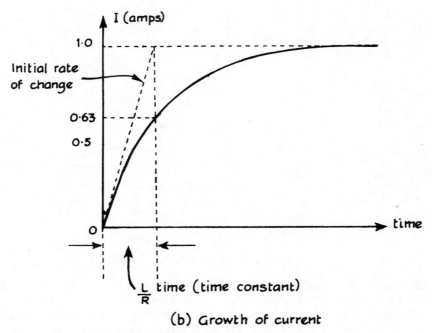

(a) LR Circuit

(b) Growth of current

Fig. 8.5 Growth of current in LR circuit.

LR Time Constant

Consider the circuit of Fig. 8.5(a) consisting of an inductor L in series with a resistance R (which may be just the resistance of the inductor). If the switch is closed, current will commence to flow but is prevented from building-up rapidly since an e.m.f. will be induced in the inductor. The back e.m.f. acts in opposition around the circuit to the applied voltage E thus reducing the rise of current. As a result, the current rises non-linearly as shown in Fig. 8.5(b). It will be seen that the rate of change of current reduces as the current rises thus causing the back e.m.f. (which is proportional to the rate of change of current) to reduce as the current rises towards a steady value settled by Ohm's law, i.e.

$$I = \frac{V}{R} = \frac{10}{10}\ 1\text{A}$$

The time constant of the LR circuit may be defined as the time taken for the current to reach 0·63 of its final steady value and is equal to L/R seconds, where L is in henrys and R is in ohms. For the values given,

$$\text{Time constant} = \frac{L}{R} \text{ seconds}$$

$$= \frac{2 \times 10^{-3}}{10} \text{ seconds}$$

$$= 0\cdot2\text{ms}$$

For practical purposes the current will reach its steady level after a period equal to 5 × time constant.

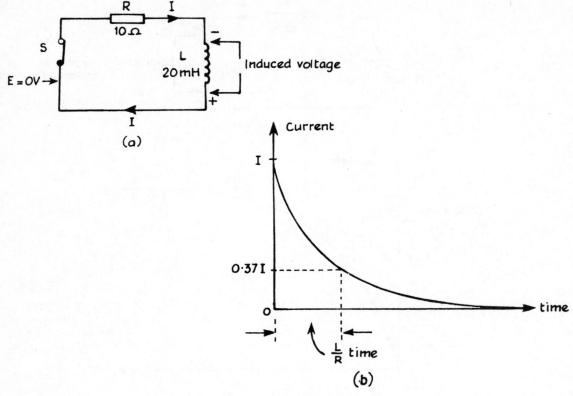

Fig. 8.6 Decay of current in an LR circuit.

If the applied voltage E is suddenly reduced to zero but the circuit is not broken, see Fig. 8.6(a), the current will start to decrease but an e.m.f. will be induced in L tending to keep the current flowing and in the same direction. The current will decrease as in Fig. 8.6(b) and will fall to 0·37 of its initial value (E/R) in a time equal to the time constant of L/R seconds. Thus an inductor tends to prevent changes of current through it, a property which is used in electronic circuits.

If an attempt is made to break an inductive circuit rapidly, a high voltage is induced in the inductor (since the induced e.m.f is proportional to the rate of change of current) which may be dangerous or damage the insulation between the turns of the inductor. This principle is put to use in car ignition coils, the starting of fluorescent lamps and the generation of flyback e.h.t. in television receivers.

Example 3

An inductor of 0·5H is connected in series with a resistor of 1kΩ across a 50V supply. Determine:

(a) the time constant of the circuit;
(b) the final value of current in the circuit;
(c) the current in the circuit after a period equal to the time constant.

Solution

(a) Time constant

$$= \frac{L}{R} \text{ seconds} = \frac{0·5}{10^3} \text{ s} = 0·5\text{ms}$$

(b) The final current flowing

$$= \frac{E}{R} = \frac{50}{10^3}\text{A} = 50\text{mA}$$

(c) After a period equal to the time constant,

Current flowing = 0·63 × the final value

$$= 0·63 \times 50\text{mA}$$

$$= 31·5\text{mA}$$

L, C AND R IN A.C. CIRCUITS

Phasor Representation

Consider the arm OA of Fig. 8.7 rotating about a fixed point O at a constant speed in an anticlockwise direction. As the arm rotates it will be seen that the height of the tip of the arm to the x-axis (X – X') varies. When the arm lies in the direction X, the height is zero and the angle (θ) between the arm and the x-axis is also zero. As the arm moves from the starting reference position the angle θ increases and the height reaches a maximum value when the arm lies in the direction Y (θ = 90°). Further rotation causes the height to reduce, reaching zero when the arm lies in the X' direction (θ = 180°). The height will again reach a maximum value when the arm lies in the direction Y' (θ = 270°) and will decrease to zero when the arm has moved to its starting position lying along the direction X (θ = 360°).

If the height of the arm from the x-axis is plotted against angle, a sinewave is produced as shown. The angle may be given in degrees or radians where 360° = 2π radians (1 radian = 57·296°).

The arm OA is the **phasor representation** of the sinewave and its length is equal to the **maximum** or **peak value** of the sinewave. The angular position of the **phasor** OA at any instant (measured from the reference direction OX) gives the angle traced out by the sinewave. After one revolution of the phasor corresponding to one cycle of the sinewave, OA will have moved through an angle of 2π radians. If the sinewave has a frequency of f cycles per second (Hz), the phasor will move with an angular velocity of $2\pi f$ rad/s or ω rad/s (where ω = $2\pi f$).

Example 4

A sinewave has a frequency of 100Hz. Determine its angular velocity (angle covered every second).

Solution

Angular velocity = $2\pi f$ rad/s

$$= 2 \times \pi \times 100 \text{ rad/s}$$

$$= 628 \cdot 32 \text{ rad/s}$$

Phase Difference

Voltages or currents found in d.c. circuits act either in the same direction or in opposite directions, but in a.c. circuits voltages or current can occur with various timing (phase) differences between their maximum peak values.

Consider Fig. 8.8(a) which shows two sinewaves v_1 and v_2 of different amplitudes and of the same frequency but with their peak values occurring at different time instants. The two sinewaves are said to have a phase difference with v_1 leading v_2 by an angle θ; although the x-axis is given in time it is related to the angle

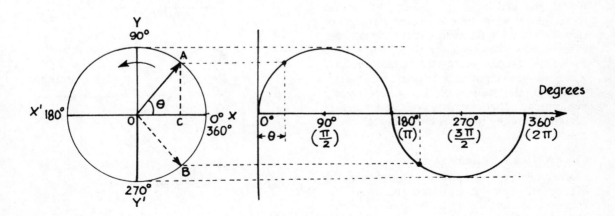

Fig. 8.7 Phasor representation of sinewave.

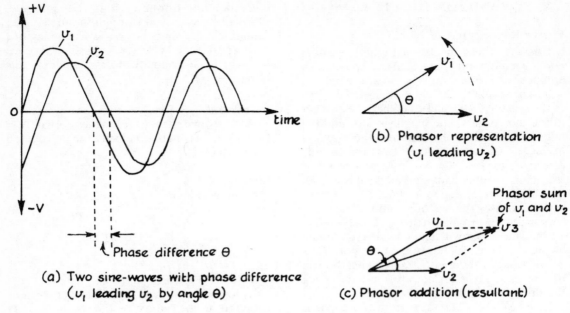

Fig. 8.8 Phase difference.

of the wave since the time period of one cycle represents 2π radian.

The sinewaves may be represented by the phasor diagram of Fig. 8.8(b) where the phasors v_1 and v_2 each have a length proportional to the peak amplitudes of the sinewave voltages and are shown with a phase difference of θ degrees. There is no need to show the phasors rotating since both sinewaves are of the same frequency and the phase difference between them will be constant. If the phasors v_1 and v_2 are added together, the result will be as in Fig. 8.8(c) where the resultant v_3 is another sinewave having the same frequency but a different amplitude from v_1 or v_2. It will be seen later in this chapter the usefulness of phasor representation of sinewaves and the importance of phase difference, which is the cause of many interesting phenomena that occur when alternating current flows in electrical circuits.

Circuit With Resistance Only

If a voltage E is applied to the circuit of Fig. 8.9(a) then at any instant when the voltage is e, the current i is given by $i = e/R$. Thus the current flowing in the circuit is proportional to the voltage at any instant, and

if the applied voltage is sinusoidal the current will be sinusoidal and will be in phase with the voltage, see Fig. 8.9(b). Voltage and current may therefore be represented by the phasors as in Fig. 8.9(c).

Since $i = \dfrac{e}{R}$ at all instants, then $I = \dfrac{E}{R}$

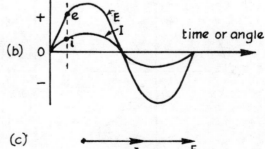

Fig. 8.9 Voltage and current phase relationship in circuit consisting of resistance only.

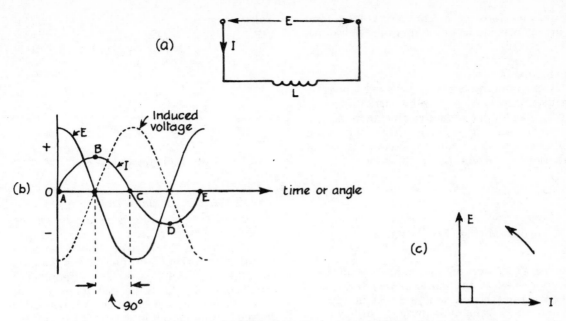

Fig. 8.10 Voltage and current phase relationship in circuit consisting of inductance only.

where I and E are the r.m.s. values. If the frequency of the applied voltage is changed and the r.m.s. value of the voltage remains constant, the r.m.s. value of the current remains constant. Thus the value of R does not vary with frequency.

Summarising, it may be said that resistance in an a.c. circuit behaves exactly the same as it would in a d.c. circuit.

Circuit with Inductance Only

Consider the circuit of Fig. 8.10(a) consisting of an inductance L henrys and assume that the resistance of the inductor is negligible. Suppose that a sinusoidal current I is passed through the inductor. Since the current is continually changing there will be a voltage induced in the inductor which is proportional to the rate of change of current. As the rate of change of current is greatest as the current passes through the zero datum line, i.e. at points A, C, E, etc., the induced voltage will be at a maximum. At points B, D, etc. where the current is constant, there will be no induced voltage.

The direction or polarity of the induced voltage will be such that it opposes the change which is causing the voltage (Lenz's Law). At instant A it is the rise of current that is causing the induced voltage thus the voltage will be in such a direction as to oppose the current rise, i.e. it will be negative. As we move towards point B the rate of rise of current decreases hence the induced voltage becomes less, until at B where the current is steady for a brief instant and the induced voltage is zero. After point B, the current starts to decrease so that the induced voltage will reverse direction so as to try to maintain the flow of current. The rate of decrease of current reaches a maximum at C and hence the induced voltage will be a maximum at this point. From C to D the rise of current is in the opposite direction and the induced voltage is positive, opposing the current rise in the negative direction. Finally, from D to E the current is decreasing and the induced voltage is in a direction such as to assist the flow of current.

Thus, if we are to force a current through the inductor, the applied voltage E must be equal and opposite to the induced voltage as shown in Fig. 8.10(b). It will be seen that the **applied voltage E leads the current I by 90°** or looking at it the other way, the current in an inductor lags the applied voltage by 90°. We may therefore represent the voltage and current in an inductive circuit by the phasors of Fig. 8.10(c).

Inductive Reactance

In an inductive circuit there is a certain ratio between the voltage and the current and this ratio is called the **inductive reactance** (X_L). It is a measure (in ohms) of the opposition offered by the inductor to the flow of alternating current and is given by

$$X_L = \frac{E}{I} \text{ ohms}$$

or rearranging, $I = \frac{E}{X_L}$ amperes

The reactance of an inductor is directly proportional to the value of the inductance (henrys) and the frequency (Hz) of the applied e.m.f. and is related to these quantities by

$$X_L = 2\pi f L \text{ ohms}$$

or $X_L = \omega L$ ohms (where $\omega = 2\pi f$).

The diagram of Fig. 8.11 shows how the reactance of an inductor varies with frequency.

Example 5

An alternating voltage of 10V r.m.s. at a frequency of 2kHz is applied to an inductor of value 5mH. Determine:
(a) the reactance of the inductor;
(b) the current flowing in the inductor.

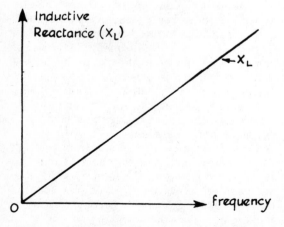

Fig. 8.11 *Variation of inductive reactance with frequency.*

Solution

(a)
$$\begin{aligned} X_L &= 2\pi f L \text{ ohms} \\ &= 2 \times \pi \times 2 \times 10^3 \times 5 \times 10^{-3} \\ &= 62 \cdot 83 \text{ ohms} \end{aligned}$$

(b)
$$\begin{aligned} I &= \frac{E}{X_L} \text{ amperes} \\ &= \frac{10}{62 \cdot 83} \text{ A} \\ &= 159 \cdot 15 \text{mA (r.m.s.)} \end{aligned}$$

Circuit With Capacitance Only

We will now consider a circuit containing capacitance only as in Fig. 8.12(a). If d.c. were applied to the circuit then no current would flow except for an initial charging current. This is not the case if a.c. is applied to the circuit and is due to the fact that whenever the voltage across a capacitor is changed a charge flows in or out of it, and thus a current must flow. With a.c. the voltage is changing continuously, hence a resulting current flows in the circuit.

Suppose a sinusoidal voltage E is applied to the circuit as in Fig. 8.12(b), then the current that flows is proportional to the rate of change of voltage ($I = C \times$ rate of change of voltage). This is a maximum at points A, C and E but zero at points B and D. Thus, as the voltage rises rapidly at A a large current will flow causing the capacitor to charge up but as the rate of rise of voltage decreases towards B the current decreases. At B when the voltage is steady for a brief instant the current will be zero. Between B and C the voltage decreases causing the capacitor to discharge and for current to flow in the opposite direction reaching a maximum at C where the rate of change of voltage is at a maximum. Between C and D the capacitor is charged in the opposite direction and the current flows in the same direction as the voltage, but reaches zero at D where the rate of change of voltage is zero. Between D and E the capacitor again discharges.

It may thus be considered that a current flows in and out of the capacitor for each half cycle of the applied voltage. As can be seen from Fig. 8.12(b), the **current leads the voltage by 90°** and this may be represented by the phasors of Fig. 8.12(c).

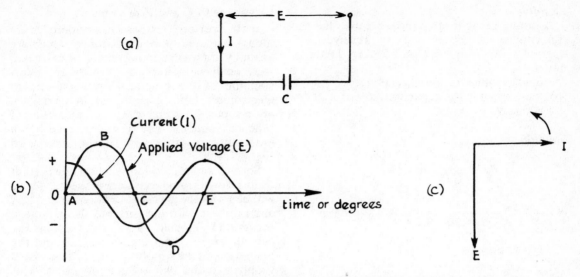

Fig. 8.12 Voltage and current phase relationship in circuit containing capacitance only.

Capacitive Reactance

In a capacitive circuit there is a certain ratio between the voltage and the current and this ratio is known as the capacitive reactance (X_c). It is a measure (in ohms) of the opposition offered by the capacitor to the flow of alternating current and is given by:

$$X_c = \frac{E}{I} \text{ ohms}$$

or rearranging, $I = \frac{E}{X_c}$ amperes

The reactance of a capacitor is inversely proportional to the value of the capacitor (farads) and to the frequency (Hz) of the applied voltage and is related to these quantities by:

$$X = \frac{1}{2\pi f C} \text{ ohms}$$

$$\text{or } X = \frac{1}{\omega C} \text{ (where } \omega = 2\pi f).$$

The diagram of Fig. 8.13 shows how the reactance of a capacitor varies with frequency.

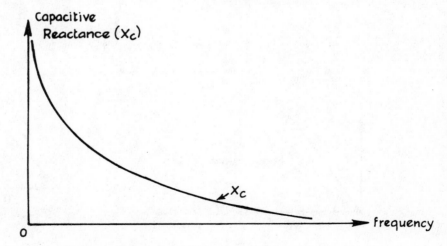

Fig. 8.13 Variation of capacitive reactance with frequency.

Example 6

A tuning capacitor in a radio receiver has a capacitance of 250pF and the receiver is operated at a frequency of 1·2MHz. Determine:

(a) the reactance of the capacitance;
(b) the current in the capacitor if there is 10V across it.

Solution

(a)
$$X_c = \frac{1}{2\pi f C} \text{ ohms}$$

$$= \frac{1}{2 \times \pi \times 1\cdot2 \times 10^6 \times 250 \times 10^{-12}} \text{ ohms}$$

$$= 530\cdot5 \text{ ohms}$$

(b)
$$I = \frac{E}{X} \text{ amperes}$$

$$= \frac{10}{530\cdot5} \text{ A}$$

$$= 18\cdot85\text{mA}$$

Circuits with *L* and *R* in series

In the previous sections we considered 'pure inductance' and 'pure capacitance' which are virtually impossible to achieve in practice and were dealt with simply to provide an understanding of the practical circuits found in electronics. For example, an inductor will always possess some d.c. resistance thus a practical inductor may be represented by an inductance in series with a resistance as in Fig. 8.14(a).

Since *L* and *R* are in series the same current *I* must flow through both components. There will be a voltage across *R* (V_R) equal to $I \times R$ and in phase with the current, also a voltage across *L* (V_L) equal to $I \times X_L$ but leading the current by 90°. In a d.c. circuit, to find the magnitude of the supply voltage (*V*) we would simply add the two voltages together. This does not solve the problem when the supply is a.c. since the two voltages have a different phase relationship to one another. These phase relationships may be taken into account by drawing the phasors for the circuit, see Fig. 8.14(b).

As the current is the common factor it can

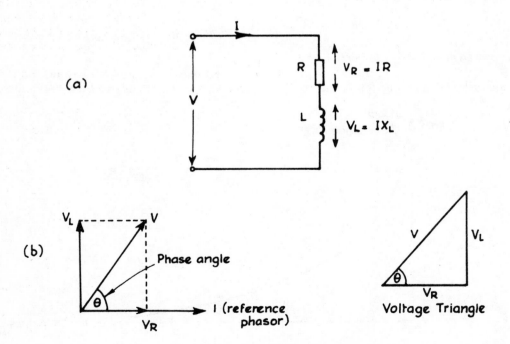

Fig. 8.14 L and R in series.

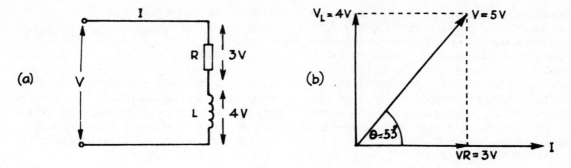

Fig. 8.15 *Phasor addition of voltages across L and R.*

be used as the reference phasor. The voltage across the resistor may be represented by a phasor in phase with the current and the voltage across the inductor by a phasor leading the current by 90°. The supply voltage V is given by the **phasor sum** as shown and is seen to **lead the current by the phase angle** θ. From the phasor diagram, a **voltage triangle** may be extracted where the sides have lengths proportional to V_R, V_L and V.

Example 7

Consider the diagram of Fig. 8.15(a) where the voltages across R and L are 3V and 4V respectively. Phasors may be drawn to scale for V_R and V_L and the resultant of the phasor addition measured to find the supply voltage V, as in Fig. 8.15(b). The phase angle θ may be measured.

The applied voltage V may be calculated from:

$$V = \sqrt{(V_R{}^2 + V_L{}^2)}$$

Using the values given in Fig. 8.15(a) gives:

$$V = \sqrt{(3^2 + 4^2)}$$
$$= \sqrt{(9 + 16)}$$
$$= \sqrt{25}$$
$$= 5\text{V}$$

Impedance

The total opposition to the flow of current of the circuit of Fig. 8.16(a) is made up of the resistance R which is constant regardless of frequency and the inductive reactance of L which varies as the frequency varies. This opposition to current flow is now given a new name **impedance** (Z) and is equal to the ratio of the applied voltage V to the current flowing I, i.e.

$$Z = \frac{V}{I} \text{ ohms}$$

If the values of R and X_L (in ohms) are known we do not simply add the values together to

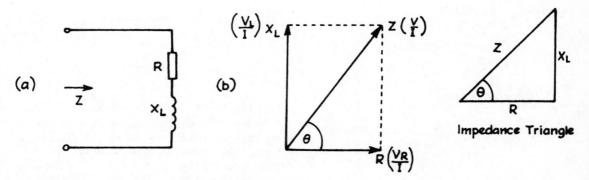

Fig. 8.16 *Impedance of L and R in series.*

find the circuit impedance, since the resistance and reactance have a different phase relationship relative to the current flowing. The circuit impedance may be found by drawing phasors as in Fig. 8.16(b) and is the simple process of dividing V_R, V_L and V by the common current component I. Thus the impedance Z is the **phasor addition** of R and X_L and the voltage triangle can be redrawn as the **impedance triangle**.

When the values of R and X_L are known, phasors for R and X_L may be drawn to scale and the resultant of the phasor addition measured to find the circuit impedance. Alternatively, the impedance may be calculated from:

$$Z = \sqrt{(R^2 + X_L{}^2)}$$

Example 8

A current of 50mA at a frequency of $1000/\pi$ Hz is passed through the series circuit of Fig. 8.17. Determine:

(a) the voltages across R and L;

(b) using phasor diagrams, the total impedance of the circuit and the voltage V across the circuit.

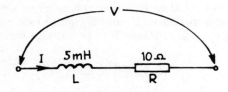

Fig. 8.17.

Solution

(a) Voltage across R

$\qquad = I \times R$

$\qquad = 50 \times 10^{-3} \times 10$ volts

$\qquad = 0{\cdot}5\text{V}$

$\quad$ Voltage across L

$\qquad = I \times X_L$

$\qquad = 50 \times 10^{-3} \times 2 \times \pi \times 1000/\pi$
$\qquad \quad \times 5 \times 10^{-3}$ volts

$\qquad = 0{\cdot}5\text{V}$

(b) $R = 10$ ohms

$X_L = 2\pi fL$

$\qquad = 2 \times \pi \times 1000/\pi \times 5 \times 10^{-3}$ ohms

$\qquad = 10\Omega$

(X_L may have been deduced from (a) since the calculated voltage across L is the same as that across R, therefore $X_L = R$.) Phasors may now be drawn to scale for R and X_L and the resultant measured to find the circuit impedance Z as in Fig. 8.18.

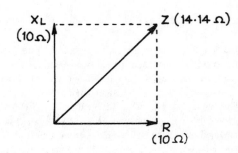

Fig. 8.18.

To find the applied voltage, phasors for V_R and V_L may be drawn as in Fig. 8.19 and the resultant measured. The above may be checked from:

$$I = \frac{V}{Z} = \frac{0{\cdot}707}{14.14}\ \text{A} = 50\text{mA (given)}.$$

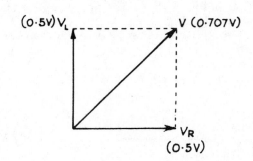

Fig. 8.19.

Circuits with *C* and *R* in series

Consider now a circuit consisting of a capacitor and a resistor in series, see Fig. 8.20(a). Since the same current I flows in both components, this is drawn as the reference phasor, Fig. 8.20(b). There will be a voltage across R equal to $I \times R$ and in phase with the

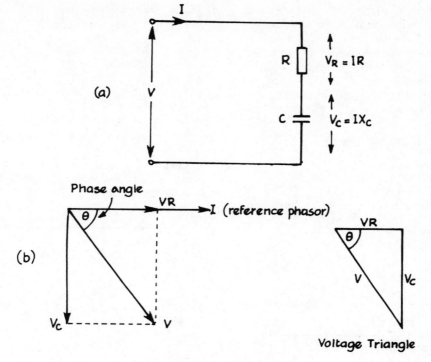

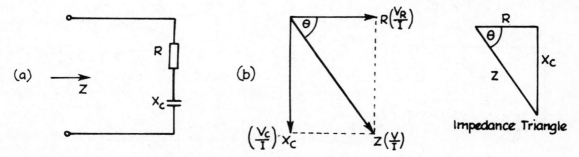

Fig. 8.20 C and R in series.

current, also a voltage across C of magnitude $I \times X_c$ but lagging on the current by 90°. The supply voltage V is given by the phasor sum of V_R and V_C and is seen to be **lagging the current by the phase angle** θ. Again, a voltage triangle may be extracted from the phasor diagram where the sides have lengths proportional to V_R, V_C and V.

When the voltage across R and C are known, phasors for V_R and V_C may be drawn to scale and the resultant measured to find V. Alternatively, the supply voltage may be calculated from:

$$V = \sqrt{(V_R^2 + V_C^2)}$$

The total opposition to the flow of current is made up of the resistance R which is constant regardless of frequency, and the capacitive reactance of C which is inversely proportional to frequency, see Fig 8.21(a). This opposition to current flow is called impedance (Z), as for the series L/R circuit is equal to the ratio of the applied voltage to the current flowing, i.e.

$$Z = \frac{V}{I} \text{ ohms}$$

To find the circuit impedance we cannot

Fig. 8.21 Impedance of C and R in series.

simply add R to X_C since the resistance and reactance have a different phase relationship to the current flowing. Thus once again, Z is found from the phasor addition of R and X_C, see Fig. 8,21(b). When the values of R and X_C are known, phasors for R and X_C may be drawn to scale and the resultant measured to find Z. Alternatively, Z may be calculated from:

$$Z = \sqrt{(R^2 + X_C^2)}$$

Example 9

If a current I of 100μA at a frequency of $2000/\pi$Hz flows in the circuit of Fig. 8.22, determine, using phasor diagrams:
(a) the impedance of the circuit;
(b) the applied voltage V.

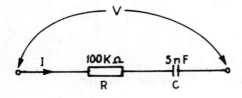

Fig. 8.22.

Solution
(a) $R = 100$kΩ (given)

$$X_C = \frac{1}{2\pi fC}$$

$$= \frac{1}{2\pi \times \dfrac{2000}{\pi} \times 5 \times 10^{-9}} \text{ ohm}$$

$$= 50\text{k}\Omega$$

Phasors for R and X_C may now be drawn to scale as in Fig. 8.23 and the resultant measured to find Z (112kΩ).

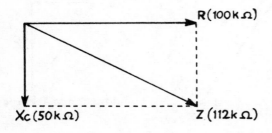

Fig. 8.23.

(b) The voltage across R (V_R)
    $= I \times R$

$\qquad = 100 \times 10^{-6} \times 10^5$

$\qquad = 10$V

The voltage across C (V_C)
    $= I \times X_C$

$\qquad = 100 \times 10^{-6} \times 5 \times 10^4$

$\qquad = 5$V

Phasors for V_R and V_C may now be drawn to scale as in Fig. 8.24 and the resultant measured to find V (11·2V).

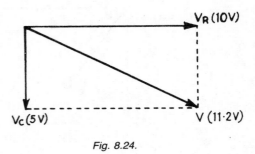

Fig. 8.24.

Circuits with L, C and R in series

Let us now consider a circuit where all three components are connected in series as in Fig. 8.25.

Since the current I is common it is drawn as the reference phasor, see Fig. 8.26. The voltage across the resistor (V_R) is in phase with the current, the voltage across the inductor (V_L) leads the current by 90° and the voltage across the capacitor (V_C) lags the current by 90°. Two conditions are illustrated; in

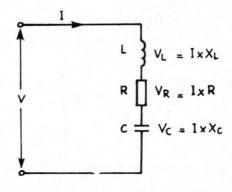

Fig. 8.25 L, C and R in series.

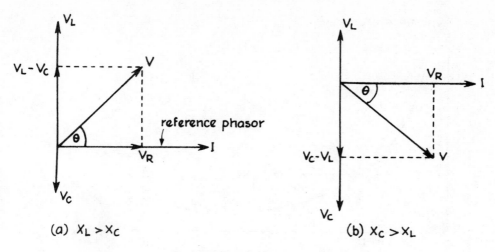

Fig. 8.26 Phasors for L, C and R in series.

Fig. 8.26(a) it is assumed that the inductive reactance is greater than the capacitive reactance, hence V_L is greater than V_C. Since the phasors for V_L and V_C act in direct opposition, the resultant of these two phasors is given by $(V_L - V_C)$. If the phasor addition of $(V_L - V_C)$ and V_R is now made, the resultant gives the applied voltage V.

Figure 8.26(b) shows the result when X_C is greater than X_L (which is the larger of the two depends upon the frequency). In this case the resultant of V_L and V_C is given by $(V_C - V_L)$. If the phasor addition of $(V_C - V_L)$ and V_R is now made, the resultant gives the applied voltage V. If the voltages across all three components are known, phasors may be constructed to scale and the resultant V measured. Alternatively the applied voltage may be found from:

$$V = \sqrt{[(V_L - V_C)^2 + V_R^2]}$$

Figure 8.27 shows how the impedance of the circuit may be obtained using phasors constructed to scale. Alternatively the impedance may be determined from:

$$Z = \sqrt{[(X_L - X_C)^2 + R^2]}$$

Assuming that the circuit values are constant there will be a particular frequency at which the reactance of L is exactly equal to the reactance of C. This results in an important condition knows as **series resonance**.

Series Resonance

The frequency (f_r) at which X_L is equal to X_C may be obtained from the intersection of the reactance graphs for L and C, see

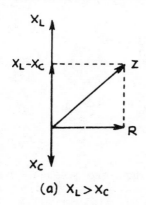

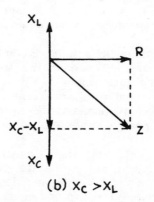

Fig. 8.27 Impedance of L, C and R in series.

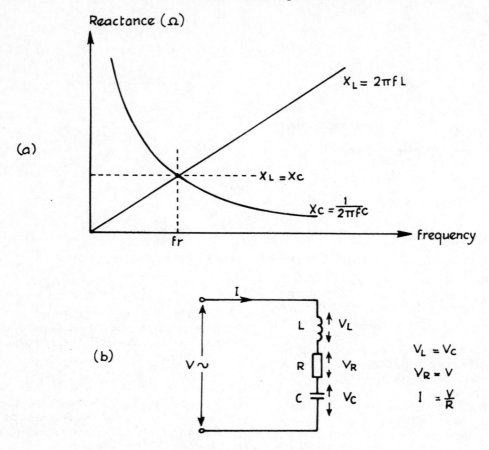

Fig. 8.28 Series resonant condition.

Fig. 8.28(a). Under this condition since the current is common, the voltages across L and C are equal (but act in opposition) and all of the supply voltage appears across R as illustrated in Fig. 8.28(b). The current then flowing in the circuit is at a **maximum** and is given by V/R.

Phasors for the series-resonance condition are given in Fig. 8.29. Since the applied voltage is the phasor resultant of V_R, V_C and V_L it is clearly equal to V_R as the resultant of V_C and V_L is zero. **At resonance** therefore, the **current I is in phase with the applied voltage**, Fig. 8.29(a).

Impedance phasors are given in Fig. 8.29(b). Again, since Z is the phasor resultant of R, X_C and X_L, the impedance at resonance is purely resistive and equal to R because the resultant of X_L and X_C is zero.

Since at the resonance frequency (f_r) $X_L = X_C$, the actual frequency at which resonance occurs may be solved from:

$$2\pi f L = \frac{1}{2\pi f C}$$

$$\text{or } f^2 = \frac{1}{4\pi^2 L C}$$

$$f = \frac{1}{2\pi \sqrt{(L C)}} \text{ Hz}$$

Example 10

Calculate the series resonance frequency when:
(a) $L = 100\mu\text{H}$ and $C = 0.005\mu\text{F}$;
(b) $L = 5\mu\text{H}$ and $C = 100\text{pF}$

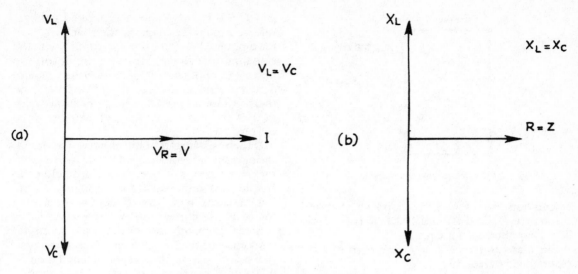

Fig. 8.29 Series resonance phasors.

Solution

(a) $f_r = \dfrac{1}{2\pi\sqrt{(LC)}}$

$= \dfrac{1}{2\pi\sqrt{(100 \times 10^{-6} \times 0.005 \times 10^{-6})}}$

$= \dfrac{10^6}{2\pi\sqrt{0.5}}$

$= 225.08\text{kHz}$

(b) $f_r = \dfrac{1}{2\pi\sqrt{(LC)}}$

$= \dfrac{1}{2\pi\sqrt{(5 \times 10^{-6} \times 100 \times 10^{-12})}}$

$= \dfrac{10^9}{2\pi\sqrt{500}}$

$= 7.12\text{MHz}$

Series Resonant Circuit Response

Figure 8.30 shows how the current in the circuit for constant applied voltage reduces as the frequency varies either side of resonance. This arises from the fact that at resonance the circuit impedance is equal to just R but away from resonance the total impedance Z increases. The resonant property of the circuit enables voltages of one frequency to be selected although voltages of several frequencies may be present. By altering the value of either L or C, the frequency at which maximum response occurs may be varied, e.g. increasing the value of L would move the peak response to the left (lower the resonance frequency) whilst decreasing its value would move the peak response to the right (increase the resonance frequency).

A further important and interesting fact that occurs at resonance may be shown by simple

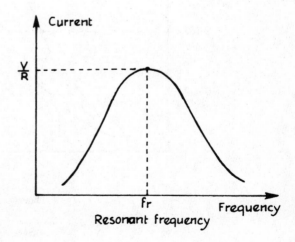

Fig. 8.30 Response of series resonant circuit.

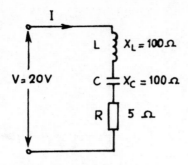

Fig. 8.31 *Example of series resonance.*

calculation, see Fig. 8.31. Suppose that at resonance X_L and X_C are 100Ω, R is 5Ω and 20V is applied to the circuit.

Since at resonance $Z = R$, the current I at resonance is given by:

$$I = \frac{V}{R} = \frac{20}{5} = 4\text{A}$$

Voltage across $L = IX_L = 4 \times 100 = 400\text{V}$

Voltage across $C = IX_C = 4 \times 100 = 400\text{V}$

Voltage across $R = IR = 4 \times 5 = 20\text{V}$
$$= \text{applied voltage}$$

We now have what appears to be a very unusual situation in that the voltages across L

and C are twenty times the applied voltage, referred to as the **magnification factor** (Q) of the circuit. This result is not in conflict with the rule that the voltages around a circuit will add up to the applied voltage, since the voltages across L and C are equal and opposite and their resultant is zero. A magnification factor of 100 or more may be met with in radio circuits.

If the resistance R of the circuit is increased, the current at resonance will be decreased, but the resistance will not have much effect at frequencies removed from resonance as the impedance is high. The effect of resistance on the response curve is shown in Fig. 8.32.

Since the bandwidth of the resonant circuit is taken to be the frequencies covered between the points where the response has fallen to 0·707 of its maximum response (3dB points), the bandwidth of the circuit with the larger series resistance will be greater but the response will be less selective, i.e. of lower Q.

Parallel Resonant Circuit

Resonance may also be achieved when an inductor is connected in parallel with a capacitor as in Fig. 8.33(a). Since it is impossible to make an inductor without

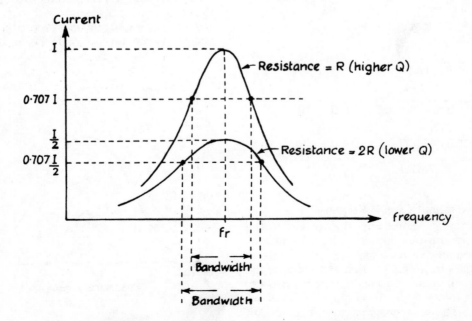

Fig. 8.32 *Effect of resistance on resonance curve of series circuit.*

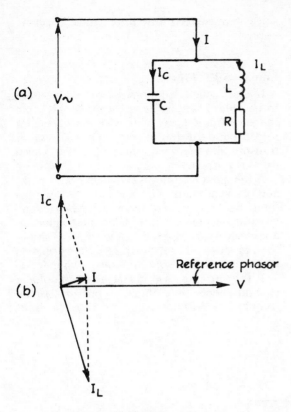

(a)

(b)

Fig. 8.33 Parallel resonance.

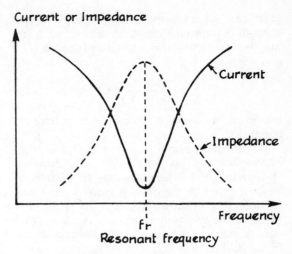

Fig. 8.34 Parallel resonance response.

resistance, a resistor R is shown in series with L but does not normally exist as a physical component.

As the applied voltage V is common to both arms of the parallel circuit, it is drawn as the reference phasor, see Fig. 8.33(b). The current I_C in the capacitive arm leads the voltage by 90°. The current I_L in the inductive arm lags the voltage by slightly less than 90° owing to the presence of the resistance R. The total current I is given by the phasor sum of I_C and I_L. There will be a frequency where I_L will be equal to I_C and under this condition I will be very small and practically in phase with V; this is the parallel-resonance condition. Thus for parallel resonance V and I are in phase, the current I is at minimum and the impedance is at a maximum. The response curve of Fig. 8.34 shows how the current I and the impedance varies as the frequency varies either side of the resonance frequency.

The effect of increasing the resistance of the coil is shown in Fig. 8.35. As the resistance is increased the response becomes less selective but the circuit bandwidth is increased. In

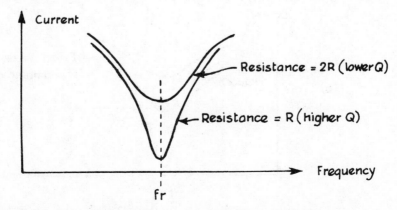

Fig. 8.35 Effect of resistance on resonance curve of parallel circuit.

practice R is kept as small as possible. When R is small compared with the reactance of L, it may be shown that the resonance frequency is given by:

$$f = \frac{1}{2\pi\sqrt{(LC)}} \text{ Hz}$$

the same as for the series-resonant circuit condition.

If the selectivity is too great, i.e. the bandwidth is too small for a particular application, the bandwidth may be increased by connecting a 'damping resistor' across the tuned circuit as shown in Fig. 8.36(a). As the value of the damping resistor is reduced, the bandwidth is increased as illustrated in Fig. 8.36(b).

The parallel resonant circuit is often referred to as a **rejector circuit** as it offers a high impedance at resonance, whilst the series resonant circuit is called an **acceptor circuit** since it presents a low impedance at resonance.

Low-pass *RC* Filter

In electronic equipment it is often necessary to be able to attenuate or suppress a certain range of frequencies lying within a particular larger band of frequencies but to pass or transmit all other frequencies; filters are used for this purpose.

A low-pass *RC* filter is shown in Fig. 8.37(a) and its symbol in Fig. 8.37(b). A low-pass filter passes low-frequency signals (ideally without loss) but severely attenuates signals of above a certain frequency. Fig. 8.37(c) shows the response where the ratio v_o/v_i is plotted against frequency. Over the range where v_o/v_i = 1, the output v_o is equal to the input voltage v_i and here the filter is passing signal frequencies without loss. As the *RC* filter

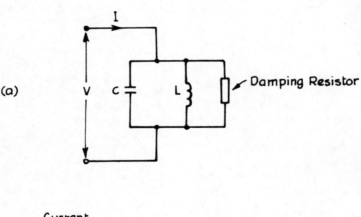

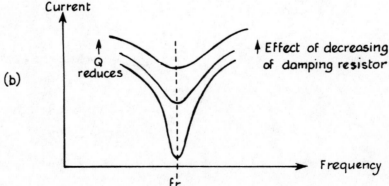

Fig. 8.36 Use of damping resistor to widen the bandwidth.

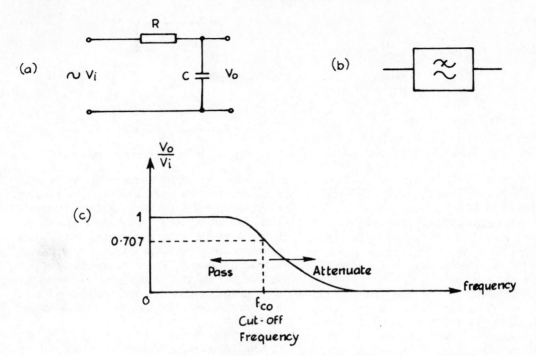

Fig. 8.37 Low-pass R–C filter.

response changes slowly from pass to attenuate, it is necessary to specify a frequency where for practical purposes the filter changes over from pass to attenuate. This frequency, called the **cut-off frequency** f_{co}, is taken to be the frequency where the output voltage has fallen to 0·707 (3dB) of the input voltage. Thus above f_{co} the low-pass filter is attenuating the input signal as the ratio v_o/v_i is less than 0·707.

The action of the low-pass RC filter may be considered as that of a potential divider, see Fig. 8.38. If the value of C is chosen so that it has a very high reactance compared with the resistance R at low frequencies, then most of

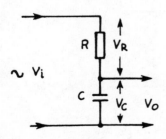

Fig. 8.38 Potential divider action of L.P.F.

the input voltage will appear across C (V_C) and little voltage will appear across R (V_R). Since V_C is the output voltage V_o, then at low frequencies the filter will be operating in the pass-band. As the frequency is raised the reactance of C falls resulting in less voltage across C but more across R. When the reactance of C is very small compared to R, there will be an extremely small voltage across C with practically all of the input voltage developed across R; here the filter is in the attenuation band (above f_{co}).

The cut-off frequency of the filter depends upon the time constant of the circuit which is determined by the CR product. At f_{co} the voltages across R and C will be equal but V_C will lag V_R by 90°.

$$\text{Thus, at } f_{co}, R = \frac{1}{2\pi f C} \ \Omega$$

$$\text{or } f_{co} = \frac{1}{2\pi C R} \ \text{Hz}$$

Example 11
In a low-pass RC filter, $R = 50\text{k}\Omega$ and $C = 100\text{nF}$. Determine the cut-off frequency.

Solution

$$f_{co} = \frac{1}{2\pi CR} \text{ Hz}$$

$$= \frac{1}{2\pi \times 100 \times 10^{-9} \times 5 \times 10^4}$$

$$= 31.8\text{Hz}$$

Thus the filter will pass frequencies from 0Hz to 31·8Hz but attenuate frequencies above 31·8Hz.

High-pass *RC* Filter

If the positions of R and C of the low-pass filter are interchanged, a high-pass filter results, see Fig. 8.39(a). The circuit symbol is given in Fig. 8.39(b) and the filter response in Fig. 8.39(c).

The filter passes frequencies down to the cut-off frequency f_{co} and below this frequency the filter changes over from pass to attenuate. It will be seen that the high-pass filter has a response which is the mirror image of the low-pass filter response.

Again the action of the filter may be considered as a potential divider, see

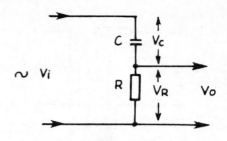

Fig. 8.40 Potential divider action of H.P.F.

Fig. 8.40. At high frequencies where the reactance of C is quite small compared with the resistance R, V_R is large compared with V_C and the filter is in the pass-band. If the frequency is reduced, the reactance of C rises resulting in more voltage across C and less across R. Below f_{co} where the reactance of C is very large compared with R, most of the input voltage appears across C with very little across R; here the filter is operating in the attenuation band.

The cut-off frequency of the filter again depends upon the CR product and f_{co} is given by:

$$f_{co} = \frac{1}{2\pi CR} \text{ Hz}$$

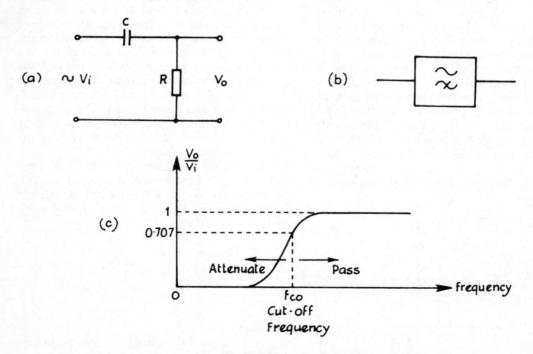

Fig. 8.39 High-pass R–C filter.

Thus if the same values as given in Example 11 are used for the high-pass filter, the filter will pass frequencies above 31·8Hz but attenuate frequencies below this figure.

QUESTIONS ON CHAPTER EIGHT

(1) A capacitor of 2000pF is charged via a resistance of 5kΩ to a d.c. supply of 20V. The time taken for the voltage across the capacitor to reach 14·14V will be:
(a) 1·414μs
(b) 0·707μs
(c) 1·414ms
(d) 4μs.

(2) A capacitor is charged via a resistance to a d.c. supply of 15V. After a period equal to the time constant the voltage across the capacitor will be:
(a) 5·0V
(b) 5·55V
(c) 9·45V
(d) 15V.

(3) A capacitor of 5μF charged initially to 100V is discharged via a resistance of 100kΩ. The approximate time for the capacitor voltage to reach 0V will be:
(a) 2·5s
(b) 0·5s
(c) 100μs
(d) 50ms.

(4) An inductor of 5mH is connected in series with a resistance of 50kΩ across a 50V d.c. supply. The time taken for the current in the circuit to grow to 0·63mA will be:
(a) 0·1μs
(b) 250s
(c) 10μs
(d) 2·5s.

(5) The reactance of an inductor is given by:
(a) $2fL$
(b) $\dfrac{1}{2\pi fL}$
(c) $2\pi L$
(d) $2\pi fL$.

(6) The reactance of a capacitor is given by:
(a) $2\pi fC$
(b) $\dfrac{1}{\omega C}$
(c) $\dfrac{2\pi f}{C}$
(d) πfC.

(7) When a sinewave voltage is applied to a circuit consisting of an inductor in series with a resistor:
(a) The current in the inductor leads the current in the resistor by 90°
(b) The voltage across the resistor leads the current by 90°
(c) The voltage across the inductor leads the voltage across the resistor by 90°
(d) The voltage across the inductor and resistor are in-phase.

(8) When a sinewave voltage is applied to a circuit consisting of a capacitor in series with a resistor:
(a) The voltage across the capacitor leads the current by 90°
(b) The voltage across the resistor and capacitor are in-phase
(c) The applied voltage and the current are in-phase
(d) The voltage across the resistor leads the voltage across the capacitor by 90°.

(9) In a series resonant circuit:
(a) The impedance at resonance is high
(b) The applied voltage and current are in-phase at resonance
(c) The voltage across the inductor and capacitor are 90° out of phase
(d) Minimum current flows at resonance.

(10) In a parallel resonant circuit:
(a) Maximum current flows at resonance
(b) The impedance at resonance is high
(c) The impedance at resonance is low
(d) The applied voltage and current are 90° out of phase.

(11) The resonance frequency of a series tuned circuit is given by:

(a) $f = \dfrac{\sqrt{(LC)}}{2\pi}$

(b) $f = \dfrac{2\pi\sqrt{L}}{C}$

(c) $f = \dfrac{1}{2\pi LC}$

(d) $f = \dfrac{1}{2\pi\sqrt{(LC)}}$.

(12) The effect of connecting a resistor across a parallel tuned circuit is to:

(a) Alter the resonance frequency
(b) Increase the bandwidth
(c) Decrease the bandwidth
(d) Decrease the current at resonance.

(Answers on page 369)

CHAPTER NINE

TRANSFORMERS AND SHIELDING

Objectives

1 To explain the transformer principle.
2 To determine voltage, current and impedance ratios and show the use of a matching transformer.
3 To consider the operation of auto and centre-tapped transformers.
4 To explain transformer losses and describe the construction of mains, audio and r.f. transformers.
5 To explain magnetic and electric shielding.

TRANSFORMERS

WHEN AN ALTERNATING current flows in an inductor there is a magnetic field around the inductor of strength that is proportional to the current flowing, see instants a, b, c and d of Fig. 9.1. Thus with a.c. there is a magnetic field that is either growing or contracting and therefore **moving**. It is the moving magnetic

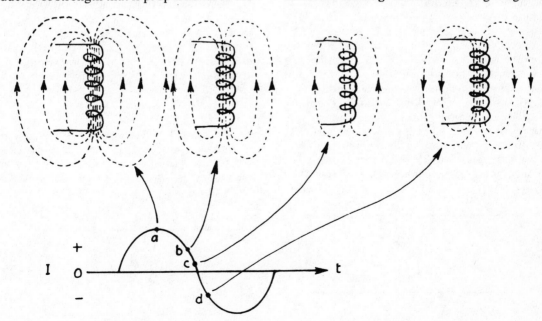

Fig. 9.1 Magnetic field associated with an inductor carrying alternating current.

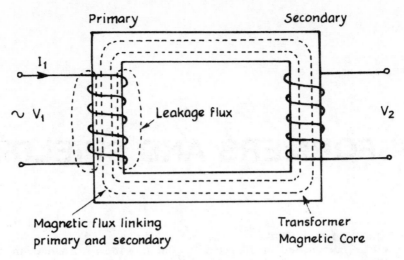

Fig. 9.2 Transformer principle.

field which cuts the turns of the inductor and induces an e.m.f. (self-induced e.m.f.) into those turns. It therefore seems reasonable that if a second coil is brought close to the first so that the moving magnetic field cuts the turns of the second coil an e.m.f. will be induced into the second coil; this is the principle of the transformer.

In most cases the two coils, called the primary and secondary are wound on a magnetic core (iron), as illustrated in Fig. 9.2. This has two effects: (i) it increases the inductance of the primary and so reduces the current that flows in the primary and (ii) it concentrates the magnetic flux so that most of it passes through the secondary winding (the portion of flux not linking with the secondary is called the leakage flux). Thus, when an a.c. supply of voltage $V1$ is applied to the primary, a current I_1 will flow. This current sets up a moving magnetic field which cuts the turns of the secondary inducing a voltage $V2$ in it. The

secondary induced e.m.f. will follow the same changing pattern of the primary applied voltage.

Voltage and Current Ratios

Let us consider an 'ideal' transformer, i.e. one with no losses and one where all of the flux set up in the primary links with the secondary. If a load R is connected across the secondary then the secondary induced e.m.f. V_s will produce a current in the secondary I_s of value equal to V_s/R, see Fig. 9.3. If the ratio of the number of primary turns to the number of secondary turns is N_p/N_s then:

$$\frac{V_P}{V_s} = \frac{N_P}{N_s} \text{ and } \frac{I_P}{I_s} = \frac{N_s}{N_P}$$

i.e. the ratio of the voltages across primary and secondary is proportional to the turns ratio, whereas the ratio of currents in primary and secondary is inversely proportional to the turns ratio.

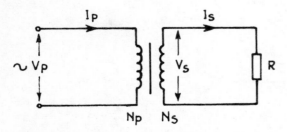

Fig. 9.3 Voltage and current ratios (ideal transformer).

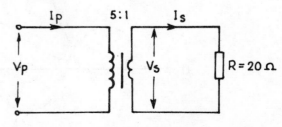

Fig. 9.4.

Example 1

If the voltage applied to the primary (V_p) of Fig. 9.4 is 50V, determine:

(a) the secondary voltage;

(b) the secondary and primary currents.

Solution

(a) Now $\dfrac{V_p}{V_s} = \dfrac{N_p}{N_s} = \dfrac{5}{1}$

$\therefore \dfrac{50}{V_s} = \dfrac{5}{1}$

or $V_s = \dfrac{50}{5} = 10V$

(b) $I_s = \dfrac{V_s}{R} = \dfrac{10}{20} = 0.5A$

Now $\dfrac{I_p}{I_s} = \dfrac{N_s}{N_p} = \dfrac{1}{5}$

$\therefore \dfrac{I_p}{0 \cdot 5} = \dfrac{1}{5}$

or $I_p = \dfrac{0.5}{5} = 0.1A$

Impedance Ratio

Consider Fig. 9.5 where R_p is the resistance or impedance 'seen' looking into the primary and let $N_p/N_s = n{:}1$.

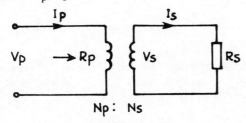

Fig. 9.5 Impedance ratio.

Now $R_p = \dfrac{V_p}{I_p}$ and $R_s = \dfrac{V_s}{I_s}$

thus $\dfrac{R_p}{R_s} = \dfrac{V_p}{I_p} \div \dfrac{V_s}{I_s}$

$= \dfrac{V_p}{I_p} \times \dfrac{I_s}{V_s} = \dfrac{V_p}{V_s} \times \dfrac{I_s}{I_p}$

but $\dfrac{V_p}{V_s} = \dfrac{N_p}{N_s} = \dfrac{I_s}{I_p} = n$

$\therefore \dfrac{R_p}{R_s} = n \times n = n^2$

or $R_p = n^2 R_s$

Thus the impedance looking into the primary is equal to the (turns ratio)^2 × the secondary impedance.

Example 2

Determine the primary impedance of Fig. 9.6 (a) and (b).

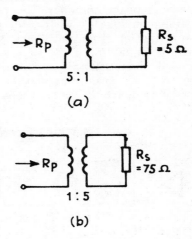

(a)

(b)

Fig. 9.6.

Solution

(a) $R_p = n^2 R_s$ ($n{:}1$ = step-down ratio)

$\qquad = 25 \times 5 = 125\Omega$

(b) Since a step-up ratio is used here ($1{:}n$),

$\dfrac{R_p}{R_s} = \dfrac{1}{n^2}$

or $R_p = \dfrac{R_s}{n^2} = \dfrac{75}{25} = 3\Omega$

Transformer Matching

If we have a signal source such as an amplifier and a load, e.g. a loudspeaker and we wish to transfer maximum power from the amplifier to the loudspeaker, then the loudspeaker resistance or impedance should be

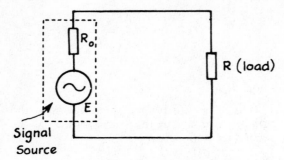

Fig. 9.7 Maximum power transfer.

equal to the output resistance or output impedance of the amplifier. This principle is illustrated in Fig. 9.7 where, for maximum power transfer from the signal source, R should be equal to R_o.

Usually the resistances are not equal and in such cases a transformer may be used for impedance matching, as shown in Fig. 9.8.

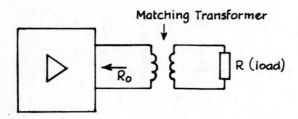

Fig. 9.8 Use of matching transformer.

When R and R_o are known the turns ratio required may be determined from

$$n^2 = \frac{R_o}{R}$$

$$\text{or } n = \sqrt{\frac{R_o}{R}}$$

The expression may be applied also to situations where maximum power is to be transferred from a transmitter to its aerial or the output of an oscillator to its load.

Example 3

An amplifier has an output resistance of 4.5kΩ and is to be matched to a 20Ω loudspeaker for maximum power transfer. Determine the turns ratio of the transformer to be used.

Solution

$$n = \sqrt{\frac{R_o}{R}}$$

$$= \sqrt{\frac{4500}{20}}$$

$$= \sqrt{225}$$

$$= 15 : 1 \text{ (step-down)}$$

Auto-transformer

The transformer illustrated in Fig. 9.2 is sometimes called a 'double-wound' transformer, i.e. having two windings. A transformer may also be constructed using a single winding with one or more tappings. The diagram of Fig. 9.9 shows an auto-transformer with a

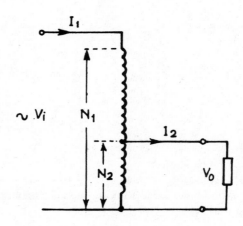

Fig. 9.9 Auto-transformer with single tapping.

single tapping. The voltage ratio is determined in the same way as for the double-wound transformer, i.e.

$$\frac{V_i}{V_o} = \frac{N1}{N2} \text{ and the current ratio by}$$

$$\frac{I_1}{I_2} = \frac{N2}{N1}$$

An auto-transformer with several tappings is shown in Fig. 9.10. The voltage ratios are given by:

$$\frac{V_i}{V_{o_1}} = \frac{N1}{N4} \ , \quad \frac{V_i}{V_{o_2}} = \frac{N1}{N3} \text{ and } \frac{V_i}{V_{o_3}} = \frac{N1}{N2}$$

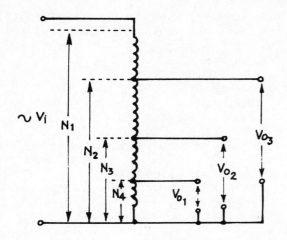

Fig. 9.10 Auto-transformer with more than one tapping.

Example 4

Sections a, b and c of the auto-transformer shown in Fig. 9.11 each have 500 turns. Determine the output voltages $V1$ and $V2$.

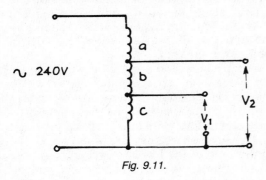

Fig. 9.11.

Solution

Turns ratio for $V1 = \dfrac{1500}{500} = \dfrac{3}{1}$

$\therefore \dfrac{240}{V1} = \dfrac{3}{1}$

or $3V1 = 240$

$V1 = 80\text{V}$

Turns ratio for $V2 = \dfrac{1500}{1000} = \dfrac{3}{2}$

$\therefore \dfrac{240}{V2} = \dfrac{3}{2}$

or $3V2 = 480$

$V2 = 160\text{V}$

Centre-tapped Transformer

Some double-wound transformers have a tapping placed at the electrical centre of the secondary winding as illustrated in Fig. 9.12(a). This results in equal voltages being developed in the two halves of the secondary winding, i.e. $V2 = V3$.

The voltage ratios are:

$$\frac{V1}{V2} = \frac{N1}{N2} \text{ and } \frac{V1}{V3} = \frac{N1}{N3}$$

Centre-tapped transformers are used with some types of full-wave rectifier where usually the centre-tap is connected to the common line or earth. Such a transformer may be designated as 300V–0–300V which means that there is 300V (r.m.s.) across each of the two halves of the secondary. This type of transformer is also used in phase discriminators due to its ability to supply equal balanced voltages.

If the secondary winding is continuous then the voltages across each half will be in-phase with one another. However, **with respect to the centre-tap** the voltages are in anti-phase with one another and may be represented by the phasor diagram of Fig. 9.12(b).

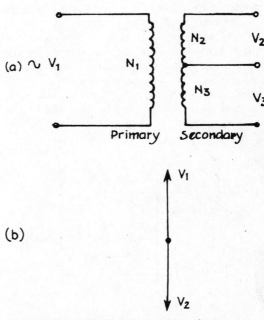

Fig. 9.12 Centre-tapped transformer.

Transformer Losses

An 'ideal transformer' has no losses and the power developed in the secondary is equal to the power supplied to the primary, or $V_p \times I_p = V_s \times I_s$. Practical transformers exhibit various power losses which means that less power is developed in the secondary than is supplied to the primary. The principal losses are:

(a) Copper Losses

The windings in a transformer are made from copper and as such each winding will have a d.c. resistance. Thus when current flows in a winding, there will be some power dissipated in the d.c. resistance of the winding. The effect of the primary winding d.c. resistance means that there will be effectively less voltage developed in the secondary and the effect of the secondary winding d.c. resistance will result in less voltage being supplied to the secondary load. Thus there will be a power loss between primary and secondary.

(b) Core Losses

If the core of a transformer were made of solid iron then an e.m.f. would be induced into it by the moving magnetic field produced by the primary winding. The e.m.f. would cause a current to circulate in the core as illustrated in Fig. 9.13(a).

The circulating currents in the core are called 'eddy currents' and would cause the core to get hot resulting in an undesirable power loss. To reduce the effect to small proportions, the core is made of thin iron laminations which are lightly insulated from one another as shown in Fig. 9.13(b). Currents will flow in the laminations, but these will be small as the flux passing down each lamination is small.

(c) Leakage flux

The useful flux in a transformer links both windings. Leakage flux links with its own turns but not both windings and its path exists largely in air. It is really wasted flux and represents a loss. Leakage flux is reduced by careful design and construction.

Practical transformers have efficiencies in the range 96–99 per cent.

Types of Transformer

Mains Transformers

These transformers operate from the mains supply of 240V r.m.s. at 50Hz and are used to supply appropriate voltages to operate integrated circuits and discrete transistors in various electronic equipment. Since modern electronic circuits require supply voltages in the range 6–50V, the transformer used is a step-down one.

The primary and secondary windings are not wound on separate limbs as drawn in theoretical diagrams. They are wound in intimate contact so that the flux induced by one winding links with the other, as illustrated in Fig. 9.14 where they are wound over the centre limb of the low-loss iron core. A core which is subjected to alternating flux is built up from laminations to reduce eddy current losses using often T and U laminations, see Fig. 9.15(a). Silicon iron is used in most

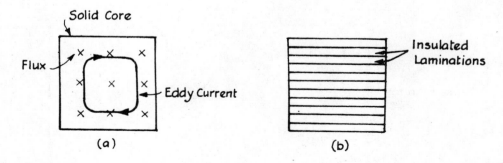

Fig. 9.13 Use of laminated core to reduce eddy-current loss.

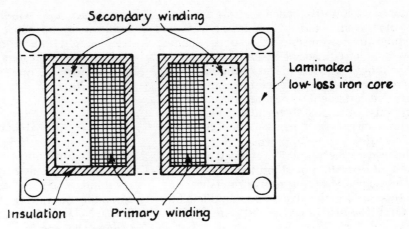

Fig. 9.14 Mains transformer construction.

modern power transformers, the addition of about four per cent of silicon to pure iron increasing its resistivity by about four times, so that the eddy current loss is reduced. Alternate groups of three to four laminations are overlapped as shown in Fig. 9.15(b) to produce a low reluctance joint thereby reducing the leakage flux that would be present with a butt joint. The silicon-iron core is normally connected to earth.

In a mains transformer where considerable power output is required, the insulated copper windings must be of sufficient diameter to carry the current without overheating. Thus the larger the power output, the larger the transformer.

Audio-frequency Transformers

Transformers of similar construction are also used at audio frequencies. Low-power audio transformers may use a core material of high permeability such as Permalloy. High-power transformers generally use silicon iron laminations since Permalloy saturates at a comparatively low flux density. Primary and secondary windings may be sandwiched as illustrated in Fig. 9.16 to improve winding coupling and reduce leakage flux.

The design of this type of transformer is more difficult than a mains transformer due to the need to achieve an even response over a band of frequencies, e.g. 30Hz to 15kHz. The size of the primary inductance limits the

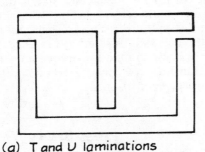

(a) T and U laminations

(b) Overlapping at joints
    (alternate 3 or 4 laminations)

Fig. 9.15 Laminated core construction.

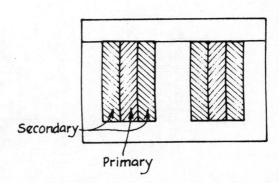

Fig. 9.16 Winding arrangement for a.f. transformer.

response at low frequencies whilst the self-capacitance and leakage inductance of the windings are responsible for response limitations at high frequencies. In addition, if one of the windings carries a d.c. component of current it will cause a reduction in inductance over that attainable without d.c. and the possibility of signal distortion. This would require a larger transformer to meet the same specification. Thus unbalanced d.c. in an audio transformer should be avoided either by push-pull operation or shunt feeding.

Interstage and output transformers were at one time used with valve audio amplifiers but are rarely found in modern solid-state circuits.

Radio-frequency Transformers

Transformers are also used at radio frequencies but the construction is generally quite different. Laminated iron cores cannot be used owing to the large eddy current loss that would occur at high frequencies and the small signals encountered in receiving equipment.

In order to reduce the size of the windings, Ferroxcube cores are commonly used. Ferroxcube is a ferrite, i.e. iron oxide having a high permeability and high resistivity (the high resistivity reduces eddy current losses). In most cases, the primary and secondary are wound as shown in Fig. 9.17(a) on an insulating tube with a solid cylinder of Ferroxcube fitted inside. In receiving equipment the primary and secondary windings may form resonant circuits and when a Ferroxcube core is used the inductance and hence the resonance frequency may be varied by moving the core in and out of the winding as in Fig. 9.17(b). Movement of the Ferroxcube

core into the winding will increase the inductance and hence reduce the resonance frequency. Often no core is used (air-cored) and the windings may be placed side-by-side or on top of one another as shown in Fig. 9.17(c).

SHIELDING

Magnetic Shielding

Consider a coil carrying current and the resultant magnetic field around the coil spreading out into the space surrounding it as in Fig. 9.18(a). If the current in the coil is **d.c.** or **low-frequency a.c.** and we wish to prevent the flux lines from intercepting other neighbouring components, the coil may be enclosed in a screening box of high permeability material such as **Mumetal** as shown in Fig. 9.19(b). The walls of the screening box form an easy (low-reluctance) path for the flux so that very little flux spreads out into areas where it would be unwelcome. The action of the screen or shield would be nullified if there were a break in the path for the flux such as V–W or X–Y. The result of such a break is illustrated in Fig. 9.18(c) where flux leaks at the break thereby reducing the effectiveness of the screening action.

It may be desirable, of course, to shield a coil from external magnetic fields and if these are d.c. or low-frequency a.c. fields, the low reluctance path offered by the walls of the screen flux will divert an external field away from the coil as illustrated in Fig. 9.19. This principle is used in the low-frequency screening of transformers, chokes, cathode ray tubes and measuring instruments.

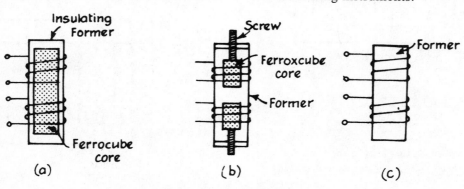

Fig. 9.17 R.F. transformers.

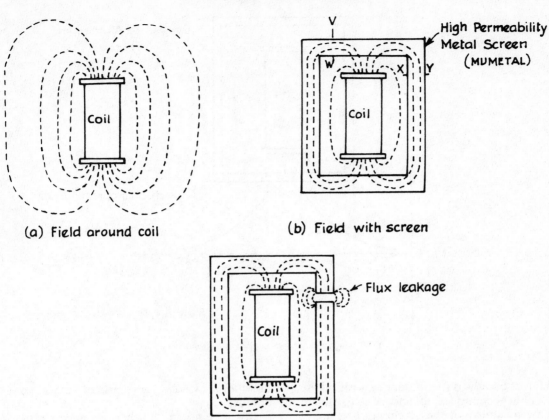

(a) Field around coil

(b) Field with screen

(c) Field with break at XY in screen

Fig. 9.18 Magnetic screening at d.c. and low frequencies.

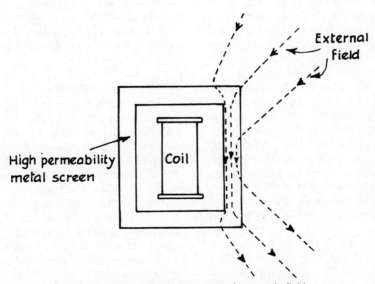

Fig. 9.19 Effect of screen on external magnetic field.

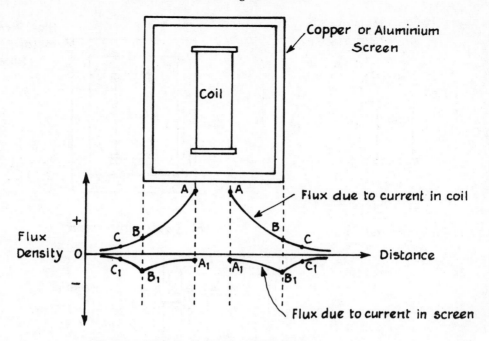

Fig. 9.20 Magnetic screening at high frequencies.

Unfortunately as the frequency is raised the screening becomes less effective due to a fall in the permeability of the screening box material. Thus at high frequencies (r.f.) a different principle is employed, see Fig. 9.20.

Here the screening box is made of a high-conductivity metal such as copper or aluminium. Since the permeability of copper is about the same as air it is useless as a flux diverter. However what the copper screen does is to act like a short-circuited secondary winding and the current induced into it sets up a magnetic field that very nearly cancels out the field external to the coil. As shown in the figure, the flux around the coil due to the current in it gradually falls off in intensity as one moves away from the coil (ABC) and spreads outside the confines of the screen. However, because an a.c. field is a moving one it cuts the walls of the screen thereby inducing a voltage into it. The induced voltage sets up a current in the screen which produces its own magnetic field. By Lenz's law this field opposes the field creating it. The field is at a maximum at point B′ but falls away on either side of the wall, A′ and C′, resulting external to the screen two fields acting in opposite

directions which **very nearly cancel one another**.

It will be noted that there is cancellation of the magnetic field due to the coil inside the screen, i.e. the effect of the screen is to reduce the inductance of the coil. To avoid a large reduction in inductance the space inside the screen should be as large as is practicable.

The principle holds good in shielding the coil from external r.f. magnetic fields.

Electrostatic Screening

No mention has been made of an 'earth' in connection with magnetic screening because earthing has nothing to do with magnetic screening but it has everything to do with electrostatic screening. Consider a component at high potential ($+V$) with respect to earth as in Fig. 9.21(a). The electrostatic field spreads out into the surrounding space to terminate on the earth line (which may be the chassis of the electronic equipment). Thus every point in space around the component is at some potential lying between $+V$ and earth, i.e. not zero potential. To remove the offending electrostatic field from other sensitive compo-

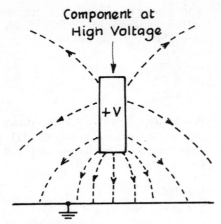

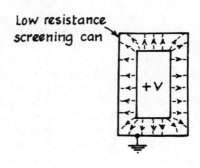

(a) Electrostatic field associated with component at high voltage

(b) Electrostatic field confined to earthed screening can

Fig. 9.21 Electrostatic screening.

nents, the component at high voltage may be enclosed in a low-resistance screening box as shown in Fig. 9.21(b) which is connected to earth. Since all points on the screening can are at earth potential the lines of the electric field will terminate on the can, thus no field will exist outside the can.

This principle holds good for steady fields even if the resistance of the screening can is not very low. However, for fast-changing fields the resistance of the screening can must be low to prevent p.d.s being set up in the screen as a result of capacitive currents induced in it. It is not essential to have a continuous metal screen and a sort of 'bird cage' is quite effective, see Fig. 9.22. It is found that very little field exists outside the cage even when the spacing between the wires

is greater than the wire diameter. This type of electrostatic screen may be useful when ventilation is required for the screened component to get rid of heat.

An electrostatic screen is sometimes fitted between the primary and secondary windings of a mains transformer, see Fig. 9.23. This reduces capacitive coupling between primary and secondary which assists in reducing the

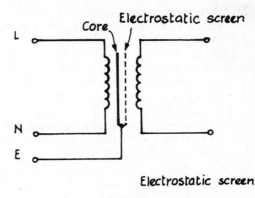

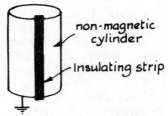

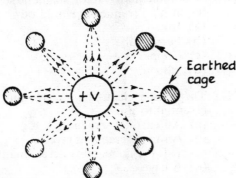

Fig. 9.22 Use of earthed cage (plan view).

Fig. 9.23 Use of electrostatic screen in transformer.

transference of mains r.f. interference to the secondary circuits. It also reduces the possibility of the establishment of potentials referenced to 'live' or 'neutral' in the secondary which is important in a mains isolation transformer.

If the primary winding were to be enclosed by an earthed copper cylinder before the secondary were wound on, it would act like a short-circuited turn and prevent normal magnetic coupling between primary and secondary. To allow magnetic coupling while providing electrostatic shielding, all that is necessary is to place a strip of insulating material between overlapping edges of an earthed non-magnetic metal cylinder. It should be noted that an earthed copper screening can will act as both a magnetic and an electrostatic shield at r.f.

QUESTIONS ON CHAPTER NINE

(1) A transformer with a step-down ratio of 4:1 has 25V applied to its primary. The secondary voltage will be:
(a) 100V
(b) 6·25V
(c) 1·5625V
(d) 2·5V.

(2) A transformer with a step-up ratio of 1:8 has 60V in the secondary. The primary voltage is:
(a) 7·5V
(b) 4V
(c) 480V
(d) 320V.

(3) The secondary current of a transformer using a 10:1 step-down ratio is 100mA. The primary current is:
(a) 1mA
(b) 10mA
(c) 1A
(d) 100A.

(4) If the secondary load of the transformer in question 3 is 100Ω, the primary voltage will be:
(a) 1V
(b) 2·5V
(c) 10V
(d) 100V.

(5) The primary current of a transformer with a step-up ratio of 1:7 is 1·4A. The secondary current will be:
(a) 9·8A
(b) 0·707A
(c) 0·2A
(d) 8·4A.

(6) A transformer with a 9:1 step-down ratio has a secondary load of 5Ω. The resistance seen in the primary will be:
(a) 0·55Ω
(b) 405Ω
(c) 45Ω
(d) 5Ω.

(7) An amplifier with an output resistance of 245Ω is to be matched to a 5Ω load. The turns ratio of the transformer used will be:
(a) 1:49
(b) 7:1
(c) 49:1
(d) 1225:1.

(8) The core of a transformer is laminated to:
(a) Reduce magnetic coupling
(b) Increase the primary inductance
(c) Reduce interference
(d) Reduce eddy current loss.

(9) To provide magnetic shielding at low frequencies it is essential to use:
(a) A screening box of high resistance
(b) An earthed screening box
(c) A screening box of high permeability
(d) A copper screening box.

(10) A suitable material for magnetic screening at high frequency would be:
(a) Iron
(b) Ferroxcube
(c) Copper
(d) Silicon.

(11) To provide electrostatic screening it is essential to use:
(a) An earthed screening box
(b) An iron screening box
(c) A low-permeability screening box
(d) A cage.

(Answers on page 369)

CHAPTER TEN

MEASURING INSTRUMENTS

Objectives
1 To describe the construction and operation of basic meters.
2 To consider instrument limitations.
3 To explain measurement errors.

THE MEASURING INSTRUMENTS used in electronic servicing should be of a standard to detect reliably the actual voltage, current, resistance or waveform levels in equipment (within stated circuit tolerances), to enable the servicing technician to make decisions on the correct/incorrect operation of the various circuits.

TYPES OF INSTRUMENT

(a) Analogue
Instruments which have a pointer that is deflected over a scale represent the quantity being measured in analogue form since the magnitude of the deflection, which moves smoothly over the scale, represents the magnitude of the quantity.

The moving-coil instrument is an example of this type, see Fig. 10.1 and its operation was described in Volume 1 of this series. In a moving-coil instrument the movement of the pointer is directly proportional to the **mean value** of the current flowing in the moving coil and the scale of the instrument is a linear one. The accuracy of measurement with this type of analogue display depends not only on the

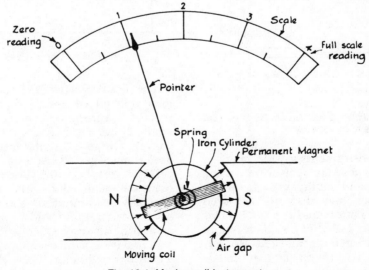

Fig. 10.1 Moving-coil instrument.

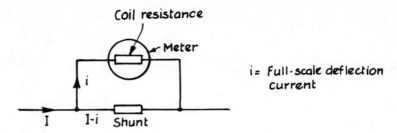

Fig. 10.2 *Use of shunt resistor to enable larger currents to be measured.*

design accuracy (e.g. 1% from one tenth of full-scale to full-scale on d.c.) but also on the estimation of the pointer position relative to the scale. To reduce reading errors, a knife-edge pointer may be used and the scale is fitted with a mirror. By aligning the pointer with its reflection in the mirror, the scale is always viewed at right angles.

The moving-coil meter is a very sensitive instrument and may require only $20\mu A$ or $2mA$ for full-scale deflection. In order to read larger currents, a portion of the total current is passed through a resistor connected in parallel with the instrument and is called a **shunt**, see Fig. 10.2.

The basic moving-coil instrument requires only a very small voltage applied to it (millivolts) to give full-scale deflection. To enable larger voltages to be measured a resistor is connected in series with the instrument called a **multiplier**, see Fig. 10.3

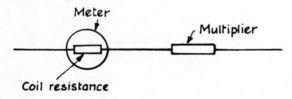

Fig. 10.3 *Use of multiplier resistor to enable large voltages to be measured.*

In 'universal' instruments a wide range of currents and voltages may be measured using switched shunts and multipliers of various values. Resistance may also be measured using an internal battery and Fig. 10.4 shows the basic principle. A battery is connected in series with the current meter and a resistor $R1$, but the circuit is broken and terminals provided for the connection of the resistance

to be measured (R_x). The value of $R1$ is chosen so that when the terminals are shorted together, the meter reads full-scale deflection but less than full-scale deflection when an actual resistance is connected between the terminals. Thus the higher the value of R_x, the less the current registered by the meter. The preset resistor $R2$ is included to compensate for the rise in the internal resistance of the battery as it ages, to maintain the calibration. The resistance of $R2$ is reduced as the battery internal resistance increases so that $R1 + R2$ remains the same.

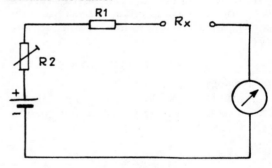

Fig. 10.4 *Principle of ohmmeter.*

The disadvantage of the moving-coil instrument is that it will operate directly on d.c. only since it is a mean or average reading instrument. However, by using a rectifier unit to convert a.c. into d.c. the instrument may be used to measure also alternating voltages and currents, see Fig. 10.5. Although the meter reads the mean value of the rectified a.c. it is normally calibrated in r.m.s. values. The r.m.s. calibration holds good only when measuring sinewaves.

A moving-coil instrument is used also in an 'electronic voltmeter' where the voltage to be measured is applied to an electronic amplifier

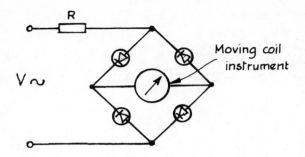

Fig. 10.5 Measuring a.c. with the moving-coil instrument.

with a high input impedance, see Fig. 10.6. D.C. or a.c. may be measured with a frequency range extending up to 1MHz or higher.

The ordinary c.r.o. discussed in Chapter 7 is another example of an analogue instrument used commonly in servicing work. Here the vertical deflection of an electron beam gives a continuous indication of the value of voltage or current to be measured. The c.r.o. is particularly useful for assessing waveform shape, peak or peak-to-peak values, frequency, periodic time, pulse period, phase difference and d.c. component of a.c. waveforms.

(b) Digital

Digital instruments produce readings of current, voltage or resistance in discrete steps. They give a read-out in direct form which is free from human reading error and have no moving parts like the moving-coil instrument. The basic ideas of a digital instrument are illustrated in Fig. 10.7.

The analogue quantity to be measured is converted into digital form, i.e. binary pulses, by an A–D converter. The pulse output of the A–D converter which is proportional to the analogue input is then decoded to operate the digital display consisting of seven segment devices (l.e.d. or liquid crystal). The display commonly uses four or five digits (plus decimal point) with an instrument reading accuracy of 0·1 to 0·8% on d.c. A large number of ranges are usually provided (e.g. 28) for universal digital instruments with voltage ranges extending from 200mV to 750V and current ranges from $20\mu A$ to 10A for both a.c. and d.c. measurements.

INSTRUMENT LIMITATIONS

All measuring instruments have certain limitations which should be considered in choosing an instrument for a particular application. The limitations include:

(a) Sensitivity; (b) Frequency range; (c) Max/min ranges; (d) A.C./D.C. current/voltage.

Sensitivity

The sensitivity of an instrument is given by $1/I_{fsd}$ ohms per volt. For example a meter

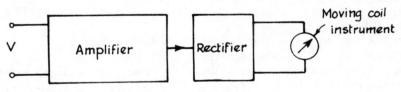

Fig. 10.6 Essentials of electronic voltmeter.

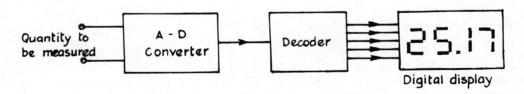

Fig. 10.7 Essentials of digital instrument.

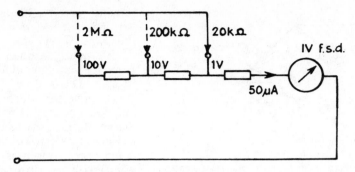

Fig. 10.8 *Effect of voltage range on internal resistance of instrument.*

reading 1V full-scale deflection which requires a current of $50\mu A$ must have an internal resistance of $1/(50 \times 10^{-6}) = 20k\Omega$. Thus the meter sensitivity is $20k\Omega/V$. A meter requiring a current of 1mA to read 1V full-scale deflection must have an internal resistance of $1/(1 \times 10^{-3}) = 1k\Omega$. Thus in this case the sensitivity would be $1k\Omega/V$.

Thus sensitivity is a measure of the internal resistance of the meter and is important as it determines the 'loading' effect when an instrument is connected into circuit. The loading effect of a multi-range meter alters when switching from one range to another but it can readily be determined if the basic sensitivity of the instrument is given, see Fig. 10.8.

In the figure it will be seen that if $50\mu A$ is required to give a full-scale deflection of 1V then the sensitivity of the instrument is $20k\Omega$ per volt. Therefore on the 1V range the instrument has an internal resistance of $20k\Omega$. Thus on the 10V range it will be ten times $20k\Omega$ (= $200k\Omega$) and on the 100V range one hundred times $20k\Omega$ (= $2M\Omega$). Therefore the loading effect decreases as the range of the instrument increases and the most accurate

measurement will be obtained on the highest range, in spite of the observed reading then being only a small fraction of f.s.d., a condition normally to be avoided.

Frequency range

Instruments will operate with their specified accuracy over only a particular frequency range, due to the effects of stray capacitance and inductance of components or bandwidth limitations of amplifiers used in the instrument. If attempts are made to measure signals with frequencies outside the specified range, low readings will generally be obtained but with occasional high reading at particular frequencies. Some typical frequency ranges for servicing-type instruments are given in Table 10.1.

MEASUREMENT ERRORS

Voltmeter Errors

The advantage of using a voltmeter of very high internal resistance is that it has a smaller loading effect upon the circuit being measured

Instrument	Input Resistance	Frequency Range
Analogue Universal Instrument	$20k\Omega/V$	0–20kHz
Analogue Electronic Voltmeter	$1M\Omega/V$	0–100kHz
Digital Universal Instrument	$10M\Omega$ on d.c. and a.c. ranges	0–50kHz
Analogue C.R.O.	$2M\Omega$	0–15MHz

Table 10.1 *Some instrument parameters*

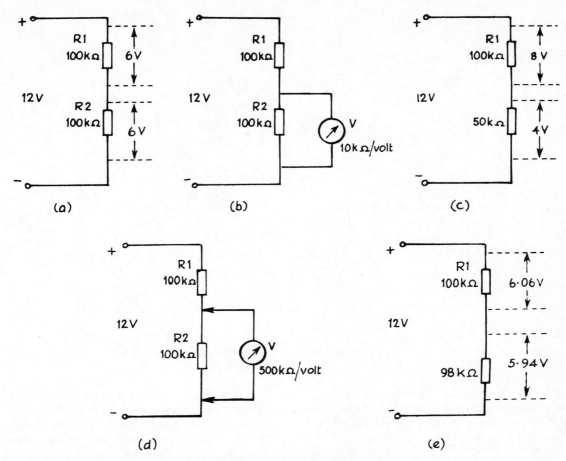

Fig. 10.9 Voltmeter error due to loading effect.

than less-sensitive instruments. This may be illustrated using the circuit of Fig. 10.9(a).

It is easy to deduce that since the resistor values are the same, the p.d. across each resistor will be the same, i.e. 6V. Suppose now that we try to measure the voltage across $R2$ with a voltmeter having a sensitivity of 10kΩ/V and an f.s.d. of 10V, see Fig. 10.9(b). The internal resistance of the meter will be 10×10kΩ = 100kΩ and since this resistance is in parallel with $R2$, the effective resistance of the combination will be 50kΩ. Thus, due to its loading effect, the voltmeter will read only 4V, an error of 33⅓%. It makes no difference if the voltmeter that is used is the most accurate instrument ever manufactured; its low internal resistance produces a large error in measurement when it is connected into circuit.

If a voltmeter having a sensitivity of 500kΩ/V and a f.s.d. of 10V is used, see Fig. 10.9(d), to measure the voltage across $R2$, the effective resistance of the combination will be 98kΩ. Thus the p.d. across each resistor will be as in Fig. 10.9(e) giving across $R2$ a voltage of 5·94V, an error of only 1%. In order to minimise errors of this type the internal resistance of the voltmeter used should be at least ten times the resistance (or impedance) of the circuit being measured.

Ammeter Errors

Although the resistance of ammeters is comparatively low, the introduction of an ammeter into a circuit can sometimes change the circuit resistance by an amount large enough to produce significant measurement

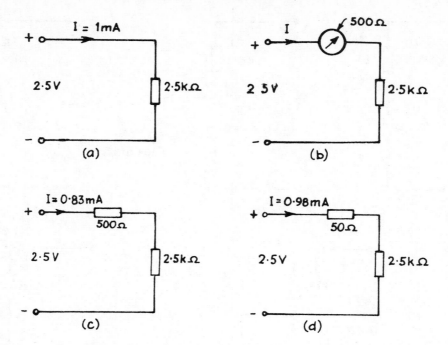

Fig. 10.10 Effect of ammeter resistance.

error. An instrument manufacturer will specify either the resistance of the ammeter or the p.d. across the terminals when reading f.s.d. For example, the p.d. across the terminals of a typical analogue universal instrument is 0·5V on all d.c. current ranges at f.s.d. Thus, when on the 1mA range the instrument resistance is $0·5/(1 \times 10^{-3}) = 500\Omega$; on the 10mA range it is $0·5/(10 \times 10^{-3}) = 50\Omega$; and on the 100mA range it is $0·5/(100 \times 10^{-3}) = 5\Omega$ etc.

Consider now that such an instrument is used to measure the current flowing in the circuit of Fig. 10.10(a). It may be calculated from the values given that the actual current flowing will be 1mA. If now an ammeter set on its 1mA range is introduced into the circuit as in Fig. 10.10(b) it is equivalent to adding an extra 500Ω in series with the 2.5kΩ resistor, see Fig. 10.10(c). The measured current flowing will be 0·83mA, an error of approximately 17%. The error may be considerably reduced if the current is measured with the instrument set on its 10mA range. The resistance of the instrument will be reduced to 50Ω and the measured value will be 0·98mA producing an error of only 2%, see Fig. 10.10(d).

Clearly, the lower the ammeter resistance in relation to the circuit resistance the less will be the measurement error. For reasonable results the ammeter resistance should be no more than one tenth of the circuit resistance.

Voltage and Current Errors

Figure. 10.11 shows two ways of connecting a voltmeter and an ammeter to measure simultaneously the forward voltage drop and the current in a p-n diode. In (a) the ammeter will measure the true current in a diode but the voltmeter will indicate the voltage drop across the diode plus the voltage drop across the ammeter. Whereas, in (b) the voltmeter will indicate the true voltage drop across the diode but the ammeter will read the diode current plus the voltmeter current. For both cases a measurement error will occur but the percentage error will depend upon the instruments chosen. In (a) the voltage error will be reduced if an ammeter is chosen with a resistance that is small compared with the diode resistance, and in (b) the current error will be reduced if the voltmeter resistance is large compared with

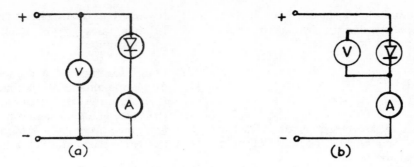

Fig. 10.11 Voltage and current errors.

the resistance of the diode. When extreme accuracy is required it is important to be aware of these difficulties.

Waveform Errors

Instruments that are used to measure a.c. quantities which produce a reading proportional to the **mean value** of the voltage or current are normally calibrated in r.m.s. terms. Usually the calibration holds good only on sinewaves since the form factor (r.m.s./mean) for a sinewave is 1.1 and this figure is taken into account in the scale calibration.

Waveforms such as the triangular wave or rectangular wave which have different form factors from the sinewave, see Fig. 10.12, will introduce a reading error on a.c. Peaky waveforms like the triangular wave will produce low readings while squarish waveforms like the rectangular wave will give high readings, when measured with an instrument

calibrated on sinewaves. Instruments which are said to be 'true r.m.s.' reading have a calibration which holds good on all waveform shapes, over the designated frequency range of the instrument.

QUESTIONS ON CHAPTER TEN

(1) A moving-coil instrument produces a deflection proportional to:
(a) the peak value
(b) the mean value
(c) the r.m.s. value
(d) the square root of the peak value.

(2) The scale of the moving-coil instrument on a.c. is calibrated in:
(a) r.m.s. values
(b) peak values
(c) mean values
(d) average values.

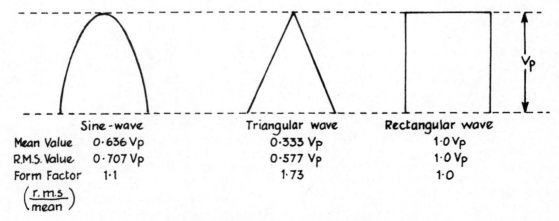

	Sine-wave	Triangular wave	Rectangular wave
Mean Value	0.636 Vp	0.333 Vp	1.0 Vp
R.M.S. Value	0.707 Vp	0.577 Vp	1.0 Vp
Form Factor $\left(\dfrac{r.m.s}{mean}\right)$	1.1	1.73	1.0

Fig. 10.12 Form factor of waveforms.

(3) An instrument has a sensitivity of 50kΩ per volt. The internal resistance on the 10V range will be:
(a) 50kΩ
(b) 5kΩ
(c) 500kΩ
(d) 5MΩ.

(4) To reduce measurement errors with a voltmeter, the internal resistance of the instrument should be:
(a) equal to the circuit resistance
(b) one tenth of the circuit resistance
(c) one half of the circuit resistance
(d) ten times greater than the circuit resistance.

(5) One advantage of a digital voltmeter over an analogue one is that:
(a) it has a greater frequency range
(b) reading errors are reduced
(c) range accuracy is always better
(d) reads true r.m.s. on a.c.

(Answers on page 369)

CHAPTER ELEVEN

POWER SUPPLIES

Objectives

1 To explain the operation of half-wave and full-wave rectifier circuits.
2 To describe the use of a reservoir capacitor and smoothing circuits.
3 To explain the operation of zener diode and transistor stabilisers.
4 To explain the principle of switched-mode power supplies and the use of over-voltage and over-current protection.
5 To describe the operation of voltage doubler circuits and need for suppression of r.f. interference.

IN VOL.1 *(Electronic Systems)* the purpose of a rectifier was discussed and in Chapter 2 of this volume the operation and construction p-n diode rectifiers were explained together with a description of a simple half-wave rectifier. It is now necessary to give further details of the half-wave rectifier circuit and to see how other rectifier circuits can be formed using p-n diode rectifiers so that a.c can be converted into a suitable d.c. for the operation of electronic equipment.

Half-wave Rectifier

The basic circuit of a half-wave rectifier is shown in Fig. 11.1. It consists of a p-n diode in

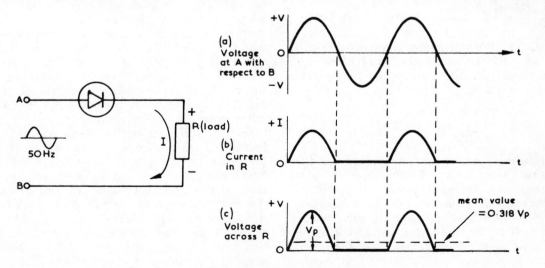

Fig. 11.1 Half-wave rectifier circuit.

series with a load (the equipment to be supplied), represented by the resistor R. The voltage to be rectified is fed between terminals A and B. This input voltage may come directly from the mains supply or from the secondary winding of a mains transformer.

Considering waveform (a) when terminal A is positive to terminal B the p-n diode will be in a forward biased state and current will flow in the direction shown through the diode and load. During the period when terminal A is negative to terminal B the p-n diode will be in a reverse biased state and no current (or a very small leakage current) will flow in the circuit. As waveform (b) shows, current flows in the load only during the positve half-cycles of the input. If the voltage drop across the rectifier is neglected, the current flowing in the load will be proportional to the input voltage. Thus with a sinewave voltage input the current in the load will consist of half sinewave (assuming a perfect rectifier). This current flowing in R will cause half sinewaves of voltage across it, see waveform (c). The voltage across R represents the output voltage of the rectifier and since it is always in one direction it is d.c.

Because there is no output during the negative half-cycles of the input, the mean value of the d.c. output is small. Now, the mean value of a half sinewave is $0.637 \times$ Peak Value but since the output across R consists of a half sinewave of voltage followed by an equal period of zero voltage the mean value will be:

$$\frac{0.637 \times \text{Peak Value}}{2} = 0.318 \times \text{Peak Value}$$

With a 240V r.m.s. mains input to terminals A and B, the mean d.c. output voltage (neglecting the voltage drop across the rectifier) would be:

$$0.318 \times \text{Vp}$$
$$= 0.318 \times 240 \times 1.414\text{V}$$
$$\simeq 108\text{V}$$

It will be noted that the polarity of the output voltage is such that the upper end of R is positive with respect to the lower end. If, however, the connections to the rectifier are interchanged, the polarity of the voltage across R will be reversed, i.e. the rectifier will conduct on negative half-cycles of the input. Thus, if the lower line (connected to B) is used as the reference or chassis line, a postive or

negative output voltage with respect to the reference line may be obtained depending upon the rectifier connections.

The half-wave circuit represents the most economical rectifier arrangement and is used for supplying equipment demanding only small current and power.

Full-wave Rectifiers

In a full-wave rectifier circuit use is made of both half-cycles of the a.c. input voltage so that the output does not remain at zero voltage for a half-cycle period as it does in the half-wave circuit. One arrangement using a centre-tapped mains transformer T1 is shown in Fig. 11.2 together with waveforms explaining the operation.

Two identical rectifiers D1 and D2 are now required supplying the common load represented by the resistor R, connected between the rectifier outputs and the transformer centre-tap. The secondary winding AC of T1 is a continuous winding with all its turns wound in the same direction but with an electrical centre-tap placed at point B. Thus, when the voltage at A is positive with respect to point B the voltage at C will be negative with respect to B and vice versa.

When A is positive with respect to B, a current I_{D1} will flow through D1 and the load in the direction shown. During the half-cycle when A is positive with respect to B, the voltage at C is negative with respect to B and so no current will flow in D2 as it will be reverse biased. During the next half-cycle when A is negative with respect to B, the voltage at C will be positive with respect to B and current I_{D2} will flow in D2 and the load in the direction shown. It will be seen that one of the diodes is conducting on each half-cycle of the input voltage and that current flows in the same direction through the load on every half-cycle, waveform (e). In consequence, there will be two half sinewaves of voltage developed across the load for each complete cycle of the input, waveform (f). The mean d.c. output voltage from the rectifier circuit is now equal to $0.637 \times$ Peak Value, i.e. twice that of the half-wave circuit, but requires twice the peak-to-peak across the full secondary winding. The current in each rectifier is half of that which whould flow in a half-wave rectifier

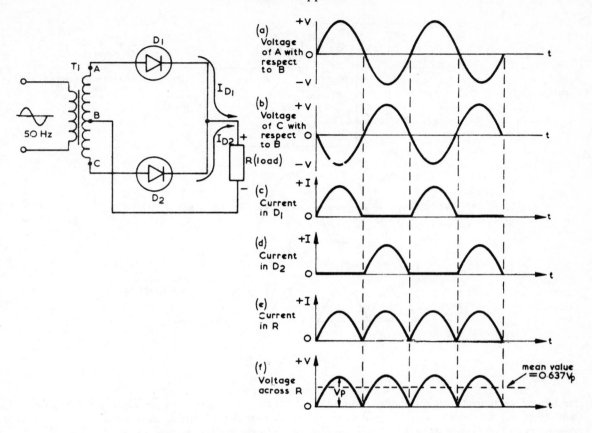

Fig. 11.2 Full-wave rectifier circuit using centre tapped transformer.

of the same current rating. Since the current flowing in the total secondary winding is effectively alternating there is no d.c. saturation of the transformer core. This is an advantage over the half-wave rectifier circuit when a transformer is used as the current in the secondary would be unidirectional and cause saturation of the core (a factor reflected in the size and cost of the transformer).

Bridge Rectifier Circuit

Another full-wave rectifier circuit known as a bridge rectifier is shown in Fig. 11.3. This uses four p-n diode rectifiers but a transformer is not essential to its operation although one may have to be used to obtain the required output voltage.

When the voltage at A is positive with resect to B, current will flow from A through D1, the load, D4 and back to B thus completing the circuit. Current cannot flow in D2 or D3 as they will be reverse biased. During the next half-cycle when A becomes negative with respect to the voltage at B, D2 and D3 become forward biased and D1 and D4 revert to the reverse bias state. Current thus flows from B, through D2 the load and D3 back to A thereby completing the circuit. Thus on each half-cycle of the input, two of the diodes are conducting and current is flowing in the same direction through the load. In consequence, there will be two half sinewaves of voltage developed across the load as in waveform (b). The mean d.c. voltage output of the circuit is 0·637 × Peak Value as for the previous full-wave circuit.

The bridge circuit has the advantage that when a transformer is required, the secondary winding need not be centre tapped. A

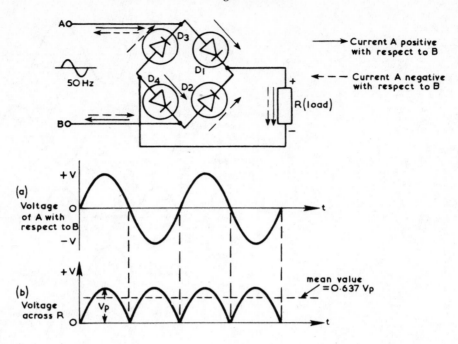

Fig. 11.3 Full-wave bridge rectifier circuit.

disadvantage is that four rectifiers are needed and that neither of the d.c. output lines is common to the inputs A or B.

Smoothing Circuits

The d.c. output of the basic rectifier circuits described is not smooth enough to act as a supply for electronic equipment. The pulsating output voltage would cause a varying performance of the electronic circuits to be fed and would result in the operation ceasing when the rectifier output dropped to a low level, i.e. when the voltage approaches zero. To produce an output voltage with only a small amount of fluctuation a smoothing circuit is required. The smoothing action can be carried out in two stages by the use of a reservoir capacitor and a filter circuit.

Use of Reservoir Capacitor

The half-wave circuit will be considered first and is shown in Fig. 11.4. A large value capacitor C1 (usually an electrolytic) has now been connected across the load R. The output

voltage from the circuit without C1 has been shown dotted in the waveform.

In the first quarter-cycle period a-b when A is positive with respect to B and the diode conducts, current will flow into the output rapidly charging C1 via the low forward resistance of the diode. In consequence, the voltage across C1 will rise to the peak of the input voltage. At every instant the voltage across the load is the same as the capacitor voltage. Immediately following instant b the input voltage (which approximately follows the dotted line) commences to fall. Since the capacitor voltage does not fall as fast as the input, the rectifier becomes non-conducting. The load current is now supplied from C1 and the capacitor discharges during the period b-c. The rate at which the capacitor discharges depends upon the time constant of C1 and the load resistance. With a large value for C1 or a high value of load resistance (small current load) the slower will be the rate of voltage decay during b-c (also d-e). At instant c when the input voltage exceeds the capacitor voltage the rectifier becomes conductive and current flows in the rectifier recharging C1 to the

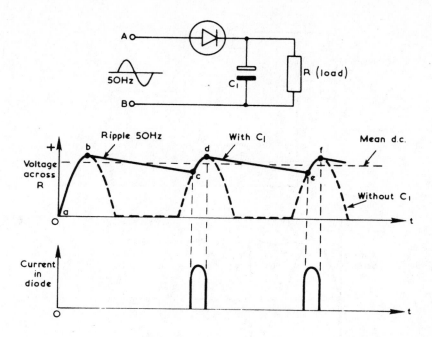

Fig. 11.4 Half-wave rectifier with reservoir capacitor.

maximum voltage. Immediately following instant d the rectifier again becomes reverse biased, current in the rectifier ceases and C1 discharges into the load.

It will thus be seen that the capacitor C1 acts as a store or reservoir of energy to supply the load current during the off period of the rectifier and for this reason is called a **reservoir capacitor**. The output voltage from the circuit is now as indicated by the solid line having the approximate shape of a sawtooth waveform. The inclusion of C1 has now raised the mean d.c. level to almost the peak level of the input voltage and has reduced the amount of ripple in the output to around 10% of its previous value. The fundamental frequency of the ripple voltage is the same as the frequency of the input voltage, i.e. 50Hz.

Current flows through the rectifier only during the brief periods corresponding to c-d and e-f, etc. (neglecting the first quarter period a-b) whereas current is supplied to the load continuously. Since the mean current passing through the rectifier must equal the mean current supplied to the load, the peak value of the current pulses in Fig. 1.4. will be much greater than the mean current. For example, with the mean load current of, say, 80mA the peak current passing through the rectifier may be typically 650mA or higher. The peak current will increase as the value of C1 is made larger and hence there is a limit to the size of the reservoir capacitor in order that the peak current rating of the rectifier is not exceeded.

The effect of a reservoir capacitor on a full-wave rectifier is shown in Fig. 11.5. An action similar to the half-wave circuit takes place but since the period b-c is approximately half that of the half-wave circuit the drop in voltage is about half that of the half-wave circuit (assuming the same CR product). Thus the ripple in the output is less which makes it easier to smooth. The fundamental frequency of the ripple is twice that of the supply frequency, i.e. 100Hz, a factor contributing to the easier smoothing of the full-wave circuit. Since there are now two pulses of current for each cycle of the input, the peak current passing through each rectifier is half that of the half-wave rectifier circuit.

In the bridge circuit the operation is

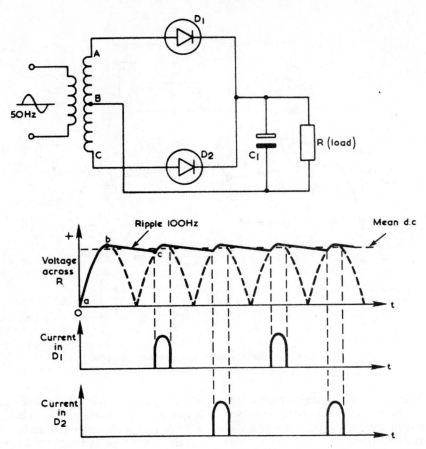

Fig. 11.5 Full-wave rectifier with reservoir capacitor.

identical but the current flowing in the secondary winding of the input transformer (a transformer will normally be used) consists of pulses acting in alternate directions, see Fig. 11.6.

Peak Inverse Voltage Rating

The maximum voltage that a rectifier will withstand in the reverse direction is known as the peak inverse voltage (p.i.v.). This maximum voltage depends upon the rectifier

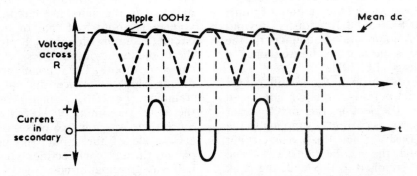

Fig. 11.6 Current in secondary winding of transformer feeding bridge rectifier.

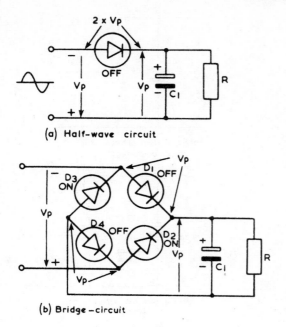

(a) Half-wave circuit

(b) Bridge-circuit

Fig. 11.7 Peak inverse voltage rating of rectifiers.

arrangement, see Fig. 11.7. In the half-wave circuit of diagram (a) the reservoir capacitor charges up to the peak value V_p of the input voltage during the conducting period of the rectifier with polarity as shown. During the non-conducting period the input voltage polarity will be as indicated resulting in a voltage between the anode and cathode of the rectifier of $2 \times V_p$ which must be within the p.i.v. rating of the chosen rectifier. For example, with a 240V mains input to the circuit, the maximum reverse voltage across the rectifier would be $2 \times 1.414 \times 240V = 678V$. To avoid breakdown of the rectifier its p.i.v. rating must be above this figure, say, 1000V.

For the full-wave circuit utilising a centre-tapped transformer, the maximum reverse voltage across each rectifier is the same as in the half-wave circuit, i.e. $2 \times V_p$ where V_p is the peak voltage across each half of the secondary winding. With the full-wave bridge circuit the p.i.v. of each rectifier is equal to the peak value of the input V_p. Why it is half that of the other full-wave circuit may be explained with reference to Fig. 11.7(b). With the peak value V_p of the input having a polarity as indicated, D2 and D3 will be conducting and C1 will be charged to V_p with polarity as shown. If D2 and D3 are thought of as closed switches it will be seen that the reverse voltage across the non-conducting rectifiers D1 and D4 is equal to V_p. Conversely, when the polarity of the input changes on the next half-cycle, D2 and D3 will be subjected to a maximum reverse voltage of V_p. This lower p.i.v. rating of the rectifiers used in a bridge circuit is an advantage over the full-wave circuit employing a centre-tapped trans-former.

Filter Circuits

The degree of smoothing produced by the reservoir capacitor is not usually adequate, so it is normally followed by a filter circuit (or a voltage stabiliser).

A common type of filter circuit found in equipment demanding small current is the resistance-capacitance filter shown in Fig. 11.8. R1, C2 forms the filter (low pass), C1 the reservoir capacitor and R the load as previously discussed. The purpose of the filter

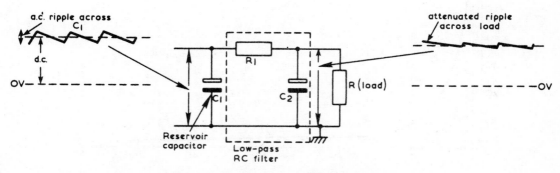

Fig. 11.8 Resistance capacitance filter circuit.

is to reduce the ripple voltage present across C1 to an acceptable level across the load without attenuating the d.c. output voltage from the rectifier. Although the voltage at C1 is a fluctuating d.c. voltage it may be considered as consisting of a d.c. voltage (equal to the mean value of the waveform) and an a.c. component representing the ripple voltage. The ripple voltage is a complex waveform and as such it is composed of a fundamental sinewave component plus harmonics. Only the fundamental sinewave component will be considered because if adequate filtering of the fundamental occurs the harmonic components will be reduced to a very low level indeed. The d.c. and a.c. components will be dealt with separately.

Capacitor C2 will not pass d.c. thus equivalent circuit for the d.c. component is as in Fig. 11.9(a). It will be seen that R1 and the load form a potential divider for the d.c. voltage (V_i) across C1. Provided that the resistance of R1 is small compared with the load resistance the d.c. output voltage (V_o) will be practically equal to V_i as required.

Considering now the a.c. component or ripple voltage v_i across C1, capacitor C2 will

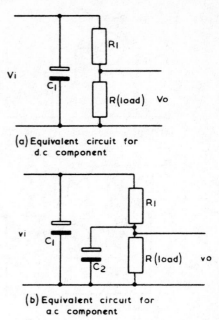

(a) Equivalent circuit for d.c component

(b) Equivalent circuit for a.c component

Fig. 11.9 RC filter circuit drawn as a potential divider.

pass this component and so is included in the equivalent circuit of diagram (b). The ease with which C2 will by-pass the ripple from the

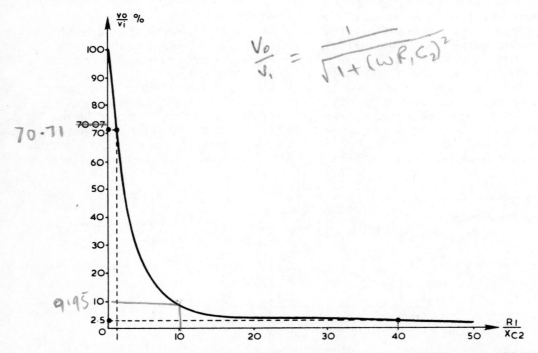

$$\frac{V_o}{V_i} = \frac{1}{\sqrt{1 + (\omega R_1 C_2)^2}}$$

Fig. 11.10 Graph showing relationship between output ripple voltage and R_1/X_{c2} ratio for RC filter.

load depends upon the reactance of C_2 (X_{c2}), given by:

$$\frac{1}{2\pi f C_2}$$

where f is the frequency of the ripple. The smaller the reactance of C2 compared with the resistance of R1, the less will be the amount of ripple voltage developed across the load. As the value of C2 is increased, the magnitude of the output ripple is reduced but the maximum value for C2 is often limited by cost and space.

Fig. 11.10 shows how the ripple voltage output from the RC filter circuit (expressed as a percentage of the input ripple) decreases as the ratio of R_1/X_{c2} is increased, assuming that the load resistance (R) is high compared with the reactance of C2. For given component values the filter circuit is more efficient in a full-wave rectifier output circuit than in a half-wave, since the ripple frequency is twice that of the half-wave rectifier.

The low-pass filter may alternatively consist of a series inductor (L1) and a shunt capacitor (C2) as shown in Fig. 11.11. The equivalent

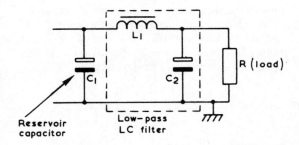

Fig. 11.11 *Inductive capacitance circuit.*

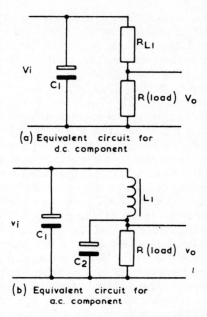

(a) Equivalent circuit for d.c. component

(b) Equivalent circuit for a.c. component

Fig. 11.12 *LC filter circuit drawn as a potential divider.*

circuit for d.c. is as shown in Fig. 11.12(a) where R_{L1} is the d.c. resistance of the inductor. C2 has been omitted because a capacitor will not pass d.c. Provided R_{L1} is small compared with R, most of the input voltage V_i will appear across the load as is required.

For the a.c. component the equivalent circuit is as shown in Fig. 11.12(b). Inductor L1 offers a high reactance to a.c. equal to $2\pi f L$, whereas C2 offers a low reactance (as for the RC filter). Since by choice of L1 value, the reactance of L1 is large compared with the reactance of C2, very little ripple voltage will

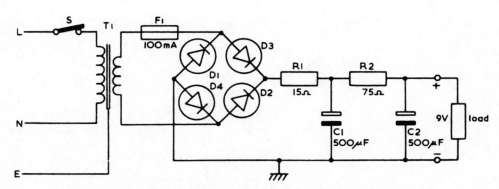

Fig. 11.13 *Power supply incorporating bridge rectifier and smoothing circuit.*

appear across the load. With typical values for L1 and C2, the output ripple voltage will be 1/100th of the input ripple or less. LC filters are more commonly used in high voltage supplies (above 200V) as it is difficult to make the d.c. resistance of L1 low enough to prevent appreciable d.c. voltage drop across it. Although more efficient than an RC filter, the LC filter has the disadvantage that the inductor is costlier and takes up more space.

An example of a low voltage power supply is shown in Fig. 11.13. Here a full-wave bridge rectifier is used fed from a step-down mains transformer T1. C1 is the reservoir capacitor followed by an RC filter R2, C2. The fuse F1 will rupture should the load current exceed 100mA or a fault occur in the power supply, e.g. C1 short-circuit. R1 is included to prevent the peak current rating of the rectifier diodes being exceeded at switch-on when C1 is uncharged. The four diodes constituting the bridge rectifier usually consists of an encapsulation of silicon diodes with four connections: two for the a.c. supply, and two for the d.c. output.

Voltage Stabilisers

As explained in Vol. 1 *Electronic Systems*, voltage regulators or stabilisers are used in power supplies to maintain a constant output voltage in spite of (a) changes in the mains supply voltage; and (b) changes in the load current. The stabiliser is placed between the smoothing filter and the load so the input to it is d.c. as in Fig. 11.14.

A number of different circuit arrangements are possible for the stabiliser and a simple arrangement using a series resistor and shunt zener diode is shown in Fig. 11.15.

A diode is chosen with a zener voltage corresponding to the required value of the stabilised output voltage (V_z). This voltage must be less than the unstabilised input voltage (V_s), the polarity of which must place the diode in the reverse bias state. The excess voltage between the input voltage and the output voltage ($V_s - V_z$) is dropped across the series resistor R. For good stabilisation the power rating of the diode should be such that it will carry a current (I_d) of about four times the expected load current (I_L). If V_s varies, I_d varies to alter the voltage drop across R to maintain a constant output voltage. For example, when V_s increases, I_d increases thereby increasing the voltage drop across R. On the other hand if V_s decreases, I_d decreases and there will be less voltage drop across R.

In practice, the output voltage does not remain perfectly stable with changes in input voltage. The degree of stabilisation depends upon the slope resistance (r_a) of the diode, see

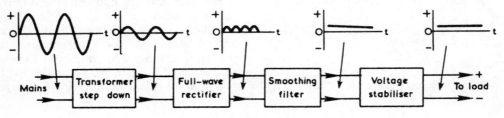

Fig. 11.14 *Basic arrangement of low voltage stabilised supply.*

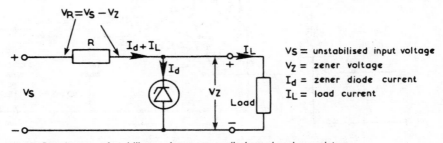

$V_R = V_S - V_Z$

V_S = unstabilised input voltage
V_Z = zener voltage
I_d = zener diode current
I_L = load current

Fig. 11.15 *Simple type of stabiliser using a zener diode and series resistor.*

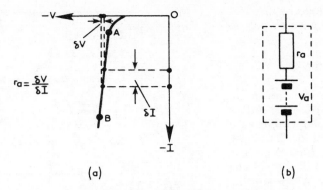

Fig. 11.16 *Reverse characteristic of zener diode and its equivalent circuit.*

Fig. 11.16(a). A zener diode may be considered as a constant voltage source represented by a battery V_A in series with its slope resistance r_a, see equivalent circuit of Fig. 11.16(b). To changes of input voltage, the series resistor R and the slope resistance r_a form a potential divider and provided r_a is small compared with R there will be little change in the output voltage. The value of r_a for a 9V zener diode when passing 10mA is typically 5Ω, whereas R may be, say, 800Ω. It is often assumed that over the portion A–B of the reverse characteristic it is straight, but in practice it is more complex. For any particular diode the larger the current, the lower is the slope resistance.

The circuit will also stabilise against variations in the current drawn by the load. Should I_L increase, the diode current would fall to try to maintain a constant voltage drop across R and hence a constant output voltage. On the other hand a fall in I_L will cause a rise in the diode current, again trying to maintain a constant voltage drop across R and hence a constant output voltage.

Under fault conditions with an o/c load as in Fig. 11.17(a), the load current will fall to zero and the diode current will increase to $I_L + I_d$ where I_L is the normal load current. Under this condition, the power dissipated in the diode will increase. If the power rating of the chosen diode is adequate then no adverse effect will result. When this is not so the zener diode may be destroyed. With a s/c load as in diagram (b) there is no output voltage and no current in the diode and all of the supply voltage is developed across R. Thus under this condition the power dissipated in R will increase, and if its power rating is insufficient it may be damaged.

Transistor Stabilisers

An improvement over the zener diode shunt stabiliser can be obtained using a transistor as the stabilising element. The transistor may be

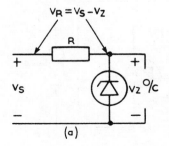
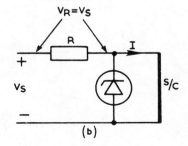

Fig. 11.17 *Zener diode stabiliser under o/c and s/c load conditions.*

connected in shunt with the load or in series with it. This has lead to designs based on two basic types of regulator.

Transistor Shunt Stabiliser

A basic shunt stabiliser is shown in Fig. 11.18. The transistor (n-p-n or p-n-p) is connected in shunt with the load with its base current supplied via a zener diode D1.

Variations in the supply voltage V_s cause variations in TR1 current and in the voltage drop across R2. Since R2 is in series with the load, variations in its voltage drop will stabilise the output voltage V_o because at all times $V_o = V_s - V_{R2}$. Suppose that V_s increase (causing a larger current in D1 and hence a larger base current in TR1) the collector-to emitter current of TR1 will increase and since this flows in R2 there will be a greater voltage drop across R2. If the increase in voltage drop in R2 is equal to the rise in V_s, the output voltage will remain constant.

It should be noted that the output voltage is equal to the zener voltage V_z of D1 plus the base-emitter voltage drop V_{be} of TR1. Since V_{be} is normally small compared with V_z the output voltage is approximately equal to V_z. Thus the only way of altering the magnitude of V_o is by using a diode with a different zener voltage. The circuit will also stabilise against load current variations. Should, say, the load current increase it would increase the voltage drop across R2 since the load current flows in R2. As a result, TR1 will conduct less (its V_{be} will fall) and there will be less current in R2 due to TR1, thereby tending to maintain a constant voltage across R2 and hence a constant output voltage.

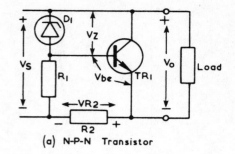

(a) N-P-N Transistor

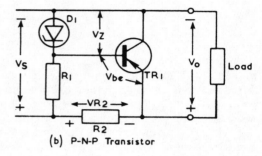

(b) P-N-P Transistor

Fig. 11.18 Transistor shunt stabiliser.

An advantage of the shunt stabiliser is that no damage is done to the transistor if the output terminals are short-circuited. This results in zero voltage across the transistor and the short-circuit current is limited by R2. Under open-circuit load conditions TR1 will conduct harder as there will be less voltage drop in R2 but the collector-emitter voltage will remain about the same. The design will normally cater for this condition and no harm will be done.

In a typical stabiliser of this type providing 9V d.c. output, variations in the mains supply to the power unit of between 190V to 250V will

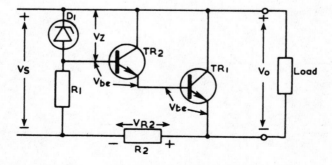

Fig. 11.19 Shunt stabiliser using cascade transistors.

result in a change of output voltage of only 0·2V. Also, a load current variation from 0mA to 125mA produces an output voltage change of only 0·25V.

The circuits of Fig. 11.18 operate by the change in TR1 base current when V_s varies. As the base current is supplied via D1, changes in the current will alter the zener voltage and hence the output voltage. An improvement in the regulation may be achieved by adding another transistor (TR2) as in Fig. 11.19.

The base current of TR1 is now supplied from TR2 emitter and the base current of TR2 will be smaller than its emitter current by the current gain of TR2. Thus if TR2 current gain is, say, 60, variations in D1 current are 60 times smaller than variations in TR1 base current, resulting in a more stable zener voltage. It should be noted that the output voltage is now $V_z + V_{be} (TR2) + V_{be} (TR1)$.

Transistor Series Stabiliser

With series type stabilisers it is arranged that any change in the unstabilised input appears across a series-connected stabilising transistor so that the output voltage across the load remains constant. An elementary circuit of this type is shown in Fig. 11.20 for use with an n-p-n or p-n-p transistor.

TR1 is the regulating transistor which is supplied with a constant base voltage V_z from the zener diode D1 fed with a suitable current via R1. As the load is connected in the emitter the arrangement forms a common collector or emitter-follower circuit, thus the emitter voltage follows the base voltage. Therefore, if the base voltage is held constant by D1, the emitter voltage and hence the output voltage will remain constant.

If, say, V_s rises causing V_o to try to rise, the V_{be} of TR1 is reduced causing TR1 collector-to-emitter resistance to increase, As a result the increase in V_s appears across the collector-to-emitter of the transistor thus restoring V_o to an equilibrium value. It should be noted that the output voltage is equal to V_z minus the V_{be} of TR1. The only way of altering the value of the output voltage from this arrangement is by altering the zener voltage.

The circuit will also deal with variations in the load current. If, say, the load current increases the V_{be} of TR1 will increase and the collector-to-emitter resistance of the transistor will be lowered. Thus less voltage is dropped across the series transistor which assists in keeping the output voltage constant. A disadvantage of the series transistor stabiliser is that if the load is short circuited, the full input voltage appears across the transistor and a large current flows. As this can lead to the destruction of the transistor some form of current limiting is desirable in series transistor stabilisers.

Use of feedback

The regulation of the basic emitter-follower stabiliser can be improved by the use of amplified feedback and a basic circuit is given in Fig. 11.21.

A potential divider comprising R3, P1 and R4 is now connected across the output and a fraction of the output voltage V_f is fed back to

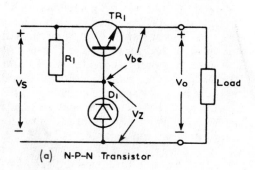 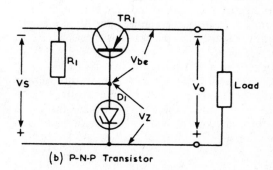

(a) N-P-N Transistor   (b) P-N-P Transistor

Fig. 11.20 Transistor series stabiliser (emitter-follower).

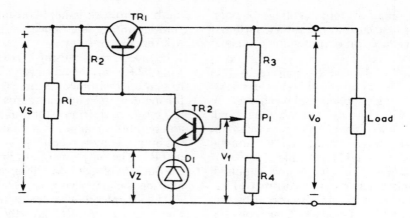

Fig. 11.21 Transistor series stabiliser using feedback and amplifier.

the base of an amplifier TR2. Here V_f is compared with a reference voltage V_z developed across the zener diode D1 and applied to the emitter of TR2. If V_o tries to depart from its steady value V_f will change causing a change in the difference voltage between V_z and V_f. This change in voltage is amplified by TR2 and applied to the base of the series regulator TR1 in such a direction that the variation in volts drop across TR1 restores the output voltage to its nominal level. The zener diode is supplied with a suitable current via R1, and R2 serves as TR2 collector load as well as passing TR1 base current.

Suppose that V_o tries to rise due to an increase in V_s or a reduction in the load current. This will cause V_f to rise resulting in an increase in the V_{be} of TR2 (emitter voltage remains constant). TR2 will thus increase its conduction and there will be a larger volts drop across R2. In consequence, the base voltage of TR1 will be reduced causing TR1 to conduct less thereby increasing its collector-emitter resistance. As a result there will be an increase in the voltage drop across TR1 thereby compensating for the rise in V_s or the reduction in load current. The output voltage will be slightly greater than prior to the variation, but if the gain of TR2 is large the difference will be small. P1 provides a means of altering the output voltage. If P1 setting increases the base voltage of TR2 it will conduct harder increasing the steady voltage drop across R2. This will turn TR1 towards the off condition thereby increasing the collector-

to-emitter resistance and lowering the output voltage. Moving P1 setting in the opposite direction will turn TR2 towards the off condition resulting in less voltage drop across R2 and TR1 turning harder on. In consequence there will be less voltage drop across TR1 collector-to-emitter and the output voltage will increase.

Another commonly used series stabiliser is given in Fig. 11.22 with TR1 connected in the common emitter configuration. The positions of D1 and R1 have been interchanged and are now fed from the stabilised side of TR1. An n-p-n transistor is still used for TR1 (but the supply has been reversed) whilst the amplifier TR2 is a p-n-p transistor. The principle of operation is similar to the previous circuit but the action is slightly different.

Suppose that V_o tends to rise due to an increase in V_s or a decrease in load current. Now, since D1 and R1 have been interchanged, the full rise in V_o is felt across R1 and is applied to TR2 emitter (the voltage across D1 remains constant). Only a portion of the rise in V_o is fed to TR2 base because of the action of the potential divider R3, P1 and R4. Thus because the emitter voltage rises more than the base voltage, the current in TR2 will be reduced. There is now less voltage drop across R2 causing TR1 to turn towards the off condition and for a larger voltage drop to occur across TR1 thereby restoring the output voltage to an equilibrium value. It will be seen that the action in TR2 is opposite to that of TR2 in the previous circuit, but TR1 operation

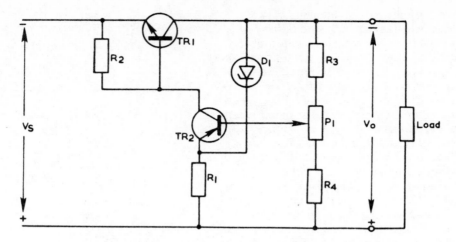

Fig. 11.22 Another common series stabiliser with feedback and amplifier.

remains the same except that the output is from the collector.

I.C. Stabiliser

Complete voltage stabiliser circuits fabricated in integrated circuit form are now in common use, one arrangement being shown in Fig. 11.23. The i.c. contains a series transistor stabiliser, a reference voltage source, an error amplifier and a current-limiting circuit.

A potential divider comprising R1, P1 and R2 is connected external to the i.c. with the feedback signal applied to one of the pins of the i.c. from P1 slider. Adjusting P1 alters the level of the stabilised output voltage. The inclusion of R3 in series with the load allows the load current to be sampled. If this rises above a predetermined value the current limit circuit comes into operation. One way of limiting the load current is to reduce the conduction of the series regulating transistor so that the output voltage is reduced once a certain current is exceeded. This protects the series regulating transistor from damage under short-circuit load conditions.

Switched Mode Power Supply

The main disadvantage of the series regulating element TR1 of Fig. 11.22 is that energy which is dissipated in the series element is lost, thereby lowering the efficiency, particularly so in a high-current power supply. Also, the heat

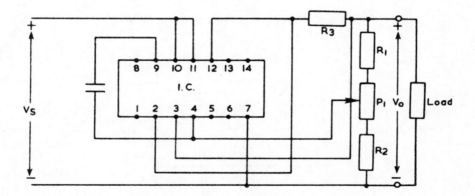

Fig. 11.23 Monolithic integrated circuit series stabiliser.

generated in the series element raises the temperature inside the enclosure of the power supply or equipment, which is undesirable.

Instead of using a series element whose resistance is varied, what is required is a series element that is ideally either fully 'on' (zero resistance) or fully 'off' (open-circuit). When fully 'on' there is no power dissipated when passing current since there is no voltage drop and when fully 'off' there is no current flowing thus there is no power dissipated. The ideal form of series element is thus a kind of 'switch' which is rapidly closed and opened at regular intervals. By varying the 'closed' to 'open' time of the switch the mean power fed to the load can be varied.

Consider the circuit of Fig. 11.24(a) where an electrical switch is used as the series element. If the switch is closed then a current I will flow in the load. However, if the switch is opened no current will flow in the load. Since continuous power is required by the load then some form of 'energy-storing' device is needed as in Fig. 11.24(b) so that current may be supplied to the load when the switch is open.

An inductor may be used as an energy store and this is featured in the basic circuit of Fig. 11.25(a). Additionally a diode D is required to provide a current path when the

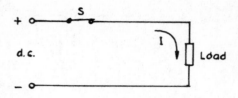

(a) Use of switch as series element

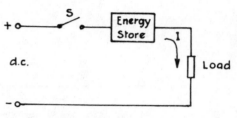

(b) Energy store required when S is open

Fig. 11.24 Idea of S.M.P.S.

switch is open. When the switch is closed, current I flows round the circuit and through the load in the direction shown producing an output voltage V_o across the load. During this time the diode is reverse biased and therefore non-conducting. The current flowing in L causes a magnetic field to be set up and energy

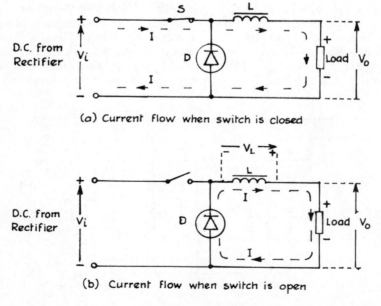

(a) Current flow when switch is closed

(b) Current flow when switch is open

Fig. 11.25 Basic circuit of switched mode stabiliser.

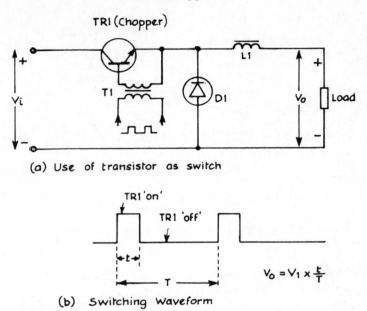

(a) Use of transistor as switch

(b) Switching Waveform

Fig. 11.26 Practical arrangement of switched mode stabiliser.

is stored in this field. If the switch is now opened as in Fig. 11.25(b), the magnetic field around L collapses, inducing a voltage into the inductor (V_L). This voltage forward biases D causing the diode to conduct thereby allowing current to flow in the load in the same direction as previously. Thus when the switch is opened, the load uses the energy stored in L with D acting as an 'efficiency diode'.

In a practical arrangement the electrical switch may be replaced by a transistor as in Fig. 11.26(a) where the transistor is either fully 'on' or fully 'off'. To switch the transistor alternately 'on' and 'off' a pulse waveform may be supplied as indicated via a transformer T1. To regulate or stabilise the output voltage all that is necessary is to detect changes in the output voltage V_o and correct it by altering the ratio t/T (the duty cycle) of the switching waveform shown in Fig. 11.26(b), since the output voltage will depend upon how much current flows when the transistor is 'on'. The idea is illustrated by the basic block schematic of Fig. 11.27. The d.c. output of the rectifier A is applied to the switching transistor B (referred to as the chopper). The chopper is driven with continuous pulses from E; a triggered monostable oscillator may be used to generate the pulses. The feedback amplifier D is used to detect changes in the output voltage and to adjust the mark–space ratio of the pulses generated in E, thereby varying the 'on' time of the chopper and hence stabilising the output voltage.

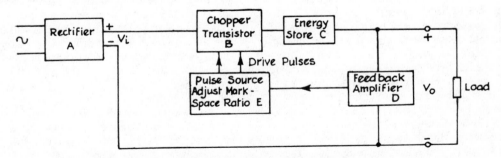

Fig. 11.27 Basic block diagram of switched mode power supply.

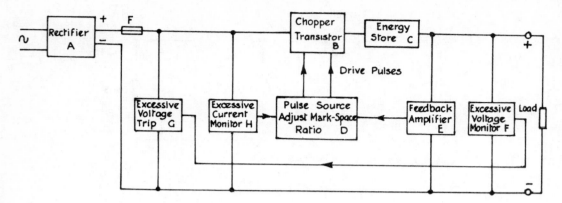

Fig. 11.28 Block schematic including over-voltage and over-current protection.

Over-voltage and Over-current Protection

To prevent damage to the circuits fed from the power supply, for example i.c.s and other voltage-sensitive circuits, it is often necessary to ensure that the output voltage of the power supply does not increase above a preset limit for any reason whatsoever, e.g. voltage transients in the mains supply or accidental internal short-circuiting to other high-voltage lines. When this form of protection is incorporated it is referred to as **excessive voltage** or **over-voltage** protection. Also, it is common to use some form of **excessive current** or **over-current** protection, particularly when a series stabiliser or switching element is used, since excessive current drawn by the load may damage the series element.

Both of these features are incorporated into the switched-mode stabiliser block schematic of Fig. 11.28. Block F monitors the output voltage and when it rises above a prescribed limit it produces an output that is applied to block G which 'trips' and blows the fuse F. The excessive voltage monitor may consist of a zener diode resistive network which produces an output when the zener voltage is exceeded. The excessive voltage trip is commonly an s.c.r. which fires during over-voltage and acts as a 'crow bar' across the d.c. input to the stabiliser. The excessive current monitor H acts as a bypass for the switching current and when this exceeds prescribed limits the monitor removes the drive pulses to the chopper, thus quickly reducing the output voltage to zero under excessive current conditions.

Voltage Doublers

In the rectifier circuits described earlier the d.c. output voltage is limited to the peak a.c. input to the rectifier arrangement. It is possible to provide d.c. outputs several times the peak a.c. input using voltage multiplier circuits. A circuit which provides a d.c. output twice that of the input voltage is called a voltage doubler and one type is shown in Fig. 11.29.

During the half-cycles of transformer secondary voltage that make point A positive with respect to point B, D1 conducts causing a current i_1, to flow charging C1 to the peak secondary voltage V_p. On the other half-cycles when A is negative with respect to B, D2 conducts causing C2 to charge to V_p by the current i_2. The d.c. voltage across the load is the sum of the voltages across C1 and C2, i.e. $2 \times V_p$. In effect the circuit is really two half-wave rectifier circuits in series resulting in twice the output voltage of a half-wave rectifier. C1 and C2 act as reservoir capacitors and if these have large values, and the load current is small, the output ripple will also be small. Since C1 and C2 are charged on alternate half-cycles the output ripple frequency will be twice that of the input frequency, i.e. 100 Hz with a 50 Hz mains supply.

An alternative doubler rectifier circuit, known as a cascade doubler is given in Fig. 11.30. During half-cycles that make point A negative with respect to B, D2 conducts charging C1 with polarity shown to the peak

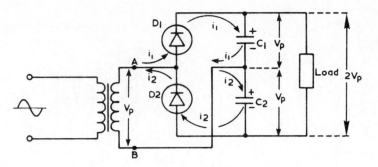

Fig. 11.29 Voltage doubler rectifier.

voltage V_p. During these half-cycles D1 will be reverse biased and thus nonconducting. On the other half-cycles when A is positive with respect to B, no current will flow in D2 as it is reverse biased. However, the voltage across the secondary winding adds to the voltage across C1 causing D1 to conduct and for C2 to charge. The total voltage applied to D1 is the peak secondary voltage V_p plus the voltage across C1 (also V_p). Thus C2 charges up to $2 \times V_p$. During these half-cycles C1 is partly discharged but is recharged on the other half-cycles.

The cascade idea can be extended to produce tripling and quadrupling of the input voltage. Voltage doublers and triplers used in e.h.t. circuits in television receivers usually employ the cascade arrangement. Although they operate on similar lines to that shown in Fig. 11.30 they are different in that the input to them is a pulse voltage waveform and not a sinewave of reversing polarity. An e.h.t. doubler with pulse input requires three diode-capacitor circuits and a tripler five diode-capacitor circuits.

INTERFERENCE

Electrical interference from such items as automobile ignition systems, fluorescent lights, refrigerators, electric motors and switching inductive circuits is impulsive in nature and a major hazard to electronic systems. It may degrade the performance of radio and television reception or audio equipment, cause low voltage semiconductor devices to fail, cause false triggering or maloperation of analogue or digital circuits and in computing systems may cause programs to 'crash'.

Impulsive interference may be conveyed in a number of ways:

(1) Direct Radiation

The interfering current flowing in the source, e.g. electric motor, radiates energy (in the form of an e.m. wave) which may be induced into the circuits of a radio receiver or other electronic equipment. The actual range of the radiation is small (up to about 50 metres) and is most troublesome in industrial environments.

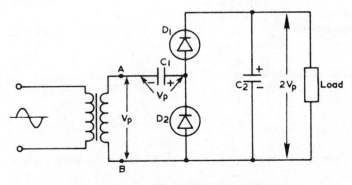

Fig. 11.30 Cascade voltage doubler rectifier.

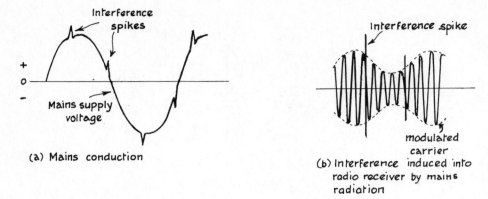

Fig. 11.31 Interference.

(2) Direct Conduction Along Mains Supply

The impulsive interference may be conducted along the mains supply, see Fig. 11.31(a) and find its way into electronic equipment usually via the power supply. It is common with systems sharing the same mains supply.

(3) Radiation From the Mains Supply

The interference may be conducted along the mains supply and re-radiated from it to be picked-up by a local receiver along with its normal signal as in Fig. 11.31(b) or induced into other items of electronic equipment. This is the predominant manner in which interference is transferred.

The following measures may be taken to reduce the effects of interference:

(a) Suppression at Source

The effects of some types of interference can be considerably reduced by suppression at the source. Electric motors, for example, produce interference if there is sparking at the brushes and this may be conveyed into the motor voltage supply. Interference of this type may be reduced by either increasing the series r.f. impedance of the supply by inserting an r.f. choke in series with each line as in Fig. 11.32(a) or by providing a low impedance path in shunt with the supply using capacitors as in Fig. 11.32(b), or a combination of both methods. To reduce direct radiation from the chokes they should be enclosed in an earthed screen.

A contactor in an inductive circuit as in Fig. 11.33 is often a source of arcing due to the inductor back e.m.f. appearing across the contacts as they open. An R–C filter con-

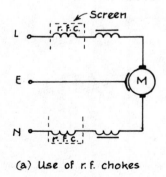

(a) Use of r.f. chokes

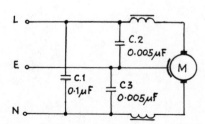

(b) Use of decoupling capacitors

Fig. 11.32 Suppression of motor brush noise.

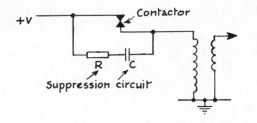

Fig. 11.33 Arc suppression.

nected as shown will damp the induced e.m.f. as the contacts open and limit the magnitude of the arcing current. This method is commonly used in car ignition systems where additionally, high resistance spark plug leads are used to suppress r.f. radiation.

When an SCR or TRIAC is suddenly switched 'on' undesirable harmonics are produced which can be a source of interference. It is thus common to fit suppression circuits as in Fig. 11.34 to prevent the harmonics from entering the mains supply and cause interference either by mains conduction to other equipment sharing a common mains supply or by direct radiation.

Two independent filters are used in Fig. 11.34, one comprising C1, C2 and C3 and the other formed by L1, L2 and C4 to prevent

the interference from being conducted into the mains supply. The filters are housed in earthed aluminium screening cans to reduce direct radiation from the filter components; the TRIAC and its firing circuit are similarly screened for the same reason.

(b) Filtering of Power Supplies to Equipment

Since r.f. interference may find its way into electronic equipment by the mechanism of mains conduction, it is common practice to incorporate suppression measures in the power supply as in Fig. 11.35.

Here an r.f. filter comprising L1, L2 and C1 is used to minimise the amount of r.f. interference finding its way to the secondary winding of the mains transformer T1. Additionally, the use of an earthed electrostatic screen between T1 windings (which reduces the capacitance between them) minimises the transference of r.f. energy to the secondary circuit. An r.f. by-pass capacitor C9 connected across the d.c. output provides a low impedance path for any r.f. interference induced into the d.c. supply. Note that the smoothing capacitor C8 does not provide a low impedance path to r.f. due to the inherent self-inductance of the electrolytic capacitors. Careful attention to r.f. decoupling throughout the d.c. supplies to the various circuits of

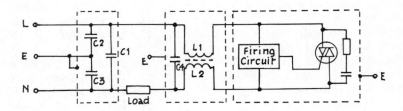

Fig. 11.34 Suppression filters to reduce r.f. interference from SCR or TRIAC.

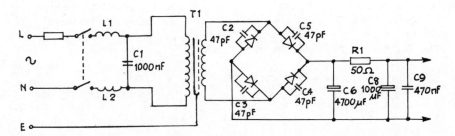

Fig. 11.35 Suppression of mains borne interference from supplies to electronic equipment.

equipment will minimise the effects of interference.

To prevent damage to the bridge rectifiers by impulsive interference each diode has an r.f. by-pass capacitor (C2–C5) connected across it.

QUESTIONS ON CHAPTER ELEVEN

Questions 1–7 refer to Fig. 11.13 on page 147.

(1) If the current flowing in the load is 80mA, the d.c. voltage present between the junction of D2, D3 and chassis will be approximately:
  (a) 2V
  (b) 12V
  (c) 16V
  (d) 80V.

(2) A suitable wattage rating for R2 with 80mA load current would be:
  (a) 500mW
  (b) 250mW
  (c) 100mW
  (d) 50mW.

(3) If D1 were to go open circuit the outcome would be:
  (a) The voltage across the load would consist of half sinewaves only
  (b) The d.c. voltage across the load would be 4·5V
  (c) The voltage across the load would be greater than normal with an increase in the ripple voltage
  (d) The voltage across the load would be slightly less than normal with an increase in the ripple voltage.

(4) With D1 open circuit there will be:
  (a) An increase in D2 peak current
  (b) An increase in the load current
  (c) An increase in D3 and D4 peak currents
  (d) A decrease in D3 peak current only.

(5) If R1 goes open circuit the effect will be:
  (a) The load current will fall to zero
  (b) The output voltage will fall to about 1V
  (c) D1 and D4 will conduct heavily
  (d) F1 will rupture.

(6) A short-circuit C1 will result in:
  (a) A large amount of ripple in the output
  (b) F1 rupturing
  (c) Smaller current in D1-D4
  (d) Load current increasing.

(7) An open-circuit C1 will result in:
  (a) No output voltage
  (b) F1 rupturing
  (c) Larger current in D1-D4
  (d) Low output voltage with an increase in ripple voltage.

Questions 8–11 refer to Fig. 11.21 on page 152.

(8) A short-circuit across the load will cause:
  (a) TR2 to conduct heavily
  (b) D1 to conduct heavily
  (c) Excessive output voltage
  (d) TR1 to conduct heavily.

(9) An open-circuit R3 will cause:
  (a) Zero output voltage
  (b) Smaller reduction in output voltage
  (c) Smaller current in TR1
  (d) Higher than normal output voltage.

(10) A short-circuited D1 will cause:
  (a) Low output voltage
  (b) Higher than normal output voltage
  (c) Zero output voltage
  (d) Small current in TR2.

(11) An open-circuited R2 will cause:
  (a) Zero output voltage
  (b) High current in TR1
  (c) High current in TR2
  (d) Higher than normal output voltage.

(12) The d.c. output voltage of a rectifier circuit may be made larger than the peak a.c. input to the rectifier by:
  (a) Using a mains transformer with a step-up ratio
  (b) Using a very large reservoir capacitor
  (c) Employing a full-wave rectifier
  (d) Using a voltage doubler.

(Answers on page 370)

CHAPTER TWELVE

DIFFERENTIATING AND INTEGRATING CIRCUITS

Objectives

1 To explain how CR networks affect the shape and amplitude of signal waveforms.
2 To show the output waveform of a CR differentiating network when fed with rectangular and sawtooth waveforms.
3 To show the output waveform of a CR integrating network when fed with rectangular and sawtooth waveforms.

THE SHAPE AND AMPLITUDE of signal wave-forms passing through the stages of an electronic circuit are particularly influenced by the presence of capacitance-resistance networks. In this chapter we shall consider how CR networks are used to achieve desired waveform shapes when fed with rectangular and sawtooth waves.

Consider first the series CR network of Fig. 12.1 when the rectangular pulses of Fig. 12.2(a) are applied to the input. The shape and amplitude of the output voltage

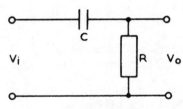

Fig. 12.1 CR Network.

across R is determined by the relationship between the CR time and the pulse duration T_p. The CR time in seconds is given by the

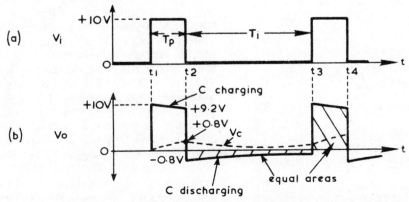

Fig. 12.2 Response of CR network to rectangular pulse ($CR \gg T_p$).

product of C (farads) and R (ohms). It will be assumed that the CR time is greater than the pulse duration. The response of the network will be explained with the aid of Fig. 12.2(b) and the diagrams of Fig. 12.3.

At instant t_1 when V_i rises the voltages present in the network are as shown in Fig. 12.2(a). As a capacitor cannot change its state of charge instantaneously, the full rise of the input voltage is initially developed across R, i.e. the capacitor passes the change of V_i and thus the voltage across the capacitor is

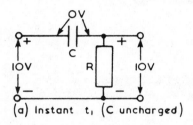

(a) Instant t_1 (C uncharged)

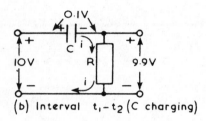

(b) Interval t_1–t_2 (C charging)

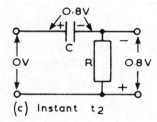

(c) Instant t_2

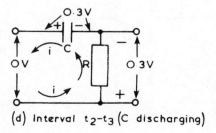

(d) Interval t_2–t_3 (C discharging)

Fig. 12.3 Diagrams showing voltages across R and C during pulse input.

initially zero. With a voltage established across R a current i will flow as shown in circuit (b) causing C to charge. This occurs during the interval t_1–t_2. As C charges exponentially the voltage across R falls exponentially. If at sometime during this interval the voltage across C has risen to 0·1V the voltage across R will have fallen by 0·1V, i.e. from 10V to 9·9V. Since it was assumed that the CR time is greater than the pulse duration, the voltage across C will only have risen by a small amount, say, to 0·8V at the end of the pulse period. In consequence, the voltage across R will have fallen to 9·2.V.

At instant t_2 the input voltage falls from +10V to 0V. This fall is passed through C to across R causing the voltage at the output to fall by 10V, from +9·2V to −0·8V. This situation is illustrated in Fig. 12.3(c) where the output voltage has reversed polarity to −0·8V and the voltage present across C is still as was assumed at the end of the charge period (0·8V). The voltage across R now causes a current i to flow discharging C as shown in circuit (d). The capacitor discharges during the interval between pulses (T_i). Suppose that during the interval t_2–t_3 the voltage across C has fallen to 0·3V, the voltage across R will also have fallen to 0·3V. If the CR time is greater than the period T_i, then at the end of this period the voltage across C will not have fallen to zero but to some small voltage depending upon the period T_i and the exact time constant.

It should be noted that at all times the algebraic sum of the voltages across C and R are equal to the input voltage V_i. When the next pulse arrives (instant t_3) and V_i rises by 10V, the output voltage also rises by 10V causing C to charge once again repeating the operation. Note that the peak voltage at the output on the second pulse is sightly lower than for the first pulse due to the charge held by C at the end of the first discharge period. Succeeding peaks will gradually lower and then settle down to a constant level. At this stage the output waveform will balance itself about zero so that the pulse area above the zero datum line is equal to the pulse area below the datum line. Thus the d.c. Component of the output wave form will be zero, which is only to be expected since the capacitor C cannot pass the d.c. component of the input waveform. The longer the time-constant, the more closely the output wave-form will resemble the input waveform.

Differentiation of Rectangular Wave

A differentiating circuit is one which produces an output that is directly proportional to the slope or rate of change of the input. The circuit of Fig. 12.1 may act as a differentiator provided the CR time is very much shorter than the pulse duration. For practical purposes the CR time should be at least one-tenth of the pulse duration T_p.

The response of a differentiating circuit to rectangular pulses is shown in Fig. 12.4. When the input voltage rises from 0V to +10V at instant t_i, so does the voltage across R as previously explained. The voltage across R causes a current to flow charging C. Since the CR time is short compared with T_p the capacitor charges rapidly and becomes fully charged during the pulse interval. As a result the voltage across R rapidly falls to zero. The output voltage remains at zero until instant t_2 when V_i falls from +10V to 0V at which point

the voltage across R also falls by 10V, i.e. from 0V to −10V. The reversal of voltage across R causes a discharge current to flow and C rapidly discharges during the pulse interval Ti. As C discharges rapidly the voltage across R falls rapidly to zero.

The differentiating circuit produces an output only when the input is changing its level; the output has a polarity that is linked to the rise and fall of the input. On the rising edge of the pulse a positive-going spike is produced but on the falling edge a negative-going spike is produced. There is no output when the input level is constant. The differentiating circuit is a high-pass filter passing only the rapid changes to the output. In the diagrams ideal pulses have been shown, i.e. having zero rise times or infinite slope. Instantaneous changes in voltage level cannot be obtained in practice.

Further examples of differentiation of pulse type waveforms are shown in Fig. 12.5. In diagram (a) a square wave input is assumed swinging equally either side of its datum line. Output spikes only appear from the differentiator when the input level changes. When the input voltage falls from +10V to

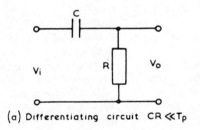

(a) Differentiating circuit $CR \ll T_p$

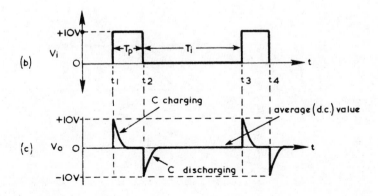

Fig. 12.4 Response of differentiating circuit to rectangular input.

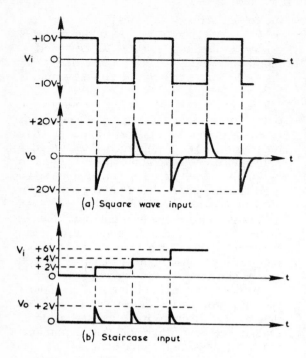

Fig. 12.5 Other examples of differentiation.

Integration of Rectangular Wave

An integrating circuit is one which produces an output that is directly proportional to the area under the input waveshape. The idea of an integrator is shown in Fig. 12.6.

Consider that the input to the integrator is a rectangular pulse of increasing duration as shown in diagram (a). Prior to instant t_1, the pulse is of zero amplitude and the integrator output, diagram (b), is zero. At instant t_2, the pulse will have an area of $x \times y$ and it will be assumed that the integrator output is a volts at this instant. If the pulse duration increases, then at instant t_3 the pulse area will be $2x \times y$, i.e. twice the area at t_2. The integrator output will now have increased to b volts and will be twice that at t_2. At a later instant t_4 the pulse area will have increased to $3x \times y$ and the integrator output will have increased to c volts and will be three times that at t_2 . . . and so on. Thus the integrator produces an output that is proportional to the area under the pulse. The output voltage shows the relative contribution of succesive equal time increments to the total area under the pulse.

A CR integrating circuit may be formed by interchanging the positions of C and R to that shown in Fig. 12.7(a) with the output taken from across the capacitor. However, the circuit will integrate only when the CR time is very much greater than the pulse duration T_p. For practical purposes, the CR time should be at least 10 times T_p.

If the integrator is fed with the rectangular wave of diagram (b), the output will be as shown in diagram (c). At instant t_1 when the input voltage rises, all of the rise will be

$-10V$ (a fall of 20V) the output falls by 20V. Whereas on a rising edge of the input the voltage rises from $-10V$ to $+10V$ (an increase of 20V) and the output does likewise.

The response of a differentiator to a staircase waveform is shown in diagram (b). Note that each time the input voltage rises it changes its voltage level by 2V. Accordingly, the differentiator produces positive-going 2V spikes corresponding to these changes.

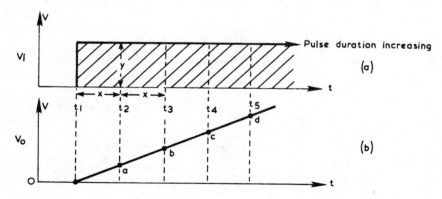

Fig. 12.6 Basic idea of integrator.

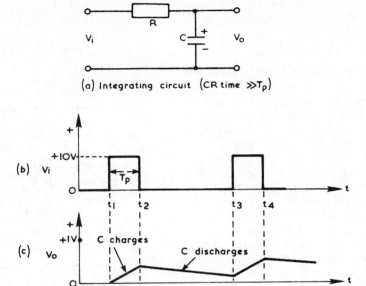

(a) Integrating circuit (CR time $\gg T_p$)

Fig. 12.7 Response of integrating circuit to rectangular input.

developed across R and a current will commence to flow charging C with polarity shown. As the CR time is long compared with T_p, the charge acquired by C during the pulse period will be small and hence the voltage across C will also be small. The voltage rises fairly linearly during this period since only a small portion of the normal exponential charging curve is used.

At instant t_2 when the input falls to zero, the fall in voltage is developed across R causing a reversal of voltage across it and a current flow in the opposite direction discharging C. If the CR time is also long compared with the interim period (t_2-t_3), the voltage across C will

fall only by a small amount. The fall in voltage will also be fairly linear since only a small portion of the normal exponential discharge curve is used.

At the end of the discharge period, the voltage across C will not be zero, thus on the following pulse C will charge to a slightly higher voltage than on the first pulse. Gradually the peak voltage of Vo will rise towards the mean value of the input with each succeeding pulse. After a number of pulses, the waveform across C will settle down to between constant levels as illustrated in Fig. 12.8. The output waveform is a sawtooth having a d.c. component equal to the mean value of the input.

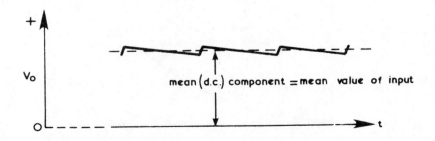

Fig. 12.8 Voltage across C after a number of pulses.

An integrator is a low-pass or smoothing filter, passing only the l.f components of the input pulse to the output.

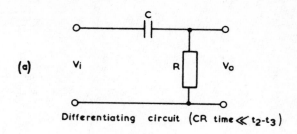

(a) Differentiating circuit (CR time $\ll t_2-t_3$)

Differentiation and Integration of Sawtooth Wave

Differentiation of a sawtooth waveform is shown in Fig. 12.9. Here the CR time must be short compared with the period t_2-t_3, in which case it will also be short compared with the period t_1-t_2. The sawtooth input consists of a rising ramp of relatively small slope followed by a falling ramp of much greater slope.

A differentiator produces an output that is proportional to the slope of the input as previously mentioned. Thus during the period t_1-t_2 the output is a constant voltage v_1, since the slope of the input is constant over this period. At instant t_2 where the input is at a peak, the slope is zero and therefore the output is zero. Between instant t_2-t_3 the output is a constant voltage v_2 but is of opposite polarity to v_1 since the slope is negative over this period. The magnitude of v_2 is greater then v_1 since the slope is greater during the falling ramp period. Thus differentiation of a sawtooth wave produces a rectangular wave. A differentiating network can therefore be used to reverse the process of integration, since integration of a rectangular wave produces a sawtooth wave.

Before dealing with the integrating of a sawtooth wave, consider the integration of the ramp voltage V_i of Fig. 12.10. Note that

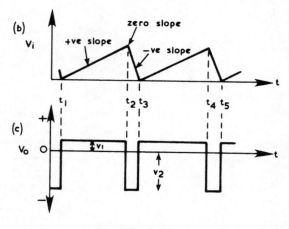

Fig. 12.9 Differentiation of sawtooth wave.

although the area under the ramp is increasing, the increase in area for successive time increments varies. Area 3 is greater than area 2 which is greater than area 1. Thus the output voltage V_o will rise at a greater rate as the rise in the input voltage progresses, producing the parabolic curve shown.

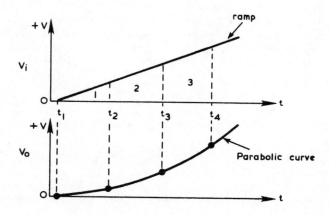

Fig. 12.10 Output of integrator with ramp input.

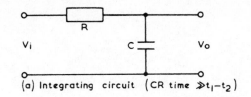

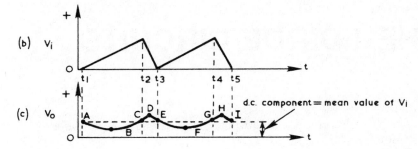

Fig. 12.11 Integration of sawtooth wave.

When the input to the integrator is a sawtooth wave having rising and falling ramp periods as shown in Fig. 12.11, the output consists of a series of parabolas as in diagram (c). During the rising ramp periods the parablas ABC, EFG, etc., are produced, whilst during the falling ramp periods the inverted parabolas CDE, GHI, etc., are produced. These parabolas will have a.d.c. component equal to the mean value of the input waveform after the circuit has reached its steady state condition.

QUESTIONS ON CHAPTER TWELVE

(1)   A repetitive rectangular pulse waveform having a pulse duration of $50\mu s$ is fed to a CR network. The network will produce a differentiated output across R if its CR time is:
(a) $2\mu s$
(b) $50\mu s$
(c) $500\mu s$
(d) 5ms.

(2)   A repetitive rectangular waveform having a pulse duration of 2ms is fed to an integrating network. The CR time of the network would probably be:
(a) $20\mu s$
(b) $200\mu s$

(c) 2ms
(d) 20ms.

(3)   When an integrating network is fed with a rectangular wave the output will be:
(a) A rectangular wave of small amplitude
(b) A series of positive and negative spikes
(c) A sawtooth wave
(d) A parabolic wave.

(4)   When a differentiating network is fed with a sawtooth wave the output will be:
(a) A rectangular wave
(b) A small amplitude parabola
(c) A series of positive and negative spikes
(d) A small amplitude sawtooth wave.

(5)   The output from a CR network fed with a square wave consists of positive and negative spikes when:
(a) An integrating circuit is used with the output across C
(b) A differentiating circuit is used with the output across R
(c) An integrating circuit is used with the output across R
(d) A differentiating circuit is used with the output across C.

(Answers on page 370)

CHAPTER THIRTEEN

OTHER DIODE CIRCUITS

Objectives

To explain the operation of the following circuits employing p-n diodes:

1 D.C. Restorers.
2 D.C. Clamps.
3 Protection circuits.
4 Limiter circuits.
5 A.M. demodulator circuits.

THE SEMICONDUCTOR DIODE may be incorporated in a variety of electronic circuits to perform different operations on signal waveforms and some will be discussed in this chapter.

D.C. Restoration

A common requirement in electronics is that of being able to alter the d.c. component of a waveform so as to set a particular level of the waveform to a specified d.c. voltage. This may be achieved using a d.c. restorer circuit. One such circuit which performs the operation of positive d.c. restoration is given in Fig. 13.1.

The circuit of diagram (a) consists of a CR network with a diode D connected in shunt with the output. As we do not wish to alter the shape of the waveform in any way, the CR time must be very long compared with the periodic time of the input waveform. Consider a square wave input having zero d.c. component as in diagram (b).

When the input voltage goes negative at instant t_i, the change in voltage is initially developed across R. The direction of this voltage will cause D to be forward biased and

the diode will conduct. When D conducts, C charges rapidly via the low forward resistance of the diode and the voltage across R quickly falls to zero. The output consists of a small negative going spike as shown in diagram (c). Between instant t_1–t_2 when the input is at a steady level the output is also steady at 0V since C is fully charged. At instant t_2 when the input suddenly rises by 10V (from −5V to +5V), the full rise is developed across R. The polarity of the voltage across R will now reverse bias the diode and it will be non-conducting. However the voltage across R will allow C to commence to discharge during the period t_2–t_3. Since the CR time is very long compared with the periodic time, C will discharge only a little during this period and in consequence the voltage across R will fall only by a small amount. At instant t_3 when the input falls by 10V, the output also falls by 10V. In doing so the output will fall just below zero causing D to become forward biased once again. As D conducts, C rapidly charges replacing the charge lost during the discharge period. From instant t_3 onwards the operation is repeated.

It will be seen that the most negative level of the input waveform has been shifted in the

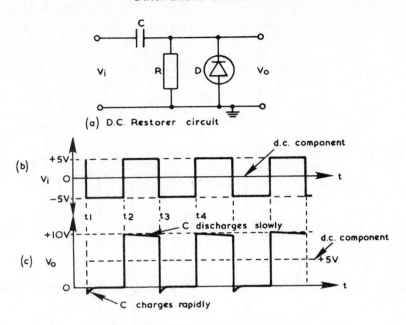

(a) D.C. Restorer circuit

Fig. 13.1 Positive D.C. restoration.

positive direction and has been restored to 0V. The d.c. component of the output waveform will therefore be +5V.

By reversing the diode connections, the circuit can be modified to perform negative d.c. restoration of the input signal as illus-

trated in Fig. 13.2. Here the diode conducts on the positive rising edges of the input waveform causing C to rapidly charge but is reverse biased on the falling edges when C commences to slowly discharge. This time the input waveform has been shifted in the

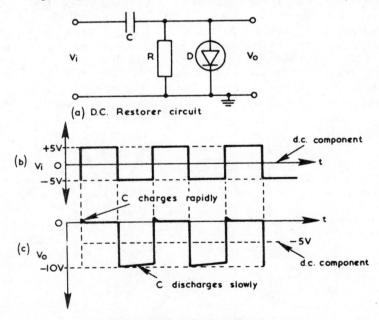

(a) D.C. Restorer circuit

Fig. 13.2 Negative D.C. restoration.

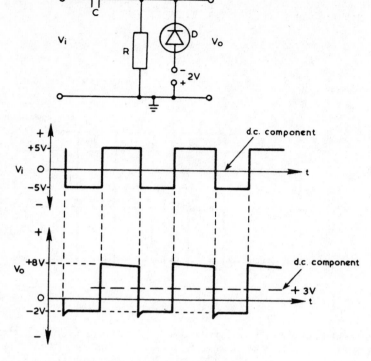

Fig. 13.3 Use of biased diode.

negative direction with its most positive level restored to 0V. The output waveform will therefore have a d.c. component of −5V.

It may be required to restore a particular level of the input waveform to a voltage value other than 0V and this can be done by biasing the diode. The idea is shown in Fig. 13.3 using a positive d.c. restorer circuit with a bias of 2V applied to the anode of the diode.

If the input waveform is the same as used previously, the diode will not commence to conduct until the voltage across R on the falling edges of the input is greater than 2V. Thus the most negative level of the input waveform will be restored to −2V instead of 0V. The output waveform will then have a d.c. component of +3V (instead of +5V when the diode is not biased). If the polarity of the bias

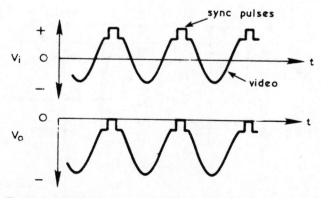

Fig. 13.4 Negative D.C. restoration of television video waveform.

voltage is reversed and the diode connections reversed then the circuit will operate as a negative d.c. restorer with the most postive level of the input waveform restored to +2V.

These d.c. restorer circuits will operate equally well on other types of input waves, e.g. sine wave, rectangular wave and sawtooth wave. Fig. 13.4. shows the action of a negative d.c. restorer when supplied at its input with a television video waveform having zero d.c. component. The output waveform has been shifted in the negative direction with the tips of the sync. pulses restored to 0V.

D.C. Clamping

Another type of circuit that may be used to alter the d.c. level of a waveform is known as a **d.c. clamp**. This operates similarly to a d.c. restorer and is used in applications where the ordinary d.c. restorer is unsatisfactory. One application of a d.c. clamp is in the setting or clamping of the black level of a television video signal waveform to a particular d.c. voltage.

An example is shown in Fig. 13.5 with the t.v. waveform given in diagram (a). Immediately following the line sync. pulse there is a brief period known as the back porch when the video signal is at black level. Suppose for simplicity that it is desirable to set the black level to 0V. The basic idea of a d.c. clamp is shown in diagram (b) with the t.v. waveform fed through the CR combination. If during the period corresponding to the back porch of the t.v. waveform the switch S is closed the capacitor will charge rapidly and point A will assume zero potential. Thus the black level of the waveform at the output will be set to 0V. When S is opened at the end of the back porch period, C will commence to discharge but if the CR time is very long compared with the period between line sync. pulse there will be little drift in the voltage corresponding to

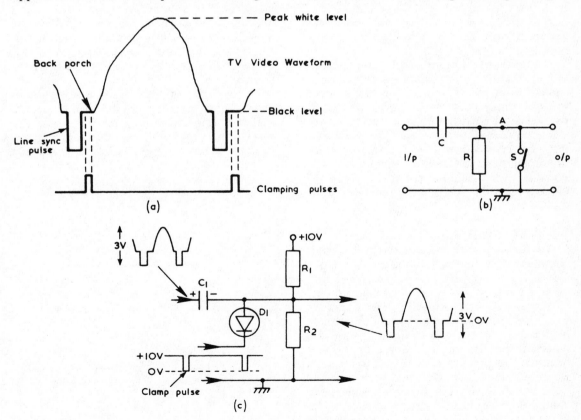

Fig. 13.5 D.C. clamp circuit.

black level. In a practical circuit the mechanical switch S is replaced by an electronic switch; a diode may be used for this purpose as illustrated in diagram (c).

To switch the diode on for a period corresponding to the back porch or a shorter duration, a clamping pulse is fed to the diode. This may be either a positive or negative pulse depending upon the circuit used, but negative clamp pulses are required here. Between clamping pulses D1 is reverse biased as its anode is returned to the potential divider R1, R2 connected across the 10V supply whilst its cathode is at +10V. When a clamping pulse arrives at D1 cathode, the cathode assumes zero potential and thus D1 conducts. This causes C1 to charge with the polarity shown and for the voltage at the junction of R1, R2 to take up zero potential thereby clamping the black level to 0V. In between clamping pulses C1 discharges very slowly via R1 (a long CR time) thus the voltage corresponding to black level does not drift to any large extent. The next clamp pulse to arrive will clamp the voltage at the output back to 0V as the charge on C1 is restored.

A number of different circuit arrangements are possible using diodes but they all work on similar principles. In place of the diode a transistor may be used as the clamp. If the voltage level corresponding to the tip of the clamp pulse is made, say, +2V the black level may be clamped to +2V instead of 0V (assuming suitable values for R1 and R2). It is possible with a suitable circuit to clamp the black level to any chosen d.c. voltage.

Limiting or clipping

Another common requirement in electronic circuits is to be able to limit the amplitude of a waveform at a particular d.c. level. A limiter or clipper circuit may be used for this purpose.

As an example consider the circuit of Fig. 13.6(a) fed with a series of positive and negative-going spikes at its input as shown in diagram (b). If during the positive spikes terminal A is positive with respect to terminal B, the diode will conduct and a current will flow in R. If the resistance of R is large compared with the forward resistance of the diode then most of the spike voltage will be developed across R and little across the diode

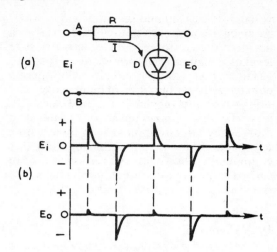

Fig. 13.6 Diode clipper or limiter.

(the output voltage will be limited to the forward voltage drop of the diode, say, 0·8V for a silicon diode). During the negative spikes point A will be negative with respect to point B and the diode will be reverse biased. Thus the negative spikes will be passed to the output. Therefore the circuit has clipped off the positive-going spikes or limited them. If the connections of the diode are reversed, the circuit will clip off the negative-going spikes leaving only the positive ones at the output.

If it is required to clip off a portion of a waveform, a biased diode limiter circuit may be used as shown in Fig. 13.7(a). Suppose that

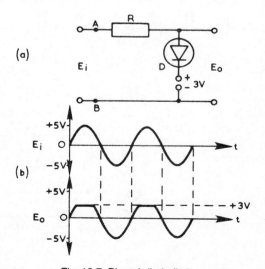

Fig. 13.7 Biased diode limiter.

it is desirable to limit the positive half-cycles of the sinewave input to the circuit to, say, +3V. If a bias voltage of 3V is connected as shown, the diode will not conduct until point A is positive with respect to point B and the input voltage is greater than 3V. Thus the portion of the input waveform below the +3V level will be passed to the output. The voltage above this level will be dropped across R when the diode conducts.

To obtain limiting on both half-cycles of the waveform to specific voltage levels, two biased diodes may be used as in Fig. 13.8. With 3V

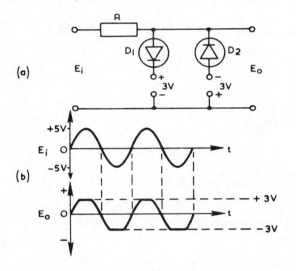

Fig. 13.8 Limiter with two biased diodes.

biasing, neither diode will conduct until the input voltage of either polarity exceeds 3V. Thus the portion of the input waveform between the limits of — 3V and +3V will be passed to the output. Outside these voltage limits, the excess voltage is dropped across R when D1 conducts above +3V and D2 conducts below −3V of the input waveform. In place of ordinary p-n diodes and bias supplies, zener diodes may be used, an example being given in Fig. 13.9.

The two zener diodes D1 and D2 must be placed in series since zener diodes conduct in the forward direction as well as the reverse direction. Suppose it is desirable to limit the sinewave input to ±6V. Diodes would be chosen with zener voltage of, say, 5·3V and the value of R chosen to provide a suitable

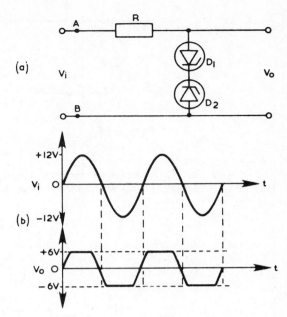

Fig. 13.9 Use of zener diodes for limiting.

current in the diodes. On the positive half-cycle of the input when A is positive with respect to B, D2 will zener when the input exceeds 6V and D1 will become forward biased. The output voltage will be limited to the zener voltage of D2 (5·3V) plus the forward voltage drop of D1, say, 0·7V, i.e. a limiting voltage of 6V as required. During the negative half-cycles of the input when A is negative with respect to B, D1 will zener and D2 will become forward biased, again limiting the output to 6V but with opposing polarity. Above and below the limiting voltages of +6V and −6V the excess voltage will be dropped across R when the diodes are conductive. As the zener characteristic is not very sharp for low voltage zener diodes, the circuit works best with zener diodes having a zener voltage greater than about 5V. To provide limiting on one half-cycle only, one of the zener diodes may be replaced by an ordinary p-n diode.

Diode Protection

Another common use for diodes is in protection circuits where they are employed to protect other components from damage due to over-voltage or voltage of incorrect polarity.

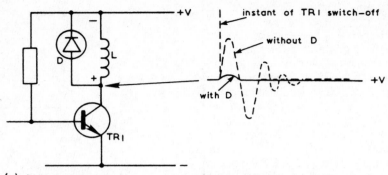

(a) Diode used to protect transistor against induced voltage of L

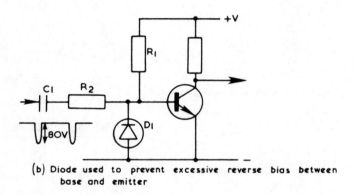

(b) Diode used to prevent excessive reverse bias between base and emitter

Fig. 13.10 Diode protection circuits.

Two examples of over-voltage protection are given in Fig. 13.10. When an inductor L is used as a load for a transistor as in diagram (a), excessive voltage may be applied between collector and emitter when the current in the transistor is cut off. Without the diode a large induced voltage (with polarity shown) may appear across the inductor when the current is cut off or rapidly reduced. This may cause the collector voltage to swing well above the + V supply line as shown causing the maximum collector-to-emitter voltage rating to be exceeded and for the transistor to be destroyed. When a diode is fitted with connections as shown, any attempt for the collector voltage to rise above the supply line potential is soon arrested as it will bring the diode into forward conduction. The conduction of the diode quickly dissipates the energy stored in the inductor and prevents the rise of collector voltage. The inductance L may be the primary winding of a transformer, the operating coil of

a relay or a choke. For a p-n-p transistor and a negative supply line the connections of the diode would be reversed.

In diagram (b) the diode is used to prevent the maximum reverse voltage across the base-emitter junction being exceeded when the base is fed with a large amplitude pulse to cut off the transistor. Forward bias for the transistor is provided by R1 and the base-emitter forward voltage drop places D1 in the reverse bias state so it has no effect. However, when the negative pulse is applied through C1 and R2 to cut off the transistor, D1 conducts and limits the maximum reverse voltage to its forward voltage drop of, say, 0·8V thus protecting the transistor. The excess voltage of the pulse is developed across R2.

Circuits employing semiconductor devices (including in particluar integrated circuits) may be damaged if voltage of incorrect polarity is applied to them. This is likely to occur when the equipment is supplied from an

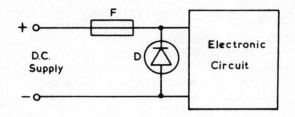

Fig. 13.11 *Use of diode for polarity protection.*

external battery the connections of which may inadvertently be reversed by the user. One arrangement for protection against accidental reverse polarity is shown in Fig. 13.11. When the supply is connected with correct polarity as shown, the diode is non conductive and the equipment works normally. If, however, the polarity of the supply is changed over, the diode will conduct thereby shorting out the supply and blowing the fuse F.

Diode Demodulator

The purpose of the demodulator or detector in a receiver is to recover the original signal information impressed on the carrier at the transmitter. In the case of a broadcast radio tranmission, the signal information consists of music and speech (audio) and either amplitude or frequency modulation of the carrier wave may be used. Here, we shall only be concerned with demodulation of a.m. waves as in a LW/MW radio receiver. The demodulator circuit used in this type of receiver is similar to that used for rectification in a power supply and operates almost identically. A basic circuit with waveforms is given in Fig. 13.12.

The circuit is shown in diagram (a). The diode D1 (point contact type) is used as the demodulator and is fed at the input with the a.m. wave shown in diagram (b) from across the tuned circuit L1, C1 which is commonly the secondary of the final i.f. transformer. If, on the positive half-cycles of the modulated carrier input point A is positive with respect to point B, D1 will conduct and a current will flow in the diode and R1. When point A is negative with respect to point B on the negative half-cycles of the input, the diode will be reverse biased and there will be no current flow.

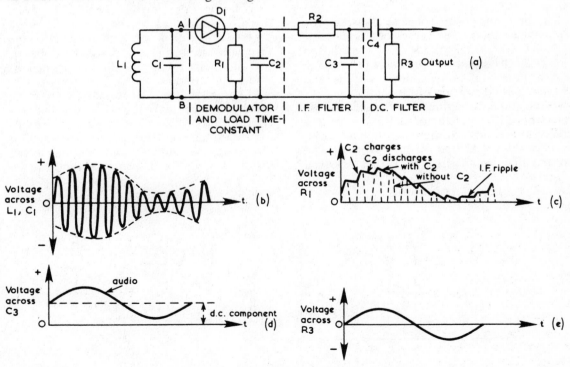

Fig. 13.12 *A.M. diode demodulator.*

Assuming that C2 is not fitted, the voltage across R1 would be as shown dotted in diagram (c) and consist of positive half-cycles only. It will thus be seen that the first operation performed on the modulated carrier is one of rectification (half-wave). To obtain maximum voltage across R1 which forms the d.c. load for D1, the value of R1 should be large compared with the forward resistance of the diode. The output of positive half-cycles contains: an i.f. component (unwanted); a d.c. component (unwanted); and the audio information (wanted). Without C2 the unwanted i.f. component would be of large amplitude and the wanted audio component of small amplitude. To improve the circuit efficiency C2 is added. The waveform across R1 is then as shown by the solid line in diagram (c). When the diode conducts on the positive half-cycles, C2 charges to the peak value of the input via the diode. During the negative half-cycles C2 discharges via R1. If the CR time of C2, R1 is long compared with the period for a half-cycle of the i.f. carrier, the voltage will fall only by a small amount during the non-conduction of the diode. It will thus be seen that C2 acts as a reservoir capacitor, charging on the positive peaks and discharging in between them. The choice of CR time for C2, R1 is important in that if it is made too long C2 will be unable to discharge fast enough when the modulation envelope is falling and would cause distortion of the audio.

Note that the addition of C2 has reduced the amount of i.f. ripple across R1 and increased the wanted audio to the peak-to-peak variation of the modulated carrier envelope. The residual i.f. ripple across R1 is then removed by a low-pass filter consisting of R2, C3. The value of C3 is chosen so that its reactance at the i.f. is small compared with R2 value but at audio frequencies its reactance is large compared with R2. This allows the unwanted i.f. to be developed across R2 but the wanted audio across C3. The voltage across C3 is then as shown in diagram (d) with the i.f. ripple removed and only the audio and a d.c. component remaining. It now remains to remove the d.c. component and this is achieved by the use of a d.c. filter C4, R3. The value of C4 is chosen so that it has a low reactance at audio frequencies compared with R3 value resulting in most of the audio appearing across R3 as is required. Since a capacitor will not pass d.c., C4 blocks the d.c. component so that the output across R3 consists of the audio component only as in diagram (e). With sinewave modulation it is not important which way round the diode is connected. If the diode connections are reversed the essential difference would be that the d.c. component would be of negative polarity (instead of positive). Since the d.c. component is blocked from the following stage its polarity is of no consequence. However, the d.c. component has an amplitude proportional to signal strength and in some receivers it is used for a.g.c. purposes. In this use the polarity of the diode connections would be important.

In practice the demodulator circuit is usually arranged as in Fig. 13.13 which shows typical component values for an a.m. transistor radio receiver. D1 is the demodulator diode with the series R1 and P1 acting as the d.c. load. C1 is the detector reservoir capaci-

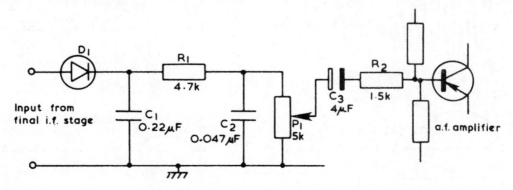

Fig. 13.13 Typical practical A.M. demodulator circuit.

tor and R1, C2 forms the i.f. filter. The d.c. component is blocked from the following stage (where it would upset the a.f. amplifier bias) by C3. The series resistor R2 'stands off' the low input resistance of the a.f. amplifying transistor from the demodulator circuit to prevent distortion of the audio signal. As well as forming part of the d.c. load for the demodulator, P1 also acts as the volume control.

QUESTIONS ON CHAPTER THIRTEEN

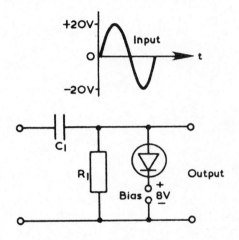

Fig. 13.14 D.C. restorer circuit.

(1) The output from the circuit of Fig. 13.14 above will be:

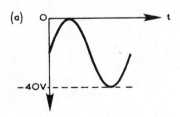

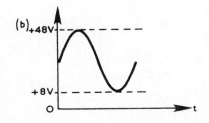

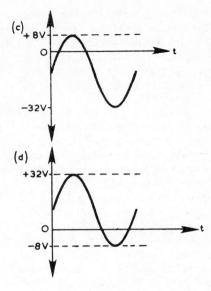

Fig. 13.15.

(2) If the diode in Fig. 13.14 above goes open circuit the effect will be:
(a) No output waveform
(b) Output almost identical to input
(c) No charge path for C1
(d) The positive peaks will be restored to 0V.

(3) To set the black level of a television waveform to a particular voltage level, which of the following would be used:
(a) A d.c. clamp
(b) A diode limiter
(c) A clipping circuit
(d) A vison demodulator.

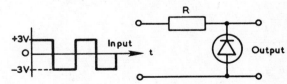

Fig. 13.16 Limiter circuit.

(4) Neglecting the d.c. voltage drop across the diode, the d.c. component present in the output of Fig. 13.16 above will be:
(a) +3V
(b) 0V
(c) −3V
(d) +1·5V.

(5) If the diode connections in Fig. 13.16 are reversed, the d.c. component present in the output will be:
(a) −1·5V
(b) −3V
(c) +1·5V
(d) +3V.

(6) A diode may be fitted across an inductor in the collector circuit of a transistor to:
(a) Stop the transistor 'bottoming'
(b) Protect the transistor from over-voltage

(c) Reduce the output capacitance
(d) Stabilise the collector current.

(7) A low-pass filter is used in an a.m. demodulator circuit to:
(a) Remove the audio signal
(b) Block the d.c. component
(c) Reduce the i.f. ripple
(d) Remove hum voltages.

(Answers on page 370)

CHAPTER FOURTEEN

VOLTAGE AMPLIFIERS

Objectives

1 To consider cascade amplifiers and the use of decibels.
2 To describe the operation and responses of a.c. and d.c. coupled voltage amplifiers, low frequency and wideband.
3 To describe the effects of using negative feedback in amplifiers and to consider circuit examples.
4 To explain the operation and responses of tuned amplifiers, r.f. and i.f.
5 To explain the use of forward and reverse gain control in receivers.

THE BASIC IDEA of a resistance loaded voltage amplifier employing bipolar and unipolar transistors was described in Chapter 5. Methods of biasing the transistor, determination of voltage gain and stabilisation of the working point were discussed. It is now necessary to consider some aspects of multi-stage amplifiers, in particular their gain, method of coupling and frequency response.

Cascade Amplifiers

If a voltage gain is required that is more than can be obtained from a single transistor amplifier, two or more stages may be connected together in cascade, i.e. the output from one stage feeding the input of the following stage. The idea is illustrated in Fig. 14.1 which shows three separate amplifier stages connected in cascade.

The overall voltage gain (A_v) of a cascade multistage amplifier is equal to the product of the individual voltage gains. For Fig. 4.1 $A_v = A_1 \times A_2 \times A_3$. If, for example, each stage has a voltage gain of 40, then for two cascaded stages $A_v = 40 \times 40 = 1600$ and for three cascaded stages $A_v = 40 \times 40 \times 40 = 64,000$. The figures given for the voltage gain of each amplifying stage should be assumed to be the voltage gain measured from the input of one stage to the input of the following stage and not the voltage gain of an isolated amplifying stage. This is important as the voltage gain of any of the individual stages may be reduced when they are connected to the following stage.

Instead of expressing the individual stage gain or overall gain of an amplifier as a pure number, as in the above example, it is frequently given in decibels. This unit which

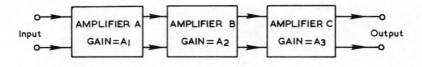

Fig. 14.1 Use of amplifiers in cascade to increase gain.

may be used to express gain or attenuation will now be considered.

Use of Decibels

Suppose that we have an amplifier as in Fig. 14.2 fed with a voltage V_i at its input. If R_{IN} is the input resistance a current I_i will flow when V_i is applied. The input power P_i is given by $V_i \times I_i$. Assume that the amplifier delivers an output voltage V_o which is applied to the load R_{LOAD} causing an output current I_o to flow. The output power P_o is given by $V_o \times I_o$.

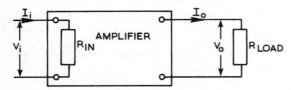

Fig. 14.2 Amplifier supplied with input power ($V_i \times I_i$) and developing output power ($V_o \times I_o$).

The power gain may be expressed as:

$$\frac{P_o}{P_i}$$

which will give a pure number. Alternatively, the power gain may be expressed as:

$$\log \frac{P_o}{P_i}$$

i.e. determine the ratio of:

$$\frac{P_o}{P_i}$$

and then find the logarithm (using tables or a pocket calculator). The unit of this ratio is called a bel; since this a rather large unit we use a decibel which is $\frac{1}{10}$ of a bel.

The power gain is then $10 \log \frac{P_o}{P_i}$ decibels (dB)

For example if $\frac{P_o}{P_i}$ is equal to 32, the power gain in decibels will be:

$$10 \log 32 \text{dB}$$
$$= 10 \times 1\cdot505\text{dB}$$
$$\approx 15\text{dB}.$$

The use of the decibel unit has a number of advantages.

(1)   A convenient number is obtained when the power ratio is large e.g. if the power ratio is 1,000,000, then in decibels it will be:

$$10 \log 1,000,000\text{dB} = 60\text{dB}.$$

(2)   If the gains of individual amplifier stages are expressed in decibels, the overall gain of a cascaded amplifier is the sum of the gains of individual stages (adding logarithms of numbers is the same as multiplying the numbers together).

An example is given in Fig. 14.3 which shows two amplifiers in cascade. If the power gain in decibels of amplifier A is +30dB and that of amplifier B is = +18dB, the overall power gain of the two amplifiers is 30 + 18dB = 48dB. Note that if the output power exceeds the input power, i.e. a true power gain, the logarithm will give a positive result (+dB). Now suppose that the power output of amplifier B is fed to some form of attenuator (for example a cable to transfer the signal power) which introduces a power loss, i.e. the power output from the attenuator is less than the power fed into it. In this case the power gain in decibels will produce a negative result (−dB). Assume that the attenuator introduces a power gain of −6dB (a loss). The overall power gain from the input of amplifier A to the output of the attenuator,

i.e. $\dfrac{P_o}{P_i}$

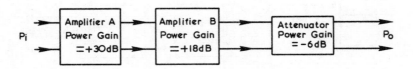

Fig. 14.3 Overall gain in decibels obtained by adding the gains of individual stages.

expressed in decibels will be $+30\text{dB} + 18\text{dB} - 6\text{dB} = 42\text{dB}$. Note that the adding is algebraic, allowing for negative signs.

(3) The human hearing sense grades loudness in a way which approximates to the decibel scale. The decibel is a convenient size as it is about the smallest change in sound intensity that the ear can detect.

Although the decibel is based on power ratios, it may be used to express voltage or current gain. If the resistance are the same at the input and the output of an amplifier, the power is proportional to:

$$V^2 \left(\text{power} = \frac{V^2}{R}\right) \text{ or to } I^2 \left(\text{power} = I^2 R\right)$$

Thus we can express voltage gain as

$$10 \log \frac{V_o^2}{V_i^2}\text{dB} = 20 \log \frac{V_o}{V_i}\text{dB}$$

and current gain as

$$10 \log \frac{I_o^2}{I_i^2} \text{ dB} = 20 \log \frac{I_o}{I_i} \text{ dB}$$

As we are more usually concerned with measuring voltage or current, these expressions are commonly used especially the one for voltage gain. A table of decibel values for power, voltage and current gain is given in Fig. 14.4. In column A we have various ratios of output/input, for ratios greater than unity (true gain) and less than unity (a loss or attenuation). Column B shows the decibel values for power ratios and column C shows the decibel values for voltage and current ratios. Note that for power ratios a change of 3dB represents a doubling or halving of the power and for voltage or current ratios a

A	B	C
Output/Input ratio	Power (dB)	Voltage & Current (dB)
$10^6 : 1$	$+60$	$+120$
$10^5 : 1$	$+50$	$+100$
$10^4 : 1$	$+40$	$+80$
$1024 : 1$	$+30$	$+60$
$512 : 1$	$+27$	$+54$
$256 : 1$	$+24$	$+48$
$128 : 1$	$+21$	$+42$
$64 : 1$	$+18$	$+36$
$32 : 1$	$+15$	$+30$
$16 : 1$	$+12$	$+24$
$8 : 1$	$+9$	$+18$
$4 : 1$	$+6$	$+12$
$2 : 1$	$+3$	$+6$
$1.414 : 1$	$+1.5$	$+3$
$1 : 1$	0	0
$1 : 1.414$	-1.5	-3
$1 : 2$	-3	-6
$1 : 4$	-6	-12
$1 : 8$	-9	-18
$1 : 16$	-12	-24
$1 : 32$	-15	-30
$1 : 64$	-18	-36
$1 : 128$	-21	-42
$1 : 256$	-24	-48
$1 : 512$	-27	-54
$1 : 1024$	-30	-60
$1 : 10^4$	-40	-80
$1 : 10^5$	-50	-100
$1 : 10^6$	-60	-120

Fig. 14.4 Table of decibel values.

change of 6dB represents a doubling or halving of voltage or current. For example, if a signal of 10mV is applied at the input of a voltage amplifier having a voltage gain of +6dB the output voltage will be 20mV; with a gain of +12dB the output voltage will be 40mV; and with a gain of +18dB the output voltage will be 80mV . . . and so on giving a doubling of the input voltage for every 6dB increase in voltage gain.

Cascade Amplifier with R–C Coupling

One method of coupling amplifier stages together in cascade is to use Resistance–Capacitance (R–C) coupling and an example is given in Fig. 14.5. Here two common emitter n-p-n transistor amplifier stages with identical component values are coupled together via R3 and C3 which form the R–C coupling. This is sometimes called capacitor coupling, since coupling is essentially via C3. The use of capacitor coupling allows the collector of one transistor to be coupled to the base of the following transistor as regards a.c. without the d.c. voltage on the collector of one stage upsetting the d.c. conditions on the base of the next stage, since a capacitor will not pass d.c. Because of the presence of C3 or any other capacitor (such as C1) in series with the signal path, the amplifier may be used only with a.c. signals.

Both stages are biased to class A using the potential divider and emitter resistor method described in Chapter 5. Silicon type transistors are assumed with base-emitter voltage drops of 0·6V. The input signal V_i is applied via C1

(which blocks any d.c. component of the signal source) to the base of TR1. C1 must have a low reactance at all signal frequencies to be passed by the amplifier. An amplified signal voltage is developed across R3 and this is applied to TR2 base via the coupling capacitor C3. The reactance of C3 must be low compared with the input resistance of TR2 input circuit which is composed of R5, R6 and TR2 base-emitter resistance all in parallel with one another. If the lowest frequency to be passed by the amplifier is, say, 160HZ and the effective input resistance of TR2 input circuit is 1·2kΩ, then the reactance of C3 should be at least 1/10 of the input resistance, i.e. 120Ω.

Now the reactance of a capacitor is given by:

$$X_c = \frac{1}{2\pi fC}$$
$$\therefore C = \frac{1}{2\pi fX_c}$$
$$C = \frac{10^6}{6·284 \times 160 \times 120}\mu F$$
$$C \approx 8 \ \mu F$$

Such a large value requires the use of an electrolytic type capacitor and due regard must be given to its polarity when connecting it into circuit (note polarity of C3). Because C3 is an effective short-circuit to signals, the input resistance of TR2 base circuit is effectively in parallel with R3 which will lower the effective load of TR1 stage and reduce its gain. Allowance must be made for this in determining the overall voltage gain required when amplifiers are coupled together.

If the lowest frequency to be amplified is,

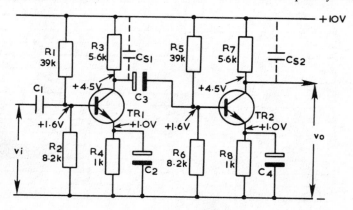

Fig. 14.5 R-C coupled transistor amplifier.

say, 100kHz then the value of C3 can be made accordingly smaller e.g. $0\cdot02\mu F$ and an electrolytic type capacitor would not be required.

The signal voltage applied to TR2 base is now amplified by TR2 stage which develops an output signal voltage across R7. This output signal voltage V_0 may be taken as shown from between TR2 collector and the negative supply line or from between TR2 collector and the positive supply line. From the signal point of view it makes no difference since positive and negative supply lines are normally at the same potential as regards a.c. The overall voltage gain of the two stages is given by the ratio of:

$$\frac{V_0}{V_i} \text{ or in decibels by } 20 \log \frac{V_0}{V_i}$$

(Strictly speaking input and output resistance should be the same. However, gain is often expressed in decibels when input and output resistance are not the same because it is convenient.)

The emitter decoupling capacitors C2 and C4 are used to prevent the gain of their respective stages being reduced by a.c. negative feedback, which will be dealt with later. For the moment it is sufficient to say that the reactance of these capacitors must be low compared with the resistors they are decoupling at the lowest signal frequency. Generally, their reactance is made about $\frac{1}{10}$ of the emitter resistors. With $1k\Omega$ emitter resistors this would indicate the use of electrolytic capacitors because of the large capacitance

required for signal frequencies below about 2kHz.

The gain-frequency response of an R–C coupled amplifier is shown in Fig. 14.6. At high frequencies the gain falls off due to the various stray capacitances present. These capacitances Cs_1 and Cs_2 are made up of a stray capacitance of the circuit and the transistor capacitance. At high frequencies these capacitance have a reactance which is low enough to appreciably shunt the collector load resistors causing a reduction of the voltage gain of the individual stages. At low frequencies the gain falls off due to the rising reactance of the coupling capacitor(s) which causes signal voltage to be dropped across them. Additionally, the rising reactance of the emitter decoupling capacitors introduces some negative feedback at low frequencies and hence some reduction in voltage gain.

The useful bandwidth of such an amplifier is the frequency-space between the frequency limits where the gain has fallen to $0\cdot707$ of its mid-band or steady reference gain level, i.e. in Fig. 14.6 the bandwidth lies from f_1 to f_2. It will be noted from columm C of Fig. 14.4 that the ratio:

$$\frac{1}{1\cdot414} \ (0\cdot707)$$

represents $-3dB$ voltage attenuation, thus at f_1 and f_2 the voltage gain will be 3dB down. Now, since power is proportional to (voltage)^2, the power will be $(0\cdot707)^2$ or $0\cdot5$ of its mid-band level; thus f_1 and f_2 are also referred to as the 'half-power' points.

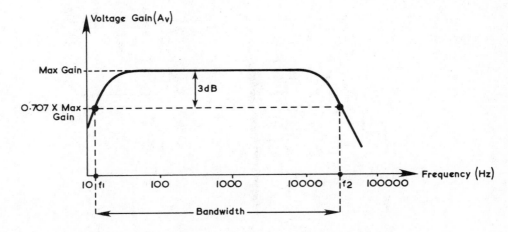

Fig. 14.6 Gain frequency response of R-C coupled amplifier.

When a comparatively wide bandwidth is required as in an audio amplifier, f_1 and f_2 may be, say, 30Hz and 16kHz respectively. If the amplifier is to be used to amplify a single frequency, e.g. a single tone test signal or the output from a transducer in electronic control equipment a much narrower bandwidth than that indicated could be tolerated.

Field effect transistors may be cascaded as for bipolar devices and use capacitor coupling between stages. However, since the voltage gain of an f.e.t. amplifier is appreciably less than a bipolar transistor amplifier, cascaded f.e.t. stages are not commonly used when high gain is required. An f.e.t. amplifier may be used with advantage as the first stage in a hybrid amplifier, see Fig. 14.7.

Noise introduced by the first stage of a multistage amplifier is particularly important because it gets amplified by subsequent stages along with the signal. Besides producing the necessary gain, an amplifier must also produce a signal-to-noise ratio that is acceptable. Now, an f.e.t. is a low noise device thus it may be advantageous to use it in the first stage of an amplifier, especially when the amplitude of the input signal is small. Apart from this, an f.e.t. has a high input resistance and thus provides less loading of the signal source which is important when the signal source is of high internal resistance, i.e. the f.e.t. will provide a better match to a high impedance source such as a ceramic pick-up. Thus the circuit of Fig. 14.7 may produce better overall results than the amplifier of Fig. 14.5.

The f.e.t. TR1 uses a potential divider R1, R2 and source resistor R5 for biasing as descibed in Chapter 5. Since R1, R2 would lower the input resistance, a stand-off resistor R3 is included which helps to decrease the effects of the potential divider on the signal source. The input signal V_i is applied via C1 to the gate of TR1 and this common source amplifier produces an amplified signal voltage across R4. From R4 the signal is coupled via C3 to the base of TR2 operating as a common emitter amplifier. After amplification the output signal voltage V_o is taken from across R9. The capacitors C1–C4 must all have a low reactance at the lowest frequency to be passed by the amplifier. As for the previous circuit only a.c. signals may be amplified.

D.C. Coupled Amplifier

If the capacitors in series with the signal path are eliminated an amplifier is then able to amplify d.c. and very low frequencies, e.g. 1 Hz or below. A basic arrangement is shown in Fig. 14.8 using two common emitter amplifiers in cascade. The coupling between TR1 and TR2 is now direct coupling or d.c. coupling. Thus the d.c. collector potential of TR1 becomes the base potential of TR2.

Assuming the same d.c. potentials on TR1 stage as in Fig. 14.5, the base of TR2 will be at +4·5V as a result of the d.c. coupling. To provide the correct base-emitter voltage drop for TR2 of, say, 0·6V the emitter resistor of TR2 may be increased (now 3·9kΩ as opposed

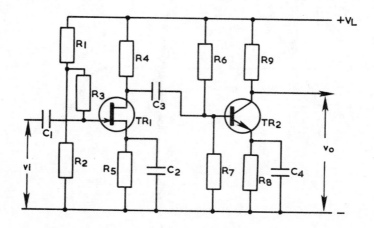

Fig. 14.7 Use of F.E.T. as first stage in R-C coupled amplifier.

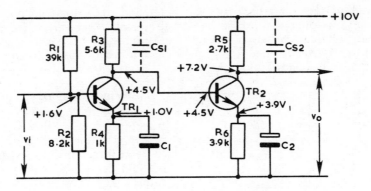

Fig. 14.8 D.C. coupled amplifier.

to 1KΩ in Fig. 14.5) to give an emitter potential of +3·9V. This will give the required base-emitter voltage drop for TR2 and will maintain the same current in it as for Fig. 14.5. To maintain the same collector-to-emitter voltage the value of TR2 collector load resistor will have to be reduced resulting in a higher collector potential for TR2 than for TR1. In a multistage amplifier, the collector potentials of successive stages will become larger and larger when this circuit arrangement is used. Also, the voltage gain of successive stages will reduce as the collector load resistor is reduced in value unless higher supply line voltage are used.

One of the problems of d.c. coupled amplifiers is d.c. drift. For example, if the collector current of TR1 changes, TR1 collector potential and hence TR2 base potential will change. This will result in a greater change in TR2 current and its collector potential, i.e.

TR2 amplifies the d.c. drift. Since the steady operating conditions of TR2 have changed it may not operate satisfactorily. In Fig. 14.8 d.c. drift is reduced by the emitter resistors R4 and R6 which introduce negative feedback since C1 and C2 are effectively open circuit to d.c. A variety of circuits have been designed to reduce d.c. drift, some employing differential amplifiers which have a low drift characteristic. These amplifiers that reduce effects of variations in temperature, supply voltage and transistor characteristics are dealt with in Chapter 16.

The d.c. coupled amplifier of Fig. 14.8 will amplify both a.c. and d.c. signals. Its gain-frequency response is shown in Fig. 14.9. The gain is now maintained down to d.c. (0Hz), but in a practical amplifier there will be some departure from level response at low frequencies and d.c. At some high frequency the gain will start to fall off due to the stray capaci-

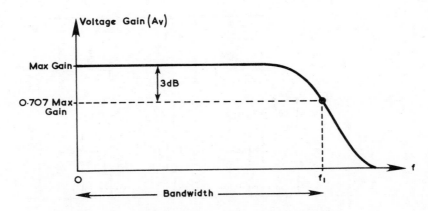

Fig. 14.9 Gain frequency response of D.C. coupled amplifier.

tances of the circuit (Cs_1 and Cs_2) whose reactance will be low enough to shunt the collector loads appreciably. The bandwidth of the amplifier is from 0 Hz to f_1 where the gain has fallen to 0·707 of its steady level.

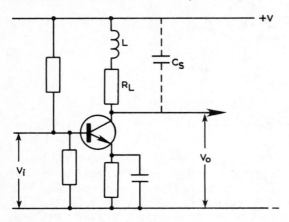

Fig. 14.10 Wide band amplifier 0Hz (D.C.) to 5·5 MHz.

To maintain the voltage gain up to a high frequency so that f_1 corresponds to, say, 5·5 MHz as in a t.v. video amplifier or 10 MHz for an oscillosope or pulse amplifier, special circuit techniques are used to reduce the effect of stray capacitance. One idea is to use a peaking coil in series with the collector load resistor as in Fig. 14.10. The load resistance R_L is kept as small as is pratical and at low and medium frequencies it is the effective load as the reactance of the peaking coil L is small. As the frequency is raised, the rising reactance of L increases the effective load impedance which compensates for the falling reactance of

Cs and maintains the gain up to a higher frequency. This arrangement is known as a shunt peaking coil circuit as the inductance is in shunt with the stray capacitance.

Transformer Coupled Amplifier

Another method of coupling is to use a transformer as in Fig. 14.11. Bias for TR1 is provided by the potential divider R1, R2; R3 is the emitter stabilising resistor. The collector of TR1 feeds the primary winding of the transformer T1, the secondary of which couples the signal to the base of TR2. Bias for TR2 is provided by R4, R5 and is supplied to the base via the secondary winding. C3 by-passes R5 as regards a.c. since without C3 the secondary current would have to flow in R5 and produce a signal voltage drop across it which would cause a loss.

As a transformer will not pass d.c. the amplifier can only be used to amplify a.c. signals. The secondary of the transformer feeds the input resistance of TR2 which will call R_i. Now the effective resistance seen at the primary is equal to $n^2 R_i$ (where n is the turns ratio) and this forms the collector load for TR1 stage. The transformer normally uses a step-down ratio (primary-to-secondary) when the input resistance of TR2 stage is low as this gives increased voltage gain for TR1 stage. Usually, the step-down ratio is limited from about 3:1 to 4:1.

The gain-frequency response for a transformer coupled stage is given in Fig. 14.12. At low frequencies the gain drops due to the falling reactance of the transformer primary

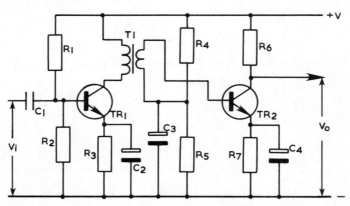

Fig. 14.11 Transformer coupled amplifier.

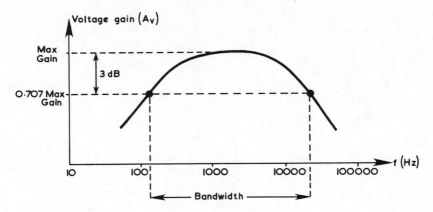

Fig. 14.12 Gain frequency response of transformer coupled amplifier.

winding which reduces the load of TR1 stage. At high frequenies the fall in gain is caused by the stray circuit capacitances as for the previous circuits. Unless the circuit is well designed, the response is inferior to that obtained with capacitor coupling and there may be unwanted peaks at high frequencies due to resonant effects between the transformer inductance and secondary load capacitance. Transformer coupling is not common in small signal voltage amplifiers but is used in power amplifiers.

Supply Line Decoupling

Consider the arrangement of cascaded amplifiers in Fig. 14.13 where i_1, i_2 and i_3 represent the signal components flowing in the output of the amplifiers. These signal currents all flow in the internal resistance R of the d.c. supply. The internal resistance of the supply whether it be a battery or a main unit is finite,

thus there will be an unwanted voltage drop V_s across it of magnitude $R(i_1 + i_2 + i_3)$.

This unwanted or spurious voltage is fed along the supply rail to all three stages together with the d.c. supply. Now the spurious voltage may find its way to the input of any of the three amplifiers. If it arrives back in-phase with the signal voltage already present then it will cause regeneration or oscillation, but if in antiphase it will cause degeneration (loss of gain). In amplifiers, the most important effect to be avoided is regeneration because if an oscillation builds up the amplifier will continue to give an output signal with no input signal.

Two measures that can be taken to reduce the amount of spurious voltage fed back along the supply rail are: (a) reduce the internal resistance of the supply to signal currents; and (b) introduce a decoupling network. Both are incorporated in Fig. 14.14.

The internal resistance of the supply to the

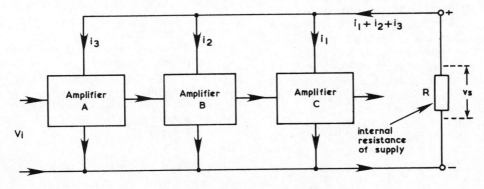

Fig. 14.13 Need for decoupling.

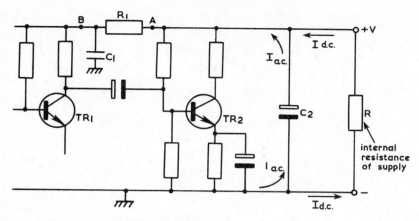

Fig. 14.14 Decoupling network in supply line.

signal currents may be reduced by placing a large value capacitor (C2) across the supply. If the reactance of C2 at low frequencies is much smaller than the internal resistance, the a.c. currents I_{ac} will be by-passed from the supply and produce little spurious voltage across it. This method is commonly used with battery-operated equipment since the internal resistance of a battery rises as it discharges. The value of C2 is of the order of 2000–3000μF. With a mains power supply C2 is formed by the final smoothing capacitor.

There is a limit to the effectiveness of C2 since doubling its value will only halve its reactance and the spurious voltage. A more effective method is to introduce a decoupling network such as R1, C1 into the line supply feed, an arrangement used with all amplifiers. If the reactance of the shunt C1 at low frequencies is made small compared with the series R1, then most of the spurious voltage appearing at A will be dropped across R1 and very little will appear across C1, i.e. at B. Thus the amount of spurious voltage fed back along the line is reduced. The larger the value of R1 the better, but its value is often restricted especially in low voltage supplies due to the voltage drop across it produced by the steady current of TR1 and any earlier stages. In an audio amplifier R1 may be 100–200Ω and C1 about 100–200μF. The same arrangement is used in r.f. amplifiers but C1 can be made smaller, say, 0·001μF to 0·1μF depending upon the operating frequencies.

Negative Feedback

Controlled feedback is used extensively in modern amplifier circuits by feeding back a fraction of the output signal to the input. If the fraction fed back is in antiphase with the input signal it is called negative feedback (n.f.b.). Whenever n.f.b. is applied in an amplifier, the gain is reduced. There would, however, be little point in reducing the gain of an amplifier if there were not benefits to be gained from the use of n.f.b. The main benefits are:

(1) The stability of the amplifier is improved, i.e. its gain remains more stable in spite of variations in the value of both active and passive circuit components with time and temperature or after component replacement and d.c. supply variations. This is important particularly with amplifiers where the gain must remain stable over long periods, e.g. in test instruments.

(2) Distortion or noise introduced by the amplifier is reduced.

(3) The frequency response of the amplifier may be improved.

(4) Input and output resistance of the amplifier may be altered to provide better matching.

There are different methods used for deriving the feedback signal and applying it to the input which will now be considered.

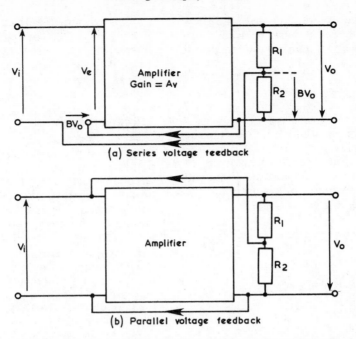

Fig. 14.15 *Voltage feedback (feedback voltage proportional to output voltage).*

Series and Parallel Voltage Feedback

With series and parallel voltage feedback, the fraction of the signal fed back in antiphase is proportional to the output voltage of the amplifier. The idea of series voltage feedback is shown in Fig. 14.15(a).

Effect on Gain

A fraction B of the output voltage, decided by the values of R1 and R2 connected across the output voltage V_o is fed back to the input and applied in series with the input signal V_i. The actual signal input to the amplifier is the difference between V_i and the feedback signal (since they are in series opposition) which we call V_e. Suppose that the gain of the amplifier without feedback is A_v and the fraction fed back in antiphase is BV_o.

Now, with feedback $V_e = V_i - BV_o$
and $V_o = A_v V_e$
$$\therefore V_o = A_v(V_i - BV_o)$$
or $A_v V_i = V_o + A_v BV_o$
or $A_v V_i = V_o(1 + A_v B)$

or $$\frac{V_o}{V_i} = \frac{A_v}{1 + A_v B}$$

but $\frac{V_o}{V_i}$ is the gain with feedback (A_v')

$$\therefore A_v' = \frac{A_v}{1 + A_v B}$$

Although the proof of the expression for gain has been shown, it is the general result that is probably more important. Consider the following example.

The voltage gain of an amplifier without feedback is 500. What will be its gain if n.f.b. is used when the fraction fed back is $\frac{1}{100}$?

Now $A_v' = \dfrac{A_v}{1 + A_v B}$

$= \dfrac{500}{1 + (500 \times \frac{1}{100})}$

$= \dfrac{500}{6}$

$\approx 83.$

Effect on Distortion

If an amplifier without feedback introduces a percentage distortion D, then when n.f.b. is applied the distortion is reduced by the factor

$1 + A_vB$. The expression for the new distortion D' with feedback can be derived in a similar way to given for gain but only the result will be given:

$$D' = \frac{D}{1 + A_vB}$$

Consider the application of the result to the following example.

An amplifier without feedback has a gain of 200 and introduces 10% distortion. What will be the distortion when n.b.f. is used and the fraction fed back is $\frac{1}{100}$?

$$\text{Now } D' = \frac{D}{1 + A_vB}$$

$$= \frac{0 \cdot 1}{1 + (200 \times \frac{1}{100})}$$

$$= \frac{0.1}{3}$$

$$= 0.033$$

$$= 3.3\%$$

Effect on Noise

Noise introduced by the amplifier is treated in the same way as distortion and is reduced by the factor $1 + A_vB$.

Effect on Frequency Response

Suppose that without feedback the voltage gain of an R–C coupled amplifier at a frequency f_1 is 100 and that at a higher frequency f_2 the gain has fallen to 80 (due to the effect of stray circuit capacitance). If n.f.b. is used and the fraction fed back is, say, $\frac{1}{100}$ the new gains will be:

At f_1

$$A_v' = \frac{100}{1 + (100 \times \frac{1}{10})}$$

$$\approx 9$$

and at f_2

$$A_v' = \frac{80}{1 + 80 \times \frac{1}{10}}$$

$$\approx 8 \cdot 9$$

Thus without feedback the gain reduction from f_1 to f_2 is 20% of that at f_1, but with n.f.b. it is only $1 \cdot 1$.% of that at f_1, i.e. the frequency response has been improved (flatter response). This of course is at the expense of a reduction in gain.

Effect on Stability

In dealing with the effect on frequency response, it was assumed that the gain of the amplifier reduced due to the effect of stray circuit capacitance. The same results are obtained whatever the cause of change in amplifier gain, e.g. if a transistor is replaced by another of the same type but with a different h_{fe}, or the supply line voltage varies. Consider the following example:

The voltage gain of an amplifier without feedback is 100 and on replacing a transistor it increases to 110 (10% increase). What will be the percentage increase if n.f.b. is used and the fraction fed back is $\frac{1}{5}$?

Gain before replacing transistor

$$= \frac{100}{1 + (100 \times \frac{1}{5})}$$

$$= 4 \cdot 76$$

Gain after replacing transistor

$$= \frac{110}{1 + (110 \times \frac{1}{5})}$$

$$= 4 \cdot 78$$

$$\% \text{ increase} = \frac{0 \cdot 02}{4 \cdot 76} \times 100$$

$$= 0 \cdot 42\%$$

Thus the stability of the amplifier has been greatly inproved.

Effect on Input and Output Resistance

With series voltage feedback, the input resistance R_i can be shown to be increased to $R_i (1 + A_v B)$ and the output resistance R_o decreased to:

$$\frac{R_o}{1 + A_vB}$$

An alternative method of applying the feedback signal to the input is shown in

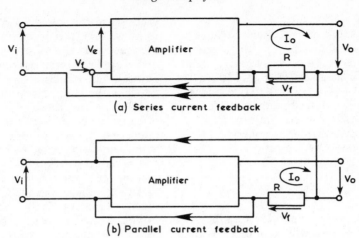

(a) Series current feedback

(b) Parallel current feedback

Fig. 14.16 Current feedback (feedback voltage proportional to output current).

Fig. 14.15(b). A fraction of the output signal voltage appearing across R2 is fed back to the input and applied in parallel with the input signal. This method of applying the feedback signal which is proportional to the output voltage, reduces the gain and distortion and improves the frequency response and stability of the amplifier as for series voltage feedback. However, it decreases both the input and output resistance of the amplifier.

Series and Parallel Current Feedback

With, so-called, current feedback a voltage is fed back to the input in antiphase with the input signal, but in this method the feedback voltage is proportional to the output current.

The feedback signal may be applied in series with the input as in Fig. 14.16(a) or in parallel with it as in diagram (b). To develop the feedback voltage V_f, a resistor R is used through which the output current I_o of the amplifier is passed.

As far as gain, noise and distortion are concerned, current feedback has the same effects as for voltage feedback; also, the frequency response is improved if the amplifier load is resistive. For series current feedback both input and output resistance are increased whereas for parallel current feedback the input resistance is reduced and the output resistance increased. The details of the four methods of deriving and applying n.f.b. are summarised in the table below.

			Effect of n.f.b. on			
Method	Voltage Gain	Stability	Distortion	Frequency response	Input resistance	Output resistance
Series Voltage	Reduced	Improved	Reduced	Improved	Increased	Reduced
Parallel Voltage	Reduced	Improved	Reduced	Improved	Reduced	Reduced
Series Current	Reduced	Improved	Reduced	Improved	Increased	Increased
Parallel Current	Reduced	Improved	Reduced	Improved	Reduced	Increased

N.F.B. Circuits

Ideas of how the basic feedback arrangements may be translated into n.f.b. circuits will now be given. An example of series voltage feedback is given in Fig. 14.17(a). This shows n.f.b. applied overall to two stages of amplification. The output voltage of TR2 is fed via R1 to across R2 in the emitter of TR1. The fraction of output voltage applied to TR1 emitter is determined by the ratio:

$$\frac{R_2}{R_1 + R_2}$$

Now, with two common emitter amplifiers, the output of the second will be in phase with the input to the first (shown by the arrow heads pointing in the same direction). However, as regards TR1 the input voltage V_i and the feedback voltage V_f are in antiphase, since one is applied to the base and the other to the emitter. The effective input signal V_e applied between the base and emitter of TR1 is equal to $V_i - V_f$ and is therefore less than the signal V_i applied to the input terminals. Thus the effect of n.f.b. is to reduce the input signal and hence the output signal which means that the gain is reduced. There is also some local series current feedback on TR1 stage (see later).

An example of parallel voltage feedback is shown in Fig. 14.17(b) where the feedback is from collector to base. The output voltage, which is in antiphase with the input over one stage of common-emitter amplification, is fed

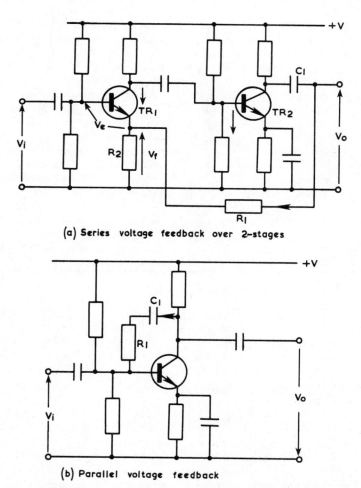

(a) Series voltage feedback over 2-stages

(b) Parallel voltage feedback

Fig. 14.17 Circuits with voltage negative feedback applied.

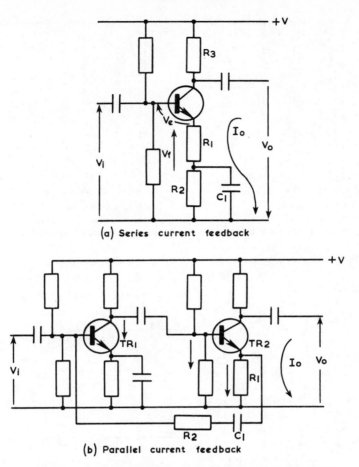

(a) **Series current feedback**

(b) **Parallel current feedback**

Fig. 14.18 Circuits with current negative feedback applied.

back to the input over one stage of common-emitter amplification, is fed back to the input via C1 and R1. The capacitor C1 blocks the d.c. and will be assumed to have zero reactance at all frequencies. Since the d.c. is blocked only a.c. feedback is considered, as also in diagram (a). The amount of feedback is determined by the value of R1 and the resistance of the input circuit.

The most common way of achieving series current feedback is shown in Fig. 14.18(a). Here an undecoupled resistor R1 is placed in the emitter circuit of the transistor. This resistor will carry the output current I_o and thus there will be a signal voltage across it that is proportional to the output signal current. This voltage V_f is the feedback voltage and it will act in opposition to the input signal V_i. Thus the effective signal V_e applied between

base and emitter is reduced since it is equal to $V_i - V_f$. Thus the voltage gain of the amplifier is reduced. The amount of feedback is settled by the ratio of R_1/R_3. The resistor R2 does not produce any n.f.b. to a.c. since it is decoupled by C1. If C1 were omitted the n.f.b. would be increased and the gain reduced to a greater degree. The presence of R1 will effect the steady d.c. at the emitter.

An arrangement for parallel current feedback is given in Fig. 14.18(b). This shows overall feedback applied over two stages of amplification. The voltage to be fed back is developed across the emitter resistor R1 of TR2 which carries the output current I_o. The signal voltage across R1 will be in antiphase with the input signal voltage V_i since it is of the same phase as TR2 base and TR1 collector. After passing through C1 (assumed to be of

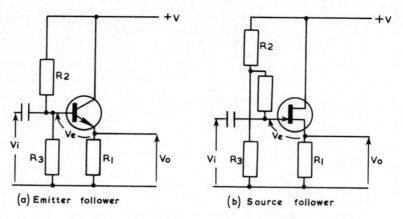

Fig. 14.19 *Emitter and source follower circuits (series voltage feedback).*

zero reactance at all frequencies) which blocks the d.c. and R2 the feedback signal is applied in parallel with the input circuit of TR1. The degree of feedback is determined by the values of R2 and the input resistance of TR1.

One of the circuit configurations of the ordinary transistor and the f.e.t. which relies on n.f.b. for its special characteristics is the emitter follower or source follower (also known as common collector and common drain), see Fig. 14.19. These circuits employ 100% series voltage feedback, since the full output voltage V_o across the emitter or source resistor acts in phase opposition to the input voltage V_i and reduces the effective input voltage V_e to a very small value. This results in (a) a voltage gain less than unity; (b) a high input resistance; and (c) a low output resistance. These features allow the circuits to be used to good advantage in matching a high resistance source to a low resistance load, i.e. to act as a buffer stage.

In practice the high input resistance of the emitter follower circuit may be limited due to the presence of the biasing resistors R2 and R3. When a very high input resistance is required, the circuit may be altered to that shown in Fig. 14.20 with components R4 and C1 added. If the reactance of C1 is considered to be zero at all frequencies, the signal voltage at point B will be the same as the emitter-signal voltage. The signal voltage at point A is the input voltage which is applied between base and the negative supply line. Since the base and emitter signal voltages are approximately the same, the signal voltage across R4

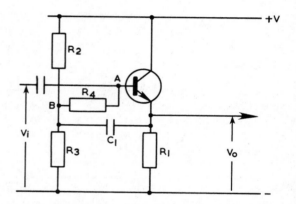

Fig. 14.20 *A Bootstrapped emitter follower.*

will be very small, i.e. the signal current in R4 will be very small. Thus the effect is that the input signal 'hardly sees' the potential divider R1, R2 or its resistance to the input signal is increased due to the presence of R4 and C1.

Frequency Selective n.f.b.

In some applications it is required to make the gain of an amplifier increase or decrease over a particular section of its frequency band. This can be achieved by including in the feedback network reactive elements, i.e. capacitors or inductors.

For example, suppose it is desired to increase the voltage gain at low frequencies to make up for a deficiency at l.f. in another part of an electronic system. Fig. 14.21(a) shows a possible circuit arrangement for obtaining the

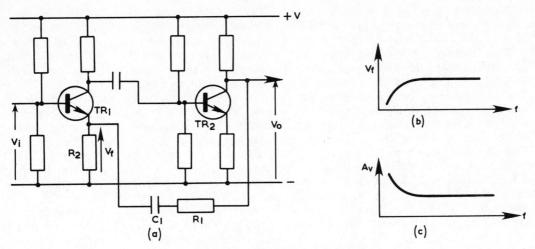

Fig. 14.21 Frequency selective N.F.B.

desired effect using series voltage feedback. The amount of feedback is settled by the values of R1, C1 and R2. If a value for C1 is chosen so that it produces a rising reactance towards low frequencies the amount of feedback voltage V_f developed across R2 will rise as in diagram (b). The voltage gain Av of the amplifier is the inverse of the curve for V_f and is shown in diagram (c). Thus the gain will rise at low frequencies producing the desired l.f. boost. By using other suitable resistance-capacitance feedback networks, low frequency cut, high frequency boost or high frequency cut can be achieved.

D.C. Feedback

When overall n.f.b. is used with a d.c. coupled amplifier such as that shown in Fig. 14.22, the feedback can be made to assist in stabilising the d.c. operating conditions of the amplifier as well as operating on the signal input.

As there is no d.c. blocking capacitor between the collector of TR2 and the emitter of TR1, d.c. variations at TR2 collector are fed back to TR1 emitter. There is a d.c. feedback loop formed (shown dotted) which will assist in correcting d.c. changes within the loop. Suppose, for example, that TR2 collector

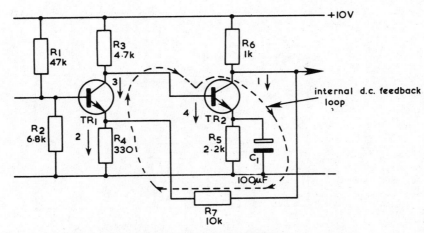

Fig. 14.22 Amplifier with A.C. and D.C. feedback.

current increases as a result of a rise in the ambient temperature causing a fall in TR2 collector voltage (indicated by the arrow marked 1). A fraction of this fall in voltage is applied to TR1 emitter (indicated by the arrow 2). Now, a fall in emitter voltage will result in TR1 collector current increasing and its collector voltage falling (indicated by arrow 3). The fall of TR1 collector voltage is applied to TR2 base (indicated by arrow 4). This will cause TR2 collector current to fall and for its collector voltage to rise which will oppose the original fall. Thus the d.c. feedback will help to stabilise the d.c. operating conditions. Other examples of d.c. feedback will be considered in Chapter 15 on power amplifiers.

I.C. Amplifier

Linear amplifiers, using similar principles to the discrete transistor circuits already described, are available in integrated circuits form and are in common use. Such i.c.s. can be designed to cover a wide range of frequencies and applications and are normally based on bipolar transistor technology. Because of the difficulty of fabricating large value capacitors in i.c. form, capacitor coupling is dispensed with to give way to direct coupling between stages within the i.c. Thus any large value coupling or decoupling capacitors that may be required have to be fitted externally to the i.c. as are any large value resistors that may be needed.

A linear i.c. amplifier will often include a mixture of common emitter, emitter follower and differential amplifier stages. Some n.f.b. is incorporated in most linear i.c.s. to provide stability of gain and d.c. stabilisation and provision is often made for additional feedback to be applied externally.

A typical form for an integrated circuit amplifier is shown in Fig. 14.23, where a combination of discrete circuits components and an integrated circuit is used. The capacitor C1 couples the input signal to the i.c. on pin 2 and the capacitor is used to block the d.c. component to and from the i.c. Capacitor C5 serves a similar purpose for coupling the output signal from pin 4. The external d.c. supply is fed to pins 1 and 7 and this provides the basic d.c. supply to the various amplifier stages within the i.c. Resistors R1 and R3 are emitter resistor which are suitably decoupled by C2 and C3. Resistors R5 and R2 are bias resistors which do not require decoupling. Resistor R4 may serve as a collector load resistor for one of the amplifiers stages. R6 and C4 provide a line decoupling network to prevent instability in the i.c. The values of the coupling and decoupling capacitors will depend upon the frequencies of the signals to be amplified; e.g. for an audio amplifier these capacitors will be in the range of, say, $1\mu F$ to $50\mu F$.

Tuned Amplifiers

A tuned amplifier is used where it is desirable to amplify a relatively narrow band

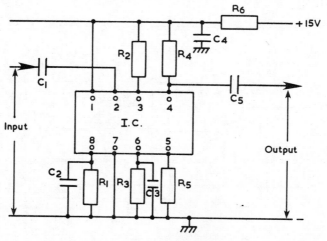

Fig. 14.23 Integrated circuit amplifier.

of frequencies to the exclusion of all other frequencies. Thus a tuned amplifier has to provide gain and selectivity. The gain may be provided by a discrete transistor stage or i.c. and the selectivity by a tuned circuit or ceramic filter.

A basic tuned amplifier stage is given in Fig. 14.24(a) using a bipolar transistor. The collector load of the amplifier is a parallel resonant circuit L1, C1 which is tuned to the centre of the band of frequencies to be amplified. Forward biasing of the transistor to class-A operation is provided by R1, R2 with R3 serving as the emitter stabilising resistor. Capacitor C3 decouples R3 to prevent n.f.b.

At the resonant frequency (f_r) the impedance of a parallel tuned circuit is high and purely resistive. The impedance at resonance is sometimes called the dynamic impedance R_D and is equal to:

$$\frac{L}{Cr}$$ where r is the tuned circuit losses.

The voltage gain of a common emitter amplifier is given by the expression:

$$Av = \frac{h_{fe} \times R_L}{R_{IN}}$$

With a tuned amplifier, the load at resonance is the dynamic impedance R_D, thus the expression for voltage gain is:

$$Av = \frac{h_{fe} \times R_D}{R_{IN}}$$

At the resonant frequency R_D is high and the voltage gain can be quite large. Away from resonance the impedance of the tuned circuit falls and thus the gain of the amplifier falls. The response of the amplifier therefore takes the form shown in Fig. 14.24(b). The bandwidth of a tuned amplifier is taken to be between the frequency limits where the gain has fallen to 0·707 of its maximum value, i.e. 3dB down from maximum gain. When the circuit losses are small, the resonant frequency is given by

$$f_r = \frac{1}{2\pi\sqrt{L.C}}$$

(f in Hz, L in henries and C in farads).

Tuning

Some tuned amplifiers use fixed tuning i.e. the frequency of operation is set by the

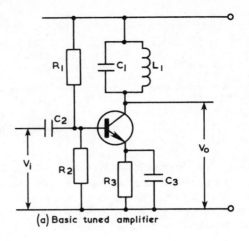

(a) Basic tuned amplifier

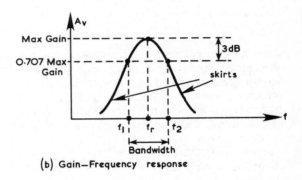

(b) Gain—Frequency response

Fig. 14.24 Tuned voltage amplifier.

manufacturer or during servicing, but in normal use the frequency is not varied. This type is found in i.f. amplifiers in receivers and in other signal applications. On the other hand, r.f. amplifiers in receivers use variable tuning so that the receiver may be set to receive a transmission on a different operating frequency.

With variable tuning, the resonant frequency may be altered by using a variable tuning capacitor or by using a variable inductor (one with an adjustable ferrite core). Alternatively, a vari-cap diode may be included in the tuning circuit so that it forms part of the circuit capacitance. Tuning is then altered by applying a variable d.c. to vary the reverse bias of the diode and hence its capacitance. These tuning methods are illustrated in Fig. 14.25.

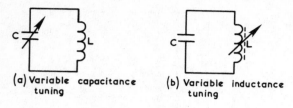

Fig. 14.25 Tuning methods.

Obtaining the Required Bandwidth

If the band of frequencies to be amplified is small, we require a tuning circuit of high selectivity or high Q factor. A high Q factor may be ensured by making the ratio

$$\frac{\text{inductive reactance of tuning coil}}{\text{tuned circuit losses}}$$

$$= \frac{2\pi fL}{r}$$

large and providing a narrow bandwidth. On the other hand if a comparatively wide bandwidth is required a tuned circuit of low Q could be used. However, a low Q tuned circuit has skirts that are not very steep and the selectivity may be inadequate. Thus to obtain

a wide bandpass with good selectivity alternative methods are used.

One method is to use a tuned circuit of high Q and to damp it with a resistor R as shown in Fig. 14.26(a). The effect of damping is shown in diagram (b). As the resistance of R is decreased, the damping is increased providing an increase in the 3dB bandwidth. The presence of R in the collector circuit of the transistor reduces the value of the effective load, so the voltage gain is less. If the gain is insufficient, further stages of amplification will be necessary.

Better selectivity can be obtained by using double tuned circuits as shown in Fig. 14.27(a). Here the two tuned circuits L1, C1 and L2, C2 of the same Q and made

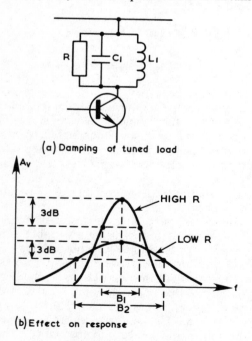

Fig. 14.26 Effect of damping.

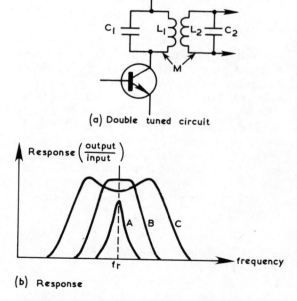

Fig. 14.27 Use of bandpass coupled tuned circuits.

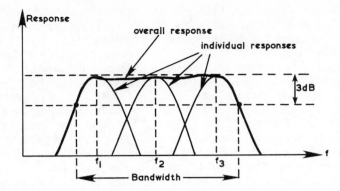

Fig. 14.28 *Idea of stagger tuning to increase bandwidth.*

resonant to the same frequency are coupled together via mutual inductance M. The actual response obtained will depend upon the degree of coupling between the two tuned circuits, see diagram (b). With weak coupling the response at A is obtained and is similar to that of a single tuned circuit. If the coupling is increased to what is termed critical coupling the flat-topped response at B is obtained. This has a bandwidth which is increased by 1·414 over that of a single tuned circuit of the same Q. Because of the flat-topped response and steep skirts of critical coupling it is the response that is often aimed for in tuned amplifier applications. If the coupling is increased still further, the response at C is obtained which has two peaks. This type of circuit is often called a bandpass circuit; when critical coupling is used it amplifies a band of frequencies by the same amount. The bandwidth of the double tuned circuit may be increased further by connecting damping resistors across it.

When a very wide bandwidth is required, a technique known as stagger tuning may be employed. This is used when a number of tuned amplifier stages are cascaded and the tuned circuit(s) of each stage are tuned to different frequencies within the band of frequencies to be amplified. The idea of this technique, illustrated in Fig. 14.28, results in an overall wide bandwidth with good selectivity.

Some examples of practical tuned amplifier circuits will now be considered under two sections: variable tuned amplifiers and fixed tuned amplifiers.

Variable Tuned Amplifiers

A variable tuned amplifier is the type used in the r.f. stages of a receiver. One example is given in Fig. 14.29 which would be suitable for a receiver operating around 100 MHZ such as a broadcast f.m. receiver. The circuit is based

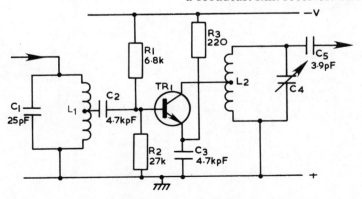

Fig. 14.29 *R.F. amplifier (100MHz) using common emitter circuit.*

on a common emitter amplifier TR1 with tuned circuits connected at input and output.

The signal to be amplified is developed across the input tuned circuit L1, C1. This is a fixed tuned circuit having a bandwidth which embraces the full frequency range of the receiver. From the input tuned circuit the signal is coupled via C2 to the base of TR1. This capacitor acts as a d.c. block. Resistors R1 and R2 provide forward bias to class-A and R3 is the emitter stabilising resistor. At first it may appear that the resistors R1 and R2 have been inadvertently interchanged, but this is in order as the circuit is using an upside down supply. Capacitor C3 decouples R3 to a.c. to prevent n.f.b. (note that as far as a.c. is concerned the negative and positive supply rails are at the same potential).

The load for the transistor is the parallel tuned circuit L2, C4 with variable tuning provided by C4. The 'upside down' supply arrangement allows one side of the variable tuning capacitor C4 to be connected to the neutral chassis line. The output from the stage is fed via a small value capacitor C5 to the next stage (normally the mixer). To prevent the input and output resistances of TR1 damping the tuned circuits unduly, the input to TR1 is obtained from a tap on L1 and the output from TR1 is fed to a tap on L2. The input and output resitances of TR1 are present between the taps on the inductors and the chassis line. Therefore, due to auto-transformer action, they will appear as larger resistances across the full tuned circuits.

More usually the r.f. stage of a receiver operating at high frequencies uses the common base configuration. A common base circuit gives a better frequency response than a common emitter circuit for a given transistor but has the disadvantage of a lower input resistance, Fig. 14.30.

Signals to be amplified are coupled to the input tuned circuit via a coupling winding L1. The input tuned circuit is formed by L2 and C1 (the circuit being completed via C2 which has a low reactance at signal frequencies). As the input resistance of TR1 is very low (tens of ohms) there is little point in making the tuning of the input circuit variable, so fixed tuning is used. The selectivity of the input circuit is therefore limited because of the heavy damping.

Base bias is provided by the potential divider R2, R3 and C3 decouples the base to the chassis line, i.e. the base is at neutral potential as regards a.c. (common base). Again an upside down supply is used which allows one side of C4 to be connected to the chassis line. Resistor R1 is the emitter d.c. stabilising resistor which is decoupled by the series combination of C2 and C3.

The collector load for TR1 is the parallel tuned circuit L3, C4 with variable tuning provided by C4. The output from the circuit is fed via the small value capacitor C5.

An f.e.t. may be used as an r.f. amplifier where its special features of low noise, higher input resistance and good signal handling are advantageous. A circuit illustrating modern practice is given in Fig. 14.31.

TR1 is a depletion mode mosfet, bias to

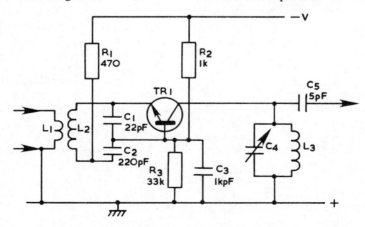

Fig. 14.30 R.F. amplifier (100MHz) using common base circuit.

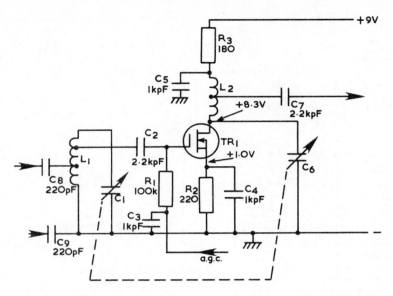

Fig. 14.31 R.F. amplifier (100MHz) using F.E.T. in common source circuit.

class-A being provided by the source resistor R2 which is decoupled by C4 to prevent n.f.b. Additionally, the bias is augmented by an a.g.c. voltage applied via R1 to the gate electrode to deal with variations in signal strength. Capacitor C3 decouples the a.g.c. line to prevent instability.

Signals to be amplified are applied via C8 and C9 to the input tuned circuit comprising L1 and C1. Variable tuning of the input circuit is provided by C1 which improves the overall selectivity of the stages. Signals from the tuned circuit are coupled to the gate of TR1 by C2 which serves as a d.c. block for the a.g.c. voltage. The gate tap on L1 allows correct matching between the input impedance of TR1 and the input circuit, thereby maintaining adequate Q and selectivity (note that the f.e.t. input impedance is only several kilohms at 100 MHZ due to its input capacitance). The drain load for TR1 is the parallel tuned circuit L2, C6 with C6 providing variable tuning. Note that for a.c. C6 is effectively in parallel with L2 since the upper end of L2 is connected to the chassis line via C5. This capacitor together with R3 forms a supply line decoupling filter. Note also the smaller values of the decoupling capacitors C3, C4 and C5 at these higher frequencies. The output signal is coupled to the following stage via C7 from a tap on L2 to

prevent undue damping of the output tuned circuit. Capacitors C1 and C6 are ganged for ease of tuning.

With a common-source or common-emitter circuit there is some capacitance between the output and input electrodes of the transistor. Although this capacitance is small (a few picofarads) it will allow feedback to occur at high frequencies which may cause the circuit to oscillate. When a common gate or common base circuit is used the capacitance between the output and input electrodes of the transistor is considerably reduced which lessons the risk of oscillation. However, with common gate or common base circuits the lower input resistance causes damping of the input tuned circuit. If the low feedback capacitance of the common gate or common base circuit could be combined with the higher input resistance of the common-source or common-emitter circuit a higher gain may be obtained without the risk of oscillation and better matching to the input tuned circuit would be achieved. This is the idea behind the cascode r.f. amplifier which uses two transistors in a combination of common emitter and common base or common source and common gate.

A cascode r.f. amplifier using f.e.ts. is given in Fig. 14.32. TR1 and TR2 form the cascode

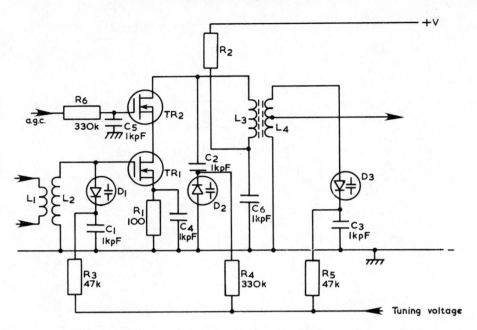

Fig. 14.32 Cascode R.F. amplifier (100MHz) using F.E.Ts. and electronic tuning.

stage with TR1 connected in common source and TR2 in common gate. As far as d.c. is concerned the two transistors are connected in series across the d.c. supply with the drain current of TR1 being the source current for TR2.

Electronic tuning is used in this circuit with three variable tuned circuits formed by L2, D1; L3, D2; and L4, D3. The vari-cap diodes D1-D3 are all fed from a common tuning line voltage via decoupling networks R3, C1 and R5, C3.

The signal to be amplified is fed to the input tuned circuit L2, D1 via a coupling winding L1. From the tuned circuit the signal is applied to the gate of TR1. Bias to class-A is provided by the source resistor R1 which is suitably decoupled by C4 to prevent n.f.b. Since the damping produced by the common source circuit is small the input circuit will have good selectivity. TR1 drives the upper transistor TR2 with the low input impedance of TR2 acting as the load for TR1, thus the gain of TR1 stage is small. Most of the voltage gain is produced by the common gate stage TR2. Capacitor C5 places TR2 in common gate by connecting the gate to chassis for signals. TR2 gate electrode could be fed from a potential

divider so that the transistor is biased correctly but in this circuit an a.g.c. voltage of positive polarity is fed to the gate to deal with varying signal strengths.

TR2 load is formed by the parallel tuned circuit L3, D2 which together with L4, D3 form a bandpass coupled circuit thus improving selectivity. The d.c. supply is fed to the drain of TR2 via the decoupling filter R2, C6 and L3. Capacitors C1, C2 and C3 act as d.c. blocking capacitors for the tuning voltage. These capacitors have a low reactance to signal frequencies and complete the a.c. circuit in their respective tuning circuits.

Fixed Tuned Amplifiers

Fixed tuned amplifiers are used in receivers for i.f. amplification. These amplifiers provide most of the receiver gain which necessitates the provision of two or more stages of i.f. amplification. One example is given in Fig. 14.33 which illustrates the method of coupling between cascaded i.f. stages.

The i.f. signal to be amplified is applied from a coupling winding L1 to the base of TR1 operating in common emitter and using a p-n-p transistor. Correct bias is provided by

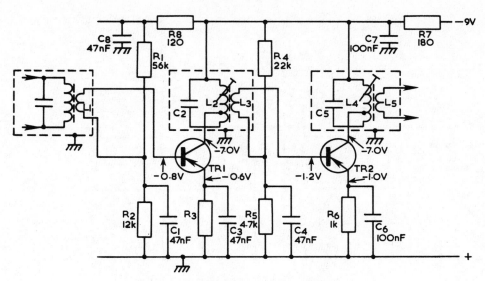

Fig. 14.33 Cascaded I.F. stages (470KHz).

R1, R2 with R3 acting as the emitter d.c. stabilising resistor and suitably decoupled by C3. Capacitor C1 by-passes R2 at i.f. to prevent loss of signal across it. The collector load for TR1 is formed by the parallel tuned circuit L2, C2 which is tuned to the i.f. of the receiver (470 kHZ in an a.m. radio receiver). TR1 collector is fed to a tap on L2 to prevent the output resistance of TR1 excessively damping the tuned circuit to maintain the selectivity.

Coupling to the base of TR2 is via a winding L3 which provides a step-down transformer action with L2. This is necessary to match to the following stage and thus prevent the comparatively low input resistance of TR2 damping L2, C2 unduly. The components C2, L2 and L3 are always enclosed in a screening can, the assembly being referred to as an i.f. transformer. The p-n-p transistor TR2 amplifies the signal applied to its base and this common-emitter stage feeds the collector load consisting of the parallel tuned circuit L4, C5. Base biasing for TR2 is provided by R4, R5 with C4 decoupling R5 to prevent loss of i.f. signal. Risistor R6 provides d.c. stabilisation and is suitably decoupled by C6 to prevent n.f.b.

The output to the following stage is coupled by the winding L5 which, together with L4, forms a further i.f. transformer. The d.c.

supply line is filtered by R7, C7 and R8, C8. Typical voltages are given with the base-emitter voltage drops (0·2V) being appropriate to germanium type transistors.

Sometimes double-tuned circuits are used but these require tapping at both primary and secondary to prevent loss of selectivity. Inductors L2 and L4 have adjustable cores so that the tuned circuits may be aligned to the intermediate frequency.

Use of i.c.

Fixed tuned amplifiers may be constructed using an integrated circuit as the amplifying element. However, an i.c. cannot provide any selectivity as tuning coils cannot be fabricated in i.c. form. When an i.c. is used, the selectivity or tuning circuit has to be provided from outside the i.c. The selectivity may be obtained from a conventional LC tuned circuit or a ceramic filter. An example showing the use of integrated circuits with ceramic filters is given in Fig. 14.34.

A ceramic filter makes use of the piezo-electric property of certain processed ceramic materials. This property is the same as found in quartz crystals which are discussed in Chapter 17. The special construction of a ceramic filter allows bandpass properties to be achieved providing good selectivity, but its

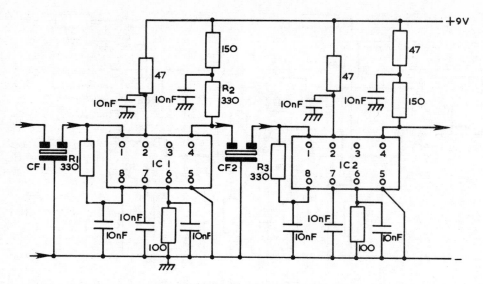

Fig. 14.34 I.F. amplifier (10·7MHz) using integrated circuits and ceramic filters.

centre frequency is not adjustable. When more than one filter is used it is important that they are all tuned to the same centre frequency. Thus the filter units are graded by the manufacturer into frequency groups and colour coded. The filters used in any i.f. amplifier must be from the same frequency group.

The ceramic filters in Fig. 14.34 are CF1 and CF2 (10·7 MHz centre frequency) and they provide the selectivity of the i.f. amplifier. Integrated circuits IC1 and IC2 produce the required gain with discrete components added externally to provide biasing, decoupling and loads, etc. as previously explained. The filters have to be matched at input and output; resistors such as R2 and R3 (330Ω) are used for this purpose.

Tuned Amplifier Responses

Typical responses for some tuned amplifier stages are illustrated in Fig. 14.35. In diagram (a) we have the response for the r.f. stage of an f.m. radio receiver such as that shown in Fig. 14.32. Diagram (b) gives the response for the i.f. stages of a radio receiver such as that given in Fig. 14.33. Finally, the response for the i.f. stages of an f.m. radio receiver such as those shown in Fig. 14.34 is given in diagram (c).

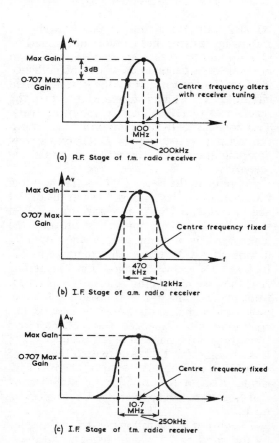

Fig. 14.35 Typical responses of tuned amplifiers.

It should be mentioned that when tuned amplifiers are cascaded with their tuned circuits resonant at a common centre frequency, there is a bandwidth shrinkage. Thus the 3dB bandwidth of the individual stages will be greater than the overall 3dB bandwidth.

Methods of Achieving A.G.C.

Automatic gain control (a.g.c.) is used in receivers to offset the effects of variations in the received signal strength. With a radio receiver the object is to provide a constant sound volume level when stations of differing signal strengths are tuned-in. With a television receiver the object is to obtain a picture of constant contrast level when tuning to stations operating on different channels (also the sound level is kept constant).

It is not intended here to deal with methods of deriving a control voltage, but to show how automatic gain control of a receiver may be achieved. With a bipolar transistor there are two ways of altering its gain: reverse gain control and forward gain control.

We will first consider reverse gain control and an example is given in Fig. 14.36. Gain control is carried out in the r.f. and/or the i.f. stages of a receiver but as an a.m. radio receiver does not usually employ an r.f. stage, control can only be applied in the i.f. stages (usually the first i.f. stage or the first two i.f. stages). To reduce the gain of TR1, the forward bias is reduced (reverse gain control). The value of the bias used on TR1 is settled by the values of R1, R2 and the magnitude of the a.g.c. voltage applied to R2. Under weak signal conditions it will be assumed that the d.c. voltage are as shown in the diagram thus producing a forward bias of 0·2V (germanium transistor). If the signal strength increases, the magnitude of the a.g.c. voltage, which is made proportional to signal strength, increases which causes the voltage at point A to move in a positive direction. As a result the forward bias on the transistor is reduced and the voltage gain of the stage is lowered. Thus an increase in signal strength causes the gain to be reduced which tends to maintain a constant output signal from the receiver. If the signal strength is now decreased, there will be less a.g.c. voltage and point A will move in a negative direction causing an increase in the bias on TR1. As a result the voltage gain of the i.f. stage will be increased thereby compensating for the reduction in signal strength. R2, C1 form a decoupling filter for the a.g.c. line.

The gain control used in television and f.m. radio receivers is usually of the forward type as there are disadvantages in using reverse control in these receivers. Since television and f.m. radio receivers employ an r.f. stage, a.g.c. may be applied to it in addition to control on the i.f. stages. An example of forward control on the i.f. stages of a television receiver is shown in Fig. 14.37.

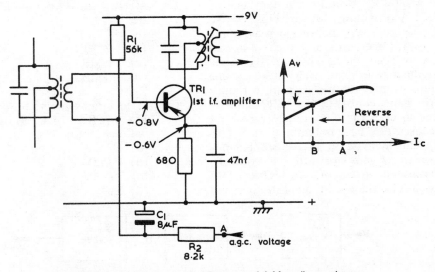

Fig. 14.36 Reverse gain control in I.F. stage of A.M. radio receiver.

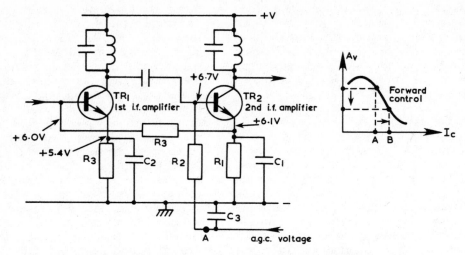

Fig. 14.37 Forward gain control in I.F. stages of television receiver.

Here the control operates on both TR1 and TR2 stages. TR2 base obtains its potential from the a.g.c. line voltage which we will assume to be approximately +6·7V under weak signal conditions. Now, the emitter voltage of TR2 will be its base voltage less its base-emitter voltage drop of, say, 0·6V (silicon transistor). Thus the emitter potential will be +6·1V as shown. TR1 receives its base potential from TR2 emitter, so TR1 base voltage will be approximately that of TR2 emitter (there will be some voltage drop across R3 due to TR1 base current). If TR1 base voltage is +6·0V, its emitter voltage will be about +5·4V providing a forward bias of 0·6V.

If the signal strength now increases, the a.g.c. voltage increases and the voltage at point A will go more positive. This will increase the forward bias of TR2 stage causing its current to increase and its gain to reduce (forward gain control). As TR2 current increases so does the d.c. voltage across R1 which causes TR1 base potential to rise. This results in an increase in TR1 current and a reduction in its gain (forward gain control). The decrease in the gain of both TR1 and TR2 compensates for the rise in signal strength and

thus tends to maintain a constant output signal from the receiver. The opposite effect will take place if the signal strength reduces causing the a.g.c. voltage at point A to become less positive and for the forward bias of TR1 and TR2 to reduce, which will result in an increase in their voltage gains.

QUESTIONS ON CHAPTER FOURTEEN

(1)   The overall voltage gain in dBs of the systems shown below in Fig. 14.38 will be:
(a) +717dB
(b) −717dB
(c) +60dB
(d) +66dB.

(2)   If the input signal to the system shown in Fig. 14.38 is 1mV, the output voltage will be about:
(a) 1V
(b) 100mV
(c) 200mV
(d) 6mV.

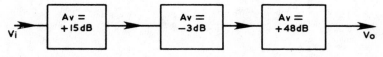

Fig. 14.38

(3) An R–C coupled amplifier will amplify:
(a) A.C. signals only
(b) A.C. and D.C. signals
(c) D.C. signals only
(d) Audio signals only.

(4) When the voltage gain of an amplifier has fallen to 0·707 of maximum gain, the response will be:
(a) 6dB down
(b) 3dB down
(c) 7·07dB down
(d) 1dB down.

(5) If the capacitor C3 becomes open circuit, the effect will be:
(a) Distorted output signals
(b) Only half-cycles will be obtained at the output
(c) No output
(d) Loss of high frequency response only.

(6) If R2 becomes open circuit the effect will be:
(a) Distorted output signals
(b) Change in TR2 d.c. potentials
(c) Smaller current in TR1
(d) No output.

(7) If R1 becomes open circuit the effect will be:
(a) No output signals
(b) Larger current in TR1
(c) Very distorted output
(d) High output signals.

(8) If the value of the resistor R1 is increased the effect will be:
(a) Change in TR1 bias
(b) Increase in n.f.b.
(c) Increase in gain
(d) Reduction in gain.

(9) If R1 and R2 have the values of 10kΩ and 500Ω respectively, the ratio of $V_f:V_o$ will be:
(a) 1:21
(b) 1:20

(c) 500:1
(d) 20:1.

(10) To obtain a narrow bandwidth in a tuned amplifier one would use:
(a) Resistance damping
(b) Stagger tuning
(c) A high Q circuit
(d) An integrated circuit.

(11) Variable tuned amplifiers are used in:
(a) I.F. amplifiers
(b) Audio amplifiers
(c) R.F. amplifiers
(d) I.C. amplifiers.

(12) A cascode r.f. amplifier may consist of:
(a) A common emitter and a common base amplifier in series
(b) A common base and common collector amplifier in parallel
(c) A common source and a common drain amplifier in series
(d) A common base and a common gate amplifier in series.

(13) A ceramic filter has:
(a) A high gain
(b) Bandpass characteristics
(c) An adjustable centre frequency
(d) A low Q.

(14) The 3dB bandwidth of an f.m. radio receiver i.f. amplifier will probably be about:
(a) 10kHz
(b) 240kHz
(c) 100MHz
(d) 5·5MHz

(15) The effect on a transistor to which forward gain control is applied when the signal strength increases is:
(a) Reduction in forward bias
(b) Increase in gain
(c) Increase in forward bias
(d) Decrease in collector current.

(Answers on page 370)

CHAPTER FIFTEEN

POWER AMPLIFIERS

Objectives

1 To explain class-A and class-B power amplification.
2 To describe operation of class-A and class-B push-pull power amplifier circuits and methods of bias stabilisation.
3 To consider transistor dissipation and the effects of load resistance value.
4 To show adjustment of mid-point voltage in class-B complementary symmetry output stage.

POWER AMPLIFIERS HAVE to provide power gain as opposed to voltage amplifiers where the need is for voltage gain. Since power is equal to $V \times I$, a power amplifier must provide appreciable voltage or current gain or a combination of both.

Need for Power Amplification

When transducers, particularly the large electrical-to-mechanical types, are used in electronics appreciable work must be done on them for satisfactory operation, thus appreciable electronic power must be supplied to them. Typical examples are a loudspeaker in an audio amplifier, a motor in a servo control system or an ultrasonic vibrator used in a flaw-detection system. If the signal source for the transducer is of low power, a power amplifier is required between the signal source and the transducer. The transducer therefore consititutes the load for the power amplifier.

Class-A and Class-B Power Amplification

Class-A operation of a power amplifying transistor is illustrated in Fig. 15.1(a). With this class of operation, the transistor is provided with a forward bias such that with the

given sinewave input, the collector current is never cut off. Operation is confined to the linear part of the characteristic, i.e. between A and C to keep non-linear distortion to a minimum. In the absence of signal drive the quiescent collector current is fairly high. If when drive is applied the output current is symmetrical on both half-cycles, the mean current is the same as the quiescent current.

Class-B operation is illustrated in Fig. 15.1(b). In power amplifiers using this method, the transistor is biased so that with sinewave drive the collector current flows for half the cycle. Thus in true class-B the forward bias is zero and the collector current in the absence of signal drive is zero. The mean current, which is less than in class-A, increases with the drive signal amplitude. Because of the need for a small forward bias to produce current flow and the inital non-linearity of the characteristic, severe distortion of the half-cycles will occur as shown. For resistive or non-resonant loads as with an audio amplifier, class-B can only be used in push-pull output stages.

Class-A Power Amplifier

A Class-A power amplifier stage is shown in

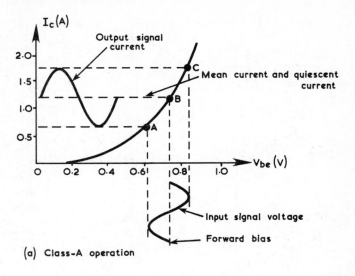

(a) Class-A operation

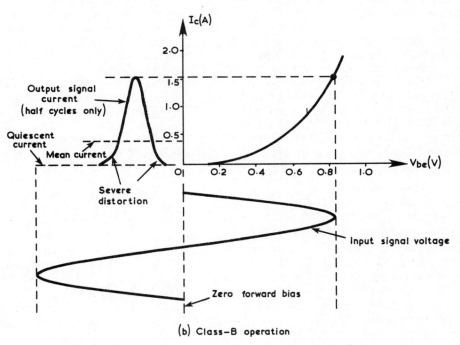

(b) Class-B operation

Fig. 15.1 Class-A and Class-B operation in power amplifiers.

Fig. 15.2. TR1 is a power type transistor and is usually fitted with a heat sink. The transistor which may be n-p-n or p-n-p is biased in the usual way by the potenial divider R1, R2 to class-A operation. Resistor R3 provides d.c. stabilisation of the operating point and is suitably decoupled by C2 to prevent n.f.b. The load for the amplifier is represented by the resistor R_L which for an audio amplifier would be a loudspeaker. Maximum power will be delivered to a load when the load resistance is equal to the internal resistance of the signal

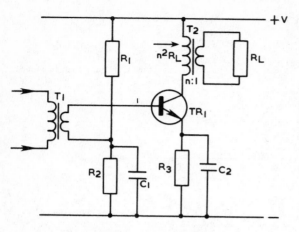

Fig. 15.2 Class-A power amplifier.

The use of a transformer eliminates the d.c. component from the load, which in the case of a loudspeaker would cause the cone to be off centre. The load seen by TR1 is equal to $n^2 R_L$.

The signal to receive power amplification by TR1 may be coupled from the previous stage (called the driver) by a transformer T1 as shown, or may be d.c. coupled. The use of a driver transformer permits correct matching between the output resistance of the driver stage and the input resistance of TR1. Normally T1 will utilise a step-down ratio. Class-A power amplifiers using a single transistor are not common but are sometimes used in the audio stages of a car radio or television receiver where the high quiescent current is not of major importance.

Although with class-A working, operation is said to be confined to be linear part of the transistor characteristic, there is always some non-linearity present which can give rise to distortion. Consider Fig. 15.3 where point B is the quiescent operating point. If a large signal is applied so that the operation is between the limits of points A and C, the output current will be distorted as shown due to the non-linearity of the characteristic. There would be a greater distortion at high power levels than lower power levels. Since with power amplifiers we are concerned with larger

source. In an audio amplifier, maximum power transfer is not the only consideration and some attention must be given to the amount of distortion present. Thus it is normal to match the load resistance to the optimum load resistance of the output transistor. The optimum load is one which gives good power transfer consistent with minimum distortion. When the actual load resistance is less than the optimum load, a transformer may be used for matching. This is the purpose of the output transformer T2 which uses a step-down ratio.

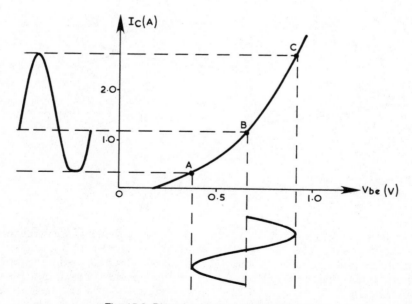

Fig. 15.3 Distortion in class-A power amplifier.

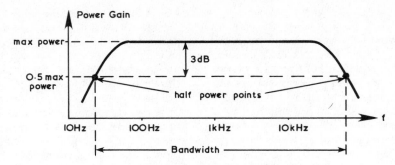

Fig. 15.4 Bandwidth of power amplifier.

signal levels than in a voltage amplifier, the power stage of an amplifier will be a key factor in determining the overall quality. Distortion of this nature can be reduced by applying a.c. negative feedback over the output stage. At the same time any n.f.b. used will assist in improving the frequency response. In Fig. 15.2 the frequency response is limited at low frequencies by the inductance of the transformers T1 and T2 and at high frequencies by the transistor and/or the transformers.

The bandwidth of a power amplifier is the band of frequencies between the limits where the power gain has fallen to half its mid-band power level, see Fig. 15.4. In decibels the half-power points are 3 dB down. The signal voltage across the load will be 0·707 of the mid-band voltage at the half-power points.

Class-A Push-pull Power Amplifier

When more power is required than can be given by a single class-A power amplifier stage, push-pull operation is invariably used. If the main requirement is low distortion, class-A push-pull is used.

A basic circuit is given in Fig. 15.5. Two power transistors TR1 and TR2 are required which are biased to class-A by their potential dividers: R1, R2 for TR1 and R3, R4 for TR2. The output currents of the transistors are combined by a centre-tapped transformer T1 to feed a common load R_L. With push-pull, equal but opposite phase drive signals are required as shown. When applied to the bases, the drive signals affect the transistors in opposite senses, i.e. as TR1 current increases on a positive half-cycle of its input, TR2

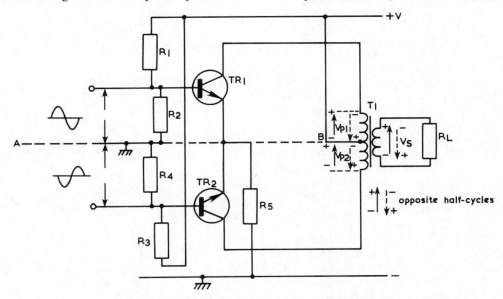

Fig. 15.5 Basic class-A push-pull power amplifier.

current decreases as its input will be on a negative half-cycle. The opposite effect occurs on the following half-cycle when the input changes polarity. Thus TR1 and TR2 collector currents are also equal and of opposite phase. Because of the centre-tapped transformer the a.c. voltages across each half of the primary winding are equal and of opposite phase (V_{p1} and V_{p2}). These primary voltages are therefore additive in developing the secondary voltage V_s. Thus the power developed in the secondary is twice that of a single transistor operating in class-A. In reality we have two identical class-A power amplifiers either side of the dotted line AB driven in antiphase with their outputs combined by the centre-tapped output transformer.

A common-emitter resistor R5 is used but this need not be decoupled since the a.c. currents in it are in antiphase and therefore there will be no n.f.b. at a.c. The resistor will provide d.c. stabilisation of both transistors in the usual way. Normally, the transistors will have closely matched characteristics, i.e. a matched pair will be used.

Class-A push-pull has the following advantages:

(1) The d.c. collector currents of TR1 and TR2 magnetise the core of the output transformer in opposite directions. Hence, with equal collector currents there is no d.c. magnetisation of the core. The output transformer can therefore be made smaller than for an equivalent class-A single transistor power stage.

(2) Because TR1 and TR2 collector currents are equal and of opposite phase, the a.c. current flowing in the internal resistance of the power supply is zero, thus supply line decoupling is simplified.

(3) Any currents in the primary of the output transformer due to 50Hz or 100Hz ripple on the d.c. supply cause magnetisation in opposite directions in the core. This results in less hum in the load compared with a single class-A stage.

(4) Because of the push-pull operation any even harmonic distortion produced by the output transistors is eliminated. Thus for the same amount of distortion, the power output may be more than twice that of a single class-A stage.

Phase Splitting Circuits

Circuits used to provide equal but opposite phase drive signals to a push-pull amplifier are called phase-splitters. A common method is to use a centre-tapped driver transformer as shown in Fig. 15.6(a).

The signal input voltage applied to the primary will produce voltages in each half of the tapped secondary as shown (represented by the arrows). On each half-cycle of the input, the voltages at either end of the secondary will be in antiphase with respect to the centre tap which is connected to a neutral point.

A transistor may be used as a phase-splitter and one example is shown in diagram (b). Here outputs are taken from the collector and emitter of the transistor which is supplied with a signal at its base. Since the collector signal voltage is in anitphase with the base voltage, and the emitter signal voltage is in phase with the base, the output signals across R1 and R2 will be in antiphase with each other. Resistor R3 is added to increase the output resistance

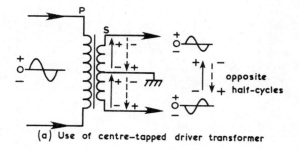

(a) Use of centre-tapped driver transformer

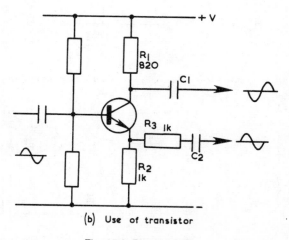

(b) Use of transistor

Fig. 15.6 Phase-splitters.

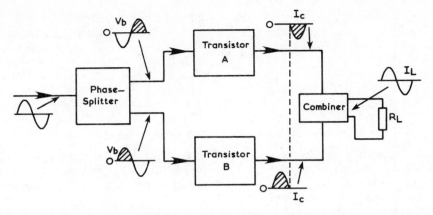

Fig. 15.7 Concept of two transistors in class-B push-pull.

of the emitter to match that of the collector. As there will be some signal loss across R3, the emitter load R2 is made larger than the collector load R1.

Class-B Push-pull Power Amplifiers

Power output transistors may be operated in class-B push-pull and Fig. 15.7 shows the basic concept. As with class-A push-pull, equal but antiphase drive signals (V_b) are required and they are derived from the phase-splitter. With class-B operation transistor A is, say, cut off whilst transistor B is conducting for one half-cycle of the input signal. During the

following half-cycle the conditions are reversed with transistor A conducting and transistor B cut off. Thus the collector current (I_C) of each transistor is composed of half-cycle current pulses as shown. These half-cycles must then be combined to produce a continuous sinewave current flow (I_L) in the load.

A basic circuit for a class-B push-pull power amplifier is given in Fig. 15.8. In true class-B both transistors should be biased to cut off, but with zero forward bias crossover distortion occurs as one transistor takes over from the other, see Fig. 15.9. To reduce crossover distortion to a minimum, both transistors are

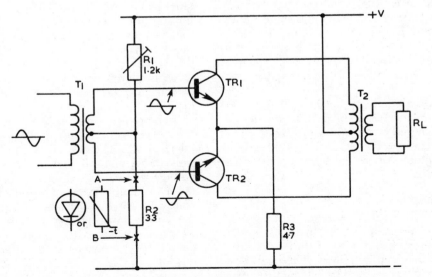

Fig. 15.8 Basic class-B push-pull output stage.

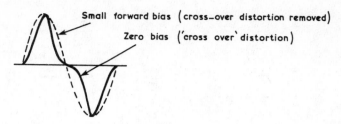

Fig. 15.9 Need for small forward bias in class-B.

given a small forward bias. In an audio amplifier crossover distortion is most unpleasant to the listener.

Antiphase drive signals are provided from the secondary winding of the phase-splitting transformer T1. A small forward bias is supplied to the bases via the secondary winding of T1 from the potential divider R1, R2. Resistor R1 is made variable so that the quiescent current in both transistors may be set to give minimum crossover distortion. This may be carried out by inserting a d.c. ammeter in series with R3 and adjusting R1 for a specified quiescent current. Alternatively, R1 may be adjusted with signal input for minimum crossover distortion, as observed on the screen of a c.r.o. connected across R_L. TR1 and TR2 should have matched characteristics, otherwise distortion will arise due to inequality in the two half-cycles of collector current. The half-cycles are combined in the load R_L because of the use of the centre-tapped output transformer T2. A common emitter resistor R3 is used which must not be decoupled since the current in R3 is composed of unidirectional half sinewaves. A decoupling capacitor would therefore build up a d.c. voltage across it which would tend to reverse bias the transistors.

The main advantage that class-B has over class-A is the low quiescent current and higher efficiency at full output. Because of the low quiescent current, class-B is always chosen for power amplifiers operating from dry batteries.

Bias Stabilisation

The small forward bias provided in class-B is rather critical. If it is too small crossover distortion will occur and if too large the quiescent current is increased. The operation of the basic circuit would be satisfactory for a fixed supply line voltage and a fixed temperature. However, if the temperature or the supply line voltage alters the circuit would be unsatisfactory for the following reasons.

(1) As the temperature rises, the base-emitter voltage drop decreases for a given emitter current (an effect that occurs in any p-n junction as explained in Chapter 2). Thus, if the bias components R1 and R2 are chosen to give the correct bias at low temperature, the quiescent current of both transistors will rise as the temperature increases. The increase in quiescent current is an important factor when the amplifier is operated from a dry battery.

(2) The bias voltage across R2 is dependent upon the supply voltage. If the supply voltage falls (assuming dry battery supply), the bias will fall resulting in crossover distortion.

The common-emitter resistor R3 will provide a measure of d.c. current stabilisation, but its value is usually limited because part of the output power of the stage is lost in R3 and the d.c. voltage drop across it subtracts from the available collector-to-emitter voltage. Its value is therefore quite small and its contribution to d.c. stabilisation consequently lowered.

To help overcome these problems either an n.t.c. thermistor or a p-n diode may be fitted in place of R2. The p-n diode idea is the most satisfactory method because if the supply line voltage alters, the voltage drop across the diode remains constant thus the bias is constant. Also, if the temperature increases, the voltage drop across the diode decreases which compensates for the decrease in voltage drop across the base-emitter junctions of the output transistors (assuming the diode and transistors are the same type, i.e. silicon). A thermistor on the other hand can only compensate for temperature varations, e.g. with a rise in temperature the resistance of an n.t.c. type will decrease causing the bias voltage to decrease and so compensate for the lower base-emitter voltage drop.

Push-pull Power Amplifier Without an Output Transformer

A class-B push-pull circuit that may be found in some portable radio receivers is given in Fig. 15.10. Now the output resistance of large and medium power transistors varies from about $5–75\Omega$, so it is possible to dispense with the output transformer and match directly between the output transistor and a loudspeaker load of suitable impedance. However, if the stage is to be used in push-pull the output current from the two transistors must be directed so that they combine in the load.

As far as d.c. is concerned TR1 and TR2 are in series across the d.c. supply and the d.c. potential at point A is half the supply potential. Because of the series connection the base of the transistors cannot be supplied with the same d.c. voltage as was used in Fig. 15.8.

Thus the antiphase drive signals have to be supplied from separate windings on the driver transformer T1. To prevent crossover distortion a small forward bias is supplied to both transistors; R1, R2 provide the bias for TR1 and R3, R4 provide the bias for TR2. Resistors R5 and R6 are for d.c. stabilisation.

For alternating currents the two transistors are in parallel and are driven in antiphase by the signals from T1 secondaries. Let us say that the signal applied to TR1 base is on a positive half-cycle, therefore the signal applied to TR2 base will be on a negative half-cycle. TR1 will thus conduct hard and TR2 will cut off (class-B operation). The potential at point A will now rise and current will flow via C1 to the loudspeaker in the direction shown by the solid line. Conversely, on the following half-cycle of the input when TR1 base is taken negative and TR2 base goes positive, TR1 cuts off and TR2 conducts hard. As a result the potential at point A falls and current flows in the opposite through the loudspeaker (and C1) in the direction shown by the dotted line. Thus TR1 supplies the current to the loudspeaker during one half-cycle and TR2 supplies the current during the

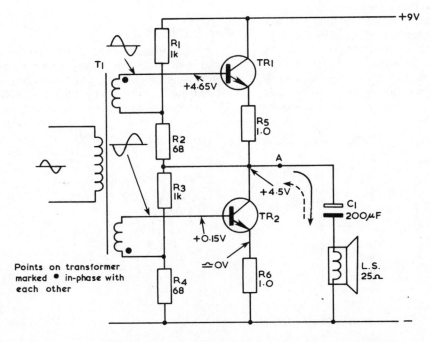

Fig. 15.10 Class-B push-pull eliminating need for output transformer.

other half-cycle. C1 blocks the d.c. from the loudspeaker and passes only the changes in potential at point A to the load. The value of C1 must be such that it offers a low reactance path to the signal currents at low frequencies. Typical voltages are given for germanium transistors. Although n-p-n transistors are shown, p-n-p transistors may be used with a reversal of the supply line potential. The circuit will operate in class-A if required but is not normally used in battery operated equipment.

An advantage of this circuit arrangement is that an output transformer is not required, which permits a more economical design. The loudspeaker may alternatively be returned to the positive supply line without affecting the principle of operation.

Complementary Symmetry Power Amplifiers

With push-pull operation the current in one transistor increases whilst the current in the other decreases. If the transistors are of the same type (two n-p-n or two p-n-p) this is acheived by driving them in antiphase. The same action can be obtained by using complementary transistors, i.e. one p-n-p and one n-p-n and driving them in-phase.

A matched pair of n-p-n and p-n-p power transistors are arranged in the basic circuit shown in Fig. 15.11 to form a complementary symmetry circuit. Because of the simpler in phase drive for this circuit, a phase-splitter is not required. Also, the output transformer may be dispensed with since the transistors

may be matched to the load as for the previous circuit.

For d.c. the two transistors are arranged in series thus the d.c. potential at point A is half the line supply potential. With no signals applied, the capacitor C will be charged to $0.5V_L$. Assuming true class-B operation for the present, when the input signal is on a positive half-cycle TR1 will be biased on and TR2 biased off. Conversely, when the input signal is on a negative half-cycle, TR1 will be biased off and TR2 biased on.

If we consider maximum drive conditions when TR1 conducts hard and TR2 is off, current is supplied to the load via the conducting TR1 and flows in the direction shown by the solid line. This causes C to discharge to zero and for the voltage at point A to rise up to a voltage equal to V_L. On the other half-cycle when TR1 is off and TR2 is conducting hard, current is supplied to the load via the conducting TR2 and flows in the direction shown by the dotted line. This causes C to charge up to the full supply voltage V_L and for the voltage at point A to fall to zero. It will be seen that the action permits the current to reverse direction in the load every half-cycle as is required.

Practical Circuit

A practial arrangement for a class-B circuit suitable for use as an audio power output stage is given in Fig. 15.12. The complementary output pair is formed by TR1 and TR2 with TR3 operating as a driver stage. The bases of

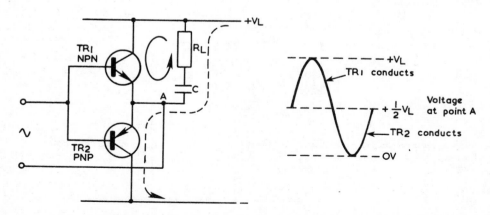

Fig. 15.11 Basic form of complementary symmetry circuit.

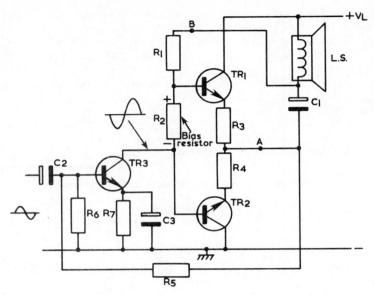

Fig. 15.12 Practical arrangement for complementary symmetry push-pull power amplifier (class-B).

TR1 and TR2 are driven in phase by the signal from across the collector load (R1) of the driver transistor TR3. Resistor R2 applies a small forward bias to TR1 and TR2 to overcome objectionable crossover distortion. The value of this resistor is chosen so that TR1 base voltage is slightly positive w.r.t. its emitter whilst TR2 base is slightly negative w.r.t. its emitter. Capacitor C1 blocks the d.c. from the mid-point A; a large value is chosen so that the reactance of the capacitor is low at all frequencies to be passed by the amplifier. Since C1 is of very low reactance, points A and B are at the same a.c. potential thus the signal voltage across R1 (TR3 load) is effectively applied between the base and emitter of both TR1 and TR2. Resistors R3 and R4 are for d.c. stabilisation of TR1 and TR2.

It was stated that the mid-point voltage was half the supply line voltage. In practice it is slighly offset from $0.5V_L$ due to the knee voltage of TR1 and the emitter voltage of TR3. With a supply of, say, 9V the mid-point voltage would be set to typically 5V to allow symmetrical operation about this voltage. It is important that the mid-point voltage remains constant.

Because of the d.c. coupling between the driver and output pair some additional d.c. stabilisation is necessary to prevent variations in the mid-point voltage. This is done by deriving the base bias for the driver from the mid-point voltage via R5, forming d.c. negative feedback. For example, suppose that the mid-point d.c. potential rises slightly due to a variation in TR3 current. This will cause the base bias on TR3 to increase and for its collector current to rise. As a result there will be a larger voltage drop across both R1 and R2 which will cause TR1 to conduct less and TR2 to conduct more. This will cause the mid-point voltage to fall, thereby compensating to some extent for the original rise. In addition to the d.c. feedback via R5 there will be a.c. n.f.b. which will assist in reducing distortion introduced by the driver and output pair and improve the frequency response.

Transistor Dissipation

Something will now be said about transistor dissipation as it is rather important. Fig. 15.13(a) shows the voltage at the mid-point and the current in the on transistor under maximum power output conditions. Now this condition does not result in maximum transistor dissipation as at first might be thought. Although the current in the on transistor is at

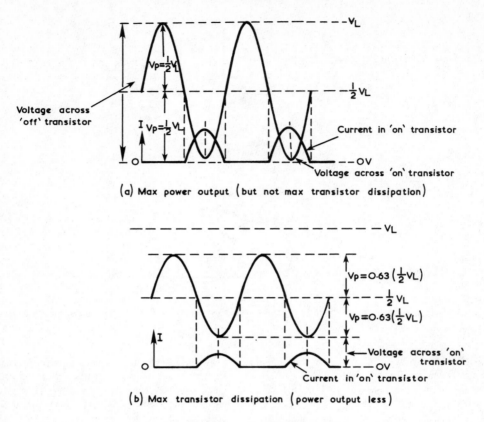

(a) Max power output (but not max transistor dissipation)

(b) Max transistor dissipation (power output less)

Fig. 15.13 Transistor dissipation in class-B.

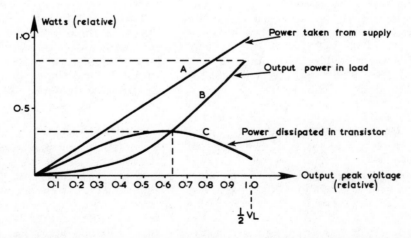

Fig. 15.14 Relationship between peak voltage across load and supply power, output power and transistor dissipation.

its greatest, the voltage across the transistor is very small (almost zero when the current is at a peak). Maximum transistor dissipation occurs at a lower level of output power when the peak voltage at the mid-point (or across the load) is equal to 0·63 of $0·5V_L$, see diagram (b).

This is also shown in Fig. 15.14. Curve A is the power taken from the d.c. supply and curve B is the power developed in the load. The difference between curve A and curve B is the power dissipated in the transistor, curve C. For example, if a d.c. supply of 10V is used for the output pair, maximum transistor dissipation will occur when the peak voltage across the load is 0·63 × 0·5 × 10 Volts = 3·15V ($\approx$ 3V).

Effect of Load Resistance on Transistor Dissipation

(a) If the load resistance is doubled, the power supplied, power in load and transistor dissipation are all halved.

(b) On the other hand if the load resistance is halved, the power supplied, power in load and transistor dissipation are all doubled.

It will be appreciated that (b) is very important because if a class-B amplifier has

been designed to supply, say, a 15-ohm load but is operated with a 7·5-ohm load, the amplifier is liable to be damaged due to excessive transistor dissipation. If the load is accidentally short-circuited, transistor dissipation will be even higher.

Setting the Mid-point Voltage

Some means of setting the mid-point voltage of the output pair may be included in the circuit and an example is shown in Fig. 15.15. An a.f. amplifier TR1 is used prior to the driver stage with d.c. coupling throughout from TR1 up to the output pair. The preset resistor R2 is included to allow the mid-point voltage to be accurately set. Adjustment of R2 alters TR1 current so altering its collector voltage, the base and collector voltages of TR2, the base voltages of TR3 and TR4 and finally the mid-point voltage.

There are two ways of setting the mid-point voltage:

(1) Under Quiescent Conditions
With a d.c. voltmeter connected between the junction of R10, R11 and the positive supply line, R2 is set for a nominal mid-point voltage of 5V (for this circuit).

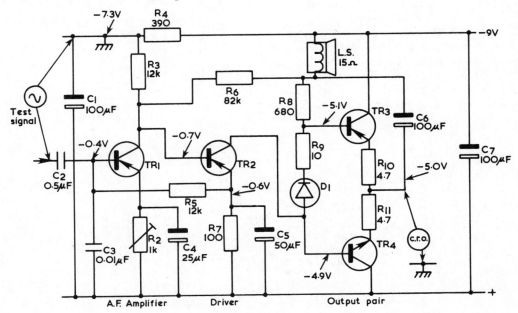

Fig. 15.15 Adjustment of mid-point voltage for class-B complementary symmetry output stage.

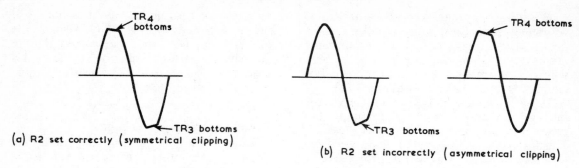

(a) R2 set correctly (symmetrical clipping)

(b) R2 set incorrectly (asymmetrical clipping)

Fig. 15.16 Waveforms obtained at mid-point during adjustment of R2.

(2) Under Dynamic Conditions

A more accurate method is to apply a test signal of, say, 1 kHz between the input to TR1 and chassis and to connect a c.r.o. between the mid-point and chassis as shown. The amplitude of the test signal is increased until clipping of the output signal just commences. R2 is then set for symmetrical clipping as indicated in Fig. 15.16(a). If R2 is set incorrectly, asymmetrical clipping will occur as shown in diagram (b), i.e. symmetrical operation about the mid-point will only occur on low level drive signals.

I.C. Power Amplifier

Power amplifiers are available in integrated circuit form, but the power output is somewhat limited to, say, about 5–10W. An example is given in Fig. 15.17 where the i.c. is included with a number of external discrete components. The transistors formed within the i.c. are often arranged in a class-B complementary symmetry circuit with the i.c. attached to a heat sink to prevent high temperatures inside the i.c. Provision may be made for external feedback to be connected to reduce distortion and improve the frequency response. The input signal to the i.c. is applied via C1 and R1 and the output from the i.c. applied via the coupling capacitor C4 to the loudspeaker load.

QUESTIONS ON CHAPTER FIFTEEN

(1) With class-B operation of a transistor, collector current flows for:
(a) 90°
(b) 180°
(c) 270°
(d) 360°
of the input cycle.

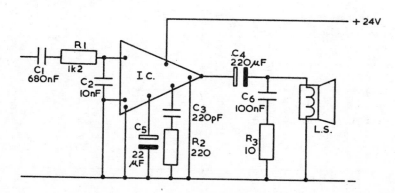

Fig. 15.17 I.C. Class-B audio power amplifier.

(2) At the half-power points of a power amplifier, the voltage across the load will be:
(a) 6dB up
(b) 6dB down
(c) 3dB up
(d) 3dB down.

(3) The voltages at either end of a tapped transformer winding are w.r.t. the tap:
(a) In phase
(b) 90° out of phase
(c) In antiphase
(d) 270° out of phase.

(4) If the load (R_L) for the amplifier shown in Fig. 15.2 on page 210 is 5Ω and T2 uses a 3:1 step-down ratio, the effective load for TR1 will be:
(a) 5Ω
(b) 15Ω
(c) 30Ω
(d) 45Ω.

(5) An audio power amplifier using a single transistor may work in:
(a) Class-B only
(b) Class-A and class-B
(c) Class-A, -B or -C
(d) Class-A only

(6) If R1 goes open circuit in Fig. 15.8 on page 213 the effect will be:
(a) No output
(b) Crossover distortion in the output
(c) Half-cycles only in the output
(d) Excessive transistor dissipation.

(7) If the mid-point voltage of Fig. 15.12 on page 217 falls, the effect will be:
(a) An increase in TR3 collector current
(b) An increase in TR1 and TR2 currents
(c) An increase in TR2 current and a decrease in TR1 current
(d) An increase in TR1 current and a decrease in TR2 current.

The following questions refer to Fig. 15.15 on page 219.

(8) The bias for the output pair is provided by:
(a) R10 and R11
(b) R8
(c) R9
(d) R9 and D1.

(9) The purpose of D1 is:
(a) Stabilise the current in TR2
(b) Stabilise the current in TR3 and TR4
(c) Reduce the n.f.b. in TR3
(d) Reduce the n.f.b. in TR4.

(10) If the 15Ω loudspeaker is replaced by one of 5Ω the effect will be:
(a) Less output power
(b) Less power taken from d.c. supply
(c) Higher dissipation in TR3 and TR4
(d) Lower dissipation in TR3 and TR4.

(11) Maximum power will be developed in the load when the peak voltage at the mid-point is:
(a) About 8V
(b) About 8·9V
(c) About 4V
(d) Exactly 9V.

(12) If R5 goes open circuit the effect on TR1 current will be:
(a) No change
(b) Slight increase
(c) Large increase
(d) Fall to zero.

(13) Resistor R6 provides:
(a) A.C. negative feedback
(b) D.C. positive feedback
(c) D.C. stabilisation of the mid-point voltage
(d) D.C. coupling between TR1 and the output pair to reduce drift.

(14) The emitter voltage of TR1 (germanium transistor) would be typical:
(a) −0·4V
(b) −1·0V
(c) −0·8V
(d) −0·25V.

(15) D.C. negative feedback is provided by:
(a) R8
(b) R5
(c) R9
(d) R3.

(16) The purpose of C7 is to:
  (a) Lower the internal resistance of the d.c. supply to a.c.
  (b) Allow a high value of load for the output pair to be used

  (c) Provide a small amount of overall positive feedback
  (d) Prevent excessive power dissipation in the output pair.

(Answers on page 370)

CHAPTER SIXTEEN

OPERATIONAL AMPLIFIERS

Objectives
1 To outline Characteristics of ideal op-amp
2 To explain limitations of practical op-amps
3 Study the use of op-amps in the inverting and non-inverting modes
4 To consider applications in summing amplifiers, differential amplifiers and integrators

---

AN OPERATIONAL AMPLIFIER, or OP-AMP for short, is a d.c.-coupled monolithic integrated circuit amplifier and is characterised by a very high voltage gain, a high input impedance and for most types a low output impedance.

A large number of OP-AMPS have differential input so that an output voltage may be obtained that is proportional to the **difference** between the two inputs (see Fig. 16.1). The two input terminals are:

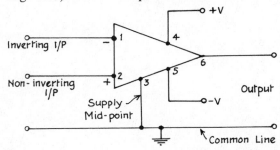

Fig. 16.1 Symbol for operational amplifier (differential input).

Pin 1 (−): the **inverting input** which produces an output voltage of opposite polarity when the other input is held constant.

Pin 2 (+): the **non-inverting** input which produces an output voltage of the same polarity when the other input is held constant.

Thus a **differential input op-amp** can be used as a '**single input**' amplifier (**inverting** or **non-inverting**) as well as a **differential amplifier**.

An op-amp will operate from a wide range of supply voltages (±3V to ±20V typically) but one pin (3) must be connected to the mid-point of the d.c. supply. With both input terminals at zero voltage, the output voltage on pin 6 will be zero. If the inverting terminal is more positive than the non-inverting terminal the output voltage will swing in the negative direction and if the input difference is sufficiently large the output will almost reach the voltage of the negative supply terminal. Conversely, if the inverting terminal is more negative than the non-inverting terminal the output voltage will swing in the positive direction and if the input difference is sufficiently large the output will almost reach the voltage of the positive supply terminal.

Ideal OP-AMP

An **ideal** op-amp has the following characteristics:

(1) Infinite input impedance
(2) Zero output impedance

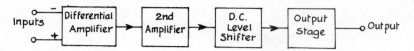

Fig. 16.2 Schematic showing basic configuration for op-amp.

(3) Infinite voltage gain
(4) Infinite bandwidth
(5) Zero output voltage when the voltages applied to the two input terminals are equal
(6) A characteristic that does not drift with temperature

Practical OP-AMP

In reality the 'ideal' op-amp does not exist of course, thus practical op-amps exhibit certain limitations. The usual i.c. op-amp configuration is shown in schematic form in Fig. 16.2. The first stage is a differential amplifier which is supplied from a constant current source and this is followed by an additional stage of amplification. To match into the output stage, a buffer/d.c. level shifter is required. The output is usually a type of complementary class 'B' output stage.

Typical characteristics of a practical op-amp are:

(1) **Input resistance** 10^5–$10^7 \Omega$
(2) **Output resistance** 50Ω–$4k\Omega$
(3) **Voltage gain**   10,000–200,000 open loop, i.e. without feedback applied

(4) Bandwidth

The graph of Fig. 16.3 shows how the open loop gain of a 741 op-amp varies with frequency. Logarithmic scales have been used because of the vast range of values to be plotted. It will be seen that the response is flat up to only 10Hz where the gain is very large (in excess of 10^5). Above 10Hz the gain falls off due to capacitive effects within the amplifier and at 1MHz the gain has fallen to unity. The op-amp is said to have a **gain–bandwidth product** of 1MHz which means that the gain at 1MHz is unity.

If the gain of the amplifier is reduced using

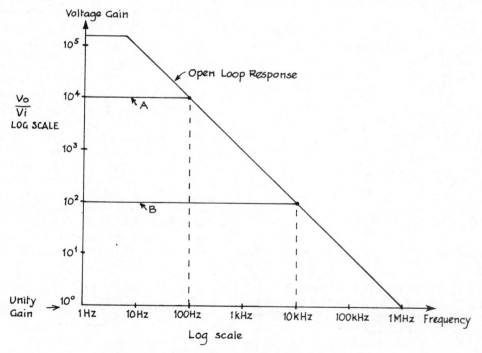

Fig. 16.3 741 Op-amp frequency response.

negative feedback (closed loop) to, say 10,000 (see later), the response will be flat up to $1MHz/10^4 = 100Hz$, response **A**. Reducing the gain to, say, 100 will result in a flat response up to $1MHz/10^2 = 10kHz$, response **B**. Thus by decreasing the gain of the op-amp its bandwidth may be widened, but note that the **gain–bandwidth product is constant**.

(5) Common-mode rejection ratio (CMRR)

When the signals applied to the two input terminals are equal, the output signal is ideally zero. A signal that is applied simultaneously to both inputs is called a **common-mode signal** and is invariably an **unwanted noise voltage**.

The CMRR is a measure of the amplifier's ability to discriminate against common mode signals, i.e. to reject noise and unwanted signals. It is defined as:

$$CMRR = \frac{\text{Differential gain}}{\text{Common-mode gain}},$$

which gives a pure number,

or

$$CMRR = 20 \log \frac{\text{Differential gain}}{\text{Common-mode gain}} \, dB$$

where Differential gain =

$$\frac{\text{Output voltage change}}{\text{Differential input voltage change}}$$

and Common-mode gain =

$$\frac{\text{Output voltage change}}{\text{Input voltage change applied to both inputs}}$$

Typically the CMRR will be in the range 80–100dB (10,000–100,000 : 1) and a high CMRR arises through the use of a differential input amplifier (Fig. 16.2). To make the CMRR as large as possible, the resistance connected to the inverting and non-inverting terminals should be made equal.

(6) Input offset voltage

Ideally the output voltage should be zero with both inputs grounded but due to imperfections an output voltage will be developed. The **input offset voltage** is the d.c. voltage that must be applied between the input terminals to obtain zero output voltage. It is typically 1mV for bipolar op-amps and 15mV for CMOS op-amps. Many op-amps are provided with a pair of terminals between which a variable resistor is connected to adjust for minimum offset voltage (Fig. 16.4).

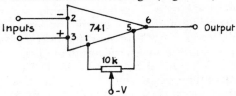

Fig. 16.4 Adjust variable resistor for minimum offset voltage (null) at output.

With any d.c.-coupled amplifier like the op-amp, **d.c. drift** in the output voltage must be kept to a low value. The main causes of drift are temperature and power supply variations. By using a differential amplifier as the input stage, with transistors connected in a balanced arrangement and formed on a single chip, d.c. drift due to temperature or supply voltage variations are minimised. Typically the variation of the input offset voltage with temperature is about $5\mu V/°C$ for bipolar op-amps and $25\mu V/°C$ for CMOS types.

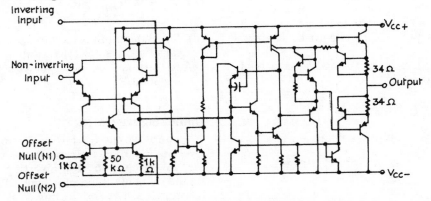

Fig. 16.5 Circuit diagram of UA747M Op-amp (one amplifier).

The circuit diagram of the uA747M dual general-purpose operational amplifier is given in Fig. 16.5. Such circuits appear complicated due to the d.c. coupling, the use of transistors as resistors and the protection circuits employed. This i.c. is characterised for operation over the full military temperature range of −55°C to +125°C.

USE AS INVERTING AMPLIFIER

The voltage gain of an op-amp can be made any specified value by using a large amount of negative feedback and the diagram of Fig. 16.6 shows the method of connection for use as an **inverting amplifier**. A resistor $R1$ is connected between the input terminal and the inverting terminal (2) of the op-amp and another resistor $R2$ is connected between the output and the inverting terminal. The non-inverting terminal may be connected to the common line as shown or via another resistor to the common line which will be considered later.

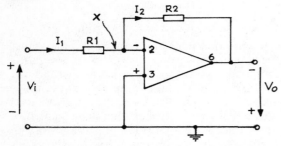

Fig. 16.6 *Op-amp as an inverting amplifier.*

Since the open loop gain of the op-amp is very high, the signal voltage appearing between pin 2 and earth must be extremely small. Thus point X is said to be a **virtual earth**.

Therefore the input voltage V_i effectively appears across $R1$,

Thus $V_i = I_1 R1$, or $I_1 = \dfrac{V_i}{R1}$

Similarly the output voltage V_o is effectively across $R2$,

Thus $V_o = I_2 R2$, or $I_2 = \dfrac{V_o}{R2}$

Since the input resistance of the op-amp is

very high, very little current flows into the op-amp itself.

Thus $I_2 = I_1$

Therefore $\dfrac{V_o}{R2} = \dfrac{V_i}{R1}$

or $\dfrac{V_o}{V_i}$ (Voltage gain) $= \dfrac{R2}{R1}$

Thus, if the values of $R1$ and $R2$ are known the voltage gain may be determined, but note that the output polarity will be opposite to the input polarity. With $R1 = R2$ we have a unity gain inverting amplifier.

Problem 1
Referring to Fig. 16.7, determine:
(a) the voltage gain of the op-amp
(b) the output voltage V_o
(c) the polarity of the output voltage
when 10mV d.c. with polarity as shown is applied to the input.

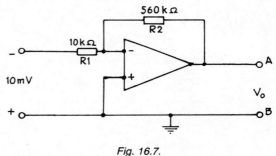

Fig. 16.7.

Solution
(a) Voltage gain $= \dfrac{R2}{R1} = \dfrac{56 \times 10^4}{10^4} = 56$

(b) V_o = Voltage gain × V_i
$= 56 \times 10\text{mV} = 560\text{mV}$

(c) Since the input is applied to the inverting terminal, the voltage at the output will be terminal A positive with respect to terminal B.

Optimising the CMRR
To improve the CMRR of the arrangement given in Fig. 16.6, the resistance connected to the inverting and non-inverting terminals should be made the same. Thus an additional resistor $R3$ may be included as shown in Fig. 16.8.

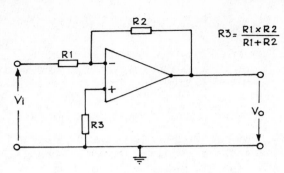

Fig. 16.8 Use of R3 to optimise the CMRR.

The value of $R3$ is made equal to the equivalent resistance of $R1$ and $R2$ in parallel, i.e.

$$R3 = \frac{R1\ R2}{R1 + R2}$$

The voltage gain of the amplifier is still given by

$$\frac{R2}{R1}.$$

Problem 2
Referring to Fig. 16.9, determine:
(a) the peak-to-peak output voltage V_o
(b) a suitable value for $R3$
when a sinewave of 2V peak-to-peak is applied at the input as shown.

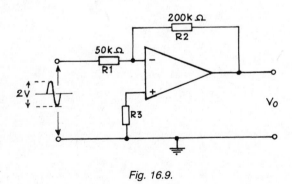

Fig. 16.9.

Solution

(a) $V_o =$ Voltage gain $\times V_i$

$$= \frac{2 \times 10^5}{5 \times 10^4} \times 2V$$

$$= 8V \text{ (in anti-phase to the input)}$$

(b) $R3 = \dfrac{R1\ R2}{R1 + R2} = \dfrac{50 \times 200}{250}\ k\Omega$

$$= 40k\Omega \text{ (39k}\Omega \text{ would probably be used).}$$

Problem 3
Referring to Fig. 16.10, sketch waveforms of the output voltage V_o when:
(a) V_i is a sinewave of peak amplitude 0·5V
(b) V_i is a sinewave of peak amplitude 1·0V

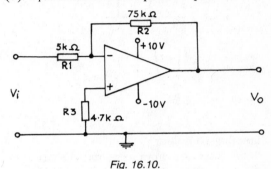

Fig. 16.10.

Solution

(a) $V_o =$ Voltage gain $\times V_i$

$$= \frac{75 \times 10^3}{5 \times 10^3} \times 0.5$$

$$= 7·5V \text{ peak.}$$ The output waveform is as shown in Fig. 16.11, bearing an anti-phase relationship with the input.

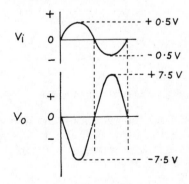

Fig. 16.11.

(b) With a supply rail of ±10V, the maximum undistorted peak swing at the output is limited to just under ±10V. Thus with a 1·0V peak input signal and a gain of 15 the output will be clipped as shown in Fig. 16.12.

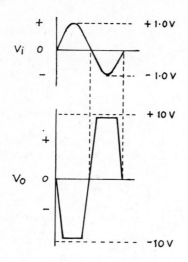

Fig. 16.12.

Summing Amplifier

The inverting amplifier may be used to obtain an output signal voltage which is proportional to the **addition** or **summation** of a number of input signal voltages (Fig. 16.13).

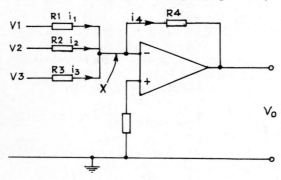

Fig. 16.13 Summing Amplifier.

As before, since the gain of the op-amp itself is very large, the signal between the inverting and non-inverting terminals is very small and point X is a virtual earth.

Thus $i_1 = \dfrac{V_1}{R1}$, $i_2 = \dfrac{V_2}{R2}$ and $i_3 = \dfrac{V_3}{R3}$

Also $i_4 = \dfrac{V_o}{R4}$.

But $i_4 = i_1 + i_2 + i_3$

Therefore $\dfrac{V_o}{R4} = \dfrac{V_1}{R1} + \dfrac{V_2}{R2} + \dfrac{V_3}{R3}$

or $V_o = \dfrac{R_4 V_1}{R1} + \dfrac{R_4 V_2}{R2} + \dfrac{R_4 V_3}{R3}$

Therefore V_o is the sum of the input voltages and the contribution of each input can be made any desired fraction by choice of resistor values. With $R1 = R2 = R3$,

$$V_o = V_1 + V_2 + V_3 \text{ (but of opposite sign)}$$

Although other methods may be used to combine signal voltages, the above arrangement has the advantage that it may be extended to a large number of inputs with minimum interaction between input sources because of the presence of the virtual earth.

Problem 4
Referring to Fig. 16.14, determine the magnitude and polarity of the output voltage V_o when d.c. voltages with polarity as given are applied to the inputs.

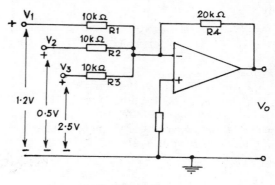

Fig. 16.14.

Solution
The voltage gain from each input

$$= \frac{20 \times 10^3}{10 \times 10^3} = 2$$

Thus V_o
$$= -(2 \times V1 + 2 \times V2 + 2 \times V3) \text{ volts}$$
$$= -(2 \cdot 4 + 1 \cdot 0 + 5) \text{ volts}$$
$$= -8 \cdot 4\text{V (i.e. } 2 \times \text{ the sum of the input voltages but of opposite sign)}$$

USE AS NON-INVERTING AMPLIFIER

The input signal is now applied to the non-inverting terminal of the op-amp. To achieve a useful non-inverting amplifier it is

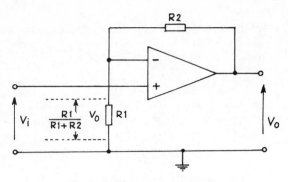

Fig 16.15 Non-inverting amplifier.

necessary to apply n.f.b. around the amplifier. The feedback cannot be applied to the non-inverting terminal as this would result in positive feedback. The feedback is thus applied as before to the inverting terminal (Fig. 16.15).

The resistors $R1$ and $R2$ act as a potential divider across the output of the amplifier to determine the fraction of signal fed back. The portion of the output signal that is fed back is

$$\frac{R1}{R1 + R2} \times V_o$$

Since the amplifier gain is very high the signal voltage appearing between the inverting and non-inverting terminals will be very small, i.e. the terminals are practically at the same potential, therefore

$$V_i = \frac{R1}{R1 + R2} \times V_o$$

Thus $\frac{V_o}{V_i}$ (voltage gain) $= \frac{R1 + R2}{R1}$

(with the output polarity the same as the input)

Problem 5
Referring to Fig. 16.16, if the triangular waveform shown is applied to the input, sketch the output waveform of the amplifier.

Solution
The voltage gain of the amplifier is

$$\frac{R1 + R2}{R1} = \frac{24 \cdot 5 \times 10^3}{2 \cdot 5 \times 10^3} = 9 \cdot 8$$

$$V_o = \text{Voltage gain} \times V_i$$
$$= 1 \cdot 6 \times 9 \cdot 8 = 15 \cdot 68 \text{V}$$

The output waveform is thus as shown in Fig. 16.17 having the same phase as the input.

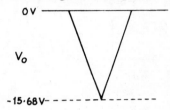

Fig. 16.17.

Voltage Follower
If the whole of the output is fed back to the inverting terminal as shown in Fig. 16.18, then V_o is practically equal to V_i. The gain of the

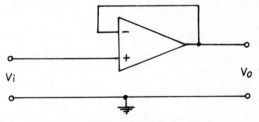

Fig. 16.18 Voltage follower.

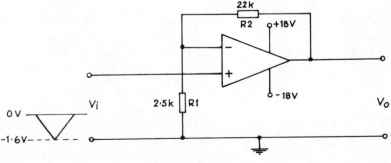

Fig. 16.16.

amplifier is almost unity and the output follows the input.

Such an arrangement may have an extremely high input resistance ($10^6 M\Omega$), a very low output resistance (0.75Ω) and a wide bandwidth.

USE AS A DIFFERENTIAL AMPLIFIER

In a differential amplifier the output voltage V_o is proportional to the **difference** between the voltages $V2$ and $V1$ applied to the inverting and non-inverting terminals of the op-amp (Fig. 16.19).

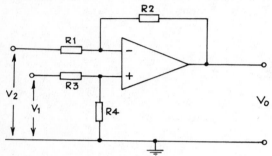

Fig. 16.19 *Differential amplifier.*

With $V1$ input grounded, the output voltage V_o (due to $V2$) = $R2/R1 \times V2$.

With $V2$ input grounded, the output V_o (due to $V1$)

$$= \frac{R4}{R3 + R4} \times \frac{R1 + R2}{R1} \times V1$$

Since the inputs produce opposite effects in the output,

Effective V_o =

$$V2 \left(\frac{R2}{R1}\right) - V1 \left(\frac{R4}{R3 + R4} \times \frac{R1 + R2}{R1}\right)$$

Let $R4 = R2$ and $R3 = R1$.

Therefore effective V_o =

$$\frac{R2}{R1}(V2 - V1), \text{ or } \frac{R2}{R1}(V1 - V2)$$

depending upon which is the larger of the two input voltages.

Thus the differential amplifier acts as a **subtractor** or **comparator**. With $R1 = R2$ the circuit behaves as a unity gain subtractor or comparator.

Problem 6
Referring to Fig. 16.20, determine V_o and its polarity when d.c. voltages are applied at the input with the polarities shown if:

(a) $V2 = 1.0V$, $V1 = 1.06V$
(b) $V2 = 1.06V$, $V1 = 1.0V$
(c) $V2 = 1.06V$, $V1 = 1.0V$, but $V1$ polarity is opposite to that shown in the figure.

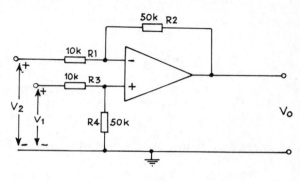

Fig. 16.20.

Solution

(a) $V_o = \dfrac{R2}{R1}(V1 - V2)$

   $= 5(0.06)$

   $= 0.3V$, with the output terminal positive to the earth line.

(b) $V_o = \dfrac{R2}{R1}(V2 - V1)$

   $= 5(0.06)$

   $= 0.3V$, with the output terminal negative to the earth line.

(c) $V_o = \dfrac{R2}{R1}(V2 - V1)$

   $= 5(1.06 + 1.0)$

   $= 10.3V$, with the output terminal negative to the earth line.

Note that the output is proportional to the **algebraic difference** of the inputs.

USE AS AN INTEGRATOR

An operational amplifier may be used as an **active integrator** by placing a capacitor in the feedback path as shown in Fig. 16.21. The performance of such a circuit is far more accurate than that of a simple CR integrator.

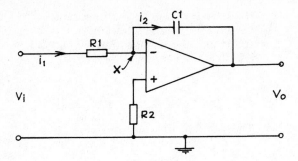

Fig. 16.21 Integrator.

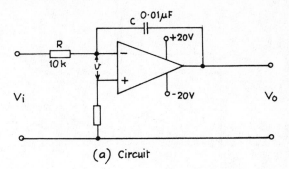

(a) Circuit

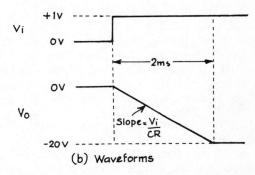

(b) Waveforms

Fig. 16.22 Constant voltage applied to input of op-amp.

Now the current in a capacitor is given by

$$i = C \frac{dy}{dt}$$

(where $\frac{dy}{dt}$ is the rate of change of voltage)

Therefore $i_2 = C1 \frac{dV_o}{dt}$

and $i_1 = \frac{V_i}{R1}$ (point X is a virtual earth)

Since $i_2 = i_1$

$$\frac{V_i}{R1} = C1 \frac{dV_o}{dt}$$

or $V_i = C1 \, R1 \frac{dV_o}{dt}$

That is the input voltage is proportional to the rate of change of the output voltage. Thus the circuit acts as an integrator. The time constant of the integrator is given by $C1 \times R1$ seconds (where $C1$ is in farads and $R1$ is in ohms). The resistor $R2$ is used to optimise the CMRR of the op-amp.

Consider the circuit of Fig. 16.22(a), where the op-amp integrator is operated from a ±20V supply. For the values given, the time-constant of the circuit is:

$0.01 \times 10^{-6} \times 10^4$ seconds
$= 0.1$ms

With $V_i = 0$V, the output voltage will be 0V and C will be uncharged. Suppose that a constant voltage of +1V is applied to the input as shown in Fig. 16.22(b). The capacitor will commence to charge and V_o will ramp down from zero as shown (note that V_o is of opposite polarity to V_i). As the voltage gain of the op-amp is very large, say 10^5, the voltage v

between the inverting and non-inverting terminals will be very small ($V_o =$ voltage gain $\times v$), thus the voltage across R is practically **constant**. Therefore C charges linearly.

The slope of the ramp is given by:

$$\frac{-V_i}{CR} \text{ volts/second}$$
$$= -\frac{1}{0.1 \times 10^{-3}}$$
$$= 10,000\text{V/s}$$

Thus after a period equal to 20/10,000s = 2ms, the output voltage will have ramped down to −20V (the limit of the negative supply line). If V_i remains at +1V after a period of 2ms has elapsed, V_o will remain steady at −20V. With a steady −1V applied to the input, V_o will ramp up linearly towards +20V (the positive limit of the supply).

If a rectangular wave having positive and negative polarity periods is applied to the input, the output will be a sawtooth with linear rising and falling sections, as illustrated in Fig. 16.23. Thus the integrator acts as a **low-pass filter** removing the high-frequency content of the rectangular input.

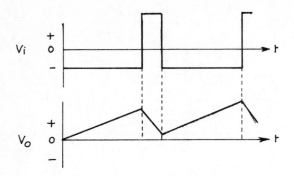

Fig. 16.23 *Integration of rectangular input.*

With suitable choice of integrator time-constant, the circuit will operate as a low-pass filter for sinusoidal signals. Here one may consider that the circuit operates as a frequency-conscious amplifier using selective n.f.b. via C. Thus at low frequencies when the reactance of C is high, there is only a small amount of n.f.b. and in consequence the gain of the amplifier is high. At high frequencies when the reactance of C is low there is a large amount of n.f.b. and the gain of the amplifier is small (Fig. 16.24).

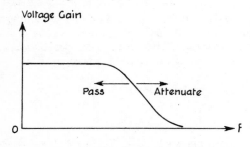

Fig. 16.24 *Low pass filter effect of integrator.*

Problem 7
Referring to Fig. 16.25, determine:

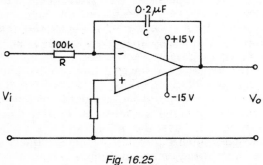

Fig. 16.25

(a) the time-constant of the integrator
(b) the output voltage after a period of 40ms following the application of a steady −0·5V to the input.

Solution
(a) Time-constant = $0·2 \times 10^{-6} \times 10^{5}$s
$$= 0·02s = 20ms.$$
(b) The slope of the output is given by

$$\frac{-V_i}{CR} \text{ volts/second}$$

$$= \frac{0·5}{20 \times 10^{-3}} = 25V/s$$

After a period equal to 40ms the output will have ramped to

$$25 \times \frac{40}{10^{3}} = 1V$$

Thus $V_o = +1V$

OP-AMP APPLICATIONS
The following list gives some of the common uses for operational amplifiers:

(1) As a general-purpose amplifier (inverting or non-inverting), providing a low drift characteristic and good noise rejection (high CMRR). Gain can easily be adjusted by altering input and feedback resistor values.
(2) As a voltage follower or buffer stage on account of its very high input impedance, very low output impedance and wide bandwidth.
(3) As a differential amplifier where its low drift, high CMRR and high gain make it suitable as an instrument amplifier, amplifying inputs from signal transducers such as strain gauges, thermocouples, etc. Also suitable in this configuration for detecting small differences in potential across circuit network components and performing subtraction of electrical voltages.
(4) As a summing amplifier in D–A converters.
(5) As an integrating amplifier for use in some types of A–D converters and ramp generators.
(6) Low-pass, high-pass and band-pass filter applications.

(7) As a logarithmic or exponential amplifier where active devices such as p–n diodes or transistors are employed as the input or feedback elements.

(8) As a sensitive switching circuit where only a very small differential input voltage is required to cause the output to switch from one level to another.

(9) As an astable or monostable multi-vibrator.

QUESTIONS ON CHAPTER SIXTEEN

(1) The input resistance of an OP-AMP is typically:
    (a) 10–100 ohm
    (b) 100–1000 ohm
    (c) 10^2–10^5 ohm
    (d) 10^5–10^7 ohm.

(2) The open-loop voltage gain of an OP-AMP is typically:
    (a) 10,000–200,000
    (b) 1000–2000
    (c) 10–200
    (d) 1–2000.

(3) If the differential gain of an OP-AMP is 1000 and the common mode gain is 2, the CMRR will be:
    (a) 1002
    (b) 998
    (c) 2000
    (d) 500.

(4) Refer to Fig. 16.26.
The voltage gain of the amplifier arrangement is:

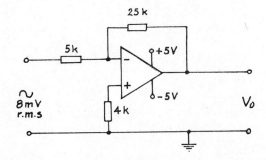

Fig. 16.26

(a) 2·78
(b) 5
(c) 6·25
(d) 125.

(5) Refer to Fig. 16.26.
The magnitude of the r.m.s. output voltage V_o will be:
    (a) 8mV
    (b) 22.4mV
    (c) 40mV
    (d) 50mV.

(6) Refer to Fig. 16.27.
The voltage gain of the amplifier is:
    (a) 5
    (b) 6
    (c) 30
    (d) 125.

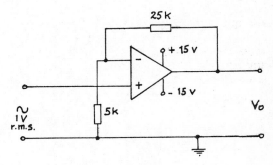

Fig. 16.27

(7) Refer to Fig. 16.27.
The peak-to-peak output voltage will be approximately:
    (a) 16·97V
    (b) 14·14V
    (c) 12V
    (d) 84.84V.

(8) Typical input and output resistances of an OP-AMP voltage follower are respectively:
    (a) 1MΩ and 10kΩ
    (b) 100MΩ and 0·75Ω
    (c) 10MΩ and 100MΩ
    (d) 2kΩ and 5kΩ.

(9) Refer to Fig. 16.28.
The time-constant of the circuit is:

(a) 0·5ms
(b) 1ms
(c) 0.25ms
(d) 50μs.

(10) Refer to Fig. 16.28.
When a constant d.c. voltage of value
shown is applied to the input, the output
will ramp up towards the positive supply
line. The slope of the ramp will be:
(a) 2000V/s
(b) 2mV/s
(c) 1000V/s
(d) 1mV/s.

(Answers on page 370)

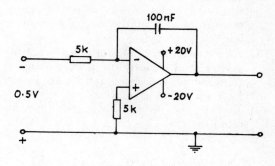

Fig. 16.28

CHAPTER SEVENTEEN

SINEWAVE OSCILLATORS

Objectives
1 To show the essential elements of an LC oscillator.
2 To explain the action of the oscillatory circuit and determine the frequency of oscillation.
3 To describe the operation of tuned collector, tuned base, Reinartz, Hartley, Colpitts and tuned load oscillators.
4 To describe the operation of crystal and R-C sinewave oscillators.

WHEN DISCUSSING AMPLIFIERS in Chapter 14 it was stated that positive feedback is to be avoided otherwise instability will arise. In some circuits, positive feedback is deliberately introduced, i.e. a fraction of the output signal is fed back in phase to the input. An amplifier with positive feedback will provide a gain of:

$$A' = \frac{A}{1 - AB}$$

where A is the gain without feedback and B is the fraction of the output that is fed back. As an example consider an amplifier with a voltage gain of 100 without feedback and with 1/100 of its output fed back to the input in phase. The gain with feedback will be:

$$A' = \frac{100}{1 - (100 \times \frac{1}{100})}$$

$$= \frac{100}{1 - 1}$$

$$= \frac{100}{0}$$

$$= \infty$$

Thus the gain with positive feedback is now infinite which means that the amplifier is providing its own input and no longer operates as an amplifier to external signal. It is now acting as an oscillator and will provide its own input and produce a continuous output independent of any external signal input. The term AB is known as the loop gain and if this is equal to or greater than unity, the gain with feedback becomes infinite and oscillation will occur. In practice the gain cannot be infinite as the signal output will become limited and thus limit the gain.

L.C. Sinewave Oscillators

Oscillators that give a continous sinewave output in the frequency range of 30 kHz to 200 MHz or so, use a frequency determining circuit comprising inductance and capacitance. These are called L.C. oscillators and Fig. 17.1 shows the basic form of all such oscillators.

An L.C. oscillator can be arranged into three parts:

    (a) A frequency determining L.C. network (the oscillatory circuit).
    (b) A feedback network.
    (c) An amplifying device.

The oscillatory circuit generates the sine-

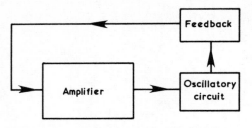

Fig. 17.1 Basic form of all L.C. oscillators.

wave oscillation and a fraction of its output is fed back via the feedback network to the input of the amplifier. After amplification the feedback signal is reapplied to the oscillatory circuit. If the gain of the amplifier is A and the fraction fed back is B, the loop gain is AB. For oscillation to occur, the loop gain must be equal to or greater than unity and the feedback signal must be reapplied in phase to the oscillatory circuit.

The Oscillatory Circuit

An L.C. oscillatory circuit is shown in Fig. 17.2(a) where the resistance r represents the resistance losses of the circuit.

Consider that C has been charged from a d.c. source to produce a voltage v between its plates with a polarity as shown. Energy is then stored in the capacitor in the form of an electric field. Because of the circuit produced by the inductor, the capacitor will discharge through the inductor causing a current i to flow as indicated. If the current commences to flow at instant t_o, see Fig. 17.2(b), it will reach a maximum at instant t_i at which time the capacitor will be fully discharged. The energy that was initially stored in C is now stored in L in the form of a magnetic field. As there is now no voltage to support the current in L, the magnetic field will commence to callapse. In doing so, an e.m.f. will be induced in L with a polarity as shown in Fig. 17.3(d). The direction of the induced e.m.f. is such that it keeps the current flowing in the same direction.

As the current decays during the interval t_1–t_2, the capacitor recharges with the polarity shown in Fig. 17.3(b) and at instant t_2 the capacitor will be fully charged. Energy has now been transferred back to the capacitor. The capacitor now discharges and current flows in the opposite direction through the inductor as in diagram (c). This occurs during

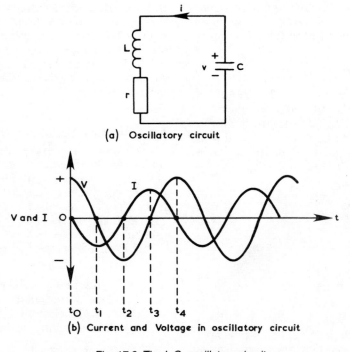

(a) Oscillatory circuit

(b) Current and Voltage in oscillatory circuit

Fig. 17.2 The L.C. oscillatory circuit.

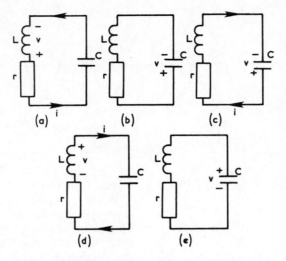

Fig. 17.3 Diagrams explaining action in oscillatory circuit.

the time interval t_2–t_3. At instant t_3, the capacitor will be fully discharged and the current in L at a maximum. As there is no voltage to support current flow, the magnetic field of L will collapse inducing an e.m.f. as shown in diagram (d). The current continues to flow in the same direction but decays during the interval t_3–t_4 as C recharges. At instant t_4, the capacitor will be fully charged with a polarity the same as it started with and the current will be zero, diagram (e). This completes one cycle of events and the process may be repeated.

It will be seen that there will be a continous exchange of energy between L and C. Because

of the presence of the circuit resistive losses r, each time current flows there will be an energy loss. Thus, unless this loss can be made up in some way, the voltage and current waveforms will gradually decay as shown in Fig. 17.4 until they are zero, when the oscillation will stop. This is called a damped oscillation.

Continuous Oscillation

If energy can be supplied to the LC circuit to replace the energy lost in r, a continuous or undamped oscillation can be maintained as shown in Fig. 17.5. When the oscillatory

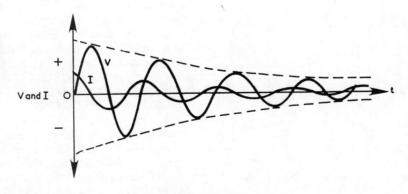

Fig. 17.4 Damped oscillation.

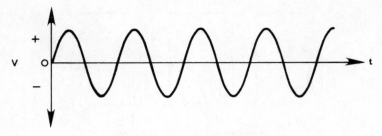

Fig. 17.5 Continuous oscillation.

circuit losses are small, the frequency of the oscillation is given by

$$f_o = \frac{1}{2\pi\sqrt{L.C}} \quad \text{L in henrys and C in Farads.}$$

L.C. Oscillator Circuits

A large number of different oscillator circuits are possible. Some are intended for fixed frequency operation and other for variable frequency operation, e.g. in test signal generators and local oscillators in receivers. In arriving at a suitable circuit, the following factors are given particular attention:

(a) Stability of Frequency (with temperature, supply voltage and load variations).
(b) Purity of Output Waveform (freedom from harmonics).
(c) Constancy of Output Level (with changes in frequency or supply voltage).

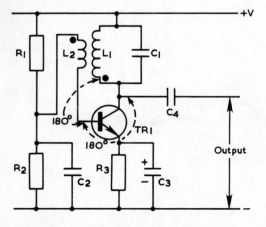

Fig. 17.6 Tuned collector oscillator (series fed).

Tuned Collector

When a bipolar transistor is used as the amplifying device, the oscillatory circuit may be placed in the collector circuit to form a tuned collector circuit as in Fig. 17.6. L1, C1 is the oscillatory circuit which determines the frequency of operation. To ensure that the oscillator is self-starting at switch-on, the transistor is given a small forward bias from the potential divider R1, R2. Feedback to the base of the transistor is via a small coupling winding L2 which is inductively coupled to L1. The turns ratio and the degree of coupling determine the amount of signal that is fed back to the base.

Also, the winding direction of L2 ensures that the feedback signal to the base is 180° out of phase with that at the collector. The oscillatory signal applied to the base produces a signal at the collector 180° out of phase with that at the base. Thus the signal arriving back at the oscillatory circuit is in phase as is required to sustain the oscillation.

Normally, the amount of feedback provided by L2 is greater than is required to make good the losses in L1, C1, i.e. the loop gain is greater than unity. Once oscillation commences, it will tend to build up in amplitude, so some means must be provided to limit the amplitude. Note that it would be very difficult to maintain exactly the right amount of feedback by means of L2; if it were to fall by a small amount the oscillation would cease even though it may have started.

In this circuit, the magnitude of the oscillation is limited by the action of R3, C3 which may be explained with the aid of Fig. 17.7. Suppose that the inital bias from R1, R2 biases the transistor to point B. After a few cycles as the oscillation builds up to a large amplitude, collector and emitter current will

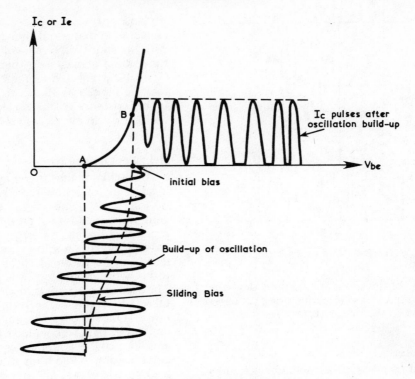

Fig. 17.7 Operation of oscillator showing action of sliding bias.

flow only during positive half-cycles. This causes C3 to become charged with polarity as shown, thereby reducing the effective base emitter forward bias. The greater the amplitude of oscillation, the larger the voltage across C3 and hence the smaller is the forward bias. As the forward bias reduces, the period for which the transistor is conducting is shortened and the energy fed to L1, C1 is less. As equilibrium is reached where the energy fed to L1, C1 is just sufficient to make up for the losses, the amplitude of oscillation remains constant. At this point the loop gain will become unity. If any change takes place, e.g. the supply voltage alters, the voltage across C3 will alter to re-establish equilibrium conditions.

The gradual decrease in bias of the transistor is sometimes called sliding bias. It will be seen that once the oscillation has reached equilibrium, the bias on the transistor corresponds to point A, i.e. class-B (in some circuits it may go into class-C). The time constant of R3, C3 is important because during the negative half-cycles when the transistor is non conducting, C3 discharges through R3 and the bias should not change appreciably during this period. The value of C3 should not be too large or the bias on the transistor will not follow changes in the amplitude of oscillation. Capacitor C2 decouples R2 to signal to prevent loss of feedback signal across R2.

An alternative tuned collector oscillator is shown in Fig. 17.8. The oscillatory circuit L1, C1 is now in shunt with the transistor and is fed via C4 (d.c. block). This capacitor will have a small reactance at the frequency of oscillation. Resistor R4 prevents the internal resistance of the d.c. supply damping the oscillatory circuit; an r.f. choke may alternatively be used for this purpose. Initial forward bias is provided by R1, R2 with C3, R3 producing the sliding bias action as for the previous circuit. The circuit action is identical with the series-fed arrangement, with the coupling winding L2 providing the antiphase feedback to the base. After inversion by the transistor the oscillatory signal is fed back in phase to L1, C1 via C4. An

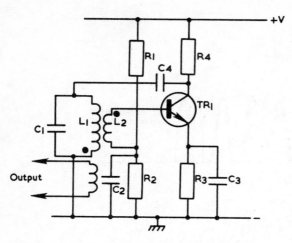

Fig. 17.8 Tuned collector oscillator (shunt fed).

advantage of the shunt fed circuit is that when C1 is to be made variable, one side of it may be connected to the common or chassis line.

Tuned Base

Instead of placing the oscillatory circuit in the collector it may be connected in the base circuit of the transistor to form a tuned base oscillator as shown in Fig. 17.9. The operation is generally similar, with L1, C1 forming the frequency determining circuit and L2 the feedback winding. The oscillatory signal applied to the base receives phase inversion by the transistor. After passing through C4 the signal receives further phase inversion by the coupling between L2 and L1 to arrive back in phase across L1,C1.

Capacitor C4 blocks the d.c. from the collector so that is not shorted out via L2. As with the shunt fed tuned collector circuit, the tuned base arrangement permits one side of C1 to be connected to the common line. L1 may be tapped as shown to prevent the low input resistance of the transistor damping the oscillatory circuit excessively.

Reinartz Oscillator

An oscillator that is commonly used as the local oscillator in a.m. radio receivers is shown in Fig. 17.10. The circuit is connected in common base with C2 grounding the base to oscillatory signals.

With the common base configuration, it is necessary for feedback through the transsitor to be between emitter and collector circuits. The oscillatory circuit is formed by L1, C1 with C1 made variable for receiver tuning purposes. Once the oscillation has started the oscillatory signal is coupled from L1, C1 to the emitter via the coupling winding L3. After amplification by the transistor the signal is fed back to L1, C1 via another coupling winding L2. The winding directions of the coupling windings ensure that the energy fed back to the oscillatory circuit meets the usual in phase requirement. Initial starting bias for the

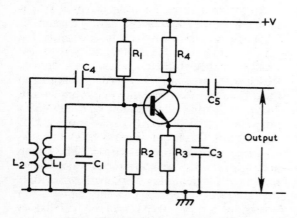

Fig. 17.9 Tuned base oscillator.

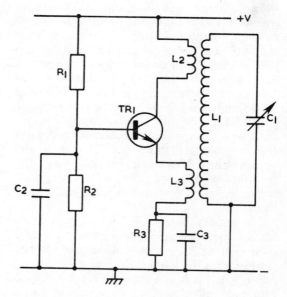

Fig. 17.10 Reinartz oscillator.

transistor is obtained from R1, R2 with C3, R3 providing sliding bias. Because of the greater isolation of the oscillatory circuit from the transistor the frequency stability of the circuit is improved.

Hartley Oscillator

In all the circuits considered so far a coupling winding has been used, but this is not essential and among a number of oscillator circuits that do not use a coupling winding is the Hartley oscillator.

A commonly used version of the Hartley oscillator is shown in Fig. 17.11. The oscillatory circuit is formed by L1, C1 but the inductor is tapped to achieve the necessary phase inversion in the external feedback circuit. L1 is a continuous winding and if, say, point A is going positive w.r.t. the tap C, point B will be going negative w.r.t. the tap, i.e. points A and B will be in antiphase with each other. The position of the tap varies the amount of feedback to the base of the transistor with the feedback signal developed between points A and C. As the tap is moved closer to point A the amount of feedback is reduced.

Starting bias is given by R1, R2 and sliding bias is produced by the action of C3, R3. When oscillations have started the oscillatory signal between points A and C, which is in anitphase with the voltage between B and C, is fed back to the base via C2 (d.c. block). The feedback

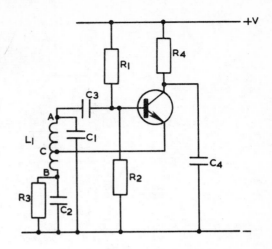

Fig. 17.12 Alternative Hartley oscillator.

signal receives a phase reversal between base and collector and thus arrives back at point B in phase to sustain the oscillation.

An alternative Hartley oscillator circuit is given in Fig. 17.12. L1, C1 form the oscillatory circuit with C2 completing the a.c. path to the common negative line. The tap on L1 is connected to the emitter and point A is connected to the base via the d.c. blocking capacitor C3. Point B at the other end of the inductor is effectively connected to the collector to a.c. via C2 and C4, both of relatively large value. Thus because of the tap on L1, points A and B are in antiphase. The phase reversal between base and collector of the transistor ensures that the feedback is in phase as is required. Resistors R1 and R2 provide starting bias and C2, R3 sliding bias. R4 is the d.c. feed resistor to the collector.

Colpitts Oscillator

Another type of L.C. oscillator that is very similar to the Hartley is the Colpitts circuit. Instead of using an inductor with a physical tap, the tap is obtained by using two capacitors. Fig. 17.13 shows the basic idea.

If two capacitors C1 and C2 are connected in series across the inductor L1, the coil will be effectively tapped at a point depending upon the relative values of the capacitors. With equal value capacitors as in Fig. 17.13(a) the tap is effectively at the centre of the inductor,

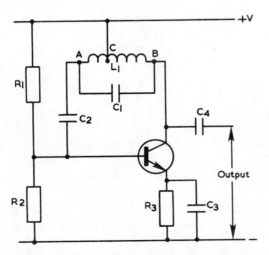

Fig. 17.11 Hartley oscillator (series fed).

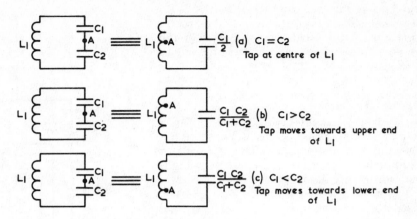

Fig. 17.13 Idea of use of two capacitors to tap coil.

i.e. as regards a.c. the potential at the junction of the two capacitors is the same as the tap. Now, the a.c. potential at the junction of the two capacitors depends upon the relative reactance of the capacitors at the signal frequency. Thus if C1 value is made greater than that of C2, the reactance of C1 will be less than that of C2 and the effective tap on L1 will move towards the upper end of the coil as in diagram (b). Conversely, when C1 value is made less than that of C2, the reactance of C1 will be greater than that of C1 and the tap will move towards the lower end of L1 as in diagram (c). Thus we have a very convenient way of adjusting the tap on the inductor to vary the amount of feedback in an oscillator.

One arrangement of a Colpitts oscillator is shown in Fig. 17.14. The oscillatory ciruit is formed by L1, C1 and C2, with C1 and C2 tapping the inductor at a suitable point.

Because of the tap produced by C1 and C2, oscillatory voltages at either end of L1 will be in antiphase as is required. The transistor provides the usual phase inversion between base and collector so that the feedback is in phase to sustain the oscillation. Capacitor C3 blocks the d.c. between base and collector but passes the a.c. from the lower end of L1 to the base of the transistor. The r.f. choke in the collector prevents the low internal resistance of the d.c. supply from shorting out part of the oscillatory circuit. Starting and sliding bias are as for the prevous ciruits.

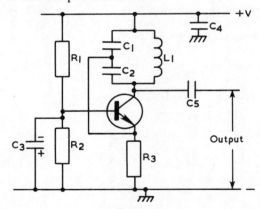

Fig. 17.15 Colpitts oscillator (series fed).

A series fed Colpitts oscillator is given in Fig. 17.15. Capacitors C1 and C2 artifically tap the inductor L1 with the tap connected to the emitter of the transistor. As regards a.c. the upper end of L1 is connected to the base

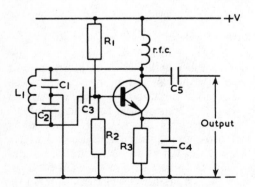

Fig. 17.14 Colpitts oscillator (shunt fed).

via C4 and C3. Thus the base and collector connections at opposite ends of L1 are in antiphase as requried. R1, R2 provide the initial starting bias for the transistor. Sliding bias is provided by C3 which charges up with the polarity shown when base current flows on the conducting half-cycles. This causes the operating point to move to class-B or class-C as the oscillation builds up.

Tuned load

When the load to be fed from an oscillator is inductive or tuned, the load can be made to form part or whole of the oscillatory circuit. An example is shown in Fig. 17.16.

Here the erase head of an audio tape recorder, which is to be fed from the oscillator, is made part of the oscillatory circuit. The inductance L of the erase head together with C1 and C2 are arranged in a Colpitts oscillator circuit. Its operation is identical to that given in Fig. 17.14. This idea provides an efficient means of transferring largish amounts of oscillatory power from an oscillator to the load.

Use of Buffer Stage

The operating frequency of an oscillator is dependent to some extent upon the magnitude of the load. When the load is reactive, i.e. capacitive or inductive, variations in the loading will effect the frequency of oscillation. The effect of variable loading can be reduced by employing a buffer stage between the oscillator and its load.

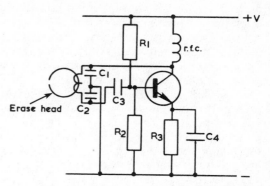
Fig. 17.16 Load forming part of oscillatory circuit.

A common type of buffer stage is the emitter-follower circuit and an example is given in Fig. 17.17. TR1 forms the oscillator transistor connected in a Colpitts circuit with the output capacitively coupled via C1 to an emitter-follower TR2. Forward bias to class-A is provided by the potential divider R1, R2 and the output is taken to the load from across the emitter resistor R3. An emitter-follower has a high input impedance so there is little loading on the oscillator. Variations in loading occur across R3 in the output circuit of TR2. Because the output impedance of TR2 is low, variations in the loading have little effect on the signal across R3. The use of TR2 thus serves to improve the frequency stability of the oscillator.

Crystal Oscillators

Some oscillator circuits make use of the piezo-electric property of a crystal in place of

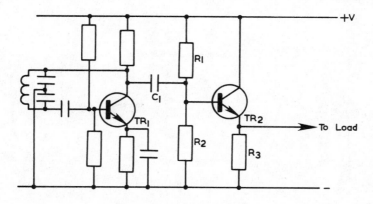
Fig. 17.17 Use of buffer stage.

an L.C. circuit to determine the frequency of operation. The piezo-electric effect occurs naturally in quartz and can be induced in certain ceramic materials. A slice of quartz cut from a complete crystal in a particular way is given conductive coatings on each side and then sealed in a glass/metal container to protect it from damage and contamination.

The operating frequency of a crystal depends upon the size of the slice; the thinner it is the higher the operating frequency. Crystals are generally available in the range of about 4 kHz to 10 MHz. For higher frequencies, the crystal slice becomes very thin and fragile. The frequency stability of a crystal is of very high order. For example, a 1 MHz crystal may be stable to within 1 Hz over long periods. For high accuracy the crystal should be maintained at a constant temperature, e.g. in a temperature-controlled oven. One important use of crystal oscillators is in transmitters where the carrier frequency must be maintained to a high degree of accuracy. If a carrier frequency above 10 MHz is required, the output from the crystal may be multiplied using a suitable frequency multiplier circuit until the desired frequency is obtained.

A crystal and its equivalent circuit are given in Fig. 17.18. From the equivalent circuit it will be seen that a crystal can be maintained in either series or parallel resonance. Series resonance is produced by L1, C1 and parallel resonance by C_p and the inductance of the series arm above its series resonant frequency. In pratice the series and parallel resonant frequencies (f_s and f_p) are quite close, differing only by about 1% or less.

The piezo-electric effect is illustrated in

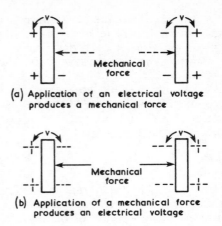

(a) Application of an electrical voltage produces a mechanical force

(b) Application of a mechanical force produces an electrical voltage

Fig. 17.19 The Piezo electric effect.

Fig. 17.19. If a slice of the crystal is subjected to an alternating voltage as in diagram (a), a mechanical force is set up which changes direction in sympathy with the polarity of the applied voltage. Thus the application of an alternating voltage gives rise to a mechanical vibration. The effect is reversible in nature, i.e. if the crystal slice is subjected to a mechanical vibration a voltage is produced between opposite faces of the crystal with a polarity depending upon the direction of the applied force, see diagram (b).

In an oscillator, the crystal is supplied with electrical energy and if the frequency of the energy is closed to the natural resonance of the crystal, a very strong mechanical vibration will be set up in the crystal. This vibration will cause a large voltage to be developed between its opposite faces (larger than the applied voltage). Thus the Q of a crystal is very large:

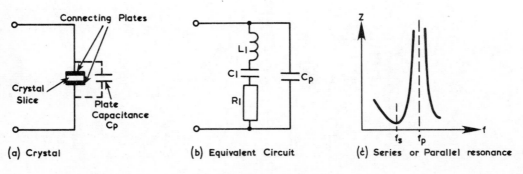

(a) Crystal

(b) Equivalent Circuit

(c) Series or Parallel resonance

Fig. 17.18 Piezo electric crystal.

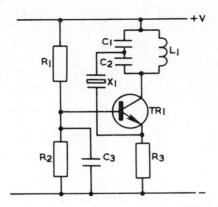

Fig. 17.20 *Crystal oscillator using series resonant mode.*

about 20,000 as opposed to, say, 200 for an L.C. circuit.

When used in oscillator circuits a crystal may be arranged to operate in its series resonant mode, at a frequency where it presents an inductive reactance or in its parallel resonant mode. An example of the series resonant mode is given in Fig. 17.20.

Starting bias for the transistor is provided by R1, R2. The collector load for the transistor is the parallel resonant circuit L1, C1 and C2 which is tuned to the desired frequency of operation. Energy is fed back from the collector to the emitter via the crystal X1. Maximum feedback will occur at the series resonant frequency of the crystal and only then will the loop gain be sufficient to sustain the oscillation. Because of the high Q of the crystal a very stable oscillation frequency is achieved.

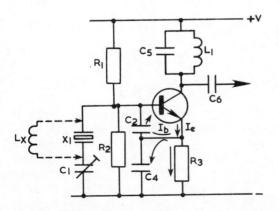

Fig. 17.21 *Oscillator with crystal presenting an inductive reactance.*

Another crystal oscillator circuit is given in Fig. 17.21. In this example the crystal is operating just above series resonant so that it prevents an inductive reactance. The crystal may therefore be replaced by an inductance L_x (shown dotted). The circuit is then more readily recognizable as a Colpitts oscillator with C2 and C4 tapping the inductor L_x. By adjusting C1, the frequency of oscillation may be altered slightly (a vari-cap diode may be included in series with the crystal to give fine adjustment over the frequency).

A portion of the oscillatory signal appearing between the base and the negative line is developed across C2 which provides the input current Ib. Due to transistor action Ib is amplified and feedback to the oscillatory circuit is provided by the larger portion of Ie that flows in C4. Since Ib and Ie are in phase, the feedback is positive and thus will maintain the oscillation. Resistors R1 and R2 provide starting bias. L1, C5 in the collector circuit is used to reject harmonics at the output.

R–C Sinewave Oscillators

When a low frequency sinewave in the range of about 10 Hz to 100 kHz is required, a Resistance–Capacitance (R–C) oscillator is normally used. This is because LC oscillators are difficult to design at low frequencies as L and C values becomes large. There are two possible arrangements for an RC oscillator and the basic principle of both types is illustrated in Fig. 17.22.

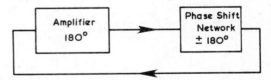

(a) R C oscillator using 180° phase shift network

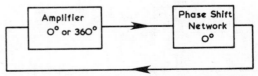

(b) R C oscillator using 0° phase shift network

Fig. 17.22 *Basic principle of R.C. oscillators.*

In diagram (a) the output of an amplifier feeds an R.C. phase shift network which introduces a phase shift of $\pm 180°$. The output from this circuit is then fed back to the input of the amplifier. If the amplifier (usually a single stage) introduces phase inversion of its input signal, the output of the amplifier will arrive back to the network in phase, i.e. the overall phase shift is 0° or 360°. If the oscillator is to give a sinewave output the phase shift introduced by the phase shift network must change with frequency. However, since the output from the phase shift network will only be in antiphase with its input at one frequency, oscillation will occur at this single frequency. For oscillations to take place, the amplifier must make up for the losses introduced by the phase shift network, i.e. the loop gain must be equal to or greater than unity.

With the other arrangement shown in diagram (b) an amplifier is used which does not provide phase inversion of its input signal, i.e. a two stage amplifier. Since the phase shift network used here does not produce any phase shift at the desired operating frequency, the overall phase shift is 0° or 360° as is required for oscillations to be established. Again, the amplifier must make up for the losses incurred in the network.

An oscillator that is based on the idea Fig. 17.22 (a), is given in Fig. 17.23. The transistor is forward biased to class-A by R3, R4 and stabilised by R6 which is decoupled by C4 to prevent n.f.b. Resistor R5 is the collector load. The phase shift network is

formed by C1, R1; C2, R2; C3 and the input resistance of the transistor. Usually, C1, C2 and C3 are the same value with R1 and R2 values made the same as the input resistance of TR1 (R_{IN}). Each CR section introduces a leading phase shift as illustrated in Fig. 17.24

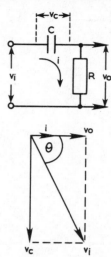

Fig. 17.24 Phase shift (θ) introduced by isolated RC section.

but the three C.R. sections must provide an overall phase shift of 180° at a single frequency. In practice, the calculation of phase shift is complicated by the fact that each R.C. section tends to load the preceding one. If variable frequency operation is required, C1, C2 and C3 may be made variable and ganged together. The approximate frequency of oscillation is given by:

$$f_o = \frac{1}{2\pi CR\sqrt{6}} \text{ Where } C = C1 = C2 = C3 \text{ and}$$

$$R = R1 = R2 = R_{IN} = R5$$

$$= 0.065 \frac{1}{CR}$$

At f_o the loss in the phase shift network is 29 and thus the h_{fe} of the transistor must be greater than 29. Since the frequency is proportional to $1/c$, a given capacitance change will produce a larger frequency variation than with an LC oscillator where frequency is proportional to $1/\sqrt{c}$.

A circuit using the principle of Fig. 17.22 (b) is given in Fig. 17.25. This circuit makes

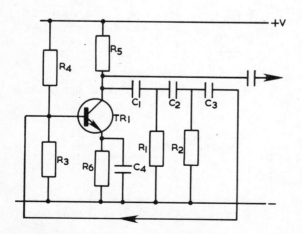

Fig. 17.23 R-C phase shift oscillator.

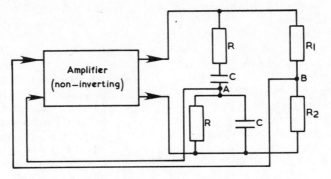

Fig. 17.25 Wein bridge R-C oscillator.

use of a Wein bridge which is shown external to the amplifier. The output from the Wein bridge is taken between points A and B and applied back to the input of a non-inverting amplifier, i.e. a two-stage common-emitter amplifier. When the bridge is balanced the output will be zero and the frequency at balance is given by:

$$f_o = \frac{1}{2\pi CR}$$

In order to produce oscillations, the bridge is operated slightly off balance by varying the ratio of R1 to R2:

at balance $\dfrac{R_2}{R_1 + R_2} = \dfrac{1}{3}$

When operated slightly off balance, the output between points A and B is in phase with the input to the network and the overall feedback is positive as is required. Only at one frequency will the phase lead, introduced by the series R.C. equal the phase lag produced by the parallel R.C. to give zero phase shift. For best operation the output resistance of the amplifier should be low and its input resistance high. The voltage gain required by the amplifier to maintain oscillation should be greater than 3.

To produce a good sinewave output from an RC oscillator, the loop gain should be made nearly to unity. If it is greater, the transistor will be driven into the non-linear part of its characteristic and the output will be distorted. The output waveform can be improved by incorporating a control in the amplifier to vary the gain. Alternatively, automatic amplitude

stabilisation may be employed. This may be achieved in the Wein bridge oscillator by replacing R1 with a.n.t.c. thermistor. Thus, as the amplitude of the oscillation increases, the voltage across the thermistor increases which causes its resistance to fall and for the bridge to come closer into balance. As a result the output from the bridge is reduced and the amplitude of oscillation is kept constant.

QUESTIONS ON CHAPTER SEVENTEEN

(1) An LC or RC oscillator circuit will oscillate if:
  (a) Loop gain is equal to unity and overall feedback is in antiphase
  (b) Loop gain is less than unity and overall feedback is in phase
  (c) Loop gain is less than unity and overall feedback is in antiphase
  (d) Loop gain is equal to unity and overall feedback is in phase.

(2) Resistance present in an L.C. oscillatory circuit will result in:
  (a) An increase in the circuit Q
  (b) Loss of energy
  (c) Less feedback being required
  (d) Lower harmonic level in the output.

(3) Sliding bias is used in an L.C. oscillator to:
  (a) Keep the oscillator amplitude constant
  (b) Make the oscillator self-starting

(c) Increase the forward bias as the oscillation builds up
(d) Bias the transistor to class-A.

(4) To increase the frequency of an L.C. oscillator:
(a) C may be increased
(b) L may be increased
(c) C may be decreased
(d) L is increased and C decreased by the same percentage.

Questions 5–7 refer to Fig. 17.6 on page 238

(5) If R1 goes open the effect will probably be:
(a) Smaller amplitude of oscillation
(b) Larger amplitude of oscillation
(c) Wrong frequency of oscillation
(d) Oscillation will fail to start.

(6) If the connections to L2 are reversed the effect will be:
(a) Oscillation will fail to start
(b) Nil
(c) Larger amplitude of oscillation
(d) Change in oscillation frequency.

(7) If L1 goes circuit the effect will be:
(a) Oscillation at low frequencies only
(b) No oscillation
(c) Oscillation at high frequencies only
(d) Intermittent operation.

(8) A circuit that would be suitable for use as a local oscillator in an a.m. radio would be:

(a) A crystal oscillator
(b) A Reinartz oscillator
(c) A series fed Hartley oscillator
(d) A Wein bridge oscillator.

(9) An oscillator that would be suitable for generating a 15 Hz sinewave would be:
(a) A crystal oscillator
(b) A Hartley oscillator
(c) A Colpitts oscillator
(d) An R.C. oscillator.

(10) The most suitable oscillator for generating the carrier of a broadcast radio transmission would be:
(a) A crystal type
(b) An R.C. type
(c) A Hartley type
(d) A Colpitts type.

(11) The main use of a buffer stage with an oscillator is to:
(a) Increase the amplitude of the oscillator output
(b) Improve the frequency stability
(c) Provide a high impedance source to the load
(d) Allow ease of tuning.

(12) Series capacitors are used to tap the oscillatory circuit inductor in:
(a) A Hartley oscillator
(b) A Reinartz oscillator
(c) A Colpitts oscillator
(d) A tuned base oscillator.

(Answers on page 370)

CHAPTER EIGHTEEN

MULTIVIBRATORS

Objectives

1 To consider the action of a transistor as a switch.
2 To explain the action of an astable multivibrator.
3 To describe synchronisation and use of an astable to produce a sawtooth.
4 To describe the operation of monostable and bistable multivibrators.

THERE ARE OSCILLATORS that are specifically used to generate non-sinusoidal waveforms. Multivibrators are in this class of oscillator, and are employed to generate rectangular waveforms. In this chapter three types of multivibrator circuit will be considered.

   (a) Astable Multivibrator
   (b) Monostable Multivibrator (also known as the Flip-Flop)
   (c) Bistable Multivibrator.

Transistor as a Switch

Multivibrator oscillators use two transistors which operate as eletronic switches. The use of a bipolar transistor as a switch is illustrated in Fig. 18.1. A transistor may be switched rapidly on and off by the application of a rectangular pulse to its base as shown in diagram (a). When the input voltage is below the level required of, say, 0·7V, to produce collector current flow, the transistor is off and only a small leakage current (Iceo) flows in the collector load R_L. Thus the voltage drop across R_L is negligible and the Vce of the transistor is almost equal to the supply line voltage V_L. When the base voltage rises above 0·7V, the transistor conducts and if supplied with sufficient base current the collector current saturates. Under this condition the collector voltage falls to a small value and is said to 'bottom'.

The fully off and fully on conditions are best seen from the load line given in diagram (b). The load line is drawn from a point on the Vce axis corresponding to the supply voltage and with a slope appropriate to the value of R_L. It will be seen that if the base current is equal to or greater than $40\mu A$, the operating point is at A. This is the fully on condition where the collector current saturates and the voltage drop across the transistor falls to a low value or bottoms. The bottoming voltage is only about 0·25V, depending upon the type of transistor used. In the fully off condition the operating point is point B where the base current is zero. An f.e.t. will operate as a switch almost identically but with a slightly higher bottoming voltage of 0·3 to 1·0V and a smaller leakage current of 1 nA.

The power dissipated within the transistor is small at point A and B. When the transistor is fully on there is only a small voltage drop across it (although the current is relatively large) and when fully off only a small leakage current flows (although the volts drop across the transistor is equal to the supply line voltage). Between the two extreme points on the load line, the transistor operates at various

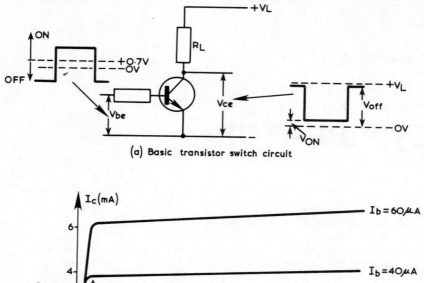

(a) Basic transistor switch circuit

(b) Operating conditions of transistor

Fig. 18.1 Transistor as a switch.

points as it changes over from the off to on condition. At point C, halfway up the load line, the dissipation is greater than at the extremes and is at a maximum. Thus if the transistor is to act as a switch, the switching time between A and B should be short so that the dissipation is small. As the power dissipation is small in the fully on and fully off conditions quite small power transistors can be used for high-speed switching.

. It would be expected that at the instant the base current is reduced to zero when switching from on to off the collector current would immediately stop flowing. In practice, it continues to flow for a short time due to what is known as charge storage. This occurs in the base region of the transistor and acts like a charged capacitor. Charge storage causes a

delay in the cut-off time of the transistor, depending on its type and construction.

Astable Multivibrator

An astable multivibrator is a free-running oscillator consisting of two cascaded RC coupled stages connected to give 100% positive feedback. A basic circuit is given in Fig. 18.2 where the outputs from the collectors of TR1 and TR2 are cross-coupled to the base of the other transistor via the coupling capacitors C1 and C2. Resistor R1 provides the base bias for TR2, and R2 provides the base bias for TR1. Resistors R3 and R4 are collector load resistors.

Assuming that R3 = R4, R1 = R2, C1 = C2, and similar transistors are used to produce a

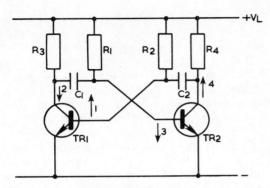

Fig. 18.2 Basic astable multivibrator.

symmetrical circuit, it may be thought that both transistors would conduct together and remain conducting since they are both biased on via their base resistors R1 and R2. In practice, however, immediately following the connection of the supply voltage, one transitor will become fully conducting and the other fully off. This is due to the cross-coupling and it is quite random which transistor becomes fully conducting initially.

Any disturbance such as a noise voltage or inequality in the two transistors (their d.c. current gains will not be identical) will produce the initial condition of one transistor conducting hard and the other being cut-off. For example, consider a noise voltage disturb-ance at TR1 base acting in the positive direction and indicated by arrow 1. Now, a rise in voltage at TR1 base will be amplified by TR1 to produce a fall in voltage at its collector (arrow 2). This fall in voltage is passed via C1 and TR2 base (arrow 3), reducing the current in TR2 and causing its collector voltage to rise (arrow 4). The rise in voltage is then passed via C2 back to TR1 base (note that it arrives back in phase with the original rise, i.e. positive feedback). This rise will receive repetitive amplification in TR1 and TR2 until TR2 is cut off by the large fall in voltage at its base and TR1 is conducting hard due to the rise in voltage at its base. This accumulative action takes place very quickly at switch on. However, the circuit does not remain in this state for very long which is explained with the aid of the waveforms in Fig. 18.3.

At time t_o, TR1 is fully on with its collector voltage bottomed, and TR2 is fully off with its collector voltage at practically the full supply line potential V_L. TR2 is held off by the negative voltage at its base.

The following reactions then occur:

(1) Since the voltage at the lower end of R1 (w.r.t. the negative line) is negative by a voltage almost equal to V_L, and the upper end of R1 is connected to $+V_L$, there is a voltage across R1 of twice the

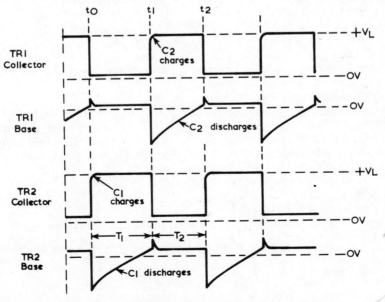

Fig. 18.3 Astable multivibrator waveforms (C1R1 = C2R2).

supply line potential. This voltage causes a current to flow in R1 thereby allowing C1 to discharge. As C1 discharges exponentially via R1, the base voltage of TR2 rises. When it has risen just a little above zero, TR2 starts to conduct.

(2)   The conduction of TR2 causes its collector voltage to fall and this fall is passed via C2 to TR1 base. As a result, the conduction in TR1 is reduced and its collector voltage rises. The rise in voltage is applied via C1 to TR2 base, increasing the conduction of TR2. As a result, TR2 collector voltage falls even further . . . and so on. The accumulative action due to positive feedback very quickly results in TR2 coming hard on and TR1 switching off. TR1 is held off due to the negative voltage at its base. Thus at instant t_1, TR2 collector voltage bottoms and TR1 collector voltage rises to $+V_L$.

(3)   There is now a voltage established across R2 that is equal to twice the supply line potential. This voltage causes a current to flow in R2 thereby allowing C2 to discharge. As C2 discharges exponentially via R2, the base voltage of TR1 rises. When it rises above zero, TR1 starts to conduct.

(4)   The conduction of TR1 causes its collector voltage to fall and this fall is passed via C1 to the base of TR2. As a result, the conduction of TR2 is reduced and its collector voltage rises. The rise in voltage is applied via C2 to TR1 base increasing the conduction of TR1 even more. Again due to the positive feedback loop, TR1 becomes fully conducting very rapidly and TR2 quickly switches off. TR1 collector voltage is then bottomed and TR2 collector voltage is equal to the line supply potential $+ V_L$.

This completes a full cycle of events at instant t_2 and the cycle will repeat itself continuously. It will be seen that neither TR1 nor TR2 remain in a stable state for long periods, hence the name astable (not stable). Rectangular voltage waveforms are available as outputs from either collector, with TR1 collector being in antiphase with TR2 collector.

The period T_1 that TR2 is off is determined by the time-constant of C1. R1 and the off period for TR1 (T_2) is determined by the time constant C2 R2. The periodic time T of the waveform is given by:

$$T = 0.69 (C1.R1 + C2.R2) \text{ s}$$

or the frequency f by

$$f = \frac{1}{0 \cdot 69(C1.R1 + C2.R2)} \text{Hz}$$

Asymmetrical Output

When the time constants C1 R1 and C2 R2 are equal, a symmetrical or square-wave output is obtained as shown in Fig. 18.3. If the time constants are unequal an asymmetrical wave (unequal mark-to-space ratio) will be produced.

An example is shown in Fig. 18.4 where C1R1>C2R2. Under this condition, TR1 will be fully on for relatively long periods and off for relatively short periods. The converse is true for TR2. An asymmetrical output may be required for instance when it is to be used to produce a sawtooth, as in a timebase.

Variable Frequency Operation

The frequency of an astable may be altered by adjusting the time constants of C1 R1 and C2 R2. Shortening either time constant will

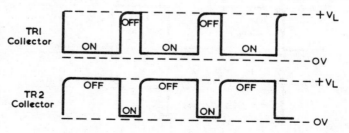

Fig. 18.4 Effect of making C1R1 > C2R2.

increase the frequency. However, if only one time constant is altered the mark-to-space ratio will be changed which may be undesirable. To maintain a constant mark-to-space ratio as the frequency is altered, the arrangement shown in Fig. 18.5 may be used.

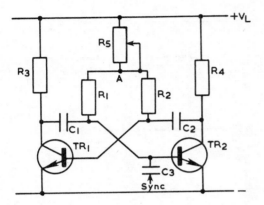

Fig. 18.5 *Variable frequency operation.*

The base bias resistors R1 and R2 are returned via a common resistor R5 to the supply line. One may consider the effect of varying R5 as altering the aiming potential for both time constants, which is illustrated in Fig. 18.6.

Since both time constants are equally affected, only one base waveform need be considered. Suppose that the aiming potential at point A as set by R5 is V_1 volts. If a coupling capacitor commences its discharge at instant t_1

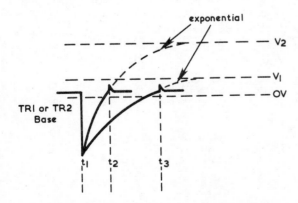

Fig. 18.6 *Effect of varying the aiming potential with R5.*

the base voltage will rise exponentially aiming for V_1. However, as soon as the voltage rises just above zero at instant t_3 the precipitate action of one transistor coming on and the other going off commences. Suppose now that the resistance of R5 is reduced to increase the aiming potential at point A to V_2 volts. When a coupling capacitor commences its discharge at instant t_1 it will aim for V_2, thus the initial slope of the discharge curve is steeper. In consequence, the base voltage will reach the cut on point for the transistor in a shorter period of time, i.e. at instant t_2. The shorter the change over period, the higher will be the frequency of operation. Thus the higher the aiming potential, the higher is the frequency of p.r.f. The variable resistor R5 may therefore serve as a frequency control. In some circuits R5 may be returned to a higher potential than the line supply voltage; this provides steep discharge curves and better stability.

An interesting situation arises if the aiming potential is a sinewave. This would cause frequency modulation of the multivibrator; a technique that is used in some video cassette recorders.

Synchronisation

The frequency stability of an astable multivibrator is not high, but it can easily be locked or synchronised to an external source of the same frequency of a frequency which is a multiple of its free-running frequency.

Synchronisation may be achieved by feeding positive going pulses to the base of one of the transistors as in Fig. 18.5 where the sync. pulse are supplied to TR2 base via C3. The effect of a sync. pulse on the base voltage waveform is shown in Fig. 18.7(a). If the sync. pulse arrives at the base when that transistor is on it will have no effect since the transistor will be bottomed. However, if it arrives when the transistor is off it will cause the base voltage to rise above zero in advance of the instant where, unaided, the transistor would normally reach the cut-on state as shown. To bring the astable exactly into synchronism with the external sync. pulses, the free-running frequency must be adjusted so that it is slightly lower than the frequency of the sync. pulses as shown in diagram (b).

Should it be desirable to lock the astable

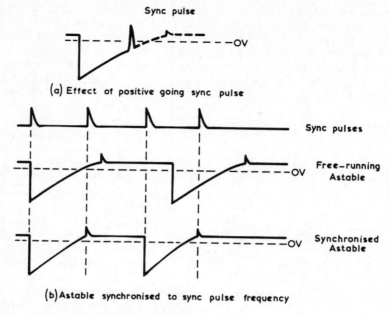

(a) Effect of positive going sync pulse

(b) Astable synchronised to sync pulse frequency

Fig. 18.7 Synchronisation of astable.

circuit to every other sync. pulse as in Fig. 18.8, the free-running frequency should be made slightly lower than the sync. pulse frequency/2. In this way, the astable acts as a frequency divider, giving one output pulse for every two sync. pulses. Higher frequency division is possible, but is not normally beyond 10 as it is then difficult to make synchronisation exact and stable.

Use of Astable to Produce a Sawtooth

A simple way of producing a free-running timebase is to use a CR sawtooth forming network and an astable multivibrator as shown in Fig. 18.9. Suppose that the mark-to-space ratio of the astable is set so that TR2 is off for long periods and on for relatively short periods as shown by the waveform for TR2 Collector.

When the transistor is off, D1 is off and C1 charges with the polarity shown towards $+ V_L$. If the time constant C1, R1 is made long compared with the TR2 off period, the rise in voltage across C1 will be fairly linear. As soon as TR2 conducts, and its collector voltage bottoms, D1 will become forward biased allowing C1 to rapidly discharge via D1 and TR2. If the on period of TR2 is long compared

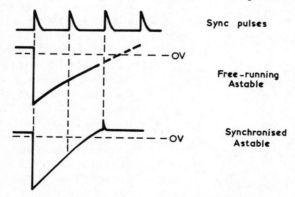

Fig. 18.8 Astable synchronised to sync pulse frequency ÷ 2.

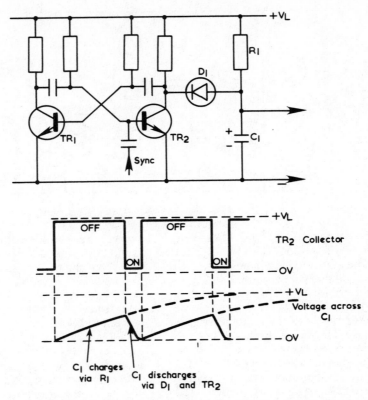

Fig. 18.9 Using an astable and CR network to produce a sawtooth.

with the discharge time of C1, the voltage across C1 will fall to zero. Thus, when TR2 goes off again, C1 will commence to charge again via R1 thereby producing a repetitive sawtooth voltage waveform across C1.

The frequency of the sawtooth waveform is determined by the frequency of the astable multivibrator and this may be locked to an external sync. source if desired. The rise in voltage across C1 corresponds to the **scan** of the timebase waveform and the fall in voltage to the **flyback** section. The longer the time-constant of C1,R1 in relation to the off time of TR2, the more linear will be the scan but the smaller its amplitude.

Monostable Multivibrator

A monostable oscillator is a triggered oscillator, i.e. not free-running and only has one stable state. At switch-on the circuit takes up this state with one transistor fully on and the other fully off. Upon the application of a trigger pulse the circuit switches over and the conducting state of the transistors are reversed. However, this is not a stable state and after a period of time determined by the circuit components it reverts to its former stable state. It remains in this state until another trigger pulse is applied.

A typical collector coupled circuit is given in Fig. 18.10. It will be seen that there is a.c. coupling between TR1 and TR2 via C2, but d.c. coupling between TR2 and TR1 via R5. At switch on, TR2 conducts hard as its base is supplied from the positive supply line via R3 and R7. Thus TR2 collector voltage is bottomed and low at, say, 0·25V. By suitable choice of R5 and R6 values, the voltage at TR1 base will be insufficient to bias TR1 on. Therefore, at switch on TR1 is off and TR2 is on; this is the stable state. It is assumed here that silicon transistors are used, but in circuits using germanium types the lower end of R6

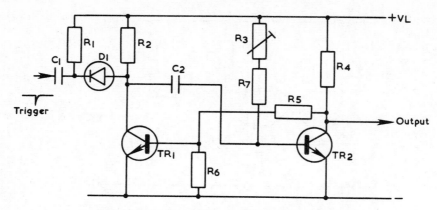

Fig. 18.10 Monostable multivibrator and trigger circuit.

may be taken to a negative potential to ensure that TR1 is fully off. As TR1 is off its collector potential will be high and C2 will be charged to practically the full line supply potential. These are the conditions prevailing prior to instant t_1 in the waveforms in Fig. 18.11. Trigger pulses are fed to TR2 base via C1 and the trigger diode D1. Since TR1 is off, both sides of the diode are at positive supply voltage. Thus, on receipt of negative trigger pulses at D1 cathode, the diode conducts and a negative going pulse is produced across R2 which is fed to TR2 base via C2.

The negative pulses applied to TR2 base at instant t_1 reduce its collector current, causing its collector voltage to rise. This rise is reflected at TR1 base causing TR1 to commence conducting. In consequence, TR1 collector voltage falls and this is passed to TR2 base via C2 turning TR2 further off. This

action is repeated quickly and often resulting in TR2 turning sharply off and TR1 coming quickly to the fully on state. TR2 is held off by the negative potential at TR2 base (in the same way as in the astable circuit). The voltage established across R3 and R7 now causes a current to flow discharging C2 through R7 and R3. This causes TR2 base voltage to rise exponentially towards $+V_L$. However, as soon as the voltage rises a little above zero TR2 commences to conduct. The resultant fall in TR2 collector potential commences an accumulative action that results in TR1 rapidly switching off and TR2 quickly coming hard on. The circuit is now back in its original stable state and will remain so until the next trigger pulse is applied. Note that when TR1 is conducting, D1 is reversed biased, thus the fall in TR1 collector potential is not fed back into the trigger pulse source.

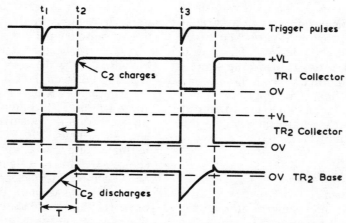

Fig. 18.11 Waveforms of monostable multivibrator.

It will be seen that at the collectors of the transistors, pulse waveforms are available having a duration T. This interval is essentially governed by the time-constant C2, R7 and R3. By varying the time-constant with the aid of R3, the duration of the pulse can be varied over quite wide limits when suitable component values are employed. Note that the p.r.f. of the monostable is determined by the p.r.f. of the trigger pulses.

Emitter Coupled Monostable

There are a number of advantages in replacing the direct coupling between TR2 collector and TR1 base with emitter coupling. A basic circuit is given in Fig. 18.12 where the direct coupling has been replaced by emitter coupling via the common emitter resistor R8.

In the stable state, TR2 is conducting as its base is returned to the positive supply line via R7, R3. The current due to TR2 flowing in R8 makes the emitter of TR1 positive and by suitable choice of values for R1 and R5, TR1 can be arranged to be cut off. When a postive trigger pulse is fed through C1 to TR1 base, the transistor conducts and its collector voltage falls. The fall in voltage is passed through C2 to TR2 base causing TR2 to turn off. As there is now no emitter current in TR2, the voltage across R8 falls a little which maintains TR1 in the on state. Capacitor C2 now discharges through R7 and R3 and when

TR2 base voltage rises a little above the voltage across R8, TR2 conducts once more. As a result of this, the voltage across R8 rises which turns TR1 off. The circuit is now back in its original stable state.

As with the collector coupled circuit, the pulse duration at the output is settled by the time constant C2, R7 and R3 and the p.r.f. of the monostable by the p.r.f. of the trigger pulses. This arrangement has the following advantage:

(a) The output may be taken from TR2 collector which is now isolated from the coupling path between transistors.

(b) Similarly, the trigger circuit is isolated from the feedback path as the trigger is applied direct to TR1 base.

(c) Greater flexibility is allowed in choosing the operating points of the transistors which is of importance in high-speed switching applications.

Use of Monostable

The main use of a monostable multivibrator is to produce a pulse of desired duration and/or a pulse with a fixed time delay. An example is given in Fig. 18.13.

Suppose that is required to produce a pulse with a particular duration having a fixed time delay from the leading edge of the pulse shown at (a). Now, if the pulse at (a) is used to trigger

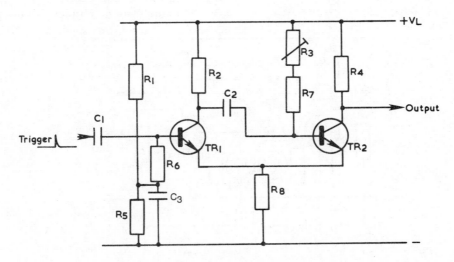

Fig. 18.12 Emitter coupled monostable multivibrator.

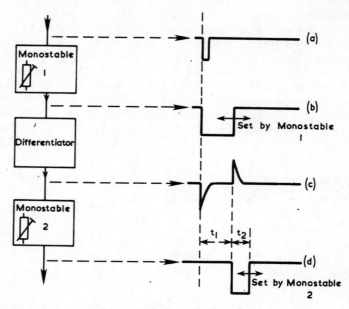

Fig. 18.13 *Use of Monostables to produce a delayed pulse.*

Monostable 1, the pulse output shown at (b) will have a width dependent upon the time-constant of this monostable and this can be set to give the duration t_1. If the output of Monostable 1 is then fed to a differentiating circuit, the output will be as at (c). By using the positive-going spike of waveform (c) to trigger Monostable 2, its output will be as at (d) with a duration t_2 set by the time constant of the monostable.

Thus, at (d) we have a pulse with a fixed time delay t_1 from the commencement of the pulse at (a) and with a particular duration t_2.

Bistable Oscillator

This type of multivibrator is extensively used in counter circuits and its basic principle was described in Volume 1. It is now necessary to study its circuit action, a typical circuits being given in Fig. 18.14.

As the name bistable implies this multivib-

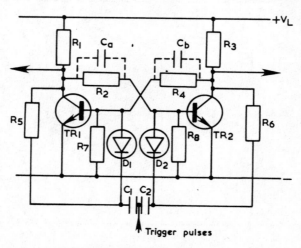

Fig. 18.14 *Bistable oscillator.*

rator has two stable states with one transistor conducting and the other cut off, producing one of its stable states. Upon the receipt of a trigger pulse the circuit changes over; the transistor that was conducting is now cut off and the transistor that was off is now conducting. This is the second stable state. The next trigger pulse to be applied causes the bistable to revert to its original stable state. A bistable is thus a triggered multivibrator.

The two transistors TR1 and TR2 are cross-coupled by R2 and R4 so that positive feedback occurs. Both transistors cannot be conducting simultaneously, except for a brief period during changeover. Thus, initially when the supply is connected one transistor is conducting and the other is cut off.

Suppose that TR1 is conducting and TR2 is cut off. As a result TR1 collector will be bottomed and, due to the low collector voltage of, say, 0·25V, the base voltage of TR2 will be insufficient to turn TR2 on (silicon transistors are assumed). Thus TR2 collector voltage will be at $+ V_L$. This is the condition illustrated in the waveforms of Fig. 18.15 just prior to instant t_1.

To change over the circuit conditions a negative going trigger pulse is required to be fed to TR1 base to switch TR1 off. The trigger pulses are applied through C1 and C2. To ensure that each trigger pulse is applied to the appropriate transistor, steering diodes D1 and D2 are employed. When TR1 is on, D1 is biased on but D2 is off. The first trigger pulse to arrive is steered through D1 to TR1 base. Here it causes TR1 to start to turn off. The

resulting rise of voltage at TR1 collector is passed via R2 to TR2 base causing TR2 to conduct. As a result TR2 collector voltage starts to fall which is passed via R4 to TR1 base causing TR1 current to reduce even further. This action is repeated rapidly many times resulting in TR1 quickly going off and TR2 rapidly coming hard on (instant t_1).

Thus the state of the circuit has been changed with TR1 cut off and TR2 conducting. The circuit will remain in this state until the next trigger pulse arrives. This pulse will be steered through D2 which is now biased on to TR2 base (D1 is off). TR2 now starts to turn off and the rise in voltage at its collector is passed on to the base of TR1 via R4. This action causes TR1 to turn on and the fall in voltage at its collector is passed to TR2 base via R2 where the effect is to further reduce TR2 current. This action is also repeated rapidly many times resulting in TR1 coming hard on and TR2 going off (instant t_2). The next trigger pulse is steered through D1 causing TR1 to cut off and TR2 to conduct (instant t_3) . . . and so on.

It will be noted that for every two trigger pulses, one complete cycle of bistable action takes place, i.e. the p.r.f. of the output at either collector is half the p.r.f. of the input trigger. Thus a bistable may be used as a ÷ 2 stage.

Speed-up Capacitors

In some bistable oscillator circuits, R2 and R4 are shunted with small value capacitors (Ca

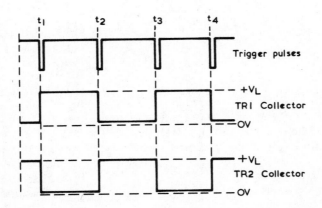

Fig. 18.15 Bistable oscillator waveforms.

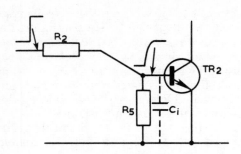

Fig. 18.16 Need for speed-up capacitor.

and Cb). These are called speed-up capacitors, and the need for them can be seen from Fig. 18.16.

When TR2 is off it may be regarded that R5 is shunted by C_i (the capacitance of the reverse biased base-emitter junction of TR2). When TR1 goes off and its collector rises as shown, R2 and C_i form a low pass filter for the step-voltage change. As a result the base waveform of TR2 would be rounded as indicated (showing the loss of high frequency components) and this would increase the switching time of the circuit. If R2 is shunted with a capacitor of suitable value, the resistor will be by-passed at h.f. and the switching time of the circuit will be reduced. Since the same argument holds good when TR1 is off, it is also necessary to shunt R4 with a speed-up capacitor.

QUESTIONS ON CHAPTER EIGHTEEN

(1) When a transistor is used as a switch and is in the fully on condition, the collector-to-emitter voltage with a 9V supply line will probably be:
(a) 9V
(b) 4·5V
(c) 2·2V
(d) 0·25V.

(2) Which of the following would result in a decrease in the frequency of the astable multivibrator ciruit of Fig. 18.2 on page 251:
(a) Smaller C1 value
(b) Larger C2 value
(c) Smaller C2 value
(d) Larger R4 value.

(3) Which of the following components faults would result in TR1 collector potential in Fig. 18.2 being permanently at $+ V_L$ volts:
(a) R2 o/c
(b) R1 o/c
(c) R4 o/c
(d) R3 o/c.

(4) In Fig. 18.2 if the capacitor C1 goes open circuit the effect will be:
(a) P.R.F. will increase
(b) Asymmetrical output
(c) No output
(d) Sawtooth output.

(5) In Fig. 18.2 if the capacitor C2 goes open circuit, the collector-to-emitter voltages of TR1 and TR2 with a supply line of 10V will be:
(a) TR1 0·25V and TR2 10V
(b) TR1 10V and TR2 0·25V
(c) TR1 0·25V and TR2 0·25V
(d) TR1 10V and TR2 10V.

(6) A d.c. voltmeter connected between the emitter and collector of TR1 or TR2 in Fig. 18.2, when the circuit is producing a square-wave output from a 10V supply, will read about:
(a) 0·25V
(b) 0·5V
(c) 5V
(d) 9·25V.

(7) There is no output from the circuit in Fig. 18.10 and the collector-to-emitter voltage of TR2 is 0·3V with a supply rail voltage of 10V. Which of the following component faults could cause these symptoms:
(a) R3 o/c
(b) TR2 base-emitter short
(c) C1 o/c
(d) TR2 emitter connection o/c.

(8) Which of the following is a free-running oscillator:
(a) An astable multivibrator
(b) A bistable multivibrator
(c) A monostable multivibrator
(d) A flip flop.

(9) The p.r.f. of the trigger applied to a bistable is 10kHz. The output waveform from one of the transistors will be at p.r.f. of:
(a) 10kHz
(b) 20kHz
(c) 1kHz
(d) 5kHz.

(10) The p.r.f. of the trigger pulses applied to a monostable is 500Hz. The output pulse will have a p.r.f. of:
(a) 250Hz
(b) 500Hz
(c) 1kHz
(d) 50 Hz.

(Answers on page 370)

CHAPTER NINETEEN

NUMBER SYSTEMS

Objectives
1 To explain binary, octal and hexadecimal number systems
2 Reasons for use of B.C.D.
3 Conversion between number systems
4 Study examples of binary addition and subtraction

IN THE **decimal** or **denary** system (base or radix 10) of which we are most familiar, we use ten digits:

$$0 \quad 1 \quad 2 \quad 3 \quad 4 \quad 5 \quad 6 \quad 7 \quad 8 \quad 9$$

Using these digits we can construct a number of any magnitude using the following columns:

Decimal Point
$$\longleftarrow \quad 10^5 \quad 10^4 \quad 10^3 \quad 10^2 \quad 10^1 \quad 10^0 \quad \cdot \quad 10^{-1} \quad 10^{-2} \quad 10^{-3} \quad 10^{-4} \quad 10^{-5} \quad \longrightarrow$$

Increasing in powers of 10   Decreasing in powers of 10

Thus, if we write   2   5   1   this means 2 hundreds +
5 tens +
1 unit

To indicate that we are using a base of 10 we should write this number as 251_{10}, but as we normally use only this numbering system the base is omitted.

Although the decimal system is convenient for human calculations it is not suitable for digital electronics, since ten different voltage or current levels would be required to specify the ten digits. It would not be difficult to assign ten voltage or current levels within a specified range, but maintaining the levels without ambiguity during processing by an electronic system would be more difficult, due to the non-linearity of devices and the effects of noise.

From earlier work it will have been noted that bipolar transistors, f.e.t.s and diodes exhibit controlled-switch characteristics, i.e. they can be placed in the fully 'on' or fully 'off' mode and are thus **2-state** or **binary** devices.

These 2-state devices are fast, reliable and inexpensive; consequently modern digital electronic systems operate on a binary or base 2 number system.

BINARY SYSTEM

The binary system is used widely in digital electronics and is the basis of machine-code language used with computers. In the binary system we use only two digits:

$$0 \text{ and } 1$$

The columns used for binary follow the same idea as for denary but are based on powers of 2 (base 2):

Binary Point
↓

$$\longleftarrow \quad 2^5 \quad 2^4 \quad 2^3 \quad 2^2 \quad 2^1 \quad 2^0 \quad \cdot \quad 2^{-1} \quad 2^{-2} \quad 2^{-3} \quad 2^{-4} \quad 2^{-5} \quad \longrightarrow$$

Increasing in powers of 2

Decreasing in powers of 2

| 32s | 16s | 8s | 4s | 2s | 1s | | ½s | ¼s | ⅛s | ¹⁄₁₆s | ¹⁄₃₂s |

Thus, if we write   1   0   1   1   this means 1 eight +
0 fours +
1 two +
1 unit
= 11 in decimal (11_{10})

Binary Fractions

In the denary system, if we move the decimal point to the right, the number is increased by a factor of ten for each column movement. Conversely, movement to the left decreases the number by a factor of ten for each column movement.

Shifting the **binary point** to the left or right again decreases or increases the number but this time by a factor of 2; for example:

$$
\begin{aligned}
1000 \cdot 0 &= 8 \\
100 \cdot 0 &= 4 \\
10 \cdot 0 &= 2 \\
1 \cdot 0 &= 1 \\
0 \cdot 1 &= 0 \cdot 5 \\
0 \cdot 01 &= 0 \cdot 25 \\
0 \cdot 001 &= 0.125 \\
&\text{etc}
\end{aligned}
$$

Thus the binary number $1101 \cdot 11$ is $13 \cdot 75$ in denary.

It should be noted that a fractional denary number cannot be expressed accurately in binary unless it consists of a sum of ½s, ¼s, ⅛s, ¹⁄₁₆s, etc.

OCTAL SYSTEM

The octal system is based on powers of 8 and uses 8 digits:

$$0 \ 1 \ 2 \ 3 \ 4 \ 5 \ 6 \ 7$$

The columns used follow the same general idea as for denary and binary but using powers of 8:

Octal Point
↓

←―――――――――― 8^3 8^2 8^1 8^0 . 8^{-1} 8^{-2} 8^{-3} ――――――――――→

Increasing in powers   Decreasing in powers
of 8   of 8

512s   64s   8s   1s   ⅛s   1/64s   1/512s

Thus, if we write   2   3   7   this means 2 sixty-fours +
                                           3 eights +
                                           7 units
                                   = 159 in denary

The octal scale is a useful shorthand way of writing binary numbers (particularly large ones). Consider the binary number 101011001111000. To convert the number into octal the binary digits are subdivided into groups of **three** and each group is converted into the decimal equivalent of that group, thus:

101   011   001   111   000   Binary

5   3   1   7   0   Decimal
                              equivalent
                              (Octal)

Thus 53170_8 is a more compact way of expressing the binary number. To convert from octal to binary is simply the reverse process; for example to express 642_8 in binary:

6   4   2   Octal

110   100   010   Binary

Thus 110100010_2 is the binary equivalent of 642_8.

HEXADECIMAL SYSTEM

The hexadecimal number system is based on powers of 16. It has become more widely used than octal due to advances made in microcomputer systems. Hex replaces octal in most microcomputers due to the reduced number of digits necessary to represent any particular binary number. Since the base is 16, sixteen symbols are required which are made up from ten digits and six alphabet characters (hybrid system):

Decimal	Hexadecimal
0	0
1	1
2	2
3	3
4	4
5	5
6	6
7	7
8	8
9	9
10	A
11	B
12	C
13	D
14	E
15	F

The column weightings are:

Hexadecimal Point

$$\longleftarrow \quad 16^4 \quad 16^3 \quad 16^2 \quad 16^1 \quad 16^0 \quad \cdot \quad 16^{-1} \quad 16^{-2} \quad 16^{-3} \quad \longrightarrow$$

Increasing in powers
of 16

Decreasing in powers
of 16

4096s 256s 16s 1s $\frac{1}{16}$s $\frac{1}{256}$s $\frac{1}{4096}$s

Thus, if we write   1   A   F   this means 15 units +
                                          10 sixteens +
                                          1 two hundred and fifty-sixes
                                  = 431 in decimal

The usefulness of Hex as a shorthand version of binary may be seen from the following:

Convert 1100111100101101_2 to Hex.

The binary number is split into groups of **four** and each group is given the Hex coding for the decimal equivalent of that group:

1100	1111	0010	1101	Binary
C	F	2	D	Hex

Thus CF2D is the Hex equivalent of the binary number 1100111100101101_2 and uses only four digits as opposed to sixteen in binary. The octal equivalent of this particular binary number is 147455 (six digits). The conversion from Hex to binary is simply the reverse process:

Convert 2FF (Hex) to binary:

2	F	F	Hex
0010	1111	1111	Binary

Hence 001011111111_2 is the binary equivalent of 2FF (Hex).

Conversion between Hex and Octal

This may be achieved by intermediary conversion to binary.

Example 1
Convert 6BC to Octal.

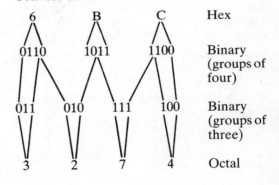

Example 2
Convert 3761_8 to Hex.

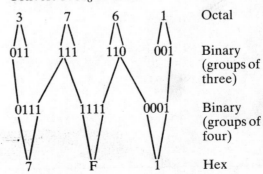

BINARY CODED DECIMAL

Although the binary system is the simplest and best for logic circuits and computers, the decimal numbering system is the one with which the majority of people are familiar. Octal and Hex are shorthand versions of binary but are not much help in conversion between binary and decimal.

To overcome these problems several binary codes have been devised to translate each denary digit into an equivalent 4-bit binary code and vice-versa.

Consider the b.c.d. form of the decimal number 3459.

D	C	B	A
Thousands decade	Hundreds decade	Tens decade	Units decade
3	4	5	9
0011	0100	0101	1001

Each digit from each decade of the denary number is coded by a block of **four** binary digits. The above result may be written as:

0011   0100   0101   1001   (b.c.d.)

or

0011010001011001   (b.c.d.)

and uses **Natural** binary coding for each decade. It will be seen that the binary digits for 0 to 9 only need be remembered since the same code is used for each decade.

Conversion from b.c.d. to binary is the reverse process:

Convert 11101101001 (b.c.d.) to denary:

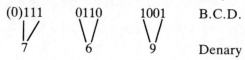

When converting to b.c.d., the fact that it is b.c.d. is not sufficient since there is a number of different b.c.d. codes in use. Table 19.1 shows the b.c.d. form for each decade. Natural binary uses 8 : 4 : 2 : 1 weighting and the second column shows 2 : 4 : 2 : 1 weighted BCD. The XS3 (excess-three) BCD is different from the other two codes in that zero is not represented by 0000. Instead, zero is represented by 0011. In natural binary code 0011 is equivalent to 3 in decimal. It will be seen by comparing the natural b.c.d. with the XS3 code that three must be added to the natural binary code sequence for the numbers 0–9 to give the XS3 sequence for numbers 0–9; hence the name 'excess-three'. Note that there is no simple weighting for the XS3 code.

Table 19.1 B.C.D. Forms

Denary Number	Natural Binary 8 : 4 : 2 : 1 BCD				2 : 4 : 2 : 1 BCD				XS3 Excess-three BCD			
	D	C	B	A	D	C	B	A	D	C	B	A
0	0	0	0	0	0	0	0	0	0	0	1	1
1	0	0	0	1	0	0	0	1	0	1	0	0
2	0	0	1	0	0	0	1	0	0	1	0	1
3	0	0	1	1	0	0	1	1	0	1	1	0
4	0	1	0	0	0	1	0	0	0	1	1	1
5	0	1	0	1	0	1	0	1	1	0	0	0
6	0	1	1	0	0	1	1	0	1	0	0	1
7	0	1	1	1	0	1	1	1	1	0	1	0
8	1	0	0	0	1	1	1	0	1	0	1	1
9	1	0	0	1	1	1	1	1	1	1	0	0

BINARY ARITHMETIC

Binary Addition

Binary numbers are added together according to the following rules:

2-Digit
$0 + 0 = 0$
$0 + 1 = 1$
$1 + 0 = 1$
$1 + 1 = 0$ (Carry 1)

3-Digit
$0 + 0 + 0 = 0$
$0 + 0 + 1 = 1$
$0 + 1 + 0 = 1$
$0 + 1 + 1 = 0$ (Carry 1)
$1 + 0 + 0 = 1$
$1 + 0 + 1 = 0$ (Carry 1)
$1 + 1 + 0 = 0$ (Carry 1)
$1 + 1 + 1 = 1$ (Carry 1)

Example 1
Find the result of $1101 + 0100$

$$1101 +$$
$$0100$$
$$= 10001$$

Example 2
Find the result of $1101 + 1111 + 0110$.

When adding three or more binary numbers together they are best added by adding two together and then adding the next on to the result:

$$1101 +$$
$$1111$$
$$= \quad 11100 +$$
$$0110$$
$$= \quad 100010$$

Example 3
Find the result of $1101 \cdot 01 + 1000 \cdot 11$.

Compound numbers are added in the same way:

$$1101 \cdot 01 +$$
$$1000 \cdot 11$$
$$= \quad 10110 \cdot 00$$

Binary Subtraction

The subtraction of one binary number from another is carried out in a computer by using what is known as the **two's complement** method as this leads to a simplification in electronic hardware.

Two's Complement Method
Consider the binary subtraction of $1101 - 1001$. The first binary number 1101 is called the **minuend** and the second binary number 1001 the **subtrahend**. To perform the calculation we find the 2's complement of the subtrahend and then **add** it to the minuend.

To find the 2's complement of the subtrahend we simply invert all of the bits (producing the 1's complement) and then add 1 to the least significant bit.

Taking	1001	(subtrahend)
inverting all bits gives	0110	(1's complement)
add 1 to the l.s.b.	+ 1	
	0111	(2's complement)

Adding the 2's complement to the minuend gives

$$1101 +$$
$$0111$$

Overflow → (1) 0100
(disregard)

Answer $= 0100$

Example 1

Find the result of 110111 − 1111 using the 2's complement method.

First we must make subtrahend the same number of bits as the minuend by adding leading 0s to the subtrahend, thus:

$$
\begin{array}{lll}
 & 001111 & \text{(subtrahend)} \\
\text{inverting all bits} & 110000 & \text{(1's complement)} \\
\text{add 1 to the l.s.b.} & +\quad 1 & \\
\hline
 & 110001 & \text{(2's complement)} \\
\end{array}
$$

Adding the 2's complement to the minuend gives

$$
\begin{array}{l}
110111\ + \\
110001 \\
\hline
\end{array}
$$

$$
\begin{array}{ll}
\text{Overflow} \rightarrow & (1)\,101000 \\
\text{(disregard)} & \hline \\
\end{array}
$$

Answer = 101000

Example 2

Find the result of 1000 − 1100.

It is clear that the subtrahend is larger than the minuend and the answer will be a negative quantity. Proceeding however as previously we have:

$$
\begin{array}{lll}
 & 1100 & \text{(subtrahend)} \\
\text{inverting all bits} & 0011 & \text{(1's complement)} \\
\text{add 1 to the l.s.b.} & +\ \ 1 & \\
\hline
 & 0100 & \text{(2's complement)} \\
\end{array}
$$

Adding the 2's complement to the minuend gives

$$
\begin{array}{l}
1000\ + \\
0100 \\
\hline
\end{array}
$$

$$
\text{No overflow} \rightarrow\ (0)\,1100
$$

Answer = 1100

No overflow indicates a negative number. To find the negative number we subtract 1 from the above result and then invert all bits thus:

$$
\begin{array}{ll}
 & 1100\ - \\
 & \quad\ 1 \\
\hline
= & 1011 \\
\text{invert all bits} & 0100 \\
\end{array}
$$

Placing a negation sign in front of it to show that it is negative produces − 0100 (−4 in decimal).

One may always check the result of binary addition or subtraction by converting the binary numbers into decimal and performing the calculation in denary.

QUESTIONS ON CHAPTER NINETEEN

(1) The binary equivalent of the decimal number 7·125 is:
(a) 111·111
(b) 111·101
(c) 111·010
(d) 111·001.

(2) The octal equivalent of the binary number 111011100 is:
(a) 13130
(b) 734
(c) 11312
(d) 821.

(3) The binary equivalent of the Hex number 3AF is:
(a) 1110101111
(b) 1111010111
(c) 1011111011
(d) 0101111111.

(4) The decimal equivalent of the natural coded BCD number 011101101001 is:
(a) 976
(b) 967
(c) 769
(d) 498.

(5) The result of adding the binary numbers 1011 + 1010 + 0110 is:
(a) 11011
(b) 10011
(c) 11010
(d) 11101.

(6) The result of the binary addition of 1001·01 + 10·111 is:
(a) 1100·111
(b) 1011·101
(c) 1101·011
(d) 1100·001.

(7) The decimal result of adding $1AB_H$ + 101101_2 + 627_8 is:
(a) 921
(b) 879
(c) 8039
(d) 1038.

(8) In general the smallest number of digits results when a binary number is written in:
(a) Hex
(b) BCD
(c) Octal
(d) Decimal.

(9) The decimal result of the binary subtraction 101101 − 100010 is:
(a) 5
(b) − 9
(c) 10
(d) 11.

(10) The decimal result of the binary subtraction 11010 − 11100·1 is:
(a) 3·5
(b) 2·5
(c) − 2·5
(d) 7.

(Answers on page 370)

CHAPTER TWENTY

DIGITAL CIRCUITS

Objectives

1 To define positive and negative logic.
2 To describe the principles of combinational logic circuits; compile truth tables and write Boolean expressions.
3 To describe the operation of S-R, D-type and JK bistables.
4 To describe the construction and operation of counters and registers.
5 To explain the operation of multi-segment displays and decoders.

IN VOLUME 1 of this series basic logic gates were introduced and examples of simple gate combinations were given. It is now necessary to consider gate combinations further and to develop more complex logic circuits.

Positive and Negative Logic

In digital circuits the logic 1 and 0 states correspond to particular electrical voltages. If the **more positive** of the two states is selected as logic 1 then the system is said to use **positive logic**, see Fig. 20.1(a). On the other hand if the **more negative** of the two states is selected

as logic 1, the system is said to use negative logic, see Fig. 20.1(b).

With logic families, e.g. TTL, CMOS, I^2L, etc. the actual logic voltage levels found in digital circuits fall within stated voltage ranges. There must be sufficient voltage clearance between these ranges so that there is no ambiguity in recognising a logic 1 voltage from a logic 0 voltage; see Fig. 20.2 which illustrates the voltage ranges for TTL. Here positive logic is assumed since the more positive of the two voltage ranges is designated logic 1. There is no reason why negative logic notation should not be used; however, it

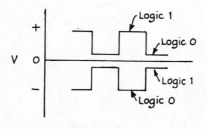

(a) Examples of Positive Logic

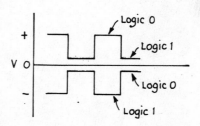

(b) Examples of Negative Logic

Fig. 20.1 Positive and negative logic.

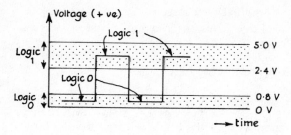

Fig. 20.2 TTL logic levels (positive logic).

should be noted that the name given to a logic gate as defined by its truth table depends upon the logic notation employed. Consider the following example:

Suppose that the voltages measured at the input and output of a 2-input logic gate are as shown in the truth table of Fig. 20.3. If **positive logic** is assumed where logic 1 = +5V and logic 0 = +0.2V, then the truth table may be redrawn as in Fig. 20.4. It will be seen that the

Inputs		Output
A	B	F
+ 0·2 V	+ 0·2 V	+ 0·2 V
+ 0·2 V	+ 5·0 V	+ 0·2 V
+ 5·0 V	+ 0·2 V	+ 0·2 V
+ 5·0 V	+ 5·0 V	+ 5·0 V

Fig. 20.3 Input & output voltages of 2-input gate.

A	B	F
0	0	0
0	1	0
1	0	0
1	1	1

Fig. 20.4 Positive logic (AND function).

A	B	F
1	1	1
1	0	1
0	1	1
0	0	0

Fig. 20.5 Negative logic (OR function).

gate behaves as an AND gate. On the other hand, if **negative logic** is assumed where logic 1 = 0.2V and logic 0 = 5V, the truth table may be redrawn as in Fig. 20.5. In this case it will be noted that the gate behaves as an OR gate!

Thus, when working on digital circuits it is important to be aware of the notation used. Positive logic systems tend to be very common but do not take it for granted that positive logic always applies. **Mixed logic** is also possible, e.g. the inputs may use positive logic and the outputs negative logic. Positive logic will be assumed throughout this chapter, unless otherwise stated.

EX-OR and EX-NOR Gates

Exclusive-OR

An exclusive-OR gate has two inputs and a single output. Its symbol is given in Fig. 20.6(a). The output from an exclusive-OR gate will assume the logic 1 state if one and only one input is as logic 1. A truth table for the gate is given in Fig. 20.6(b). It will be seen that unlike the OR gate, output is not obtained when both inputs are at logic 1, i.e. it excludes this condition. Since an output is obtained only when the input logic levels are **different**, it is sometimes referred to as a **non-equivalence** gate.

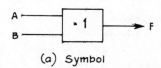

(a) Symbol

Inputs		Output
A	B	F
0	0	0
0	1	1
1	0	1
1	1	0

(b) Truth Table

Fig. 20.6 Exclusive-OR gate.

Exclusive-NOR

An exclusive-NOR gate performs the opposite function to the exclusive-OR gate. Its symbol and truth table are given in Fig. 20.7. It will be seen that output (logic 1) is obtained

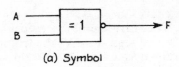

(a) Symbol

Inputs		Output
A	B	F
0	0	1
0	1	0
1	0	0
1	1	1

(b) Truth Table

Fig. 20.7 Exclusive NOR-gate.

only when the inputs are the same or coincident. It is thus often referred to as a **coincident** or **equivalence** gate.

Boolean Expressions

Boolean or **Switching** Algebra is a convenient way of representing the action of logic gates or systems and is simpler than truth tables, particularly when there is a large number of inputs. The symbols used relate to the fundamental logic gate operations of AND, OR and NOT:

Combinational Logic

Logic gates are frequently used in combination with one another to produce complex logic systems and some further examples will be considered here.

Example 1

A self-service petrol pump will deliver petrol (F) if the grade selector is set at either 4-star (A) or 2-star (B) and the cashier switch (C) is also operated. Draw a logic circuit that will implement this requirement giving the Boolean expression at the output and the truth table. A suitable logic circuit is given in Fig. 20.8(a) requiring an OR gate G1 and an AND gate G2. The Boolean expression for the output is F = (A + B) . C.

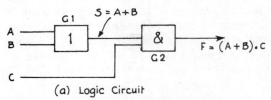

(a) Logic Circuit

Fig. 20.8(a) Logic circuit of petrol pump.

In drawing up a truth table for combinational gates it is useful to tabulate the output of any intermediate gate(s) as shown in Fig. 20.8(b).

Logic Function	Boolean Expression

AND$\qquad\qquad$ F = A . B (where . means AND)
F (the output) is at logic 1 if the inputs A and B are both at logic 1.

OR$\qquad\qquad$ F = A + B (where + means OR)
F is at logic 1 if A or B is at logic 1.

NOT$\qquad\qquad$ F = $\bar{A}$ (where $\bar{A}$ means the opposite of A)
F is at logic 1 when A is not at logic 1.

Thus for NAND and NOR we have:

$\qquad$NAND$\qquad\qquad$ F = $\overline{A . B}$

$\qquad$NOR$\qquad\qquad$ F = $\overline{A + B}$

and for EX–OR and EX–NOR we have:

$\qquad$EX–OR$\qquad\qquad$ F = (A . $\bar{B}$) + ($\bar{A}$. B)

$\qquad$EX–NOR$\qquad\qquad$ F = (A . B) + ($\bar{A}$. $\bar{B}$)

Inputs to G1		Output	Input	Output
A	B	S	C	F
O	O	O	O	O
O	1	1	O	O
1	O	1	O	O
1	1	1	O	O
O	O	O	1	O
O	1	1	1	1
1	O	1	1	1
1	1	1	1	1

Intermediate Output (G1)

Inputs to G2

(b) Truth Table

Fig. 20.8(b) Logic circuit of petrol pump.

Here we see that the intermediate output (S) has been listed for the four combinations of the inputs A and B. The output at S thus provides one of the two inputs together with C for the AND gate G2. However, it will be noted that the four combinations of inputs A and B have been listed twice. This is because that for every combination of A and B, input C can be at logic 1 or logic 0. The listing thus gives a **full truth table**.

Example 2

A video cassette recorder is required to rewind the tape from right-to-left when the R button is operated but to fast-forward the tape from left-to-right when the F button is operated. The control system will need to provide two outputs, X to operate the rewind motor and Y to operate the fast-forward motor ('1' signifies output and '0' no output). A safeguard should be incorporated to protect the tape from breaking should the F and R buttons be operated simultaneously. Draw a logic circuit that will meet these requirements. Give the Boolean expression at each output and draw up a truth table.

A suitable logic circuit is given in Fig. 20.9(a) using two AND gates and two inverter gates. It will be seen that output is obtained from G1 only when the R button is operated and the F button is not operated. Similarly an output is obtained from G2 only when the F button is operated and the R button is not operated. If both R and F buttons are operated simultaneously no output is obtained at X or Y so neither motor will turn. These conditions are confirmed by the truth table of Fig. 20.9(b).

Example 3

In an industrial process control an alarm (F) is to be given if two liquid containers A and B

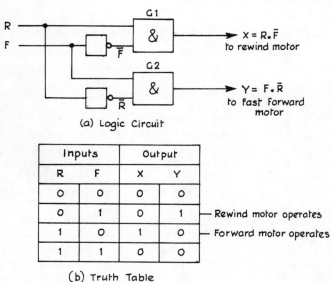

(a) Logic Circuit

Inputs		Output	
R	F	X	Y
O	O	O	O
O	1	O	1
1	O	1	O
1	1	O	O

— Rewind motor operates

— Forward motor operates

(b) Truth Table

Fig. 20.9 Logic circuit for VCR motor control.

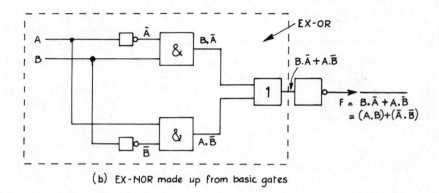

(a) Logic Circuit

(b) EX-NOR made up from basic gates

Inputs		Output	
A	B	F	
0	0	1	— Both containers empty
0	1	0	
1	0	0	
1	1	1	— Both containers full

(c) Truth Table

Fig. 20.10 Logic circuit for liquid container alarm.

are either both full (1) or both empty (0). No alarm is to be sounded if only one container is empty or only one container is full. Draw a logic circuit that will implement this requirement and produce a truth table. The required logic circuit is given in Fig. 20.10(a). This is an equivalence or Exclusive-NOR gate. The gate function may be implemented using basic logic gates as illustrated in Fig. 20.10(b). Sensors would be required to detect the empty and full levels of the containers and the truth table of Fig. 20.10(c) confirms that the alarm will sound only when the sensors indicate that both containers are empty or both are full.

Example 4

An electrical machine should only operate (X) if one and only one of two switches S and T are operated and a safety guard (Q) is in position. Draw a logic circuit that will implement this requirement and produce a truth table.

The logic solution is an EX-OR gate and an AND gate connected as shown in Fig. 20.11(a). The truth table is given in Fig. 20.11(b); note again the use of an intermediate output in forming the full truth table. The use of the EX-OR gate permits one and only one switch to operate the machine.

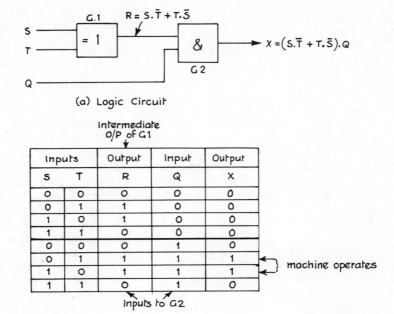

(a) Logic Circuit

Inputs		Output	Input	Output	
S	T	R	Q	X	
0	0	0	0	0	
0	1	1	0	0	
1	0	1	0	0	
1	1	0	0	0	
0	0	0	1	0	
0	1	1	1	1	machine operates
1	0	1	1	1	
1	1	0	1	0	

Fig. 20.11 Logic circuit for machine control.

Example 5

Using NAND gates only, draw logic diagrams to perform the OR and NOR operations. Fig. 20.12(a) and (b) show how 2-input NAND gates may be arranged to perform the OR and NOR operations. Note that when the 2 inputs of the NAND gate are commoned it behaves as a NOT gate.

There are many attractions in standardising with a single type of gate (NAND or NOR), particularly with large-scale integration. The NAND and NOR gates are 'universal', i.e.

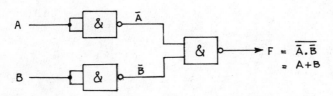

(a) Use of NAND gates to produce OR function

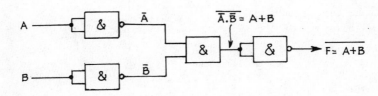

(b) Use of NAND gates to produce NOR function

Fig. 20.12 NAND gate standardisation.

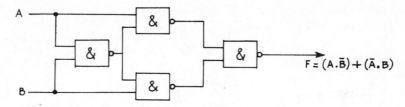

Fig. 20.13 Use of NAND gates to produce Exclusive-OR.

any other type of gate may be synthesised by using just NAND or NOR alone. The diagram of Fig. 20.13 shows how the Exclusive-OR function may be implemented using just NAND gates.

Example 6

Draw a truth table for the logic diagram of Fig. 20.14 including the intermediate outputs X, Y and Z. From the truth table deduce a simpler form for the arrangement. The truth table is given in Fig. 20.15. It will be seen that the arrangement effectively performs the NAND function, thus the logic diagram may be replaced by a 2-input NAND gate.

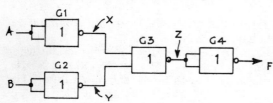

Fig. 20.14

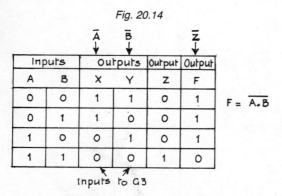

Inputs		Outputs		Output	Output
A	B	X	Y	Z	F
0	0	1	1	0	1
0	1	1	0	0	1
1	0	0	1	0	1
1	1	0	0	1	0

$F = \overline{A.B}$

Inputs to G3

Fig. 20.15 Truth table for Fig. 20.14.

Fan-in and Fan-out

The **fan-out** of a logic gate is the maximum number of basic logic gates that the gate may supply simultaneously without causing the

output logic level to fall outside its specification.

The diagrams of Fig. 20.16 show the Output/Input logic level profiles for a standard TTL logic gate. Diagram(a) shows that it has a HIGH output (logic 1) window from 2·4V to 5V and will provide a source current of 400μA. The LOW output (logic 0) window is from 0V to 0·4V and will sink currents up to 16mA. Diagram(b) shows that the HIGH input level is from 2V to 5V with an input current of 40μA. The LOW input level is from 0V to 0·8V with an input current of 1·6mA.

Thus if (a) is the output profile of one TTL device and (b) is the input profile of another TTL device, it can be readily seen that the maximum number of devices that (a) can drive simultaneously is 400μA/40μA = 10, or 16mA/1·6mA = 10. Therefore the fan-out is 10 in either the LOW or HIGH output state. Thus a standard TTL gate has a fan-out of 10.

The **fan-in** of a logic gate is the maximum number of separate inputs which may be applied to the gate. In many cases fan-in is limited by the switching speed of the gate (propagation delay) since one limit on the switching speed is the increase in stray capacitance arising from adding more separate

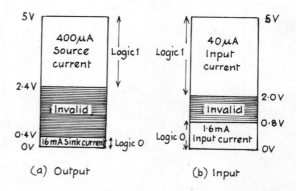

(a) Output   (b) Input

Fig. 20.16 TTL output/input logic profiles.

inputs. Sometimes fan-in expanders may be used to increase the fan-in figure.

I.C. Packaging

The main reason for the growth of digital integrated circuits is that they are more reliable, smaller and lighter than discrete circuits; they require fewer circuit connections, can be mass produced and are thus cheaper. Also, complex digital circuits can be fabricated in i.c. form that would be uneconomical using alternative techniques. I.C.s for logic circuit families may be divided broadly into those based on bipolar transistor techniques, e.g. TTL and ECL, and those employing metal oxide semiconductor devices, e.g. NMOS, CMOS, etc.

An integrated circuit consists of a single crystal chip of silicon on which is formed an electronic circuit containing both active and passive component elements. The silicon chips are placed into packages in which they will be used. The pins of the package are connected by wire bonding to the chip circuit. It is the pins of the package to which are connected supply voltages, input and output signals and external components. There are three i.c. packages in common use:

Dual-in-line

This is the most common package (Fig. 20.17(a)) and consists of a circuit mounted on a lead frame and encapsulated with a plastic compound. Some types are

hermetically sealed and use a ceramic encapsulation with glass for the hermetic sealing. The dual-in-line package is available in 8-pin, 14-pin, 16-pin, 18-pin, 20-pin, 28-pin and 40-pin versions.

Flat Package

This type is intended for direct surface mounting by soldering on to the printed circuit board (Fig. 20.17(b)). The encapsulation is usually of ceramic with hermetic sealing. This type is available in 10, 14 and 16-pin versions and provides a rigid and reliable circuit-board connection.

TO Package

The TO metal package of Fig. 20.17(c) is similar to that used for discrete transistors and is available with 8, 10 and 12 pins.

Integrated circuits range from small scale integration (up to 100 components per chip) to very large scale (up to 10 000 components per chip). Thus, even with s.s.i. there is room on a chip for a number of basic logic gates. Some common multiple gate i.c.s using the dual-in-line package are shown in Fig. 20.18.

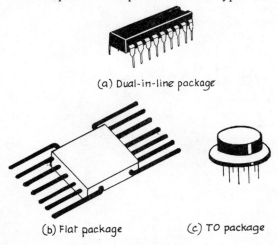

(a) Dual-in-line package

(b) Flat package   (c) TO package

Fig. 20.17 I.C. packages.

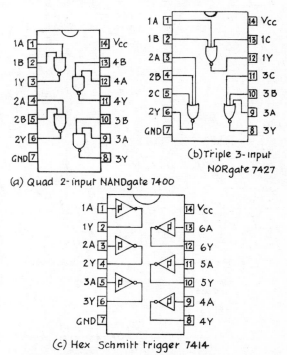

(a) Quad 2-input NANDgate 7400

(b) Triple 3-input NORgate 7427

(c) Hex Schmitt trigger 7414

Fig. 20.18 Examples of multiple gate I.Cs.

Half-Adder

A digital computer or calculator must be able to add binary numbers according to the rules:

A		B		SUM
0	+	0	=	0
0	+	1	=	1
1	+	0	=	1
1	+	1	=	0 and CARRY 1

This may be achieved using a combinational logic circuit, see Fig. 20.19.

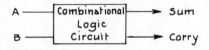

Fig. 20.19 Addition of binary numbers.

Inspection of the rules shows that the relation between A, B and the SUM columns requires the use of the EX-OR function, thus the required combinational logic circuit is as shown in Fig. 20.20. This is known as a 'half-adder'.

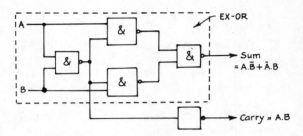

Fig. 20.20 Half-adder logic circuit.

Full-Adder

In the addition process, an electronic 'adder' must be capable of adding three binary digits: digit A, digit B and the 'carry digit' from the previous column according to the rules.

Two half-adders are required to perform this process and the combinational logic circuit becomes a 'full-adder', see Fig. 20.21.

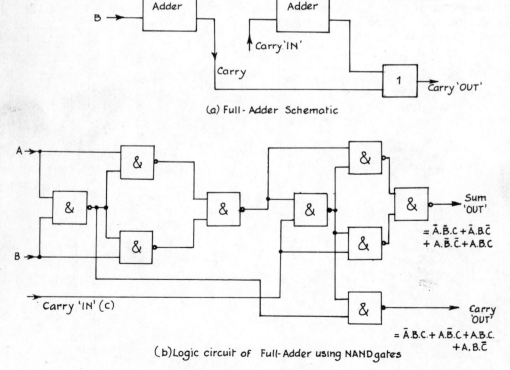

(a) Full-Adder Schematic

(b) Logic circuit of Full-Adder using NAND gates

Fig. 20.21 Full adder.

A	B	CARRY IN	SUM	CARRY OUT
0	0	0	0	0
0	0	1	1	0
0	1	0	1	0
0	1	1	0	1
1	0	0	1	0
1	0	1	0	1
1	1	0	0	1
1	1	1	1	1

Parallel Adder

Two multi-digit binary numbers may be added serially, i.e. one column at a time, or in parallel where all columns are added simultaneously. In serial addition each pair of digits from the two binary numbers is presented to a full-adder in a timed sequence from a memory store (shift register); this is a relatively slow process compared with parallel addition where the answer is produced almost instantaneously.

Figure 20.22 shows the basic idea of a 4-bit parallel binary adder such as the SN7483. This is capable of adding together two 4-bit binary numbers but requires four full-adders as shown. The logic states given on the diagram illustrate the operation when adding the two binary numbers P and Q (1101 + 1110) where P1 and Q1 are the least significant digits. The carry-in (Ci) terminal of the l.s.d. full-adder is permanently hard-wired to logic 0.

Considering the operation in pairs of digits, P1 and Q1 are added in FA1, producing a sum of logic 1 and a carry out (Co) of logic 0. In FA2 the digits P2 and Q2 are added to the carry-in, producing a sum of logic 1 and a carry-out of logic 0. Full-adder FA3 adds together P3, Q3 and the carry-in digit, resulting in a sum of logic 0 and a carry-out of logic 1. Finally, FA4 adds together P4, Q4 and the carry-in digit, producing a sum of logic 1 and a carry-out of logic 1.

Two 4-bit full adders may be used together to produce an 8-bit full adder.

A parallel adder may be used as a combined

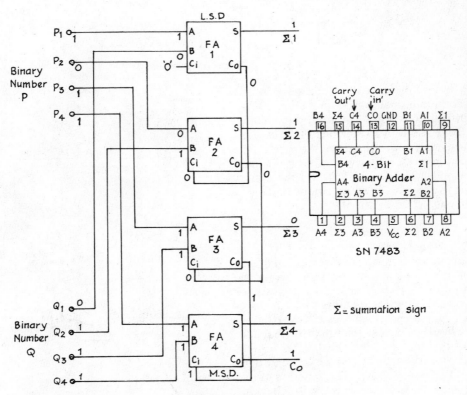

Fig. 20.22 Parallel adder.

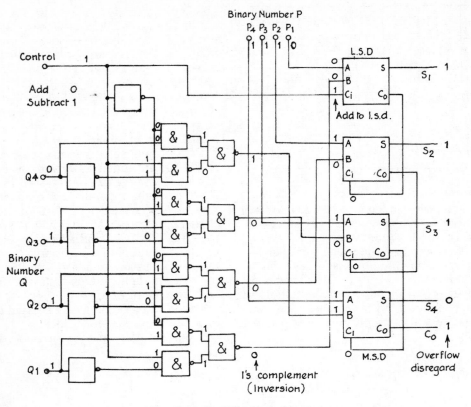

Fig. 20.23 Parallel adder/subtractor.

adder/subtractor with the addition of some extra combinational logic circuit (Fig. 20.23). A control line is used to initiate the change-over from addition to subtraction. The logic states given on the diagram show it in the subtraction mode (Binary Number P — Binary Number Q). The full-adders add the Binary Number P to the 2s complement of Binary Number Q.

Binary Comparators

Binary comparators are combinational logic circuits that are used for comparing the magnitude of parallel binary input words or bytes or checking for equality. The arrangement of Fig. 20.24 which uses EX-NOR gates may be used to check the equality/inequality of two 4-bit binary words. The AND gate gives out a logic 1 for equality (match) or logic 0 for inequality (non-match). This combinational circuit may be utilised for security checking where, say, Binary Word A is a stored code

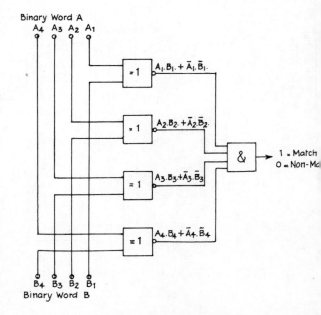

Fig. 20.24 4-bit equality comparator.

and Binary Word B is the pass code which must match the stored code before the AND gate will operate to permit access, use of machine, etc. Obviously an 8-bit comparator would give better security, as $2^8 = 256$ codes would be available. It could be arranged that after, say, three non-matches the security checker would be inhibited thus preventing unauthorised access, etc.

It is sometimes necessary to know whether a Binary Number A is greater than, less than or equal to another Binary Number B. This requires the use of a **magnitude comparator**. The basic idea may be grasped by considering a 1-bit magnitude comparator (Fig. 20.25). This arrangement will indicate whether binary digit A is greater than, less than or equal to binary digit B and its operation is summarised in the truth table on page 282.

It will be seen that G2 provides a logic 1 at its output only when bits A and B are of equal

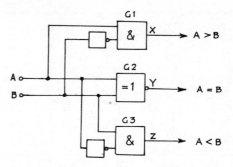

Fig. 20.25 1-bit magnitude comparator.

magnitude. The inverter gate at G1 input ensures that G1 gives out a logic 1 only when bit A is greater than bit B; similarly G2 gives an output only when bit A is less than bit B in magnitude.

This idea may be extended for comparison of the magnitude between binary numbers of any number of bits, but at the expense of an

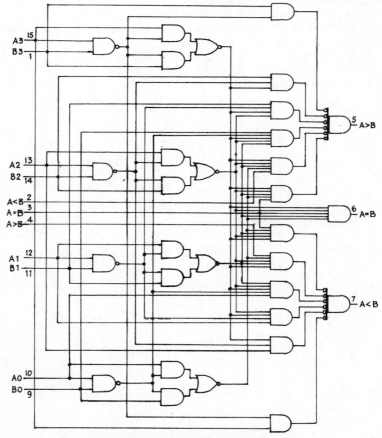

Fig. 20.26 4-bit magnitude comparator (7485).

| Inputs | | Outputs | | |
A	B	X A > B	Y A = B	Z A < B
0	0	0	1	0
0	1	0	0	1
1	0	1	0	0
1	1	0	1	0

increase in the complexity of the combinational logic circuit. Figure 20.26 shows a 4-bit magnitude comparator (7485).

DIODE MATRIX ENCODER/DECODER

Encoder

An encoder has a number of inputs, only one of which is in the logic 1 state and a digital code is generated for the input in the logic 1 state. Each input will therefore generate its own unique code when in the logic 1 state.

A diode matrix encoder is shown in Fig. 20.27 where the switches represent the inputs and Y_0–Y_3 is the output of the encoder. The arrangement could be used to generate a

binary code for each key depressed on an alphanumeric keyboard. Supposing for example that switch S4 is closed. This will cause diodes D1 and D2 to conduct producing at the Y_0 and Y_1 outputs +5V (logic 1) with the Y_2 and Y_3 outputs remaining at 0V (logic 0). The table below shows the unique binary codes generated for each key when closed.

Switch closed	Y_3	Y_2	Y_1	Y_0
S1	0	0	0	0
S2	0	0	0	1
S3	0	0	1	0
S4	0	0	1	1
S5	0	1	0	0
S6	0	1	0	1
S7	0	1	1	0
S8	0	1	1	1
S9	1	0	0	0
S10	1	0	0	1

With the four output lines, the arrangement is capable of generating sixteen unique codes thus a maximum of 16 switches may be used.

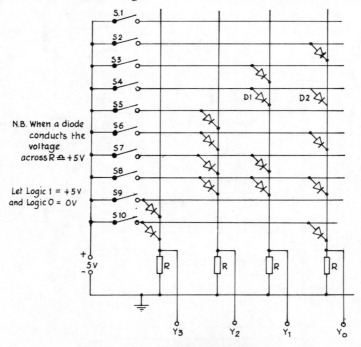

N.B. When a diode conducts the voltage across R ≜ +5V

Let Logic 1 = +5V and Logic 0 = 0V

Fig. 20.27 Diode matrix encoder (10–4 line).

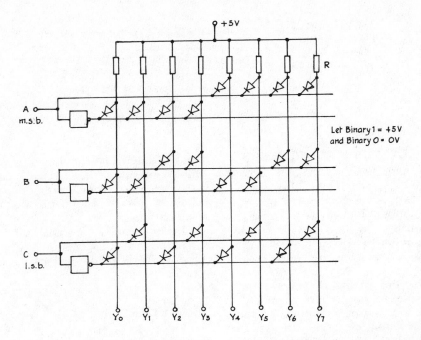

Fig. 20.28 Diode matrix decoder (3–8 line).

Decoder

With, say, 128 switches seven output lines would be used providing 128 unique codes.

A decoder performs the opposite function of an encoder, i.e. for each of its input codes one and only one output line is excited (logic 1 or logic 0). The arrangement of Fig. 20.28 shows a diode matrix decoder which will decode a 3-bit binary code at its input to provide a logic 1(HIGH) on one of its output lines Y_0–Y_7 for each code applied at its input.

The table below shows the relation between the input codes and the state of the output lines.

| Input code | | | Output state | | | | | | | |
A	B	C	Y_7	Y_6	Y_5	Y_4	Y_3	Y_2	Y_1	Y_0
0	0	0	0	0	0	0	0	0	0	1
0	0	1	0	0	0	0	0	0	1	0
0	1	0	0	0	0	0	0	1	0	0
0	1	1	0	0	0	0	1	0	0	0
1	0	0	0	0	0	1	0	0	0	0
1	0	1	0	0	1	0	0	0	0	0
1	1	0	0	1	0	0	0	0	0	0
1	1	1	1	0	0	0	0	0	0	0

The above scheme could be used to decode the digital code in a remote control system or data transmission system where each code represents a particular function and the presence of a logic 1 on a particular output line will initiate that function.

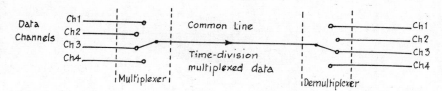

Fig. 20.29 Multiplexer–Demultiplexer principle.

MULTIPLEXER/DEMULTIPLEXER

A digital multiplexer acts like a fast operating rotary switch connecting signals from various data channels, one at a time, into a common output line as illustrated in Fig. 20.29 which shows the basic principle. Thus in the common line, the data signals from the various input channels are **time division multiplexed**.

At the other end of the system, the time division multiplexed data signals in the common line have to be sorted out into the various channels and a demultiplexer may be used for this purpose which performs the opposite function to that of the multiplexer. The principle of Fig. 20.29 is used in data transmission systems where data is sent serially over a common single line. To ensure, for example,

that channel 1 data applied at the multiplexer input appears at the channel 1 output of the demultiplexer, some form of synchronising must be used between the multiplexer and demultiplexer.

In practice the mechanical switches of Fig.20.29 are replaced by logic gates which are operated in sequence by binary coded channel address signals.

4-To-1 Line Digital Multiplexer

The logic diagram of Fig. 20.30 shows an arrangement for multiplexing 4 digital data channels into a common output. To select up to 4 channels a 2-bit binary address is required which is applied to the channel address inputs A and B. For example, with the **enable** line

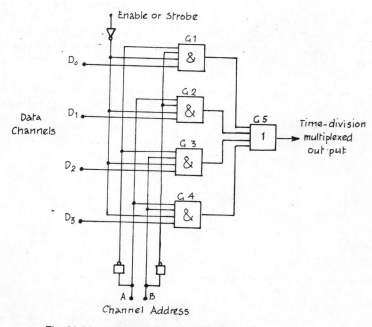

Fig. 20.30 4-to-1 line digital multiplexer.

LOW and with A = 0, B = 0 the AND gate G1 will be enabled and the data applied to the D_0 input will appear at the output of the OR gate G5. The table under shows the particular input channel connected to G5 output for the four possible address inputs applied to A and B.

Enable	Address B	A	Data channel connected to G5 o/p
LOW	0	0	D_0
LOW	0	1	D_1
LOW	1	0	D_2
LOW	1	1	D_3

The channel address may be obtained from a counter. By applying a strobe pulse (active LOW) to the enable line, the switching may be effected at a particular time instant.

4-To-1 Line Demultiplexer

The logic circuit of a demultiplexer is given in Fig. 20.31. Data from the common line is applied to one input of G5 with a strobe or enable (LOW) applied to the other input. The binary coded channel address is applied to the address inputs A and B. With, for example, A = 0, B = 0 the input data will appear at the output of Y_0. The table under shows the output NAND gate which is active for the four possible channel address combinations.

Strobe	Channel Address B	A	Output NAND gate active
LOW	0	0	G1
LOW	0	1	G2
LOW	1	0	G3
LOW	1	1	G4

SEQUENTIAL LOGIC CIRCUITS

In sequential logic circuits, the output depends upon binary signals which have already been applied over some previous period of time. A sequential system must therefore possess some 'storage' or 'memory'

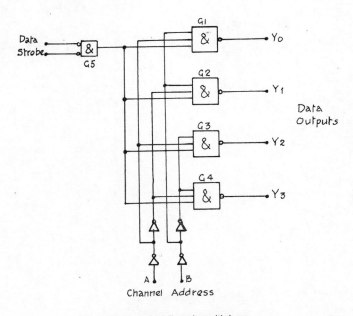

Fig. 20.31 1-to-4 line demultiplexer.

device. It should be noted that combinational logic elements are also involved in sequential systems.

Bistable Element

A bistable is a simple memory or storage element and has two stable states. Once the device has been put into one state it will remain in that state until a signal is applied to change it to its new second stable state. If the power supply is disrupted, the state to which the bistable will return when power is restored is indeterminate.

The basic principle of the bistable oscillator was dealt with in Chapter 18 and it will now be shown how the bistable can be formed from logic gates.

S-R Bistable

The SET-RESET bistable is the fundamental bistable element and its symbol is given in Fig. 20.32(a). It has two inputs SET (S) and RESET (R) and two outputs Q and $\bar{Q}$, where $\bar{Q}$ means the opposite of Q, i.e. if Q = 0 then $\bar{Q}$ = 1 and vice-versa. The S-R bistable may be formed from two cross-coupled NOR gates as shown in Fig. 20.32(b).

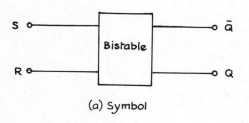

(a) Symbol

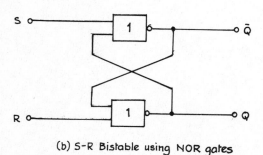

(b) S-R Bistable using NOR gates

Fig. 20.32 S-R bistable.

Operation

S = 0, R = 0. When power is applied to the bistable, the Q and $\bar{Q}$ outputs will take up opposite logic states. Suppose that initially that Q = 0 and $\bar{Q}$ = 1 and that S = 0, R = 0, as shown in Fig. 20.33.

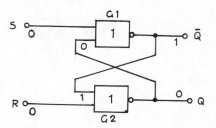

Fig. 20.33 S = 0, R = 0 (no change-store).

It will be seen from the logic states on the diagram that this is a stable operating condition. Since Q = 0, both inputs to G1 will be at logic 0 and its output at logic 1. Since $\bar{Q}$ = 1, one of the inputs to G2 will be at logic 1 thus its output must be at logic 0. It follows that Q holds $\bar{Q}$ at logic 1 and $\bar{Q}$ holds Q at logic 0.

S = 1, R = 0. Suppose now that input S is taken to the logic 1 state with input R remaining at logic 0. The initial state is therefore as in Fig. 20.34(a). The application

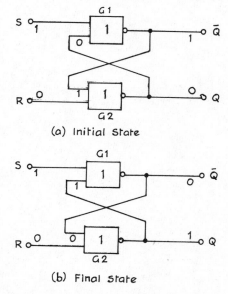

Fig. 20.34 S = 1, R = 0 (set Q to logic 1).

of a logic 1 to G1 from the S input will cause the $\bar{Q}$ output to change state to logic 0 as shown in Fig. 20.34(b). This results in both inputs to G2 becoming logic 0 causing the Q output to change state to logic 1. If the S line is now returned to logic 0 it will be seen that the Q output remains at logic 1 ($\bar{Q} = 0$). The logic 1 need only be applied to the S input momentarily since the feedback between gates causes the bistable to memorise the instruction. It should be noted that a further logic 1 applied to S has no effect once $Q = 1$.

S = 0, R = 1. Supposing now that after setting the Q output to logic 1, the R input is placed at logic 1 with the S input held at logic 0. The initial state is then as in Fig. 20.35(a). The application of the logic 1 to G2 from the R input will cause the Q output to change state to logic 0. This action results in both inputs to G1 assuming the logic 0 state and for the $\bar{Q}$ output to change to logic 1, see Fig. 20.35(b). Again the logic 1 need only be applied momentarily. If the R input is returned to logic 0 it will be seen that the Q output will remain at logic 0.

S = 1, R = 1. If the S and R inputs are simultaneously set at logic 1, see Fig. 20.36, then both the Q and $\bar{Q}$ outputs will be at logic 0. If then the S and R inputs are returned to

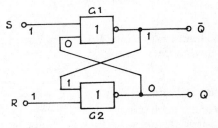

Fig. 20.36 S = 1, R = 1 (output state indeterminate).

logic 0 the output will be indeterminate depending upon the relative switching speed of the two gates, i.e. if G2 is the faster gate the Q output will be set at logic 1 but if G1 is the faster the $\bar{Q}$ output will go to logic 1. Because of the uncertainty of the output state, the condition $S = R = 1$ must be avoided.

As with other logic devices, we may draw a truth table for the S-R bistable which summarises its operation, see Fig. 20.37. In the table, the column Q_n represents the state of the Q output **prior to** the application of the inputs S and R and Q_{n+1} represents the state of the Q output **after** the application of the listed inputs at S and R.

The S-R bistable may be constructed from NAND gates as shown in Fig. 20.38.

Typical applications for S-R bistables in-

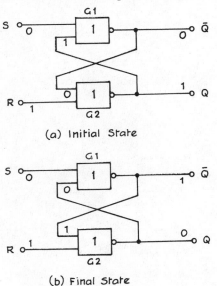

(a) Initial State

(b) Final State

Fig. 20.35 S = 0, R = 1 (reset Q output to logic 0).

S	R	Q_n	Q_{n+1}	
0	0	0	0	} No change (store condition)
0	0	1	1	
1	0	0	1	} Q output SET at Logic 1
1	0	1	1	
0	1	0	0	} Q output RESET at Logic 0
0	1	1	0	
1	1	0	?	} Indeterminate output state
1	1	1	?	

Fig. 20.37 Truth table for S-R bistable.

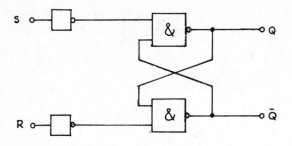

Fig. 20.38 S-R bistable formed from cross-coupled NAND gates.

clude temporary stores for binary information and switch debouncing.

Switch Debouncer

When mechanical switches are used to provide logic inputs to digital circuits, 'contact bounce' can lead to problems as the contacts are closed. The effect of the bounce is to produce several pulses when only **one** should have been produced. The S-R bistable can be used to eliminate multiple output, see Fig. 20.39. On the first make the Q output is set to logic 1, the remaining bounces have no further effect. In the 'off' position of the switch, the logic states are as shown in the diagram. On the first make, the Q output will be set at logic 1 (Q̄ at logic 0) since the S input will take up the logic 1 state and the R input the logic 0 state. As the switch contacts break, both the S and R inputs will assume the logic 0 state and thus the output will remain unchanged. On the next make when S = 1 and R = 0 the Q output will remain in the logic 1 state since the bistable was previously 'set'.

Clocked S-R Bistable

It is often desirable to control synchronously all operations in a digital logic system and this may be achieved using 'synchronising' or 'clock' pulses. By using clock pulses generated by a stable oscillator it is possible to 'gate' or 'clock' the logic levels at the S and R inputs into the bistable at some precise instant in time. The clocking may be implemented on the leading edges of the clock pulses as in Fig. 20.40(a) or on the trailing edges as in Fig. 20.40(b).

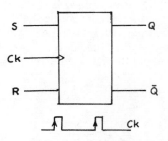

(a) Clock Pulse active HIGH

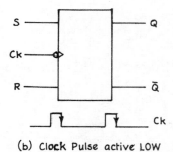

(b) Clock Pulse active LOW

Fig. 20.40 Clocked S-R bistable symbols.

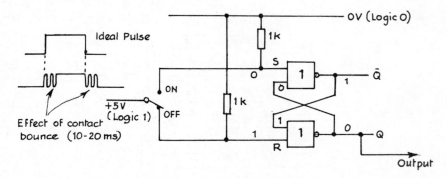

Fig. 20.39 Use of S-R bistable as switch debouncer.

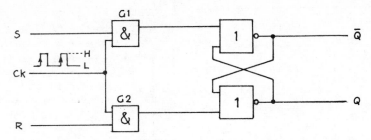

Fig. 20.41 *Method of producing a clocked S-R bistable (clock pulse active HIGH).*

Fig. 20.41 shows one way of producing a clocked S-R bistable, clock pulse active HIGH. When the clock pulse is LOW, the output from the AND gates G1 and G2 will be LOW. Changes in the logic conditions at the S and R inputs will have no effect and the bistable will be in the 'store' mode. When the clock pulse input goes HIGH on its leading edge, the outputs of G1 and G2 will correspond to the S and R inputs respectively and the bistable may change state accordingly. This bistable may change state therefore only when the clock input is HIGH. The complete truth table for the clocked S-R bistable is given in Fig. 20.42.

Additional inputs S_D and R_D may be provided (direct SET and direct RESET) as illustrated in Fig. 20.43. These inputs may be used to SET the Q output of the bistable to logic 1 or RESET it to logic 0 independently of

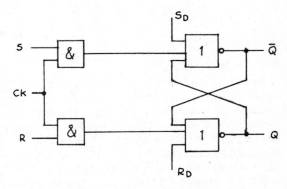

Fig. 20.43 *Use of S_D and R_D (Preset & Clear) inputs.*

the state of the S, R and Ck inputs. The S_D and R_D inputs are 'forcing' inputs and are sometimes called the PRESET and CLEAR inputs respectively.

Inputs			Output	
Clock	S	R	Q_n	Q_{n+1}
0	0	0	0	0
0	0	0	1	1
0	0	1	0	0
0	0	1	1	1
0	1	0	0	0
0	1	0	1	1
0	1	1	0	0
0	1	1	1	1
1	0	0	0	0
1	0	0	1	1
1	0	1	0	0
1	0	1	1	0
1	1	0	0	1
1	1	0	1	1
1	1	1	0	?
1	1	1	1	?

Q_n = state prior to application of inputs

Q_{n+1} = state after application of inputs

} Indeterminate

Fig. 20.42 *Truth table for clocked bistable.*

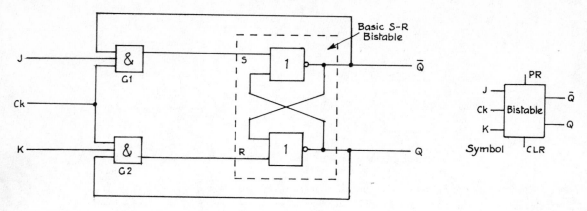

Fig. 20.44 J-K bistable.

The J-K Bistable

The J-K bistable is essentially an S-R bistable with additional logic circuitry to eliminate the indeterminate output that occurs when S = R = 1. One possible circuit arrangement is given in Fig. 20.44. It is a clocked bistable and it is provided with two input terminals (J and K); these are 'preparatory' inputs, i.e. they prepare the circuit for a change under the control of the clock input. Feedback from the Q and $\bar{Q}$ outputs and the two AND gates provide a **clock steering function** and the condition J = K = 1 is now permissible resulting in a predictable output. Direct SET and Direct RESET (PR and CLR) may also be provided, see logic circuit symbol.

It will be seen that the Q and $\bar{Q}$ outputs as well as the preparatory inputs J and K determine which input of the basic S-R bistable receives the clock pulse. For example,

consider that initially Q = 0 and $\bar{Q}$ = 1, a logic 1 is applied to J and a logic 0 to the K input. Because of the feedback, then when a clock pulse is applied (active high) the upper AND gate G1 will be operative and the lower AND gate G2 inoperative. Thus the logic states of J and K are transferred to the S and R inputs of the basic S-R bistable, setting the Q output to logic 1 and the $\bar{Q}$ output to logic 0.

If now a logic 1 is applied to the K input and a logic 0 to the J input, then on the next clock pulse G2 will be made operative and G1 inoperative. As a result the Q output will be reset to logic 0 and the $\bar{Q}$ output to logic 1.

In principle, the results set out in the truth table of Fig. 20.45 will apply. The table illustrates the versatility of the J-K bistable which may be summarised as follows:

(1) If J = K = 0 there will be no change in the output state when a clock pulse is applied

J	K	Q_n Before clock pulse	Q_{n+1} After clock pulse
0	0	0	0
0	0	1	1
0	1	0	0
0	1	1	0
1	0	0	1
1	0	1	1
1	1	0	1
1	1	1	0

Fig. 20.45 Truth table for J-K bistable.

(the bistable is then in the HOLD condition).

(2) If J = 1, K = 0 the Q output is placed in the 1 state and the Q̄ in the 0 state when a clock pulse is applied (the bistable is then in the SET condition).

(3) If J = 0, K = 1 the Q output is placed in the 0 state and the Q̄ in the 1 state when a clock pulse is applied (the bistable is then in the RESET condition).

(4) If J = K = 1, the Q and Q̄ outputs reverse states on the receipt of each clock pulse (the bistable is then in the TOGGLING mode).

It will therefore be appreciated that there are more modes available with this type of bistable due to the use of the preparatory inputs J and K.

Race-Around Condition

If the Q and Q̄ outputs of the J-K bistable change state before the end of the clock pulse, the input conditions to the AND steering gates of Fig. 20.44 will change. The effect is that Q oscillates between 1 and 0 for the duration of the clock pulse, see Fig. 20.46, and at the end of the clock pulse period the output is indeterminate.

The condition can be avoided if the clock pulse period is short compared with the 'propagation delay' (switching time) of the bistable. Because this requirement is rarely met in practice with modern high-speed integrated circuits, the race-around condition led to the development of the Master–Slave bistable.

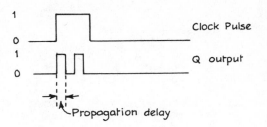

Fig. 20.46 Race-around condition.

Master–Slave J-K Bistable

This type of J-K bistable does not suffer from the 'race-around' condition and the basic idea of its operation is illustrated by Fig. 20.47.

There are now two bistables, the 'Master' and the 'Slave', with the Slave driven from the Master. The switches S1 and S2 are arranged so that when S1 is closed, S2 is open and vice versa. On the leading edge of the clock pulse S1 is closed and the input is clocked into the output of the Master. At this time the Slave bistable will not change since switch S2 is open. When the clock pulse changes state once more on its trailing edge, S1 opens disconnecting the input from the Master. At the same time, since S2 is closed the output of the Slave is made to follow the output of the Master. Because S1 is open, any feedback applied in an actual circuit cannot affect the output of the Master.

It will now be shown how this basic principle is applied to the J-K bistable, a circuit arrangement of which is given in Fig. 20.48.

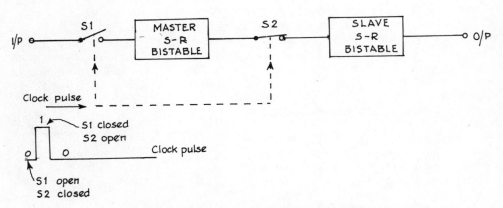

Fig. 20.47 Basic idea of Master–Slave J-K bistable.

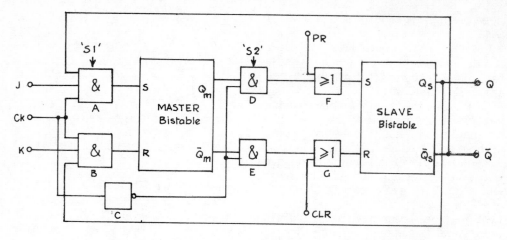

Fig. 20.48 Circuit arrangement for J-K Master–Slave bistable.

As with the basic J-K bistable, feedback is applied from the output (of the SLAVE) to the clock steering gates A and B. This configuration eliminates the 'race-around' condition and a predictable output results for the condition J = K = 1.

Operation

The AND gates A and B effectively replace 'S1' of Fig. 20.47 and the AND gates D and E replace 'S2'. When the clock pulse goes to logic 1 on its leading edge, the Master is enabled via gates A and B but due to the inverter gate C, the Slave is disabled. The following initial conditions will be assumed:

Qs = 0 , Qm = 0 , J = K = 1,
Clock pulse = 0   and PR = 0
Q̄s = 1 , Q̄m = 1   CLR = 0

(1) When the clock pulse changes from 0 to 1 on its leading edge, the output of gate A will go to logic 1 but the gate B output will be in the logic 0 state. Since gate A and B outputs are the S and R inputs of the Master, the Qm output of the Master will be set at logic 1 (Q̄m = 0). At this time the Slave is disabled as gates D and E are inoperative.

(2) When the clock pulse changes from logic 1 to logic 0 on its trailing edge, gates A and B are disabled, but gates D and E are enabled. Thus the Qm and Q̄m outputs of the Master become the inputs of the Slave, i.e. Qs goes to logic 1 and Q̄s goes to logic

0. The change in the output states of the Slave has no effect on the Master since gates A and B are inoperative.

(3) On the leading edge of the next clock pulse when it goes from logic 0 to logic 1, the output of gate A is set at 0 and the output of gate B to logic 1. This resets the Master outputs to Qm = 0 and Q̄m = 1. On the trailing edge of the clock pulse, the Slave follows the Master and the Slave outputs are reset to Qs = 0, Q̄s = 1.

When the Master–Slave Bistable is operated in this way it is said to be a 'toggle' bistable (T-Bistable). Waveforms summarising the modes of operation of the Master–Slave Bistable are illustrated in Fig. 20.49.

The J-K bistable is a very important and flexible logic device and forms the basis of counting circuits which are considered in the next section. Fig. 20.50 shows how the T-bistable is constructed by tying the J and K terminals together (now called the T-terminal). When T is at logic 0, the state of the bistable will not change when the clock input goes to logic 1. However when T is at logic 1,

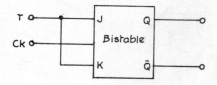

Fig. 20.50 T-bistable.

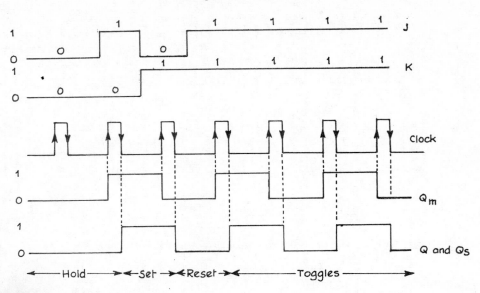

Fig. 20.49 *Waveforms illustrating operation of Master–Slave J-K bistable.*

the bistable will change state each time the clock input goes to logic 1 (high).

COUNTERS

Asynchronous Binary Counter

A common method of producing a binary counter is to use a number of Master–Slave J-K bistables wired as 'toggle' bistables as shown in Fig. 20.51. The pulses to be counted are applied to the clock input of bistable A and

it will be seen that the output of bistable A provides the clock input to bistable B; the output of bistable B provides the clock input to bistable C, and so on. Negative-edge triggering is used, i.e. the 'slave' output of any bistable changes state on the negative-going edge of its clock input. A common 'clear' line (clear LOW) is used to reset all Q outputs LOW. During counting the 'clear' line is held in the HIGH state. With this particular circuit both Q and Q̄ outputs are made available, but this is not always the case.

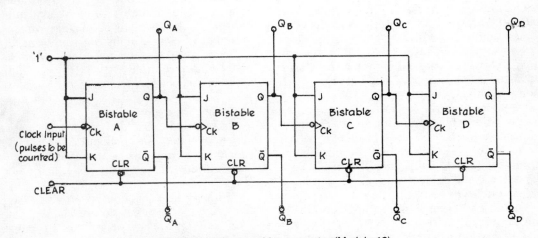

Fig. 20.51 *Asynchronous binary counter (Modulo-16).*

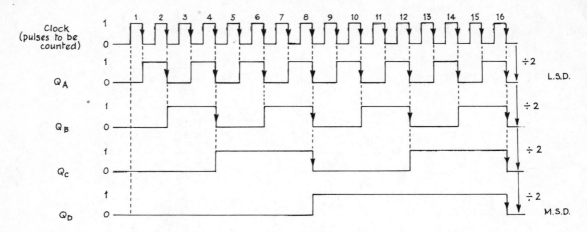

Fig. 20.52 Waveforms showing operation of asynchronous counter of Fig. 20.51.

Operation

Assume that the counter has been reset by taking the 'clear' line LOW, i.e. $Q_A - Q_E$ outputs will all be LOW (logic 0). The waveforms given in Fig. 20.52 depict the operation during counting.

On the leading edge of the first clock pulse the 'Master' of bistable A will be set at logic 1 and on the trailing edge, the logic 1 from the 'Master' will be transferred to the output of the 'Slave', i.e. Q_A will be set at logic 1. Since the Q output is the clock input of bistable B, the 'Master' of bistable B will be set at logic 1 (but not its 'Slave') at this time. Thus at the end of the first clock pulse, the binary output of the counter will be 0001 (note that Q_A provides the least significant digit).

On the leading edge of the second clock pulse the Master of bistable A will be reset to logic 0 and on the trailing edge of the clock pulse the Slave of bistable A will be reset to logic 0. It will be remembered that the Master of bistable B has already been set at logic 1, thus when the Q_A output goes LOW, the Slave of bistable B will be set to logic 1. Since the output of bistable B is connected to the input of bistable C, the Master of bistable C will be set to logic 1 (the Slave of C will not change until the output of bistable B goes LOW). Thus at the end of clock pulse 2, the output of the counter will be 0010.

On the leading edge of the third clock pulse, the Master of bistable A will be set at logic 1 and on the trailing edge the Slave of bistable A

will be set at logic 1. Q_A will change from logic 0 to logic 1 and the Master of bistable B will be reset to logic 0. At the end of clock pulse 3, the output of the counter will be 0011.

This procedure continues and at the end of 15 clock pulses the counter output will be 1111. Upon receipt of clock pulse 16, the counter will be reset to 0000.

Modulus

Any number of bistables can be cascaded in this way to form an n-bit counter. The arrangement of Fig. 20.51 is referred to as a 4-bit counter since there are 4 binary bits or digits in the coded output. A 5-bit binary counter will count up to decimal 31 and reset on clock pulse 32, but requires 5 bistables of course. The modulus of a binary number system is the decimal equivalent which that number of bits or digits can represent, e.g.

3-bit binary counter = 2^3 = 8 — Modulo-8
4-bit binary counter = 2^4 = 16 — Modulo-16
8-bit binary counter = 2^8 = 256 — Modulo-256

Propagation Delay

In practice there is a small delay between the application of a clock pulse to any stage of a counter and its output assuming the appropriate logic level as illustrated in Fig. 20.53.

With an asynchronous counter or 'ripple' counter, the bistables do not change state at the same instant, causing the propagation delays to become accumulative. For example,

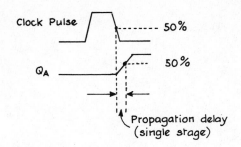

Fig. 20.53 Maximum counting rate limited by propagation delay.

when the counter output is 0111 then on the eighth clock pulse all the bistables change state. However Q_D cannot change until Q_C changes, Q_C cannot change until Q_B changes and Q_B cannot change until Q_A changes. Thus, if the propagation delay of each stage is 20 ns, a time delay of 80 ns will elapse before the counter output finally settles to 1000. Because the change of state appears to 'ripple' through the counter, the asynchronous counter is also known as a **ripple-counter**.

Bidirectional Binary Counter

The asynchronous binary counter previously described is a FORWARD counter or an UP counter since it counts 'up' from zero. It is often required to be able to count 'down' from a pre-determined value to zero. A counter operating in this mode is referred to as a DOWN counter or REVERSE counter.

From the truth table given in Fig. 20.54 it will be seen that the **total** value stored in both Q and $\bar{Q}$ at the end of any clock pulse is constant and equal to decimal 15. Clearly the previous counter will count 'down' if the $\bar{Q}$ outputs are used. By using suitable combinational logic a **Bi-Directional** counter may be constructed. One possible circuit arrangement is given in Fig. 20.55.

To provide the reversible function with a single counter it is necessary to introduce a control line as shown. When the control line is set at logic 1 the upper set of AND gates are enabled but the lower set of AND gates are disabled (by the inverter gate) and the counter is in the UP count mode. When the control line is set at logic 0, the upper set of AND gates are disabled but the lower set are enabled; the counter is then in the DOWN count mode.

Count UP Mode

The control line will be held at logic 1 and if the clear line is taken LOW the counter outputs will all be reset at logic 0. The clear line is then taken HIGH. When the clock pulses (the pulses to be counted) are applied at the counter input, the counter will count up as

Clock Pulse No.	Output States									
	Q_D	Q_C	Q_B	Q_A			$\bar{Q}_D$	$\bar{Q}_C$	$\bar{Q}_B$	$\bar{Q}_A$
0 (16)	0	0	0	0			1	1	1	1
1	0	0	0	1			1	1	1	0
2	0	0	1	0			1	1	0	1
3	0	0	1	1	Count 'Up'	Count 'Down'	1	1	0	0
4	0	1	0	0			1	0	1	1
5	0	1	0	1			1	0	1	0
6	0	1	1	0			1	0	0	1
7	0	1	1	1			1	0	0	0
8	1	0	0	0			0	1	1	1
9	1	0	0	1			0	1	1	0
10	1	0	1	0			0	1	0	1
11	1	0	1	1			0	1	0	0
12	1	1	0	0			0	0	1	1
13	1	1	0	1			0	0	1	0
14	1	1	1	0			0	0	0	1
15	1	1	1	1			0	0	0	0

Fig. 20.54 Truth table for binary counter of Fig. 20.51.

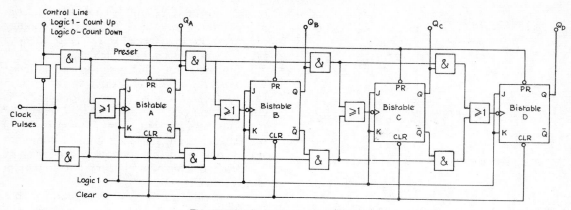

Fig. 20.55 Reversible (up-down) counter.

previously described for Fig. 20.51 with the upper set of AND gates connecting the Q output of each bistable to the clock input of the following bistable via an OR gate. After 15 clock pulses the counter will register 1111 at its outputs.

Count DOWN Mode

If now the control line is taken to logic 0, the counter will count down from 1111. On the leading edge of the first clock pulse, the Ck input of bistable A will go HIGH and the Master of bistable A will be reset. The Ck input of bistable B will remain LOW since $\bar{Q}_A$ is logic 0. On the trailing edge of the clock pulse, the Slave of bistable A will be reset to logic 0 and $\bar{Q}_A$ will change to logic 1. Throughout this interval, the Ck input of bistable B has remained LOW. The counter output is now 1110.

On the leading edge of the second clock pulse, the Ck input of bistable A will go HIGH and the Master will be set. At the same time

the Ck input of bistable B will go HIGH and its Master will be reset to logic 0. On the trailing edge of the clock pulse, the Slave of bistable A will be set to logic 1 and the Slave of bistable B will be reset to logic 0. The counter output is now 1101.

This operation continues down the counter with the counter output being decremented by one for each clock pulse input.

Decade Counter

It is often desirable to be able to count to a base N which is not a power of 2. For example, to count to a base of 10 is a common requirement as this is the basis of the denary number system of which we are more familiar.

For a decade or divide-by-10 counter we require a chain of n bistables such that n is the smallest number for which $2^n > N$, e.g. for N = 10 (decade counter), n = 4. A feedback gate is then added so that on a count of 10 all outputs are reset to logic 0. Inspection of the

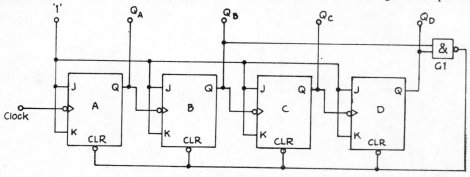

Fig. 20.56 Asynchronous decade counter.

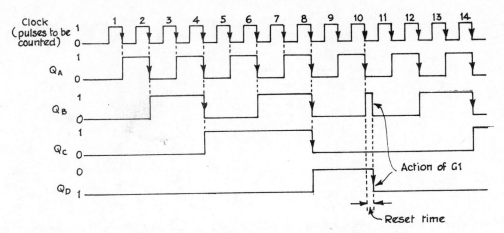

Fig. 20.57 Waveforms showing operation of decade counter.

truth table for a binary counter shows that at a count of 10 the output states are:

$$Q_D = 1, \quad Q_C = 0, \quad Q_B = 1, \quad \text{and} \quad Q_A = 0$$
$$(1010).$$

However, for a decade counter we require **all** of the outputs to be in the logic 0 state at a count of 10, i.e. the Q_D and Q_B outputs must be reset back to logic 0 at a count of 10. One way of achieving this is as shown in Fig. 20.56.

The four bistable stages are wired as toggle bistables with the pulses to be counted applied to the first stage. When a count of 1010 is reached, the output from the NAND gate G1 goes LOW which is applied to the 'clear' inputs of all stages, resetting all outputs to logic 0. The timing waveforms for the counter are shown in Fig. 20.57. Note that on the 10th input pulse the counter outputs are all at logic 0; this is providing that the propagation delay (reset time) of the CLEAR inputs is short (typically 50 ns for TTL devices). Unequal

reset times from the CLEAR to the output of individual bistables may cause unreliable operation, e.g. if bistable B has a shorter reset time than bistable D, then bistable B input to G1 will go LOW before bistable D input, with the result that bistable D will not clear. It will be seen that the counting sequence recommences on the 11th input pulse.

Synchronous Counters

In synchronous counters the counting sequence is controlled by means of the pulses to be counted (clock pulses) which clock **all** of the bistable stages in synchronism. This effectively removes the relatively large propagation delay associated with asynchronous counters. The propagation delay of synchronous counters is equal to the **propagation delay of a single bistable stage** plus the delay of any control gates required. Another advantage of synchronous counters is that no 'glitches' appear

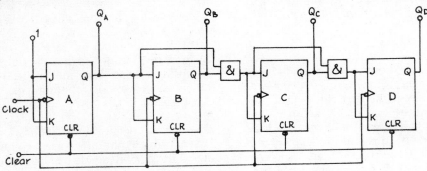

Fig. 20.58 4-bit synchronous counter.

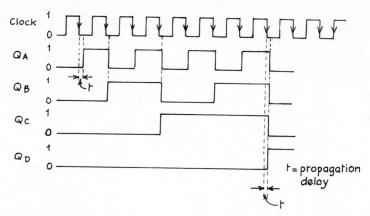

Fig. 20.59 *Waveforms of synchronous counter showing effect of propagation delay (non-accumulative).*

in the output of any decoding gate connected to the counter, since all bistables change state at the same time; hence no strobe pulse is required for the decoding gates.

One method of producing a synchronous binary counter is shown in Fig. 20.58, with associated waveforms given in Fig. 20.59. Master–slave bistables are invariably used. In the synchronous mode of operation, the appropriate input signals are gated into the masters of all bistables on the leading edge of the clock pulse. On the trailing edge of the clock pulse the new values of the count are transmitted synchronously to the bistable outputs, i.e. into the slaves.

It will be noted that the clock pulses are fed directly to each bistable and that the J and K inputs are tied together, but only in bistable A are they connected to logic 1. The J and K inputs of bistable B are connected to the Q output of bistable A, but the J and K inputs of bistables C and D are driven from the AND gates G1 and G2 which are supplied with signals from the input and output of the previous stage.

Circuit operation

Assume that the counter has initially been cleared so that the binary output is 0000. On the leading edge of the first clock pulse, the master of A will be set to logic 1. Since the J and K inputs of all other bistables are at logic 0, the masters of these bistables will not change. On the trailing edge of the clock pulse the slave of A will be set at logic 1, thus the counter output will be 0001.

On the leading edge of the second clock pulse, the master of A will be reset to logic 0. Since Q_A is at logic 1, the master of B will be set to logic 1. Bistables C and D will be unchanged. On the trailing edge of the clock pulse, the slave of A will be reset to logic 0 and the slave of B will be set to logic 1. The counter output will be 0010.

On the leading edge of the third clock pulse, the master of A will be set at logic 1. Since Q_A is at logic 0, bistable B will not be affected neither will bistables C and D. On the trailing edge of the clock pulse, the slave of A will be set at logic 1. The counter output will then be 0011.

On the leading edge of the fourth clock pulse the masters of bistables A and B are reset to logic 0. Since both Q_A and Q_B are at logic 1, the master of C will be set to logic 1 because G1 operates. On the trailing edge of the clock pulse, the slaves of A and B will be reset to logic 0, while the slave of C will be set at logic 1, that is the slaves of A, B and C all change state in unison. The counter output is now 0100.

It will be seen that the ripple-through delay has now been removed and the outputs of all bistables change state in synchronism. Reversible synchronous counters may also be constructed.

Divide-by-n Synchronous Counters

Synchronous counters are available commercially that will divide by a number which is not a power of 2, but these are more difficult to design than the asynchronous type. Figure

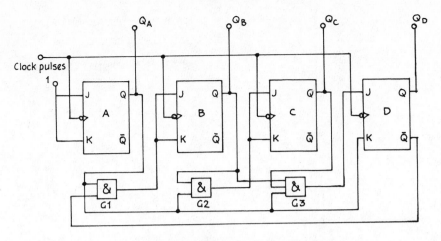

Fig. 20.60 Synchronous decade counter.

20.60 shows an arrangement for a synchronous decade counter. The 3-input AND gate G3 causes bistable D output to return to logic 0 after the tenth pulse while G1 prevents bistable B output going to logic 1 on the tenth pulse.

LATCHES

A latch is a D-type bistable, the symbol of which is given in Fig. 20.61. One method of implementing a D-type bistable is shown in

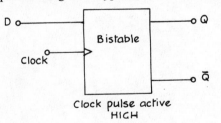

Fig. 20.61 D-type bistable (latch) symbol.

Fig. 20.62. It will be seen that it consists essentially of an S–R bistable (G4 and G5) with the addition of control gates G2 and G3 and an inverter gate G1. There is only one input, the D-input (D stands for data) and the bistable uses clocking. The inverter gate ensures that the S and R inputs of G4 and G5 are always complementary thereby removing the hazard that exists in an S–R bistable when $S = R = 1$.

The waveforms of Fig. 20.63 illustrate the basic action of the latch. When the clock pulse is in the active HIGH state (logic 1), G2 passes the logic level present at the D-input to the S input of G4, and G3 passes the inverted level present at the D-input to the R input of G5. If the clock pulse is LOW (logic 0) then the S and R inputs to G4 and G5 are at logic 0.

Suppose that when the clock pulse goes to the HIGH state the D-input is at logic 1, (Fig. 20.63(a)). Thus the inputs to G4 and G5 will be $S = 1$ and $R = 0$, causing the Q output

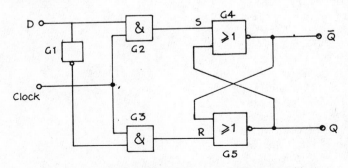

Fig. 20.62 A method of producing a D-type bistable.

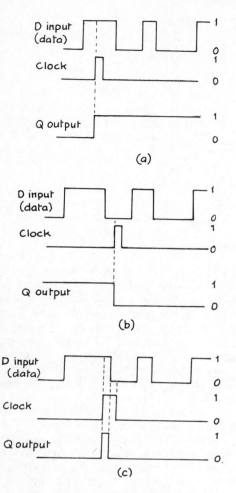

Fig. 20.63 Clocking data into the Q output.

to be set at logic 1, i.e. the same as the input data. When the clock pulse ceases the Q output will remain at logic 1, i.e. it has 'latched' to the data. Conversely if the D-input is at logic 0 when the clock pulse is in the HIGH state as in Fig. 20.63(b), the inputs to G4 and G5 will be $S = 0$ and $R = 1$. This will cause the Q output to be reset to logic 0, the same as the input data. Again, when the clock pulse ceases, the Q output will remain 'latched' at logic 0. Thus the latch acts as a memory and retains the last 'instruction' given to it by the D-input when the clock pulse is in the HIGH state. If the data at the D-input changes during the period that the clock pulse is in the HIGH state, the Q output will follow that data (Fig. 20.63(c)).

A truth table for the latch is given below:

Clock	D-input	Q_n	Q_{n+1}
0	0	0	0
0	0	1	1
0	1	0	0
0	1	1	1
1	0	0	0
1	0	1	0
1	1	0	1
1	1	1	1

where Q_n = state of Q output prior to clock pulse, and Q_{n+1} = state of Q output after the application of the clock pulse.

D-type bistable latches are available in TTL and CMOS i.c. technology and the example given in Fig. 20.64 is for the TTL 8275 Quad Bistable Latch. This employs four D-type

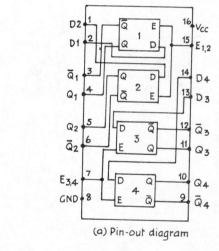

(a) Pin-out diagram

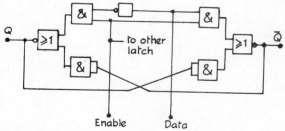

(b) Logic Diagram *each* latch

Fig. 20.64 Quad bistable latch (8275).

bistables. Separate 'enable' lines to latches 1, 2 and 3, 4 permit individual control of each pair of latches. The 'enable' pulse acts like a clock pulse and initially data is transferred on the leading edge of the pulse. While the enable pulse is in the HIGH state, the Q output follows the data input. When the enable pulse falls, the input data is retained at the Q output. Both Q and $\bar{Q}$ are accessible.

REGISTERS

When several bistables are connected together so that they store related data, the assembly is referred to as a **register**. A **shift register** is a register in which the data may be moved serially to the left or right and some types are reversible. A shift register is a temporary store of data. In a digital system or computer they are used to move data to and from a central memory or to store the interim results of arithmetic processes; the ability to shift data one place to the left or right is an essential requirement to some binary arithmetic operations.

There are many arrangements for shift registers and some of the more common types will be considered.

Basic Shift Register

A basic shift register may be constructed from a series of D-type bistables as shown in Fig. 20.65(a) which illustrates a shift-right shift register. Alternatively, J–K bistables may be used as shown in Fig. 20.65(b). The use of an inverter gate between the J and K inputs converts the J–K bistable into a D-type bistable. The operation is as follows:

(1) Assume that all bistables have been reset so that the Q_A–Q_D outputs are at logic 0.
(2) If the D input of bistable A is set at logic 1 then on the first clock pulse, the Q_A output will be set at logic 1 with the other outputs remaining at logic 0.
(3) Assume that the data input is now returned to logic 0. On the second clock pulse the Q_A output will be set at logic 0 but since the output of bistable A was previously at logic 1 and is applied to the D input of bistable B, the Q_B output will be set at logic 1. The Q_C and Q_D outputs remain at logic 0. It will be seen that the logic 1 has shifted one place or stage to the right.
(4) The operation continues in this way with the logic 1 shifting one place to the right

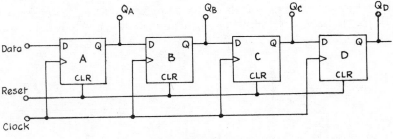

(a) 4-bit Shift Register

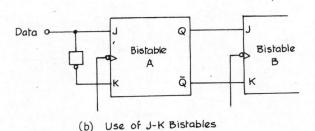

(b) Use of J-K Bistables

Fig. 20.65 Shift register (shift right).

on each clock pulse. After the fifth clock pulse, the logic 1 will have shifted completely through the register and all outputs will be at logic 0; the register is now empty.

The truth table below shows the propagation of the logic 1 through the register from left to right.

Clock pulse no.	Q_A	Q_B	Q_C	Q_D
0	0	0	0	0
1	1	0	0	0
2	0	1	0	0
3	0	0	1	0
4	0	0	0	1
5	0	0	0	0

In practice the input data to the register may consist of various combinations of logic 1s and 0s and the waveforms of Fig. 20.66 illustrate the propagation of the binary digits 1011 through the register, assuming that data is transferred on the positive-going edge of the clock pulse. Note that after the 4th clock pulse the four bits of data are stored in the register; they will remain there if clocking of the register ceases. To move the data serially out

of the register, clocking must recommence and here it is assumed that it starts on the 5th clock pulse. At the end of the 8th clock pulse the data will have shifted completely through the register and all outputs will be at logic 0.

In this mode, the shift register operation may be described as **Serial In – Serial Out** (SISO). However it should be noted that the data once clocked into the register is available in parallel form at the Q_A–Q_D outputs, thus the shift register also provides a facility of **Serial In – Parallel Out** (SIPO). This latter facility is very useful in a digital system as the data is available simultaneously, for example 8 bits of data may be clocked in serially to an 8-bit register and the whole byte may be taken out in a single operation. Thus the basic shift register will provide the **serial-to-parallel conversion** of data.

Parallel Loading

It is often required to be able to load the register with parallel data, i.e. to load all of the bits into the register simultaneously. This is sometimes referred to as 'broadside' loading. A common example of this is in parallel-to-serial conversion; the data word is loaded into the register in parallel form and then clocked out in serial form. There are many circuit arrangements for parallel loading and one

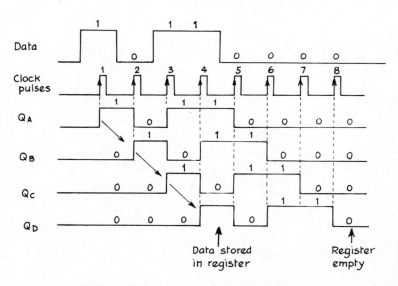

Fig. 20.66 *Waveforms showing propagation of 1011 through shift register.*

example is given in Fig. 20.67 which shows a method of parallel loading using the **preset** and **clear** inputs (preset and clear LOW). When the 'enable' line is LOW, the parallel data inputs A, B and C are inactive and the PR and CLR terminals of the D-type bistable are HIGH. The shift register then operates in the normal shift-right mode, the serial data input being D_A and the serial output being Q_C. The data may also be read in parallel form once the data has been loaded using the outputs Q_A–Q_C.

A HIGH on the 'enable' line will permit parallel loading. Only input A need be examined since all the parallel inputs are the same. Suppose input A is HIGH (logic 1) when the enable line goes HIGH. This will cause the PR of bistable A to go LOW and the CLR to go HIGH. Thus the bistable will be preset so that the Q_A output is HIGH (logic1) irrespective of its previous state. Similarly, if input A is LOW (logic 0) the PR of bistable A will go HIGH and the CLR will go LOW. The bistable will thus be reset so that the Q_A output is LOW (logic 0). Thus the Q_A output will follow the data applied at the A terminal.

It is important to note that with this system a clock pulse is not required for parallel loading.

The shift register of Fig. 20.67 may be used in any of the following modes:

(a) Serial In – Serial Out (SISO)
(b) Serial In – Parallel Out (SIPO)
(c) Parallel In – Serial Out (PISO)
(d) Parallel In – Parallel Out (PIPO)

Reversible Shift Registers

The shift registers previously considered are capable of shifting data only to the right. There are applications, however, where data shift to the right or left is desirable; a **reversible shift register** must therefore be used. The circuit diagram of Fig. 20.68 shows one arrangement of implementing a reversible SISO shift register. It will be seen from the diagram that the principle of operation is unchanged. Under the control of the shift control line (logic 1 for right shift – logic 0 for left shift) the combinational logic gates effectively reverse the order for left shift.

For left shift, the upper AND gates are made operative by the control line and the Serial In data from the shift left terminal is applied to the input of bistable C. The output of this bistable drives bistable B and so on.

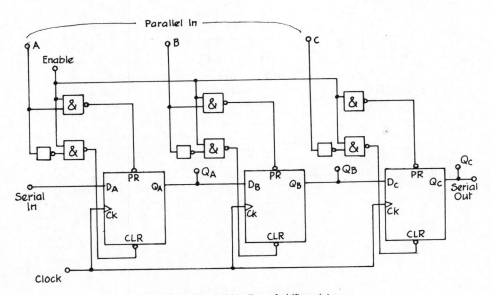

Fig. 20.67 Parallel loading of shift register.

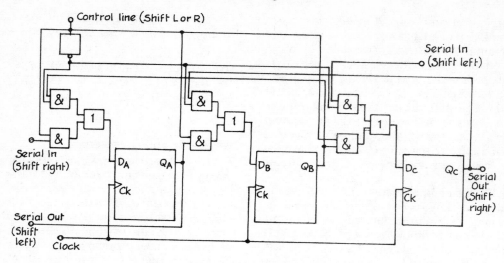

Fig. 20.68 Reversible shift register.

When right shift is selected the lower set of AND gates are made operative and the serial input is applied to the input of bistable A which drives bistable B, and so on.

Some reversible shift registers have the parallel loading facility previously referred to thus providing enhanced versatility.

DISPLAY DRIVER/DECODERS

7-segment displays using l.e.d. and liquid crystal segments were described in Chapter 6. It will now be shown how the binary signal output from a digital circuit may be decoded and hence used to drive the display segments. Consider the arrangement in Fig. 20.69 where

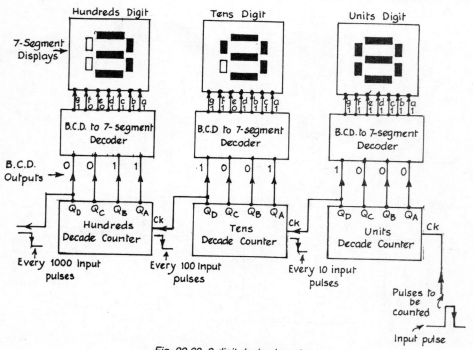

Fig. 20.69 3-digit decimal read out.

decade counters are used to operate a 7-segment display providing a 3-digit decimal read-out. Three separate counters are employed arranged as the 'Units', 'Tens' and 'Hundreds' decade counters thus providing binary-coded decimal (b.c.d.) outputs. The pulses to be counted are applied to the clock input of the 'units' counter, the Q_D output of which is used as the clock input of the 'tens' decade counter. The Q_D output of the 'tens' counter is then used as the clock input of the 'hundreds' decade counter; this idea may be extended to increase the number of digits used in the display.

It will be appreciated, of course, that although a decade counter counts input pulses from 0 to 9 and then resets on the 10th pulse, the actual read-out from the bistable stages is in **binary**. However since only the binary digits equivalent to 0–9 in decimal are involved in the output from each decade counter, the output is said to be in binary-coded decimal. To operate the 7-segment displays the counter

outputs must be 'decoded' using 4–7 line decoders. The diagram shows the decoder output states after 398 pulses have been applied to the input of the 'units' counter.

Decoders

A **decoder** is a combinational logic circuit that is used to decode or translate a number of input binary lines into a number of output lines where for a given binary input, **one** of the output lines goes HIGH all other lines being LOW or vice versa.

A simple arrangement is the **2-to-4 line decoder**, a logic circuit of which is given in Fig. 20.70. The logic states shown on the diagram illustrate the operation for a binary input of 11. In this arrangement a LOW (logic 0) is obtained on only one of the output lines for each binary code on the input, see the truth table of Fig. 20.70(b). Thus the presence of a logic 0 on a particular output line identifies the binary code on the input; this is the **decoding**

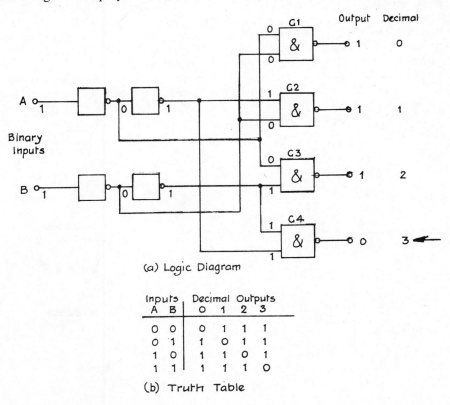

(a) Logic Diagram

Inputs		Decimal Outputs			
A	B	0	1	2	3
0	0	0	1	1	1
0	1	1	0	1	1
1	0	1	1	0	1
1	1	1	1	1	0

(b) Truth Table

Fig. 20.70 2-4 line decoder.

process, i.e. 2-line binary to 4-line decimal. The idea of Fig. 20.70(a) may be extended to provide 8 output lines from 3 binary input lines or 16 output lines from 4 binary input lines, etc. but at the expense in the complexity in the number of logic gates used in the combination.

B.C.D. -to- 7-Segment Decoder

A B.C.D. -to- 7-segment decoder has 4 input lines and 7 output lines and is formed from a combinational logic circuit. We need not concern ourselves with the actual logic circuit as the decoder is normally available as an integral i.c. package containing the combinational logic circuit together with driver output stages to operate the various segments. For each 4-bit b.c.d. code applied at the input the 7 output lines take up logic states (HIGHS or LOWS) so that the desired numeral is displayed.

The arrangement of Fig. 20.71 illustrates how the decoder/driver is used to operate a 7-segment l.e.d. display (common-cathode type). When any of the output lines a–g of the decoder are HIGH (+5V), the l.e.d. array connected to that output is turned on, illuminating particular segments of the display. The series resistors (R) in the output lines limit the current in each l.e.d. to about 20 mA.

A truth table for the decoder is given in

Inputs				Outputs						
D	C	B	A	a	b	c	d	e	f	g
L	L	L	L	H	H	H	H	H	H	L
L	L	L	H	L	H	H	L	L	L	L
L	L	H	L	H	H	L	H	H	L	H
L	L	H	H	H	H	H	H	L	L	H
L	H	L	L	L	H	H	L	L	H	H
L	H	L	H	H	L	H	H	L	H	H
L	H	H	L	H	L	H	H	H	H	H
L	H	H	H	H	H	H	L	L	H	L
H	L	L	L	H	H	H	H	H	H	H
H	L	L	H	H	H	H	H	L	H	H

Fig. 20.72 Truth table for B.C.D. -to- 7-segment decoder.

Fig. 20.72 where a HIGH (H) represents +5V and a LOW (L) indicates 0 V.

Two control inputs are provided on the decoder of Fig. 20.71. The L.T. (Lamp Test) terminal is used to check that all outputs go HIGH when the L.T. terminal is taken LOW. Under this condition all segments of the display should be illuminated, thus displaying numeral 8. The L.T. terminal is a master input and overrides any other input to the decoder. The BL (Blanking) terminal input is used to

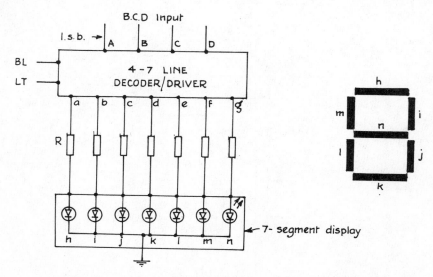

Fig. 20.71 B.C.D. -to- 7-segment decoder/driver for l.e.d. display.

place the decoder outputs a–g in the LOW state irregardless of the state of the b.c.d. input and thus turns off the display. This control input is normally used to turn off leading zeros in a numeric display of digits, such as in a pocket calculator, to make the display easier to read and to reduce consumption.

Liquid Crystal Display

Liquid crystal displays are also 7-segment devices and will thus require a 4–7 line decoder for displaying numerals 0 to 9. When a voltage is applied between the Backplate (BP) and the segment, that particular segment is opaque

(black). On the other hand, if no p.d. exists between a segment and the backplate, that segment is transparent.

To prevent chemical deterioration and hence increase life expectancy, the display is normally driven by a square-wave applied to the Phase (PH) input of the decoder, see Fig. 20.73. The diagram shows the logic states for an input that will result in the display of numeral 3. It will be noted that for this condition the decoder outputs g and f are logic 1 and logic 0 respectively. These states are also shown in diagrams (a) and (b) of Fig. 20.74 together with the square-wave input and output of the respective EX-OR gate. It will be seen that the square-waves fed to the

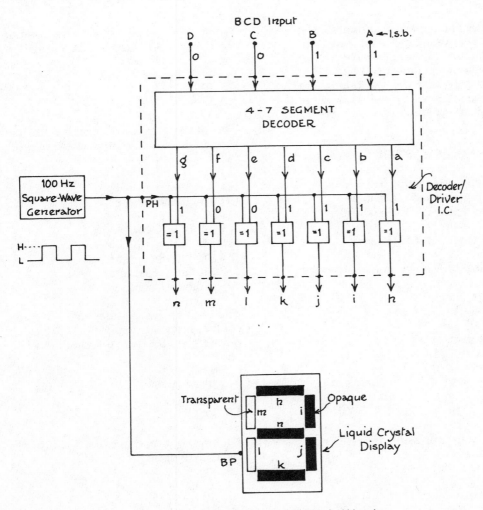

Fig. 20.73 Liquid crystal decoder/driver i.c.

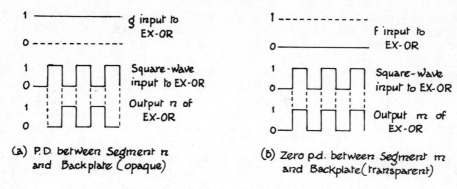

Fig. 20.74 *Waveforms explaining operation of liquid crystal display.*

backplate and segment n are in antiphase, i.e. a p.d. exists between the backplate and segment n, whereas the square-waves fed to the backplate and segment m are in phase, i.e. no p.d. exists between the backplate and segment m. Thus segment n will be opaque and segment m transparent.

QUESTIONS ON CHAPTER TWENTY

(1) An example of negative logic is:
(a) 0V (logic 1), −5V (logic 0)
(b) +5V (logic 1), 0V (logic 0)
(c) −1V (logic 1), −5V (logic 0)
(d) −5V (logic 1), 0V (logic 0).

(2) The truth table shown under gives the logic states for a:
(a) NAND gate
(b) EX-NOR gate
(c) EX-OR gate
(d) NOR gate.

A	B	F
0	0	1
0	1	0
1	0	0
1	1	1

(3) The Boolean expression $F = \overline{A + B}$ represents a:
(a) NAND gate
(b) EX-OR gate
(c) NOR gate
(d) EX-NOR gate.

(4) When $S = 1$ and $R = 0$, the output states of an S-R bistable are normally:
(a) $\bar{Q} = 1$, $Q = 0$
(b) $\bar{Q} = 0$, $Q = 1$
(c) $Q = 1$, $\bar{Q} = 1$
(d) $Q = 0$, $\bar{Q} = 0$.

(5) The outputs of a J-K bistable reverse state on each consecutive clock pulse if:
(a) $J = 1$ and $K = 0$
(b) $J = 1$ and $K = 1$
(c) $J = 0$ and $K = 1$
(d) $J = 0$ and $K = 0$.

(6) A 4-bit binary counter is a:
(a) Modulo-4 counter
(b) Modulo-8 counter
(c) Modulo-16 counter
(d) Modulo-2 counter.

(7) The output logic states of a decade counter after the application of 10 clock pulses from the RESET condition will be:
(a) 0000
(b) 1010
(c) 1001
(d) 1011.

(8) The propagation delay of a J-K bistable (TTL) is typically:
(a) 20 s
(b) 20 ms
(c) 20 vs
(d) 20 ns.

(9) The most likely output states of a 2-to-4
line decoder when the input lines are
both at logic 0 are:
(a) 0 0 0 0
(b) 0 0 1 1
(c) 1 1 1 1
(d) 0 1 1 1.

(10) The Q outputs of an UP/DOWN counter
are $Q_A = 1$, $Q_B = 1$, $Q_C = 0$ and
$Q_D = 1$. The $\bar{Q}$ outputs will be:
(a) $\bar{Q}_A = 0$, $\bar{Q}_B = 0$, $\bar{Q}_C = 1$ and $\bar{Q}_D = 0$
(b) $\bar{Q}_A = 1$, $\bar{Q}_B = 1$, $\bar{Q}_C = 0$ and $\bar{Q}_D = 1$
(c) $\bar{Q}_A = 1$, $\bar{Q}_B = 1$, $\bar{Q}_C = 1$ and $\bar{Q}_D = 0$
(d) $\bar{Q}_A = 0$, $\bar{Q}_B = 0$, $\bar{Q}_C = 1$ and $\bar{Q}_D = 1$

(Answers on page 370)

CHAPTER TWENTY ONE

WAVEFORM GENERATION

Objectives
1 To explain the operation of a Miller integrator ramp generator.
2 To consider triangular waveform generation.
3 To explain the use of Schmitt trigger and unijunction oscillator circuits.
4 Outline operation of 555 timer.

THIS CHAPTER IS concerned with the generation of waveforms for testing, timing, timebase and other applications and in particular the action of integrated circuits which act as waveform sources or waveform shapers.

MILLER INTEGRATOR

Miller Effect

In any inverting amplifier such as that shown in Fig. 21.1, there will be some small capacitance existing between the output and input terminals, C_f (the feedback capacitance) and also a small input capacitance between the input terminal and the common line, C_i. For

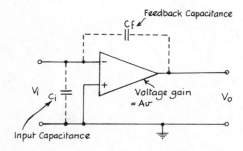

Fig. 21.1 Input and feedback capacitance of inverting amplifier.

example, with a bipolar transistor connected in common emitter the feedback capacitance is between collector and base (C_{cb}) and the input capacitance is between base and emitter (C_{be}).

At low frequencies these capacitances may be ignored without affecting the amplifier gain. At high frequencies however, feedback via C_f can significantly affect the gain of the amplifier. The feedback capacitance is amplified by the gain of the amplifying device and appears as a much larger capacitance in parallel with the input capacitance C_i; this is known as the 'Miller Effect'. The effective input capacitance is given by

$$C_{eff} = C_i + C_f(1 + A_v)$$

where A_v is the voltage gain of the amplifier. For example, if $C_i = 15pF$, $C_f = 4pF$ and $A_v = 60$,

$$C_{eff} = 15 + 4(61) = 259pF$$

The increase in the input capacitance will cause the amplifier gain to fall off at high frequencies. Thus for an amplifier operating at high frequencies C_{eff} must be kept small. However, the 'Miller Effect' is put to good use in the generation of ramp and triangular waveforms.

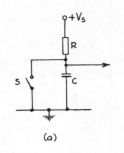

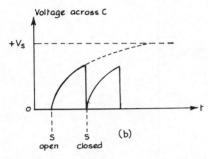

Fig. 21.2 Simple form of ramp generator.

Ramp Generator

A simple form of ramp generator is shown in Fig. 21.2(a). When S is open, C charges via R towards the supply voltage V_s. If S is closed before C fully charges, C will discharge rapidly via the switch. On opening the switch once again the capacitor will recharge and so on, producing across C a reasonable sawtooth waveform. This type of waveform is put to use as the timebase waveform in c.r.o.s. and v.d.u.s but it has many other applications as well. The non-linear rise of voltage due to the exponential charging of C which worsens as the ramp grows (Fig. 21.3), would be unsuitable for use in timebase applications where a linear ramp is required.

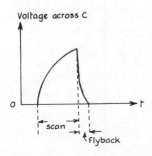

Fig. 21.3 Non-linear ramp (SCAN).

The linearity of the ramp may improve by using a higher supply voltage and causing the switch to close before the markedly non-linear part of the exponential charging curve is reached (Fig. 21.4). For example, with a 200V supply, a 20V ramp may be obtained with a linearity error of less than 10%. The smaller the ramp amplitude the less will be the linearity error and thus it may be necessary to employ some amplification to obtain a useful output voltage.

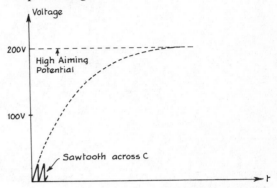

Fig. 21.4 Use of high supply voltage to improve linearity of the ramp.

A very large improvement in ramp linearity may be achieved by using a 'Miller Integrator' (op-amp integrator), (Fig. 21.5). Here negative feedback is deliberately introduced via C. If the switch S is open, C charges linearily since the voltage across R remains practically constant and the output ramps down with a slope $= -V_s/CR$ volts/second (see op-amp integrator, Chapter 16). The output voltage will return to zero when the switch is closed,

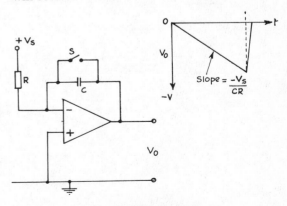

Fig. 21.5 Miller integrator.

which rapidly discharges C. By regularly opening and closing the switch a continuous sawtooth wave may be generated.

In reality the electrical switch is replaced by an electronic one and a JUGFET may be used for this purpose, see TR1 of Fig. 21.6. When the ramp control pulse is low at $-6V$, D1 is 'on' and TR1 is held 'off'. The output of the op-amp then ramps up with a slope of $-V_R/C1\ R1$. When the ramp control pulse

goes high to $+10V$, D1 is 'off' and TR1 is 'on' (saturated). $C1$ then quickly discharges via TR1 causing the output to return to zero; the width of the positive section of the ramp control pulse determines the 'hold-off' time of the ramp. This type of circuit is suitable for a low-frequency timebase application. A monostable oscillator may be used to generate the trigger waveform for application to D1.

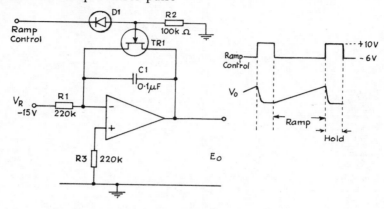

Fig. 21.6 Low frequency ramp generator using Miller integrator.

Triangular Wave Generation

The simplest way to generate a triangular wave is to use the principle illustrated in Fig. 21.7 since a triangular wave may be obtained by integrating a square wave. A

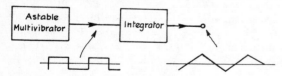

Fig. 21.7 Principle of triangular wave generation.

practical arrangement based on this principle is given in Fig. 21.8 and uses two op-amps, one connected as an astable multivibrator and the other as a Miller Integrator. The frequency of the astable is determined mainly by the time-constant $C1R1$ and the values of $R2$, $R3$; for the values given the frequency of oscillation will be about 200Hz. The square-wave output from A1 is then applied to the Miller integrator A2. When the square-wave output from A1 is at its most positive level (V_{pos}), the integrator will ramp down with a slope of

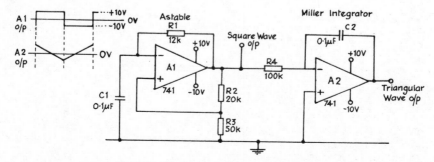

Fig. 21.8 Circuit for triangular wave generator.

$-V_{pos}/C2\ R4$ and when the output from A1 is at its more negative level (V_{neg}) the integrator will ramp up with a slope of $-V_{neg}/C2\ R4$.

Another circuit arrangement is given in Fig. 21.9 which uses the same principle but employs an op-amp Schmitt trigger in lieu of the astable. The op-amp Schmitt trigger (which is considered in the next section) employs positive feedback via $R2$ and switches as the ramp voltage passes through each of its two threshold levels set by $R1$ and $R2$ values. The frequency of the triangular wave output is given by

$$f = \frac{R2}{4R1\ R3\ C1}\ \text{Hz}.$$

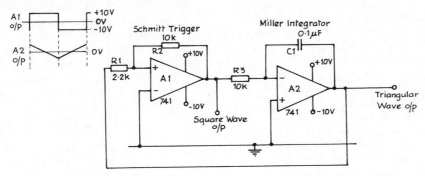

Fig. 21.9 Triangular wave generator using a Schmitt trigger and Miller integrator.

SCHMITT TRIGGER

A Schmitt trigger is a level-sensitive circuit that can have only one of two possible output states. It changes state very rapidly when specific trip points are reached and its main uses include:

(a) reshaping of pulses with long rise and fall times
(b) squaring sinewave signals
(c) level detection

Because of its ability to reshape pulses and eliminate noise it is found as a standard logic gate in most i.c. families.

Basic Operation

A discrete circuit using transistors together with waveforms illustrating the operation are given in Fig. 21.10. When the input to TR1 is zero, TR2 is biased 'on' via $R2$ and $R3$ from TR1 collector. The current in TR2 produces a p.d. across $R4$ which holds TR1 in the 'off' state. In this state the output voltage from TR2 collector is low. However, the circuit values are usually chosen so that when TR2 is 'on' it is not saturated, thus permitting a faster switching speed.

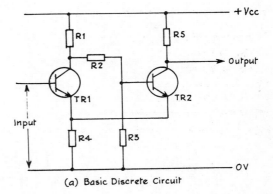

(a) Basic Discrete Circuit

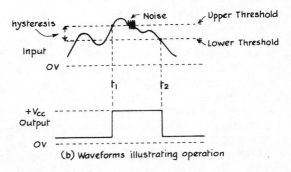

(b) Waveforms illustrating operation

Fig. 21.10 Schmitt trigger operation.

When the input voltage is increased so that it becomes practically equal to the voltage on TR2 base, i.e. it equals the p.d. across $R4$ plus the forward bias required for TR1 base–emitter junction, TR1 commences to conduct. The resultant fall in TR1 collector voltage causes a fall in TR2 base voltage and thus a reduction in TR2 current. As the current in TR2 reduces, the current in TR1 increases which results in a further fall of TR1 collector voltage and TR2 base voltage. This regenerative action results in TR1 rapidly switching 'on' and TR2 rapidly switching 'off'. All of this occurs at instant t_1 when the input reaches the **upper threshold level**. The output from TR2 collector is now in the high voltage state.

This circuit condition persists until the input voltage falls below a lower level, the **lower threshold** when TR1 rapidly switches 'off' and TR2 rapidly switches 'on'. The circuit thus possesses 'hysteresis' and the reason for this is that when TR2 switches 'off', the voltage on its base falls; thus to switch TR1 'off' the input voltage must fall just below TR2 base voltage. This occurs at instant t_2 when the output voltage reverts to the low state.

It will be noted from Fig. 21.10(b) that noise present on the input and appearing above the lower threshold is eliminated at the output. Two further uses of the Schmitt trigger are illustrated in Fig. 21.11. Diagram (a) shows how the circuit may be used to reshape pulses which have long rise and fall times; the output pulses have very fast rise and fall times (propagation delay of the order of 16ns). Diagram (b) shows how the circuit may be used to 'square' a sinewave signal; variations of the input outside the threshold levels have little effect on the output and a good square wave is obtained as the switching is rapid.

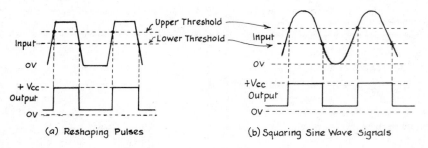

Fig. 21.11 Use of Schmitt trigger.

Schmitt Trigger I.C.

A common Schmitt trigger in the TTL family is the 7414 i.c. which has six Schmitt triggers included in one package (Fig. 21.12(b)). Note the negation sign in the circuit symbol given in Fig. 21.12(a); the output is HIGH when the input is below the lower threshold (inverting Schmitt trigger). With a supply voltage of 5V, the 7414 has an upper threshold of about 1·7V and a lower threshold of about 0·9V thus giving a voltage hysteresis of 0·8V. The propagation delay of each trigger is typically 15ns.

Another common Trigger in the TTL range is the 7413 which is a dual NAND Schmitt trigger having four inputs to each gate; the

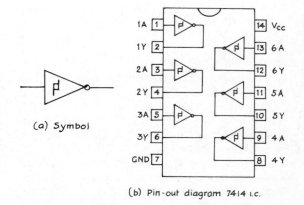

Fig. 21.12 Hex Schmitt trigger i.c. (7414).

Fig. 21.13 NAND Schmitt trigger.

circuit symbol is given in Fig. 21.13. A NAND Schmitt is essentially a NAND gate followed by a Schmitt trigger. The input to the trigger will be in the HIGH state only when all of the inputs to the NAND gate are in the LOW state.

Schmitt trigger devices are also available in CMOS, such as the 4584 (Hex inverting Schmitt) and the 4093 (Quad 2-input NAND Schmitt). These devices have an upper threshold of 2·9V and a lower threshold of 1·9V giving an hysteresis of 1·0V with a 5V supply.

Op-Amp Schmitt Trigger

An op-amp may be connected to form a Schmitt trigger circuit and one arrangement is given in Fig. 21.14. The input signal V_i is applied to the inverting terminal and positive

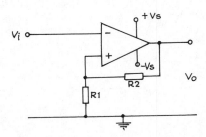

Fig. 21.14 Op-amp Schmitt trigger.

feedback via $R2$ is applied to the non-inverting terminal; the fraction of the output voltage that is fed back is given by

$$\frac{R1}{R1 + R2} \times V_0.$$

As a result of the positive feedback, then at switch-on and with $V_i = 0V$ the output voltage will rapidly assume either positive or negative saturation, i.e. V_o will be equal to approximately $+V_s$ or $-V_s$. Assume that V_o takes up positive saturation of $+V_s$ volts.

Let $V_s = \pm 5V$, $R2 = 8k\Omega$ and $R1 = 2k\Omega$.

Therefore the voltage at the inverting terminal will be

$$\frac{2}{2 + 8} \times 5 = +1V.$$

If V_i is increased in the positive direction from zero, V_o will remain in positive saturation until $V_i = +1V$. As soon as V_i is slightly greater than $+1V$ the output of the op-amp will rapidly switch into negative saturation ($-5V$) causing the voltage applied to the non-inverting terminal to change rapidly to $-1V$. The output will remain at negative saturation as long as V_i is more positive than $-1V$.

If V_i is now gradually reduced until V_i is just slightly negative of $-1V$ the output of the op-amp will switch back rapidly into positive saturation. Thus in this case, the upper and lower threshold voltages are $+1V$ and $-1V$ respectively, an hysteresis of 2V. By altering the value of $R1$ relative to $R2$, the hysteresis may be varied.

Schmitt Trigger Astable

A Schmitt trigger may be connected to form an astable multivibrator as shown in Fig. 21.15. This uses a 4093 2-input NAND Schmitt trigger having threshold values of 2·9V and 1·9V, i.e. a hysteresis of 1V

As will be noted, one input (A) is permanently connected to $+V_d$ (logic 1). Assume that the output V_o has just been switched to the HIGH state. At this instant input B must be LOW (logic 0) and the capacitor C discharged. C now charges at a rate determined by the time-constant CR seconds. When the voltage across C (V_c) reaches the upper threshold of $+2·9V$ both inputs of the

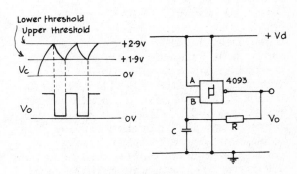

Fig. 21.15 Schmitt trigger astable.

NAND Schmitt trigger are HIGH and the trigger output rapidly goes LOW. This action causes C to discharge via R at the same rate until the voltage across C falls below the lower threshold of +1·9V. Input B is then in the LOW state and the output switches back to the HIGH state. As the waveforms show, C alternately charges and discharges between the upper and lower threshold values.

Schmitt Trigger Monostable

A Schmitt trigger monostable multivibrator using a 4093 NAND Schmitt trigger is shown in Fig. 21.16.

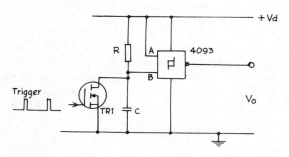

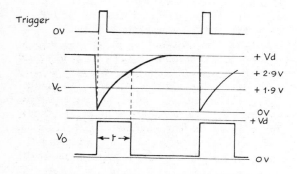

Fig. 21.16 Schmitt trigger monostable.

In the absence of a trigger pulse input, TR1 (an n-channel enhancement mosfet) is non-conducting and C is fully charged to $+V_d$. Inputs A and B are thus both HIGH and the output V_o is LOW. When a positive trigger pulse is applied to TR1, the transistor turns fully 'on' causing C to discharge rapidly. As a result, input B of the NAND Schmitt trigger goes LOW and the output switches to the HIGH state. The capacitor then charges up via R towards $+V_d$ but when the voltage across C

(V_c) reaches the upper threshold, the trigger output reverts back to the LOW output state. Thus a positive-going pulse is obtained at the output with a duration t which is dependent upon the CR time-constant.

UNIJUNCTION TRANSISTOR OSCILLATOR

The construction and operation of the u.j.t. was considered in Chapter 6 but the main features are repeated in Fig. 21.17. The device consists of a small bar of n-type silicon with ohmic contacts at either end (B1 and B2). A p–n junction is formed between the emitter lead and the bar by alloying an aluminium wire to the bar. In use, B2 is made positive w.r.t. B1 and in the absence of any voltage on the emitter the resistance between B2 and B1 is high (5–10kΩ). Thus the bar acts as a potential divider for the voltage applied between B2 and B1. The actual potential close to the p-region depends upon the position of the emitter lead which is usually arranged so that the potential is 0·4 to 0·8 of the voltage between B2 and B1.

Suppose that the B2 to B1 voltage is 20V and that the potential close to the p-region is $0·75 \times 20 = 15$V. If the voltage supplied between emitter and B1 is less than 15V, the p–n junction will be reverse biased and no emitter current will flow. However, if the voltage between emitter and B1 exceeds 15V by a

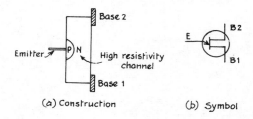

(a) Construction   (b) Symbol

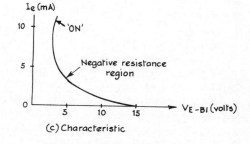

(c) Characteristic

Fig. 21.17 U.J.T.

small amount, say 0·6V, the p–n junction will be forward biased and emitter current will flow. The flow of current between emitter and B1 reduces the resistance between these terminals causing more current to flow. Thus the emitter current rises and the emitter-to-B1 voltage drops. After passing through a negative resistance region the current rapidly builds up and above a particular emitter current the voltage drop between emitter and B1 rises slightly.

Use as an Oscillator

A u.j.t. is suitable for use in SCR/Triac firing, timer and oscillator circuits and a typical arrangement is given in Fig. 21.18. The u.j.t. is arranged as a relaxation oscillator which generates a sawtooth waveform at the emitter by the charging of $C1$ via $R1$ and $R2$ and the rapid discharging of $C1$ via the u.j.t.

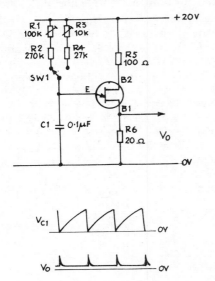

Fig. 21.18 U.J.T. oscillator for producing timing pulses.

At switch-on, $C1$ is uncharged, thus the emitter potential is zero and the u.j.t. is 'off'. As $C1$ charges via $R1$ and $R2$ towards the supply rail, the voltage across $C1$ rises exponentially. When the voltage across $C1$ exceeds the potential close to the p-region, the p–n junction becomes forward biased causing emitter current to flow. $C1$ will therefore rapidly discharge via the emitter-to-B1 and

$R6$. At the end of the discharge period the u.j.t. becomes reverse biased and the device goes 'off'. $C1$ then recommences charging via $R1$ and $R2$ and the cycle is repeated. Each time $C1$ discharges the current in $R6$ produces a positive-going pulse in the output.

Varying the time-constant by altering the value of the preset $R1$ will vary the repetition rate of the output pulses. SW1 will thus allow the oscillator to operate at one of two preset repetition rates. The pulse output is suitable for use as firing pulses for an s.c.r. or the pulses may be supplied to a monostable such as the 555 timer to generate repetitive pulses of width specified by the 555 timer.

555 TIMER I.C.

There is a number of i.c. timers in common use, such as the 555, 556 and the ZN 1034. These i.c. devices provide a **change of output voltage state** after a **predetermined time interval** which is the action of a **monostable multivibrator**. In the monostable mode the 555 timer is capable of producing accurate time delays over a wide range (μs to several minutes).

555 Monostable Operation

The i.c. package pin-out and the internal circuits of the 555 are given in Fig. 21.19, together with the necessary external components. The **external** timing components R_A and C are connected as shown. In the absence of a trigger pulse the $\bar{Q}$ output of the S–R bistable is HIGH and the discharge transistor TR1 is 'on' holding the output LOW. The three internal resistors $R1$, $R2$ and $R3$ form a potential divider so that $\frac{2}{3}V_{cc}$ appears at the inverting input of comparator 1 and a voltage of $\frac{1}{3}V_{cc}$ appears on the non-inverting input of comparator 2. The other input of comparator 2 is connected to the trigger input which is taken to $+V_{cc}$ via R_B, thus the output of comparator 2 is LOW. The outputs of the two comparators control the state of the internal S–R bistable.

With no trigger applied, the $\bar{Q}$ output is HIGH and TR1 is 'on' holding pin 7 at almost zero volts, thus preventing C from charging and at the same time the output on pin 3 is LOW, see waveforms of Fig. 21.20. When a

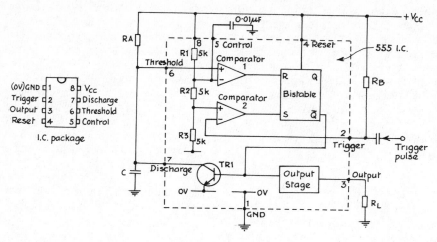

(0V)GND	1	8	Vcc
Trigger	2	7	Discharge
Output	3	6	Threshold
Reset	4	5	Control

I.C. package

Fig. 21.19 555 timer i.c.

negative-going trigger pulse is applied on pin 2 the output of comparator 2 goes HIGH (comparator 1 output is LOW) which SETS the bistable. This action causes the $\bar{Q}$ output to go LOW, TR1 to turn 'off' and for the output on pin 3 to switch to the HIGH state (instant t_1).

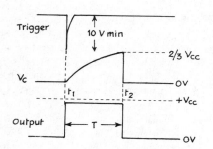

Fig. 21.20 Waveforms showing operation of 555 monostable.

C now charges exponentially via R_A and the voltage across C (V_c) rises towards $+V_{cc}$. When the voltage at the junction of R_A, C just exceeds $\frac{2}{3}V_{cc}$, the output of comparator 1 goes HIGH which RESETS the bistable. The $\bar{Q}$ output goes HIGH which causes TR1 to conduct and C to discharge rapidly. At the same time the output goes LOW, instant t_2. The duration T of the output pulse is the time taken for C to charge from zero up to $\frac{2}{3}V_{cc}$, thus $T = 1.1CR_A$ seconds.

Applications of the 555 Monostable

The circuit arrangement of Fig. 21.21 shows how the 555 may be connected to provide a 20s time delay. S1 is the **start** switch which when operated momentarily takes the trigger input (pin 2) down to zero voltage from $+V_{cc}$ and causes the output on pin 3 to go HIGH and for the l.e.d. to come 'on'. The capacitor C then charges via R_A towards $+V_{cc}$. After a period of 20s, C will be charged to $\frac{2}{3}V_{cc}$ and the output will go LOW. The l.e.d. will then be extinguished. The switch S2 allows the timing to be interrupted by taking pin 4 to zero voltage and thus acts as a **reset** switch.

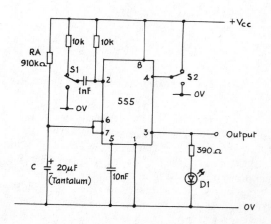

Fig. 21.21 20-second time delay.

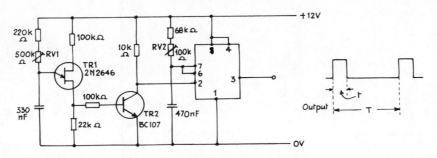

Fig. 21.22 Simple pulse generator.

The circuit of Fig. 21.22 shows a simple pulse generator using a 555 timer in the monostable mode. TR1 is a u.j.t. oscillator which provides trigger pulses for the 555. The trigger pulses are inverted by TR2 so that they are negative-going at the 555 trigger input on pin 2. The periodic time T of the output pulses on pin 3 is adjusted by RV1 and the pulse width t is adjusted by RV2. For the component values given, $T = 100$–250ms and $t = 20$–80ms.

A further application of the 555 is illustrated in Fig. 21.23 where use is made of the control input (pin 5 of the i.c.). By imposing an external voltage on this pin, the internal reference levels of $\frac{2}{3}V_{cc}$ and $\frac{1}{3}V_{cc}$ may be shifted above or below the normal reference levels hence affecting the duration of the output pulse. In the monostable mode, pin 5 can be swung between 45% and 90% of V_{cc}.

Thus if a rising ramp is applied to pin 5 the pulse output of the timer may be width-modulated. For applications where the control facility is not required, pin 5 is decoupled to the 0V line with a capacitor.

555 as an Astable

The 555 may also be connected to operate as an astable multivibrator as shown in Fig. 21.24. The output is then a train of pulses with width and frequency determined by the external timing components. Pins 2 and 6 of the i.c. are connected together which allows C to charge and discharge between the threshold level of $\frac{2}{3}V_{cc}$ and the trigger level of $\frac{1}{3}V_{cc}$.

When power is applied to the i.c., C charges via R_A and R_B towards V_{cc}. As soon as the voltage across C reaches $\frac{2}{3}V_{cc}$ the output changes state. This causes C to discharge via

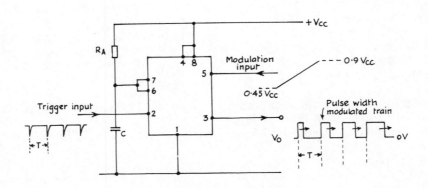

Fig. 21.23 Pulse width modulator.

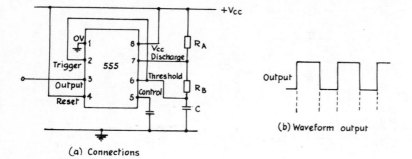

Fig. 21.24 555 as an astable.

R_B and the internal discharge transistor towards 0V. When the voltage across C falls to $\frac{1}{3}V_{cc}$, the circuit again changes state. This results in the internal discharge transistor turning 'off' allowing C to charge via R_A and R_B once again.

To achieve a symmetrical output $R_B \gg R_A$ and the frequency will primarily be determined by R_B and C,

$$f = \frac{1}{1.4CR_B} \text{ when } R_B \gg R_A$$

If some control over the mark-to-space ratio of the output is required the external timing components may be arranged as in Fig. 21.24(c). Here C will charge via D1 and R_A but discharge via D2 and R_B. Hence R_A sets the mark and R_B the space.

QUESTIONS ON CHAPTER TWENTY ONE

(1) A common method of producing a triangular wave is to:
 (a) Integrate a square wave
 (b) Differentiate a sawtooth wave
 (c) Differentiate a sine wave
 (d) Integrate a sawtooth wave.

(2) A Schmitt trigger has an upper threshold level of 1·8V and a lower threshold level of 0·9V. The voltage hysteresis is therefore:

(a) 2
(b) 2·7V
(c) 0·9V
(d) 1·62V.

(3) Refer to Fig. 21.18.
The repetition rate of the output pulses may be decreased by:
 (a) Decreasing C1 value
 (b) Decreasing R6 value
 (c) Reducing R1 value
 (d) Increasing R2 value.

(4) Refer to Fig. 21.19.
With $R_A = 2.2\,k\Omega$ and $C = 100\,nF$, the duration of the output pulse will be:
 (a) 0·242 ms
 (b) 22 μs
 (c) 0·22 ms
 (d) 0.22 s.

(5) Refer to Fig. 21.22.
If RV1 resistance is increased, the effect on the output will be:
 (a) Increase in both pulse repetition rate and pulse duration
 (b) Increase in pulse duration only
 (c) Decrease in pulse repetition rate only
 (d) Decrease in pulse duration only.

(Answers on page 370)

CHAPTER TWENTY TWO

MICROPROCESSOR-BASED SYSTEMS

Objectives

1 To define common terms.
2 Outline and explain operation of minimum micro-based control system.
3 Explain microprocessor operation during an instruction.
4 List common faults, outline fault finding aids and test programs.

MICROCOMPUTERS ARE USED extensively in offices, factories, shops, booking agents, airports, etc. where the **handling and manipulation of data** is of prime importance. These computing systems usually take the form of a keyboard, v.d.u., printer, disc drive, microprocessor and supporting chips. Such systems are concerned with the storage of scientific and engineering records, stock control, production of bills, hotel and travel reservations, aircraft/train time schedules, etc.

Microprocessor-based systems, on the other hand, are used where the main concern is the **control of external devices and equipment**. Such systems are used commonly in industry for the control of industrial processes and plant machinery; heating, ventilation and air conditioning plant for office blocks; and the control of items of domestic equipment such as video tape recorders and washing machines. The minimum requirement for these systems consists usually of a microprocessor chip and a number of supporting integrated circuits.

BITES, BYTES AND WORDS

In microprocessor-based systems, the signals which are sent or received from outside devices or equipment, or the signals which are stored in the systems' memories, are referred to as 'Data'. These data signals are binary-coded digital signals consisting of **high** and **low** logic levels, see Fig. 22.1.

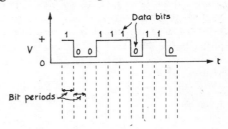

Fig. 22.1 Train of data bits.

Each **low** or **high** voltage state in the pulse train is called a **data bit** (or just **bit** for short) and each bit is allocated a particular time interval, called a **bit period**. Data bits can be sent in serial form, i.e. one bit following another using a single line (**single data bus**) or in parallel form using eight or sixteen lines (eight-bit or sixteen-bit data bus), see Fig. 22.2.

Data signals that are transferred between the various integrated circuits forming a

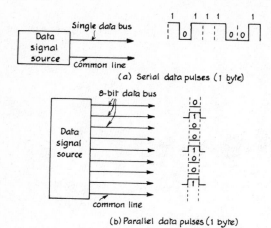

(a) Serial data pulses (1 byte)

(b) Parallel data pulses (1 byte)

Fig. 22.2 Serial and parallel data.

Word length is by common agreement kept to multiples of 8-bits and a group of 8-bits is called a **byte**. Half of a byte, i.e. 4-bits is called a **nibble**. Thus a system using a word size of 16-bits has a word made up of two data bytes, see Fig. 22.3. An 8-bit data word is capable of providing $2^8 = 256$ different 8-bit binary codes, whereas a 16-bit data word is capable of providing $2^{16} = 65536$ different 16-bit binary codes.

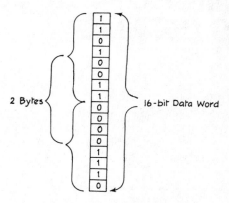

Fig. 22.3 16-bit parallel data word.

microprocessor-based control system are sent in **parallel form**, as this is a fast and convenient way of handling data. Serial data transfer is normally reserved for sending data over large distances where only a single data line is required. Also some peripheral devices in a computer system, e.g. v.d.u.s and some printers operate with serial data only.

A group of data bits handled within a computing system is called a data **word**. The number of bits making up a word is standard for a particular microprocessor. For most second-generation microprocessors the word length is 8-bits but in others it is 16-bits and can be as high as 64-bits. It does not matter how long or short is the standard length, it is still defined as a word.

PROGRAM INSTRUCTIONS

At the heart of a microprocessor-based control system is the microprocessor itself which carries out the system's program as a series of **instructions** which allows the tasks to be implemented in an orderly manner. The instructions are stored in the program memory (Fig. 22.4), as a sequence of binary codes.

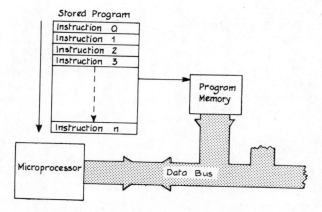

Fig. 22.4 The stored program concept.

Writing down a program in binary codes is very tedious but is alleviated by writing the program instructions in **Hexadecimal**. A program written in hexadecimal is often referred to as **Machine Code**.

As the program is carried out, the microprocessor executes each instruction stored in the program memory commencing at Instruction 0 and proceeding until Instruction *n* (the final instruction) has been completed. Each instruction in the program memory consists of two parts:
(a) the OPERATOR code, and (b) the OPERAND.

The Operator Code

This defines the **operation** to be performed during the execution of the instruction. Common operator codes include LOAD, STORE, ADD, SUBTRACT, COMPARE, JUMP and SHIFT. An operator code is usually one byte long thus its 8-bits can identify 256 different codes. In practice the **instruction set** of a microprocessor consists of about 80 operator codes.

The Operand

This part of the instruction contains the binary numbers on which the operator code (op-code) operates. The binary number (usually written down in HEX) may be data, i.e. a number to be stored in a particular location or the address of a particular location into which data is to be stored. The operand may be one or two bytes in length but for some op-codes it is zero bytes, i.e. these op-codes do not require an operand.

It should be noted that at 'machine level' a microprocessor-based system deals only in binary thus the operator code and operand when written down in HEX are simply numbers. Since a list of instructions written down as HEX numbers is not very informative to humans, the op-codes are usually written in a symbolic alphabetic code, i.e. in the form of **mnemonics** which is more meaningful when reading.

Consider the example of a simple machine code program in Table 22.1, based on the Motorola 6800 instruction set.

It should first be mentioned that data may be stored in a number of different areas within a microprocessor-based system and that each 'location' where binary data is stored is given an unique **address**. Each address is described by a binary number as far as the machine is concerned, but when writing an address down it is put into its HEX equivalent. In Table 22.1(a) the addresses used in the program memory run from 0020 to 0027 (HEX) and the table also shows some instructions with the op-code written in HEX. To make the op-code more meaningful when composing a program, it is usually written down in its

Table 22.1 Simple Machine Code Program (6800)

Address	Instruction		Operand	Meaning
	HEX Op-code	Mnemonic Op-code		
0020	86	LDAA	26	Load into accumulator A the binary equivalent of the HEX number 26
0022	8B	ADDA	36	Add to accumulator A the binary equivalent of the HEX number 36
0024	B7	STAA	0100	Store the contents of accumulator A in the address 0100 (HEX)
0027	3F	SWI		Soft-ware interrupt (program ends)

(a) Op-code in HEX and mnemonic form

Address	Instruction	
0020	10000110	← Op-code 86
0021	00100110	← Operand 26
0022	10001011	← Op-code 8B
0023	00110110	← Operand 36
0024	10110111	← Op-code B7
0025	00000001	← Operand 0100 (digits 01)
0026	00000000	← Operand 0100 (digits 00)
0027	00111111	← Op-code 3F

(b) Actual binary codes placed in program memory

mnemonic form, also shown in Table 22.1(a). It will be noted that in table (a) there are gaps left in the addresses. This is to allow for the number of bytes required by the instructions. For example, the instruction LDAA 26 requires 2 bytes whereas the instruction STAA 0100 requires 3 bytes. The full address list is given in table (b) which shows the actual binary codes placed in the memory locations with 1 byte at each location.

The Fetch-Execute Cycle

During the implementation of a program, the microprocessor **fetches** each instruction in turn from the program memory. It determines the action to be carried out and then **executes** the action. Upon completion of the instruction, the next instruction is fetched from the memory. The 'fetch phase' and the 'execute phase' constitute the rhythmic beat of a computer, see Fig. 22.5.

These two phases are known as the 'instruction cycle' of a computer system. When carrying out the 'fetch phase' of an instruction, the microprocessor is able to determine from the first byte (op-code) of the instruction the number (if any) of the remaining bytes of the instruction. Thus, prior to execution, the microprocessor fetches the required number of bytes which make up the complete instruction.

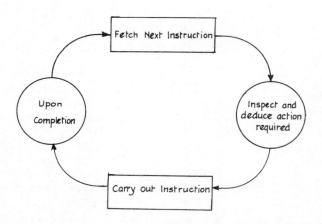

Fig. 22.5 *The rythmic beat of a computer.*

MINIMUM MICROPROCESSOR-BASED SYSTEM

The block schematic of Fig. 22.6 shows the essential 'hardware' meeting the minimum requirement for a microprocessor-based control system. The inidividual items will now be described.

(1) Microprocessor

This item provides the rhythmic beat of a computer system and consists of a large number of logic gates, buffer stages and a few shift registers manufactured on a single integrated circuit chip (usually a 40-pin dual in-line package). A microprocessor acts as a kind of universal digital circuit and serves as the **central processing unit** (c.p.u.) of the computer system. It executes arithmetical problems, logic comparison, data transfer and control operations that are presented to it as a sequence of instructions, step-by-step under the control of the systems program.

Three popular microprocessors are the Zilog Z80, the Intel 8080 and the Motorola 6800. Although the internal circuits of these types are different, they are all 8-bit microprocessors, thus the data word length is 8-bits and they communicate with the outside via three separate buses – data, address and control, which will be considered later.

Fig. 22.7 shows in simplified form the internal structure of a typical microprocessor.

Programming instructions received one by one from the program memory (ROM) and entering the microprocessor via the data bus are held in the **Instruction Register** so that any particular instruction being carried out can be interpreted. The **Instruction Decoder and Control** block **decodes** the instruction held in the instruction register and manipulates data around the internal bus so that the instruction is carried out. In order to accomplish this, it makes use of **control signals** sent along internal control lines to the various blocks within the microprocessor.

The **ALU** (Arithmetic Logic Unit) is the circuit where arithmetical and logic operations are performed. A typical operation for the ALU would be the addition of two binary numbers or the ANDing of a pair of binary numbers. The results of operations carried out by the ALU are stored in a register called the **Accumulator**.

It is most important that during the implementation of a program the microprocessor keeps track of the memory location from which the next instruction is to be taken. This

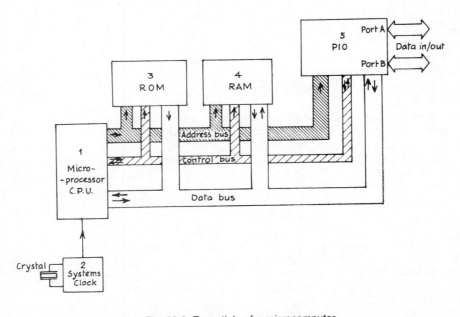

Fig. 22.6 Essentials of a microcomputer.

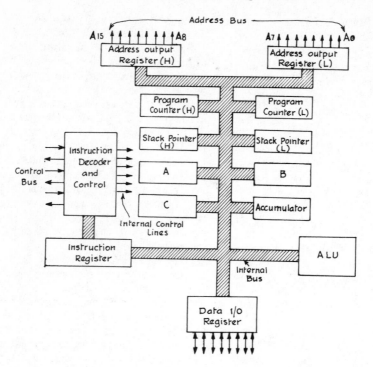

Fig. 22.7 Simplified internal structure of a microprocessor.

is the function of the **Program Counter** which consists of two 8-bit registers. The program counter always holds the memory address of the next instruction to be carried out. During the execution of an instruction, the program counter is incremented so that on completion of the instruction it holds the memory address of the next instruction to be accessed from the program memory.

The memory addresses from which programming instructions are received (ROM) or where data is temporarily stored (in RAM) are applied to the 16-bit address bus via **Address Output Register Buffers**. These devices have two functions. They amplify the microprocessor signals so that they are capable of driving the external memory devices and hold the addresses steady until they have been accepted by the external memory.

Data enters or leaves the microprocessor via the **Data I/O Register** which is bidirectional. This device holds the binary data signals steady until they are ready for acceptance by the stages or devices internal or external to the

microprocessor. The send/receive data facility of the Data I/O Register is controlled by signals from the Instruction Decoder and Control block.

During the implementation of a program, some memory space will be required to store interim results or to transfer the data held in the microprocessor registers during an 'interrupt'. Most microprocessors have at least one input pin reserved for an 'interrupt request' which when activated will cause the microprocessor to abandon the current instruction sequence and to jump to another area of the systems program. After the interrupt has been dealt with, the microprocessor will call back the data from the memory space so that the main program can continue. The memory space reserved for temporary use is called the RAM stack and the **Stack Pointer** holds the address of the next unused location in the RAM.

Additional registers are often used; registers A and B which may be used as temporary registers and register C (processor status register).

Microprocessor Comparison

Internal architecture, operation and facilities vary from one processor to another. They vary in the number of specialised and general-purpose registers used, maximum speed of operation, number of data and address lines, number of basic instructions and addressing modes available and in their overall capabilities. Some features are shown in Table 22.2 for three popular microprocessors.

Table 22.2 Comparison of popular microprocessors

Microprocessor	Word size	Number of address lines	Number of registers	Max. clock frequency	Package	Voltage
Zilog Z80 (NMOS)	8-bits	16	18 × 8-bit 4 × 16-bit	4MHz	40 pin	5V
Motorola 6800 (NMOS)	8-bits	16	3 × 8-bit 3 × 16-bit	2MHz	40 pin	5V
Intel 8080 (PMOS)	8-bits	16	3 × 8-bit 6 × 16-bit	0.8MHz	40 pin	5V

(2) Systems Clock

To synchronise operations within the computer system, a stable clock signal is required and this is generated by the systems clock, block 2 of Fig. 22.6. The frequency of the clocking signal is usually a few megahertz for the popular microprocessors but can be as high as 10MHz for the more specialised processors. Frequency stability is ensured by using a quartz crystal for the master timing. The systems clock may be on board the microprocessor chip or external to it.

The microprocessor is fed with the clock signal from block 2 and internally generates non-overlapping antiphase clock signals ϕ_1 and ϕ_2, see Fig. 22.8. These clocking signals are used inside the microprocessor and for synchronising the actions of other blocks such as the RAM and ROM.

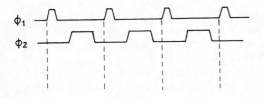

Fig. 22.8 Non-overlapping clock signals generated by microprocessor.

(3) ROM

The set of instructions or program is stored normally in a memory external to the microprocessor. In control applications such as the control of a domestic washing machine where the program is fixed, it is permanently stored in a ROM (read only memory).

A ROM is a non-volatile memory, that is, its contents are not lost when power is removed. Each location within the memory is capable of storing a **high** or **low** voltage (logic 1 or 0), the levels of which are fixed by permanent connections during programming by the manufacturer. Most modern ROMs are word-organised and Fig. 22.9 shows the basic idea of a ROM storing 1024, 8-bit bytes (or words). Each byte is stored in a known location or at a particular 'address' and during implementation of the system program the stored bytes are output from the ROM under the control of the microprocessor. To identify each stored byte, the microprocessor must provide an address and in this case an 8-bit binary address ($2^8 = 1024$) is required to address the 1024 byte locations. The address decoder converts the 8-bit binary address to one of 1024 output lines, each of which will identify a single stored byte.

The data output from each memory position is placed byte-by-byte into a temporary store called a latch which may be formed from eight

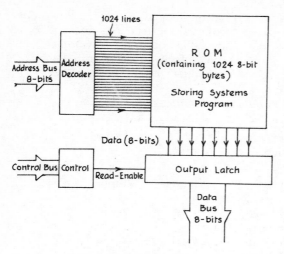

Fig. 22.9 Read only memory.

be at some specified location or address so that it can later be retrieved and Fig. 22.10 shows the basic idea.

A RAM is a volatile store, so that its contents are lost when the power is removed and each location where a **high** or **low** voltage (logic 1 or 0) is stored may be formed from a bistable element. If a RAM capable of storing 1024, 8-bit words is used, it will be seen that the addressing required is the same as for the ROM of Fig. 22.9. However, data can be written into or read from these locations, thus a bidirectional latch is needed. Signals from the control bus control the enabling of the latch during the write or read operations and provide a means of placing the latch in the read or write mode, thus altering the flow of data to or from the data bus.

D-type bistables. A signal fed along the control bus produces a 'read-enable' signal which activates the latch output thus placing the data on to the data bus, byte-by-byte.

(4) RAM

The RAM acts as a temporary store for data which may be changing from instant to instant, unlike the fixed operating program held in the ROM. For example, if the microprocessor is carrying out multiplication or division of input data, interim results may be stored temporarily in the RAM and then retrieved later. Alternatively, the program may call for the data from, say, five input transducers to be sequentially stored in the RAM. Once in the RAM, the data may be recalled and manipulated upon by the microprocessor at a later instant. In some control systems such as control of a washing machine or video tape recorder, data relating to 'user commands' entered via selector buttons on the machine, may be stored in the RAM to implement a particular section of the systems program from the ROM. Upon completion of the section of program the data stored in the RAM is erased and may be replaced at a later time with new data.

It is thus evident that a RAM is a type of memory which can have data written into it or read from it (Read and Write Memory). When data is stored temporarily in the RAM it must

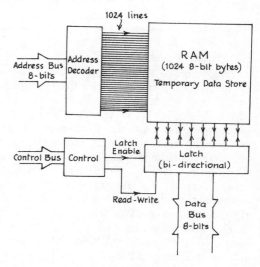

Fig. 22.10 RAM.

(5) PIO

During the running of a program a microcomputer needs to communicate with various input and output devices, accepting data from them or sending data to them. This may be achieved through the use of **input and output ports**, each port consisting of eight parallel terminals or lines. The microprocessor may have to communicate with many peripheral devices through these ports and the system must be organised so that the microprocessor communicates with only one device at a time;

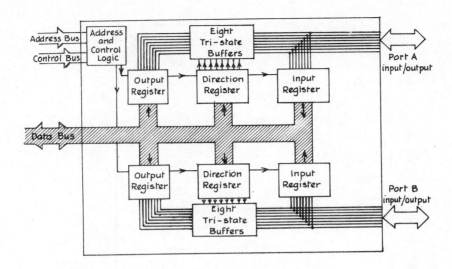

Fig. 22.11 Programmable input/output I.C. (simplified).

attempting to talk with several devices simultaneously would result in chaos. One port may be permanently connected as an input port and the other as an output port. However, to improve the versatility it is useful to be able to program the ports so that they may both be used as input or output ports, or some lines on each port may be designated input lines and others output lines. This requirement led to the development of **programmable input/output** (PIO) i.c.s., see Fig. 22.11.

Each port has associated with it three registers and a set of tristate buffers. The direction register is used to program the individual lines of the port as input or output lines by controlling the state of the tristate buffers. Progamming is initialised by applying suitable logic levels on the data bus to the direction register. The input and output registers of each port store the data at input and output. All three registers are under the control of the address and control block which provides a 'chip select' signal for each port and a read/write signal for the input/output registers.

Bus Lines

Data Bus

Most microprocessors use an eight-bit binary word and thus require an eight-bit data bus, i.e. one with eight lines in order to transmit simultaneously eight bits of data (parallel data transfer). 'Data' can be taken to mean signals received from input transducers or signals sent to output devices, programming instructions taken from the ROM or interim results stored in the RAM. Since a microprocessor must be capable of transmitting data to and from the c.p.u., the data bus must be bidirectional.

Address Bus

The address bus usually has 16 lines which allows the various memory locations in the ROM, RAM or PIO to be selected. With a 16-line address bus the c.p.u. is able to address $2^{16} = 65536$ locations or 64K locations (1K = 1024 locations). A common way of showing how the addresses of the various memory locations have been allocated within a computer

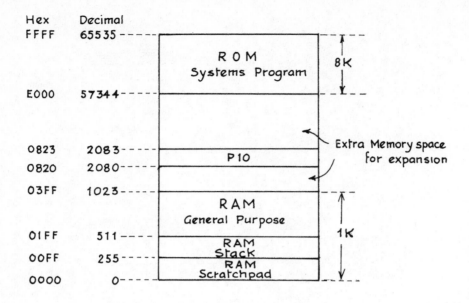

Fig. 22.12 Memory map.

system is by a **memory map**, see Fig. 22.12. This shows that the ROM systems program is located between addresses 57344 and 65535 and the RAM 'scratchpad' (where the c.p.u. stores interim results) is allocated addresses 0 to 255. Data stored in the input and output registers of the PIO are also considered to be memory addresses and occupy four bytes (addresses 2080 to 2083). Thus by placing a particular address on the address bus, the microprocessor can select the appropriate memory store. The actual selection is normally carried out by the 'address decoder'.

Control Bus

The control bus is used for control purposes within the computer system and typically there may be ten lines, some of which are input control lines to the microprocessor and others which are output control lines. One output control line is the $\overline{\text{Read}}$ line which has a logic 0 on it when the c.p.u. wishes to read data from a memory location; a logic 1 is placed on this line when the c.p.u. does not need to be read. Another output control line is the $\overline{\text{Write}}$ line which has a logic 0 placed on it when the c.p.u. wishes to write into a memory location. Input

control lines are used for the systems clock and the use of interrupts.

Microprocessor Operation during Instruction

Consider the simple instruction in plain language 'LOAD THE ACCUMULATOR WITH A NUMBER (2F) WHICH MAY BE FOUND AT MEMORY LOCATION 0020'. The mnemonic form of this instruction (based on the 6502 instruction set) is LDA 20 00 and the machine code is AD 20 00. Suppose that this instruction appears in the program memory at the following addresses:

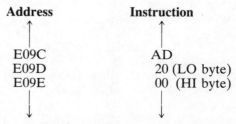

Address	Instruction
↑	↑
E09C	AD
E09D	20 (LO byte)
E09E	00 (HI byte)
↓	↓

During the implementation of this particular instruction the following steps or machine clock cycles will occur.

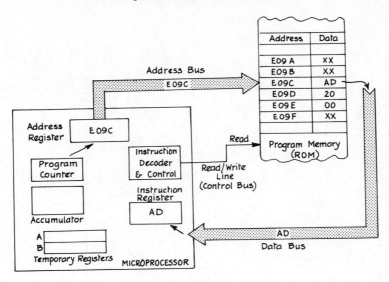

Fig. 22.13 Clock cycle 1.

Clock Cycle 1

The program counter places in the address register the binary equivalent of the address E09C which is fed to the ROM via the address bus (Fig. 22.13). The control section of the microprocessor also supplies a 'read' signal to the ROM via the control bus. As a result, address E09C is read and the binary equivalent of the op-code AD is passed into the data bus and fed to the instruction register. The instruction decoder then decodes the op-code AD.

Clock Cycle 2

The program counter is incremented to E09D and this is placed in the address register (Fig. 22.14). The binary equivalent of E09D is fed to the ROM via the address bus and a 'read' signal is sent along the control bus to place the ROM in the 'read' mode. Address E09D is read and the LO byte of the operand (20) is placed on the data bus. Its binary equivalent is sent to temporary register A where it is stored.

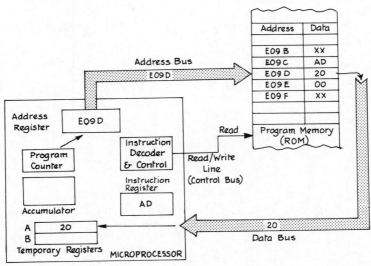

Fig. 22.14 Clock cycle 2.

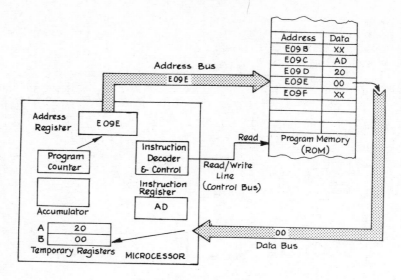

Fig. 22.15 Clock cycle 3.

Clock Cycle 3

The program counter is incremented to E09E and this is placed in the address register (Fig. 22.15). The binary equivalent of E09E is fed to the ROM via the address bus and a 'read' signal is sent along the control bus to keep the ROM in the 'read' mode. Address E09E is read and the HI byte of the operand (00) is placed on the data bus. Its binary equivalent is sent to temporary register B where it is stored.

Clock Cycle 4

The address 0020 is transferred from the temporary registers A and B to the address register (Fig. 22.16) and its binary equivalent is sent along the address bus to the RAM (where this address is assumed to be). A 'read' signal is also supplied via the control bus placing the RAM in the 'read' mode. The contents (2F) of address 0020 is then placed on the data bus and fed to the microprocessor to be loaded into the accumulator.

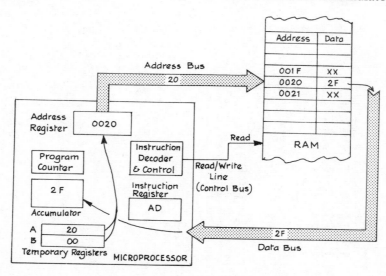

Fig. 22.16 Clock cycle 4.

The four clock cycles together constitute the **fetch-execute cycle** for this particular instruction. If the systems clock operates at 1MHz, the complete instruction takes 4µs.

SEMICONDUCTOR MEMORIES

The RAM and ROM memory stores have already been introduced briefly and in this section additional information will be given along with descriptions of other semiconductor memories (PROM, EPROM and EAROM) to be found in microprocessor-based systems.

RAM (Read-Write Memory)

A RAM is a memory store where data can be stored or retrieved randomly (Random Access Memory). Semiconductor RAMs are **volatile** stores, when power is removed the content of the memory is lost; when the memory is powered up once again the content is 'garbage'.

Store Organisation

Each 'bit' of data is stored in a unique location within the memory. The capacity of a store is normally quoted in **kilobits**. The prefix

'kilo' does not stand for 1000 as is usual, but for 1024. Thus 30 kilobits = 30K = 30 × 1024 = 30720 bits.

Fig. 22.17 shows the organisation of a 1K store with 32 rows and 32 columns. Each of the 1024 squares represents the location for one-bit (a logic 0 or 1). Any location may be specified by its row and column address, for example bit 'n' may be specified as x_0/y_3 and bit 'm' by x_{30}/y_{27}.

To 'write' or 'read' data, each location must be addressed with the address given in binary code. The 32 rows and 32 columns of a 1K RAM may be specified by a 5-bit binary code. To decode the 5-bit binary address, row and column each require a 5-to-32 binary-to-decimal decoder.

RAMs may be **bit** or **word** organised. With a 'bit' organised RAM, each address identifies a single bit, whereas for a 'word' organised RAM each address identifies a single word (of usually 4 or 8 bits). Thus with a word-organised RAM, a single byte of 8-bits may be written into or read from each unique address.

Cell Structure

Static RAM cells are usually formed by flip-flops, fabricated in i.c. form using bipolar or CMOS technology. A static RAM cell is

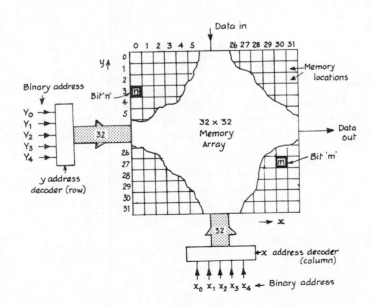

Fig. 22.17 Standard 1k RAM.

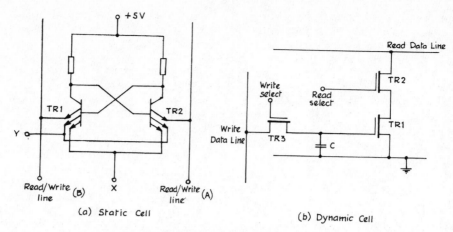

Fig. 22.18 Static and dynamic RAM cells.

given in Fig. 22.18(a) based on bipolar transistor technology. The term 'static' is used to denote that data once placed in the cell 'remains there' until power is removed.

A 'dynamic' RAM cell is shown in Fig. 22.18(b). This type of memory cell relies for its action on temporary storage of charge in a capacitory C. A disadvantage is that the charge in C gradually leaks away, which means that the data stored in the cell has to be 'refreshed' periodically (typically every 2ms); for this reason the memory is called 'dynamic'.

In computer systems, RAMs are used as temporary data stores and are used for storing systems programs when input from tape or disc.

ROM (Read Only Memory)

ROMs are essentially **non-volatile**, high-speed, high-density, random-access storage devices. Data is stored as a pattern of **highs** and **lows** (logic 1s and 0s) using combinational logic circuitry with 'permanent' connections which determine the stored data rather than flip-flop elements. The term 'random access' means that the access time to the information stored at a particular address is the same irrespective of the address and the previous location addressed.

Most modern ROMs are word organised and Fig. 22.19 shows the basic idea of a 16-bit diode matrix ROM organised as 4 × 4-bit words. To identify 4 words a 2-bit binary address (A_0 and A_1) is required. The binary address is decoded by a 2-to-4 line decoder to supply the Y address lines to the diode matrix. The diagram of Fig. 22.20 shows the ROM memory.

During manufacture, bits of a word are programmed **low** by placing a diode at the intersection of a bit line and a word line. A particular word is accessed by making the appropriate word line **low**. Note that a **low** on a

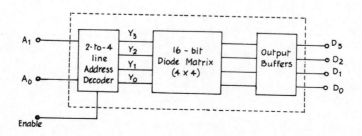

Fig. 22.19 16-bit diode matrix ROM.

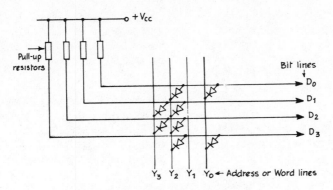

Fig. 22.20 Diode matrix ROM.

word address line will cause any diodes connected to conduct and the bit line will assume approximately zero potential (logic 0). A **high** ($+ V_{cc}$) on a word address line will cause any connected diodes to be 'off' and the bit line(s) assume the logic 1 state. The truth table given in Table 22.3 shows the output or 'stored' words as each address line in turn is taken **low** (all other address lines remaining **high**).

In practice the word length is commonly 4 or 8 bits and typically a ROM may store 256, 1024 or 4096 words. With many modern ROMs, bipolar or CMOS transistor circuitry replaces the diodes in the matrix but the basic operating principles remain the same. In computer systems ROMs find various uses: storing systems programs; character generators; code converters and look-up tables.

Table 22.3 Truth table for diode matrix

Y_0	Y_1	Y_2	Y_3		D_0	D_1	D_2	D_3	
0	1	1	1		0	1	1	0	Stored Word 1
1	0	1	1		1	1	1	1	2
1	1	0	1		0	0	0	0	3
1	1	1	0		1	0	0	1	4

PROM (Programmable ROM)

This type of ROM is produced so that programming may be carried out after production, often by the purchaser. When the PROM is made, the bits of the memory are either all **high** or all **low**. Programming causes some of the bits to reverse state.

A common method of producing a ROM is to include in each storage cell a fusible link (titanium tungsten), see Fig. 22.21. With the fusible links intact, if any of the address lines is taken **low** all output bit lines will be **low** and the memory is 'blank'. Programming of the memory entails the 'blowing' of some of the

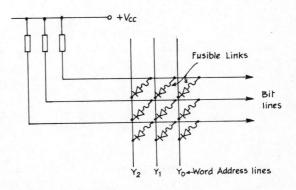

Fig. 22.21 Diode matrix PROM (memory blank).

fusible links causing the appropriate bits to reverse to the **high** state. If a particular bit is to be programmed **low** the link is left intact.

Once a PROM has been programmed it effectively becomes just a ROM. A PROM is a **non-volatile** memory store.

EPROM (Eraseable Programmable ROM)

With this type of PROM the programming is not an irreversible process. The memory contents may be erased and the PROM reprogrammed. An EPROM can be recognised by the 'quartz window' at the top of the i.c. package, see Fig. 22.22.

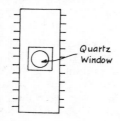

Fig. 22.22 EPROM I.C. package.

Programming of a memory cell is achieved by the storage of a charge in a MOS transistor using a 25–50V pulse. Erasure of the EPROM contents is carried out by exposing the memory matrix to shortwave ultraviolet light through the quartz window.

Some EPROMs do exhibit a sensitivity to ambient light; this does not erase them but they may malfunction when minute photo-electric leakage currents are generated. It is thus prudent to cover the quartz window after programming has been carried out.

EPROMs are **non-volatile** memory stores and are particularly useful when developing a systems program since changes are usually needed as the development proceeds.

EAROM (Electrically Alterable ROM)

With this type of PROM, the contents of the memory matrix can be erased electrically using high voltages and then reprogrammed. This removes the distinct disadvantage of the need for a u.v. source when an EPROM is used. Also an EAROM requires only about one second for erasure as opposed to about 10–30 minutes for the EPROM. Another advantage of the EAROM is that depending upon size, erasure can be confined to individual bits, bytes or blocks of bytes whereas an EPROM must be erased in total.

Once programmed, an EAROM is a **non-volatile** store and may be used for developing systems programs as for the EPROM.

Some details of common memory i.c.s. are given in Table 22.4.

An important parameter of memories is 'Access Time' which is the time elapsing from applying an address to a memory location to when data appears at the output of the location. The shorter the access time, the higher is the rate at which data may be retrieved from a memory.

MAGNETIC STORES

In computer systems, data and programs may be stored in the form of magnetic fields on tape and disc to produce **non-volatile** memory stores.

Table 22.4 Details of common integrated circuits

I.C.	Type	Family	Bit capacity	Configuration	Number of pins	Access time (ns)
8×350	Static RAM	TTL	2048	256 × 8	22	40
4256–15	Dynamic RAM		262144	262144 × 1	16	150
82S183	PROM	TTL	8192	1024 × 8	24	60
10149	PROM	ECL	1024	256 × 4	16	20
2708	EPROM	NMOS	8192	1024 × 8	24	450
3400	EAROM		4096	1024 × 4	22	900

Magnetic Tape

Magnetic tape used in the computer industry is usually between 3.8mm and 25.4mm wide, about 0.025mm thick and is made from polyester coated with a 100μm thick layer of magnetic oxide.

Commonly, 9-track or 7-track tape is used and with each track is associated a read/write head. As the tape (stored in reels) is transported passed the read/write heads, bytes of data are recorded sequentially on to the tape as shown in Fig. 22.23. With 9-track tape, eight tracks are used for the data and the other track is used for the parity bit (error protection). A group of bytes is recorded or read together and is known as a **block**. Each block of data bytes is separated by an unrecorded section of tape about 1.5cm in length which allows the tape to be positioned for recording and replay. The exact number of data bytes in each block can be varied and is determined by the software program. Large reels of tape often hold 750m of tape or more and the tape transport system allows the transfer of data bytes at rates between 300–1200 kilobytes/s.

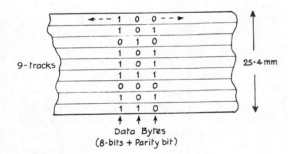

Fig. 22.23 *Recording data bytes on magnetic tape.*

If binary data is **directly recorded** so that a logic 1 is represented by positive magnetisation and a logic 0 is represented by negative magnetisation as shown in Fig. 22.24(a) then the tape track magnetisation will be as in Fig. 22.24(b). Since the replay head produces an output voltage only when there is a flux change, there will be no output when a string of 1s or a string of 0s is present in the data.

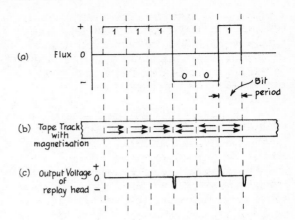

Fig. 22.24 *Problem when data is recorded directly onto tape.*

It is thus necessary to **encode** the data before it is recorded to ensure that there are appropriate flux changes. There are a number of encoding methods in use but a common one is NRZ 1 (Non-Return-to Zero), see Fig. 22.25. The data signal to be recorded is encoded in a special way so that a **logic 1 produces a flux change** and a **logic 0 no flux change**. Since the polarity of the output voltage from the replay head is not part of the code, a **decoder** is required to produce a logic 1 when a voltage pulse is present and a logic 0 when there is no pulse present at the start of each bit period. Other encoding methods include phase encoding (PE) and frequency modulation (FM).

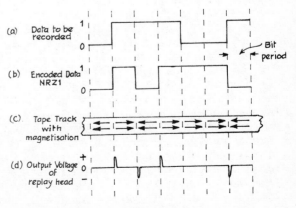

Fig. 22.25 *Encoding the data prior to recording.*

Apart from reel-to-reel recorders, digital cassette or cartridge recorders are also available. These are designed to give constant tape tension and the stopping, starting, reverse and forward movement of the tape is under digital control. Digital cassette and cartridge recorders can be single-track, 2-track or 4-tack and often use 'phase encoding' with capacities of about 10^6 bytes for cassette and 20×10^6 bytes for cartridge. Data transfer rates of up to about 60 kilobytes/s may be achieved.

Audio cassette recorders using tape with mono audio tracks may also be used to store and replay computer programs. During record, however, it is necessary for the computer to convert the logic signals into audio tones which can be recorded directly on to tape (2100Hz for logic 0 and 1300Hz for logic 1). When the recorded signals are replayed, the computer terminal must convert the audio tones back into logic 1s and 0s.

Because with a mono audio recorder only one track can be recorded at a time, data is recorded sequentially bit-by-bit. Thus data transfer rates are low (about 160 bytes/s).

Magnetic Disc

There are two main types:

Hard Disc

These rigid discs are often made from aluminium using a magnetic coating of ferric or chromium oxide. The concentric tracks on which data is recorded are divided into a number of sectors, see Fig. 22.26(a). Each sector holds a number of 16-bit words. A typical disc may have 256 tracks with a separate read/write head for each track and use 32 sectors (each holding 128 words).

The disc revolves horizontally during read and write, see Fig. 22.26(b), at about 3400 rev/min. Data bits are recorded sequentially on each track but since a large number of tracks and heads is used, 256 bits may be recorded simultaneously. Thus very high data transfer rates (about 400 kilobytes/s) may be achieved for a single disc. Greater data transfer rates may be obtained if a stack of discs (usually 10) is simultaneously recorded/replayed with moving heads. As for magnetic tape the logic signals are encoded prior to recording and often 'phase encoding' is employed.

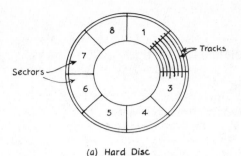

(a) Hard Disc

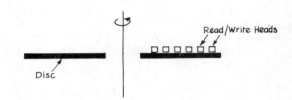

(b) Disc with fixed heads

Fig. 22.26 Hard disc.

Floppy Disc

Floppy discs are made from Mylar coated with ferric oxide and were originally 19.7cm in diameter, but smaller versions (12.7cm in diameter) known as 'mini-floppies' were later developed. The disc is enclosed in a protective plastic sleeve and there is a slot in the sleeve through which the read/write head enters, see Fig. 22.27(a). Data is stored in tracks on the disc which is divided into sectors. The large disc has about 77 tracks with 26 sectors per track and is capable of storing 128×8-bit bytes per sector. Its data transfer rate is about 250 kilobytes/s.

The disc is spun at 360 or 300 rev/min by a belt-driven drive shaft which enters via the central hole in the disc. An additional small index hole is used for defining the beginning of the tracks using a light source and optical sensor.

During record or playback the head is driven radially across the disc by a stepper motor, see Fig. 22.27(b) and touches the disc, unlike with the hard disc. To prevent accidental erasure of stored data, an adhesive

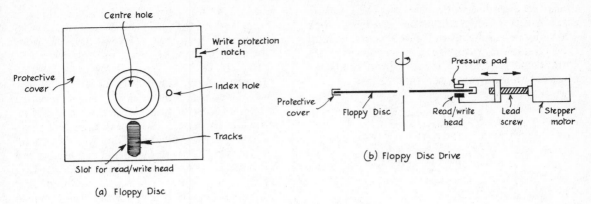

Fig. 22.27 Floppy disc.

tab may be placed across the 'write protection notch'. The logic signals must be encoded prior to recording and the encoding method is usually 'frequency modulation'. As only a single head is employed the data is recorded serially bit-by-bit.

U.A.R.T.

It has been seen that the various component parts of the minimum microprocessor control system of Fig. 22.6 manipulate and support the flow of data around the system in parallel form, byte-by-byte. There are, however, a number of peripheral devices which operate with serial data only, e.g. serial printers, floppy disc units and cassette tape recorders. Thus in order for a microprocessor-based system to send data to such units, parallel-to-serial conversion is required. Conversely, when data is sent from a floppy disc unit to be, say, stored in RAM, serial-to-parallel conversion is needed. In addition, it may be necessary for a microbased control system to communicate with a remote v.d.u. terminal via a single bus data link using serial data transfer.

The i.c. device which allows a computer system to communicate in serial form with the various peripheral devices is a **Universal Asynchronous Receiver/Transmitter** (UART). This is a **support chip** (like the PIO) provided by the microprocessor manufacturer and can be connected to the system's buses as shown in Fig. 22.28. An UART is 'universal' in the sense that it can be programmed to produce the correct form of transmission to be compatible with a wide range of peripheral devices.

With asynchronous data transfer, the time between the transmission of one character and the next is not fixed. For example, the codes generated by the keyboard of a v.d.u. terminal are random and depend upon the typing speed of the operator. However, to be able to recognise each data bit, each character block

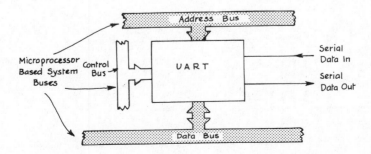

Fig. 22.28 Universal asynchronous receiver/transmitter.

must be encoded so that the receiving station can detect exactly when the character block commences and thus pull into synchronism at the data bit rate. In asynchronous data transfer it is common to use 'start' and 'stop' bits for this purpose, see Fig. 22.29.

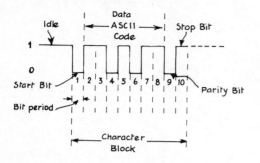

Fig. 22.29 Asynchronous data transfer.

In the absence of any transmission code the serial data line rests in the **high** or 'idle' state. To indicate when the transmission of a data byte is about to commence, the start of a character is preceeded by a 'start' bit of logic 0. Immediately following the start bit is the 7-bit character code, such as ASCII or EBCDIC. Bit 8 is used for parity checking using either

odd or even parity. The character block is completed by the 'stop' bit which returns the line to the **high** state. Every asynchronous character block is encoded in this format.

The UART is a dedicated large-scale integrated circuit and Fig. 22.30 shows the essential component blocks. The rate at which data is processed must be maintained accurately and this is achieved by the use of a clock oscillator in the 'Receiver Timing and Control' section which during reception is enabled and inhibited by the 'start' and 'stop' bits. During transmission the 'Transmitter Timing and Control' determines the data transmission rate and character block organisation. Also included is the essential serial-to-parallel conversion during reception and parallel-to-serial conversion for transmission. The UART may be under the control of the microprocessor which communicates with it via the 'control' input lines and keeps track of the state of data manipulation by the UART via the 'status' line outputs. Through the control line inputs the microprocessor is able to adjust the character length and parity (odd or even) during transmission, to make the character block compatible with the peripheral device.

When many devices are connected to a

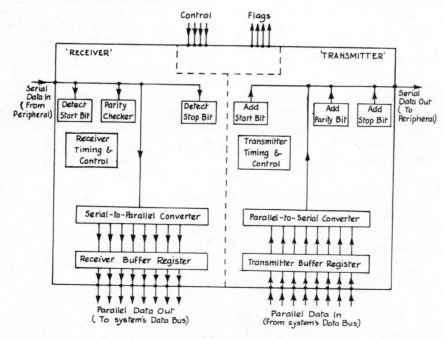

Fig. 22.30 Schematic of UART.

common data bus, they normally communicate with the data bus via 'tristate' buffers to avoid conflict between the various devices. For example, the 'Receiver Buffer Register' of the UART would be connected to the data bus via tristate buffers, see Fig. 22.31. If, say, a logic 1 is applied to the 'enable' terminal of each buffer, the register output is able to drive the data bus at logic 1 or logic 0 level (2-states). On the other hand, if a logic 0 is applied to the enable terminals the buffers are disabled and assume a high impedance state (the third state). Under this condition, the buffer register will neither 'drive' nor 'load' the data bus.

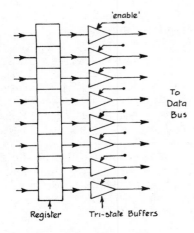

Fig. 22.31 Use of tri-state buffers.

CRYSTAL-CONTROLLED ASTABLE

Astable multivibrators may be used as clock oscillators. Figure 22.32(a) shows a TTL astable multivibrator formed from NAND gates connected as inverters where the frequency of oscillation is controlled by the values of R and C, producing at the output a rectangular pulse train of equal mark-to-space ratio.

Where a precise clock frequency is required, the circuit may include a crystal as shown in Fig. 22.32(b). Here the crystal locks the frequency of oscillation to the series resonant mode of the crystal. This type of circuit is often used to generate the clock waveform for a microprocessor.

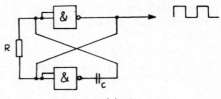

(a) TTL Astable Multivibrator

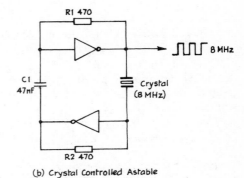

(b) Crystal Controlled Astable

Fig. 22.32 Astable oscillators.

AUTOMATIC RESET

During the execution of a program there may be an equipment power failure, thus it is usual to include a feature known as 'automatic reset' on power-up so that, when power is re-established, the microprocessor commences carrying out the program instructions at the **first** instruction.

One type of reset circuit is shown in Fig. 22.33. When power is applied C1 charges up via R1 producing across C1 a rising voltage. This rise is sensed by the Schmitt trigger and is converted into a clean fast edge when its input level reaches a predetermined value. The

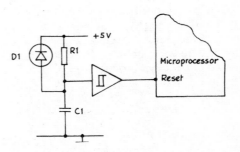

Fig. 22.33 Automatic reset.

output from the Schmitt trigger, after application to the 'Reset' input of the microprocessor, causes the microprocessor to fetch the address of the first instruction from ROM and load it into the program counter. D1 discharges C1 via the +5V power line during power failure or at switch-off so that, when power is re-established, C1 commences to charge up once again.

FAULTS IN MICROPROCESSOR SYSTEMS

Circuit boards used in microprocessor systems are composed predominantly of integrated circuits supported by some discrete components such as capacitors, resistors and transistors.

Typical Faults

Faults that can occur fall into the following categories:

(a) I.C. Failure

An i.c. may fail due to defects in its internal logic circuits or due to an open-circuit or short-circuit of internal connections to the pins of the i.c. Many i.c.s which have been destroyed by overheating show visual signs of being faulty, thus they may be cracked or look burnt. I.C.s that have previously been replaced may have bent or even missing pins. Equipment that has been operated in a damp, dusty or contaminated condition may have corroded i.c. contacts. When there are obvious visual signs of an i.c. being faulty it should be replaced, taking care to ensure that it is fitted the right way round.

(b) Open-circuit Faults

Open-circuit faults are very common. They may be due to 'dry' soldered connections, breaks in the printed circuit, i.c.s making poor contact with their holders or poor contact on circuit-board edge connectors. Such faults may be located by visual inspection with the aid of a magnifying glass or gentle tapping of the circuit board and its i.c.s.

(c) Short-circuit Faults

The most common cause of short-circuits is 'whiskers' formed from strands of wire or solder which bridge adjacent tracks of the printed circuit board or 'blobs' of solder which short together adjacent pins of an i.c. Most microprocessor boards have tracks which are very close together and are easily bridged by whiskers. An effective remedy is to brush the printed circuit with a small brush dipped in alcohol. Visual inspection with the aid of a magnifying glass may help to locate such faults.

(d) Other Faults

These include:
(1) Power supply failures due to an internal fault causing low or zero output voltage. An external circuit fault may cause the fuse to rupture or cause low output voltage due to excessive current flow. Disconnecting the circuit board from the power supply may assist in locating the fault.
(2) Mains-borne interference or other spurious e.m. radiation resulting in voltage spikes, is a major enemy to digital signals leading to the possible corruption of data and sometimes causes a system to 'crash'. Voltage spikes can cause the destruction of i.c.s. Mains-borne interference is normally protected against by r.f. filtering at the mains input.

Aids to Logical Fault Finding

(1) Logic Probes

These hand-held probes (Fig. 22.34) are used normally for static testing of the logic 1 and 0 levels which are indicated usually by red and green l.e.d.s. They give the following indications when the point under test is as stated:

Point under Test at	Indication
Logic 1	Red 'on' and green 'off'
Logic 0	Red 'off' and green 'on'
Floating or Tristate	Red 'off' and green 'off'

The probe may be powered from the circuit under test or from an external power source but in this case the negative line must be commoned with the system's earth.

Fig. 22.34 Logic probe.

Most logic probes also offer some pulse detection by 'pulse stretching' short duration input pulses to about 100ms which is long enough to give a visible indication on the l.e.d.s. The full versatility of a particular probe can be achieved only by studying the manufacturer's instruction sheet.

When checking static logic levels on i.c.s. always check on the actual i.c. pins rather than on printed circuit lines or board connections, to avoid missing o/c lines.

(2) Logic Pulsers

These compact pulse generators are similar in appearance to logic probes. Pulsers normally have tristate output, which means that they can pulse **high** or **low** but present a high impedance when not operating. This feature permits the pulser to be left connected to the circuit under test without loading the line or point to which it is connected.

Pulsers will usually deliver either a single pulse, a group of four pulses or a continuous train of pulses (at about 1kHz). To use the pulser, its tip is connected to the circuit under test and the appropriate pulse option is selected (usually by a slide switch). The pulser then automatically drives the circuits connected to it, producing a brief change in logic state which may be detected by a logic probe or c.r.o.

A pulser output may be used during fault finding to:

(a) Provide slow or fast clocking of a counter, thus replacing its normal clock input.
(b) Provide trigger pulses for monostables or clock pulses for flip-flops.
(c) Check bus and printed circuit lines for continuity, in conjunction with a logic probe.
(d) Check for short-circuits on printed circuit lines, in conjunction with a current probe.

(3) Current Probe

A current probe or tracer is a small pencil-like, hand-held tester with a tip that contains a magnetic field sensor. The tip does not have to touch the point under test as the sensor detects the magnetic field set up by the current flow in the circuit under test. The probe is provided with an indicating l.e.d. and a sensitivity control.

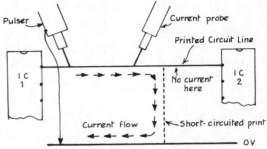

Fig. 22.35 Use of current probe to check for s/c print.

Figure 22.35 shows how a current tracer and logic pulser may be used to check for a short-circuit between printed circuit conductors. With the supplies to the i.c.s switched 'off', the output of the pulser is set to give continuous operation and is applied at the output of IC1. With the current tracer placed close to the pulser, its sensitivity control is adjusted until its l.e.d. just illuminates. The current tracer is then moved to the right towards IC2 until its l.e.d. fails to illuminate, thus pin-pointing the area of the short-circuit.

A current tracer may also be used to investigate open-circuits in printed circuit tracks and components such as resistors and power supply short-circuits, for example a short between $+ V_{cc}$ and earth.

(4) Logic Clips and Monitors

A logic clip (Fig. 22.36) is a device that will clip easily on to a standard dual in-line i.c.

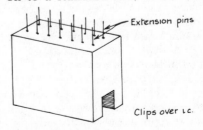

Fig. 22.36 Logic clip.

package to bring out the pins for testing. A logic probe or voltmeter may then be attached to the extended pins for testing, thus reducing the risk of accidental shorting-out of pins. Logic clips with 16, 28 or 40 pins are usually available.

A logic monitor (Fig. 22.37) is a device which clips on to the i.c. under test to indicate instantly the logic state of each pin by means of l.e.d.s. The monitor derives its power from the i.c. supply regardless of which pins the power is applied to. Logic monitors are most useful for analysing the static logic state of an i.c. or the low-frequency dynamic state. They are usually available to clip on to 14- or 16-pin dual in-line i.c.s.

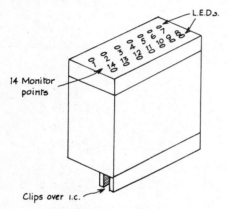

Fig. 22.37 Logic monitor.

(5) *Oscilloscope*

The oscilloscope, although the most useful instrument for general fault-finding on a wide range of traditional analogue and digital equipment is somewhat limited in its usefulness in microprocessor-based systems. One reason for this is that an ordinary c.r.o. is unable to display simultaneously the signals present on an 8-line data bus or a 16-line address bus. Secondly, the signals on these buses are not necessarily of regular content and an ordinary c.r.o., which is designed to display **repetitive** waveforms, would be unable to achieve synchronisation to obtain a meaningful display.

The use of an ordinary c.r.o. is thus confined to the display of the repetitive clock signal pulses, measuring their risetimes or investigating the presence of spurious pulses on d.c. supply lines.

(6) *Logic Analyser*

A logic analyser is a specialised item of test equipment that is designed to record the logic levels at a number of points simultaneously. It will provide more detailed and searching tests on digital circuits and microprocessor circuits in particular, than the test devices previously considered.

Logic analysers are provided typically with 8, 16 or 32 input channels, see Fig. 22.38 (8-channel) which can be used to study the logic signals on the data, address or control bus of a microprocessor system or its input/output ports. The signals applied to the input channels are sampled at specified instants and then stored in the **analyser's memory**. Once in the analyser's memory, the data may be read at leisure over and over again to provide a repetitive and continuous display.

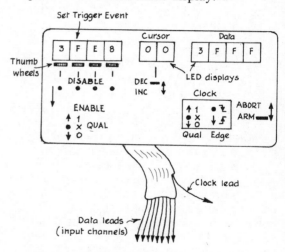

Fig. 22.38 Logic analyser.

Trigger Event. To enable the user to investigate particular areas of a data sequence, all analysers provide a 'trigger' or 'event' selection feature which defines the instant about which data is to be captured by the analyser's memory. The 'trigger event' is a previously defined 'word' or pattern of binary digits which is set by the user prior to commencing the recording process.

Recording commences when the analyser is '**armed**' at which point data applied to the input channels is continuously recorded, that is, written into the analyser's memory. During

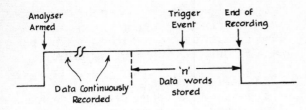

Fig. 22.39 Data recording sequence.

this period, see Fig. 22.39, the data applied is continuously compared with the 'event' data word and when a 'match' occurs the recording process continues for a further number of data words. The number '*n*' of data words stored depends upon the storage capacity of the analyser's memory (typically 128 to 1024 words) and is a form of negative time recording with some data words recorded prior to the trigger event and some after it.

Most analysers permit extra conditions to be placed on the trigger event, the trigger 'qualifier'. This feature allows the user to set the trigger event to occur, say, after '*n*' repetitions of the trigger word or '*n*' clock cycles after it.

Clock and Clock Qualifier. An analyser requires a clock signal to clock the channel data words into its memory. The clocking signal may be provided either from the system under test or from the analyser's own internal clock. When using the system's clock, leading or trailing edge triggering may be selected by the user. The analyser's internal clock which may operate at frequencies several times that of the system's clock is useful for showing up unwanted 'glitches' in the data waveform.

In some circumstances it may not be necessary to store data on all clock cycles. Thus an extra input known as a 'clock qualifier' may be provided to select particular clock edges when data is present. The clock and clock qualifier are ANDed together so that a 'qualified clock signal' is produced, only when the clock qualifier is in the logic 1 state. This permits, for example, the read/write control line of the RAM memory to act as a clock qualifier, so that the analyser monitors the data on the data bus during the read (or write) operation only.

Display Modes. Logic analysers usually permit two main forms of display. One display mode provides a data listing (Fig. 22.40), where each data word sampled on a clock edge is displayed in a suitable code such as binary, hexadecimal or ASCII.

In the example shown, data on the data bus of a microprocessor-based system is listed by

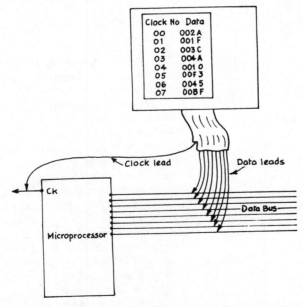

Fig. 22.40 Data listing (Data Domain).

the analyser as the clock cycles develop. To be able to interpret the data, however, the user must know what to expect on the bus for the particular instruction being executed and the point in the program where the instruction appears.

The other main form of display is the data timing display (Fig. 22.41) , where the logic waveforms on each input channel are displayed one under the other, on a c.r.o. that is either external or built into the analyser.

In the example shown, data on the address bus of a microprocessor-based system is displayed as a series of waveforms, one for each channel. A movable cursor is provided so that the component bits of each byte may be studied. This type of display mode is not really suitable for reading the addresses on the address bus; a data-listing display would be more useful. The data-timing display would be more suitable for checking the outputs of a counter, for example.

As for the previous example, in order to be able to interpret the display of addresses the user would need to know the particular addresses and their order in the system's

program. For example, during the execution of a program the program counter may be placing ROM addresses on the address bus but at other times RAM or port addresses.

(7) Signature Analyser

The main disadvantage of a logic analyser for fault-finding in a microprocessor system is the sheer volume of information that the instrument is capable of displaying and the time required by the user to analyse each byte of data, especially since it may be necessary to observe and analyse data flow at several points along the system's buses.

A **signature analyser** (Fig. 22.42), is an instrument that has been specially designed for field service work and allows the user to interpret a complex data pulse train by one simple reading of its unique 'signature'. Unlike the logic analyser, the instrument is provided with only one data probe, a clock probe and additionally stop and start probes.

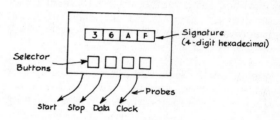

Fig. 22.42 Signature analyser.

The block schematic of Fig. 22.43 illustrates the basic idea behind the operation of a signature analyser. The instrument works synchronously using the **clock signal** from the **system under test** for a period defined by the 'start' and 'stop' pulses. At each clock cycle the signals on the data probe input, which can be connected to any **single** line of the system's buses, are sampled and classified into logic 1 or logic 0 by the threshold detector and then fed to G1. When a stop pulse is applied to the S–R bistable, its Q output goes **high** which allows G1 to operate and for the logic levels from the threshold detector to be applied to the shift register. This is a special type of register using feedback and including a modulo-2 adder.

When a stop pulse is received, the Q output of the bistable is set **low** which disables G1 and prevents further data from entering the shift

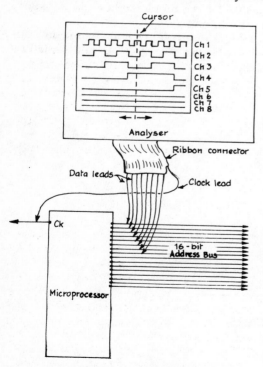

Fig. 22.41 Data timing (Timing Domain).

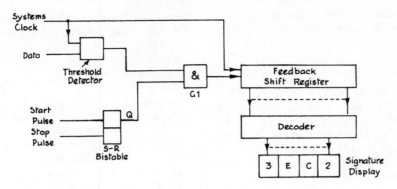

Fig. 22.43 Basic idea of signature analyser.

register. The content of the register is then decoded and fed to the display. The hexadecimal number in the display is the 'signature' of the data that was contained in the shift register.

During fault-finding, the signature analyser is used to check the signatures at various test points or 'nodes' and to compare with those signatures taken at the same point when the equipment was operating correctly. Identical signatures indicate that the data at the test point is correct, whereas different signatures indicate that the data at the test point is incorrect. The success of the method requires a means of generating suitable data pulse trains at the various test points. One way of achieving this is to place the microprocessor in the 'free-run' condition, which causes the addresses on the address bus to cycle continuously through all possible values from 0000 to FFFF (16-bit bus) and to use the most significant address line (A15) as the source of the start and stop signals. Incorrect signatures can then be traced through the system until a correct signature is found, with the point of demarcation indicating possibly a faulty i.c. or open-circuit line.

TEST PROGRAMS

When a microprocessor-based system is operating normally using its working program, the data supplied, for example, to one of its output ports may be present on the data bus for only a few microseconds and the supply of data may occur rather infrequently, say every two minutes. It would be useful during fault-finding if a special test program could be run to execute the supply of data more frequently so that, say, the data could be displayed as a repetitive waveform on a normal c.r.o. Additionally, if special test programs are available, full testing of the address decoder, the operation of the RAM during read and write at every location, the correct addressing of the program ROM and its contents noted during read or aspects of CPU operation could be checked using a logic or signature analyser.

It is standard fault-finding procedure to utilise special test programs that will exercise all parts of a system so that operation can be checked. That programs may be stored in PROM or EPROM and inserted in place of the normal program ROM. Sometimes a spare i.c. socket is provided for this purpose on the system's board. More sophisticated systems may have a test program written into the system's program as a matter of course.

ASSEMBLER INSTRUCTION CATEGORIES

When program instructions are written with the op-code in mnemonic form, the program is said to be written in **assembly** or **assembler language**. In practice the assembler language abbreviations for one type of microprocessor are quite similar to those of another, although the HEX codes may be quite different.

A typical microprocessor may execute a hundred or so different machine instructions and to understand the meaning of each op-code would appear to be a difficult task.

Fortunately, many instructions can be classified as being a member of a particular group or category.

Data Transfer

Instructions in the 'data transfer' category move or transfer data between the various registers within the microprocessor or between the microprocessor and a memory location. Typical data transfer instructions are LOAD and STORE which in mnemonic form for the 6502 microprocessor are written as:

Mnemonic	Meaning
LDA	Load accumulator with memory data
LDX	Load index register X with memory data
LDY	Load index register Y with memory data
STA	Store accumulator data in memory
STX	Store index register X data in memory
STY	Store index register Y data in memory

Arithmetic and Logic

Program instructions in this category manipulate data to perform arithmetic or logic operations on the data which is either in a specified register of the microprocessor or a memory location. Typical instructions in this group are ADD, SUBTRACT, LOGIC AND, LOGIC OR and LOGIC EX-OR which in mnemonic form for the 6502 are written as:

Mnemonic	Meaning
ADC	Add memory data to accumulator with carry
ASL	Shift left one bit (memory or accumulator)
INC	Increment memory by one
DEC	Decrement memory by one
AND	'AND' memory data with accumulator data
ORA	'OR' memory data with accumulator data
EOR	'EX-OR' memory data with accumulator data
SBC	Subtract memory data from accumulator data with borrow

Test and Branch

A programming task that is frequently met with is to perform one of two alternative processing operations depending upon the result of a specified test or comparison. For example, suppose that a microprocessor-based system is used to control the temperature of a heater at a 'set' temperature. We can represent the steps in flow-diagram form as shown:

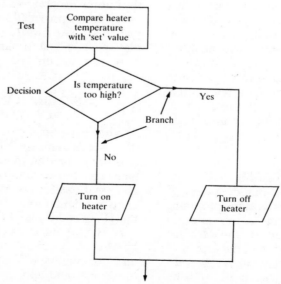

It will be seen that after carrying out a 'test', the microprocessor, through its program instructions has to decide what to do, and 'branch' accordingly.

Typical instruction mnemonics in this category for the 6502 are:

Mnemonic	Meaning
BMI	Branch on result minus
BPL	Branch on result plus
BNE	Branch on result not zero
BEQ	Branch on result zero
BCC	Branch on carry clear
BCS	Branch on carry set

QUESTIONS ON CHAPTER TWENTY TWO

(1) The word length of a microprocessor is limited to:
(a) 4 bits
(b) Any number of bits
(c) 16 bits
(d) 8 bits.

(2) A 16-bit data word is capable of providing a maximum of:
(a) 256 codes
(b) 16 codes
(c) 15 codes
(d) 65536 codes.

(3) Each program memory instruction in a microprocessor based system can consist of:
(a) An OP-code and an OPERAND
(b) An OPERAND and a BCD code
(c) An OP-code and a MACHINE code
(d) An OPERAND and a FETCH code.

(4) The results of operations carried out by the ALU are stored in:
(a) The status register
(b) The address register
(c) The accumulator
(d) The instructions register.

(5) A line carrying a $\overline{\text{Write}}$ signal will be found on:
(a) The data bus
(b) The control bus
(c) The program ROM
(d) The address bus.

(6) Parity bit insertion, prior to data transmission, is carried out by the:
(a) PIO
(b) CPU
(c) UART
(d) CRTC.

(7) Which of the following does NOT have two-way data flow:
(a) ROM
(b) RAM
(c) PIO
(d) CPU.

(8) When executing an instruction, the function of the program counter in a microprocessor is to:
(a) Hold the address of the next unused location in RAM
(b) Hold the address of the next unused location in ROM
(c) Hold the memory address of the next instruction to be executed
(d) Count the number of times the program is executed.

(9) Into which category does the assembler instruction ADDA 36 fit:
(a) Test and Branch
(b) Arithmetic and Logic
(c) Jump
(d) Data transfer.

(10) In the high impedance condition, the output of a data bus tri-state buffer should be:
(a) At or near the logic 1 level
(b) At or near the logic 0 level
(c) Between logic 0 and logic 1 levels
(d) Able to assume the level of the bus line.

(Answers on page 370)

CHAPTER TWENTY THREE

POWER CONTROL

Objectives

1 To explain the use of the SCR in a.c. and d.c. power control.
2 To explain the operation of inverter power supplies.
3 To consider the use and charging of batteries in portable equipment.

THERE ARE MANY instances in industrial electronics where it is desirable to control the amount of a.c. or d.c. power fed to equipment. Examples include the control of power supplied to lighting and heater circuits and the speed control of a.c. and d.c. motors. For the smooth control of power, modern controllers make use of the **thyristor** (SCR) and the **triac**, the characteristics of which were considered in Chapter 6.

A.C. CONTROL

It will be recalled that when the anode voltage of an SCR is made sufficiently positive with respect to the cathode, the SCR comes 'on' and the current in the device rises to a large value, being limited only by external circuit resistance (Fig. 23.1), for $I_g = 0$. Normally the SCR is turned 'on' by supplying the control gate with current and only a short pulse of current is required. Once the SCR has

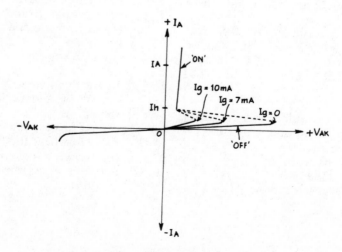

Fig. 23.1 SCR Characteristic.

'fired' the gate supply may be removed and the device will remain in the 'on' state. To switch the SCR 'off' it is necessary to reduce or remove the anode voltage so that the current falls below the holding value I_h.

The average a.c. power supplied to a load may be controlled using either **phase control** or **burst firing**. Phase control consists of controlling the period during each cycle of the a.c. supply that the supply current is allowed to flow in the load. Burst firing entails allowing current to flow in the load for a whole number of input cycles over a given time interval.

Half-Wave Circuit

Figure 6.2 illustrates the basic ideas behind the control of a.c. power to a load using phase control. The SCR selected for use in the circuit of Fig. 23.2(a) will have a forward breakdown voltage in excess of the peak a.c. input voltage so that it only comes 'on' when a trigger pulse is applied to the gate of the device. As the input is a.c. the SCR can conduct only during the positive half-cycles when the anode is positive with respect to the cathode (half-wave circuit).

If the phase of the trigger pulses are slightly delayed on the start of the positive half-cycles of the input voltage the SCR will not fire until, say, instants X. Current will commence to flow in the load at these points and continue until instants Y, when the anode voltage has reduced to zero thereby permitting the current in the SCR to fall below the holding level I_h. Note from the waveform of Fig. 23.2(b) that there is no current in the load prior to instant X, nor is there any voltage across the load, the input voltage being effectively across the SCR during this period. It will be seen that the

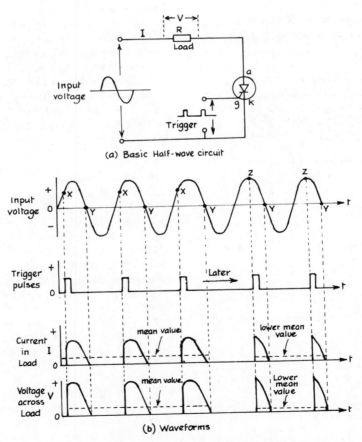

(a) Basic Half-wave circuit

(b) Waveforms

Fig. 23.2 Use of SCR to control power in load using phase control.

current in the load and the voltage across it are in the form of **unidirectional** pulses and the power in the load is given by the product of the mean values of current and voltage.

If the commencement of the trigger pulses is delayed further into the start of the positive half cycles of the input, so that the SCR does not fire until instants Z, current will flow in the load for a shorter period of each input cycle as shown. This will result in lower mean values of current and voltage and less power developed in the load. Thus, by gradually retarding or advancing the phase of the trigger pulses, smooth control over the power supplied to the load may be achieved.

Although the current in the load is pulsating, the thermal inertia of a lamp load or the mechanical inertia of a motor load will smooth out the effect of the pulsations.

Effect of Inductive Load

When the load in an SCR power control circuit contains inductance as in Fig. 23.3(a),

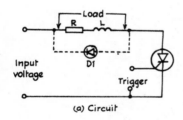

(a) Circuit

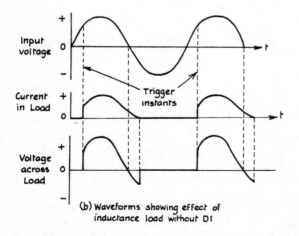

(b) Waveforms showing effect of inductance load without D1

Fig. 23.3 Inductive load and use of flywheel diode.

the current flowing in the load does not fall to zero at the instant the supply voltage passes through zero into a negative half-cycle. The effect is shown in the waveforms of Fig. 23.3(b). As soon as the load current commences to fall, an e.m.f. is induced into the inductance L with a polarity that tends to maintain the flow of current (Lenz's Law). The current in the load falls at a slower rate than the fall of the input voltage until it becomes less than the holding value, when the SCR switches 'off'. Due to the voltage induced into L, the voltage across the load exhibits negative-going blips.

Thus when inductance is present in the load it reduces the time available each cycle for the SCR to recover from the 'on' condition, the effect becoming more pronounced as the ratio of L/R increases.

To prevent current flowing in the load during the negative half-cycles of the supply, a **flywheel diode** D1 is connected across the load as shown. During the positive half-cycles of the input, D1 is reverse biased and thus non-conducting. As soon as the voltage across the load tries to reverse, D1 becomes conductive and provides a low resistance path for the inductive current, allowing the SCR to switch 'off'. The load voltage will in fact reverse by an amount equal to the forward voltage drop of D1.

Full-Wave Control

One method of achieving full-wave power control is shown in Fig. 23.4(a), where two SCRs are connected in inverse parallel. SCR1 is able to conduct when terminal A is positive with respect to terminal B on positive half-cycles of the input, while SCR2 can be made to conduct when terminal A is negative w.r.t. terminal B on the negative half-cycles of the input.

It will be seen from the waveforms of Fig. 23.4(b) that the timing of the trigger pulses will cause SCR1 to come 'on' at points X during the positive half-cycles and for SCR2 to come 'on' at points Z during the negative half-cycles of the input. SCR1 will switch 'off' at points W and SCR2 will switch 'off' at points Y as the input voltage falls to zero each half cycle. Thus SCR1 and SCR2 alternatively provide the load current but the contribution

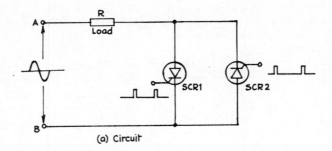

(a) Circuit

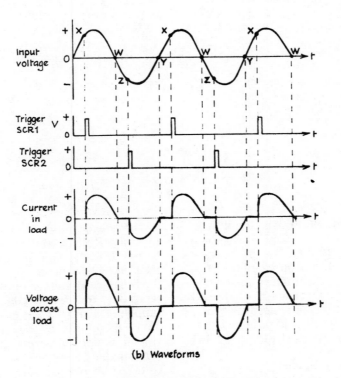

(b) Waveforms

Fig. 23.4 Full-wave power control.

of one is in the opposite direction to the other, i.e. the load current is a.c. The power developed in the load is the product of the r.m.s. values of load current and load voltage. By gradually altering the phase of the trigger pulses with respect to the start of each half-cycle, the power supplied to the load may be varied smoothly.

Note that the applied trigger pulses are positive w.r.t. to the cathode of the SCR thus separate trigger sources would be required since the cathodes of SCR1 and SCR2 are connected to different sides of the supply voltage rail. One can recognise from this circuit the difficulty in isolating the trigger source from the a.c. supply voltage and one possible solution is to use an opto-coupler.

An alternative way of achieving full-wave

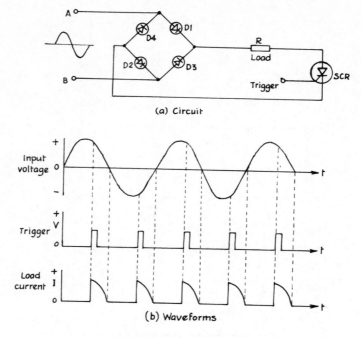

(a) Circuit

(b) Waveforms

Fig. 23.5 Full-wave bridge control.

control is to use a diode bridge circuit as in Fig. 23.5 which requires only one SCR. When A is positive w.r.t. B, say, on the positive half-cycles of the input, the anode of the SCR is positive w.r.t. its cathode and when triggered diodes D1, D2 and the SCR will conduct. Similarly, when A is negative w.r.t. B, the anode of the SCR is still positive w.r.t. its cathode and when triggered, diodes D3, D4 and the SCR will conduct.

Thus current flows in the load during each half-cycle of the input voltage but is uni-directional in the load. The SCR will automatically revert to the 'off' condition each half cycle as the input falls to zero. The waveform of voltage across the load is of the same shape as the current waveform. Again, by varying the trigger instant the mean power supplied to the load can be controlled.

Another full-wave controller is shown in Fig. 23.6(b) featuring a triac instead of an SCR. A triac can be made to conduct when T2 is positive w.r.t. T1 or when T2 is negative w.r.t. T1, see characteristic of Fig. 23.6(a). Thus the triac can be used to supply current to the load on each half-cycle of the input.

The trigger pulses for the triac are derived from a *CR* phase-shifting network. On each half-cycle of the input C1 is charged via R1 and RV1 and when the voltage across C1 exceeds the break-over voltage of the diac (about 30V typically), the diac conducts briefly thereby supplying a trigger pulse to the triac which 'fires'. As soon as the triac conducts the supply voltage is applied across the load. The triac will remain in the 'on' state until the input voltage falls back to zero on each half-cycle, see waveforms of Fig. 23.6(c).

The instant that the triac 'fires' depends upon the phase shift introduced by the *CR* network and its attenuation. For example, with RV1 set to minimum resistance, the phase shift and the attenuation is small so that the diac conducts very early on during each half cycle and the voltage across C1 very nearly follows the input, resulting in almost full power being applied to the load. On the other hand, with RV1 set to maximum resistance, the phase shift is almost 90° but, due to the higher attenuation of the network, the triac firing may be delayed up to about 170° as the voltage across C1 rises towards the 30V

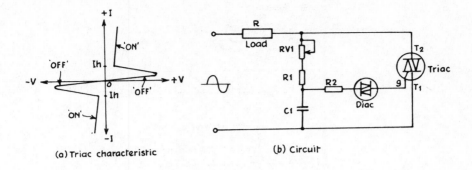

(a) Triac characteristic

(b) Circuit

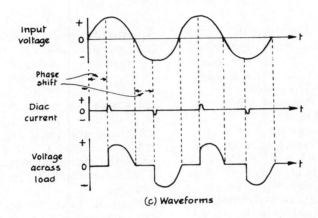

(c) Waveforms

Fig. 23.6 Full-wave controller using Triac.

break-over voltage. Thus under this condition the triac will conduct for only about 10° each half-cycle, resulting in very much reduced power to the load. Therefore, by adjusting RV1, smooth control over the power to the load may be achieved. This type of circuit arrangement is suitable for use as a lamp dimmer or for motor speed control.

D.C. CONTROL

There are many applications which require the control of the amount of power fed to a load from a **d.c. voltage source**, from either a rectifier unit or a battery. This occurs particularly in the control of d.c. motors used in pump, fan and conveyor-belt applications, as well as in trolley buses, trains and mine hoists.

When a thyristor is used in a.c. power control the current in the thyristor is reduced to zero by the reversing nature of the a.c. input voltage as it passes through the zero datum line. This method of turning-off a thyristor is called **natural commutation**. In d.c. power control the source voltage remains steady, thus to turn-off a thyristor an external circuit is required to reduce the thyristor current to zero; this is referred to as **forced commutation**.

One method of achieving forced commutation is to switch a charged capacitor in parallel with the control thyristor so that the capacitor applies a reverse voltage across the thyristor, thereby reducing the thyristor current to below its holding level. This idea is used in the circuit arrangement of Fig. 23.7 where the current in the load is controlled by the main

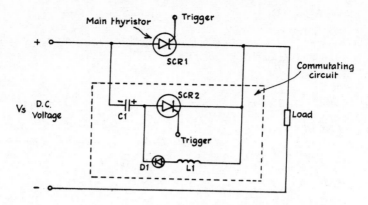

Fig. 23.7 Use of commutating capacitor.

thyristor SCR1. The auxiliary thyristor SCR2 is used to switch the commutating capacitor $C1$ in parallel with SCR1 at the appropriate instant. D1 is used for charging $C1$ with reverse voltage via $L1$. The operation of the circuit will now be described using the simplified diagrams of Fig. 23.8.

Assume that $C1$ is charged with polarity as shown in Fig. 23.7 and that a trigger pulse has just been applied to SCR1, turning it 'on'. At this time SCR2 is 'off' and D1 is also 'off', thus the circuit is as in Fig. 23.8(a) where a current I flows in the load. After a period depending upon the amount of power to be fed to the load, a trigger pulse is applied to SCR2 turning it 'on'. This action effectively places $C1$ in parallel with the main thyrsitor SCR1, as in Fig. 23.8(b). The reverse voltage from $C1$ causes a current I_c to flow in SCR1 as the

capacitor discharges. Note, however, that I_c is in the opposite direction to I in SCR1, causing the current in SCR1 to reduce to zero and for the thyristor to switch-off.

At the instant SCR1 switches-off, SCR2 is still conducting, thus the circuit is as in Fig. 23.8(c). $C1$ now charges towards V_s via SCR2 and the load, causing a voltage to build-up across $C1$ with polarity as shown. When the charging current reduces to zero SCR2 switches-off. The current in the load is then zero.

When the next gating pulse is applied to SCR1 causing it to turn 'on', a voltage is established across the load once again (Fig. 23.8(d)). This action causes D1 to conduct and for the voltage across $C1$ to reverse direction as it charges via $L1$. The polarity of the voltage across $C1$ is then in its

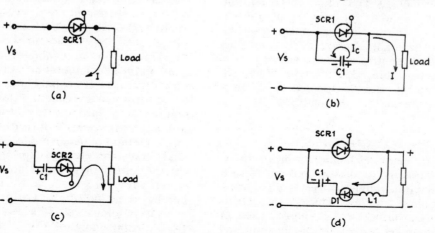

Fig. 23.8 Diagrams explaining operation of circuit of Fig. 23.7.

original state and the circuit is ready for the next commutation sequence when SCR2 is gated 'on'.

In summary it will be seen that SCR1 (the main thyristor) is turned 'on' regularly by trigger pulses applied to its gate, causing the d.c. supply voltage to be applied across the load. The commutating circuit simply provides a means of switching-off SCR1, causing the load voltage to reduce to zero. By varying the 'on' to 'off' time of SCR1, the amount of d.c. power supplied to the load can be controlled.

When the load is inductive a flywheel diode is connected across the load as in Fig. 23.9 to permit the turn-off process of SCR1 to be unhindered by the load inductance. Alternative methods of achieving commutation with a d.c. supply include the use of pulse transformers or resonant circuits.

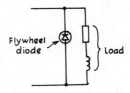

Fig. 23.9 Flywheel diode required for inductive load.

INVERTER POWER SUPPLIES

An inverter power supply is a power unit that produces an **a.c. output power from a d.c. input**. The frequency of the a.c. output may be 50Hz but is commonly 400Hz or higher. The d.c. input source is usually a battery system. Inverter power supplies are used for the following main reasons:

(1) There are many instances where batteries are the only source of power, such as in cars, vans and submarines, whereas the equipment or instruments to be operated are designed to be powered from a.c. supplies.
(2) Standby supplies obtained from batteries are essential for certain critical or life-support apparatus in the event of an interruption in the a.c. mains supply. Examples include lighting in hospital operating theatres, sophisticated instruments in airport control centres and the storage and processing of data in mainframe computers.

Block Schematic

The essentials of a fixed frequency thyristor inverter are shown in block schematic form in Fig. 23.10. The thyristor inverter stage converts the d.c. input into an a.c. output by the sequential switching of a number of thyristors. As the magnitude of the a.c. output from the inverter stage is limited to the d.c. input (say, 12 or 24V), a transformer is used to increase the a.c. to a higher value to operate the equipment which forms the inverter load. Because the a.c. output waveform of the inverter stage is rich in harmonic content whereas the load usually requires a sinewave supply, a filter is used at the transformer output.

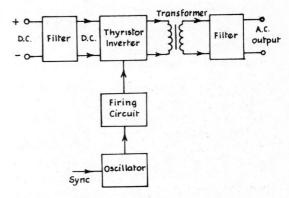

Fig. 23.10 Block diagram showing essentials of a fixed frequency thyristor inverter.

The frequency of the a.c. output is determined by the oscillator which may be voltage controlled or fixed in frequency using highly accurate crystal control. Additionally the oscillator may have a synchronising facility so that it may be synchronised to other a.c. supplies. The firing circuit is responsible for generating the firing pulses for the inverter in the correct sequence and will normally incorporate pulse amplifiers in addition to the firing pattern generator. An input battery filter is used to remove the high switching currents of the inverter from the battery to improve its storage capacity and life.

Basic Inverter Circuits

The circuit of Fig. 23.11 shows the basic principle involved in inverter switching. Thyristors S1 and S2 act simply as switches and are

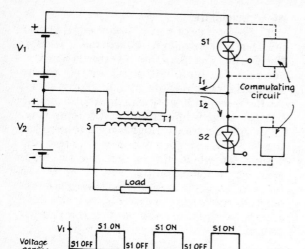

Fig. 23.11 Basic principle of inverter.

switched 'on' alternatively by trigger pulses applied to their respective gates. As the input to each thyristor is d.c. there is no natural commutation, thus in order to switch each thyristor 'off' an external forced commutating circuit has to be used. These circuits may utilise commutating capacitors as described previously.

When S1 is 'on' (S2 'off') a current I_1 flows in the primary of T1 and the supply voltage $V1$ is developed across the primary winding. When S2 is 'on' (S1 'off') a current I_2 flows in T1 primary but in the opposite direction to I_1 and the supply voltage $V2$ is developed across the primary winding. Thus an alternating rectangular voltage is developed across T1 primary having a peak amplitude equal to $V1$ or $V2$ ($V1 = V2$). The transformer will step-up this voltage to the value required by the equipment load.

Bridge circuits may also be used for inverters and the basic principle is illustrated in Fig. 23.12. Again, since the input is d.c. an external commutating circuit is needed for each thyristor to switch it 'off'. Unlike the previous circuit a split d.c. supply is not required.

In the bridge circuit the thyristors are triggered 'on' in pairs. S1 and S4 are 'fired' together as are S2 and S3 with each pair triggered alternatively. With S1 and S4 triggered 'on' (S2 and S3 'off') a current I_1 will flow in the primary winding of T1 and the d.c. supply voltage $V1$ will be developed across T1 primary. When S2 and S3 are 'fired' (S1 and S4 'off') a current I_2 flows in the primary and the d.c. supply voltage will again be developed across the primary winding but with opposite

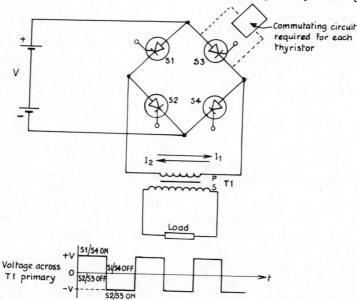

Fig. 23.12 Basic principle of bridge inverter.

polarity. Thus an a.c. rectangular voltage will appear across T1 primary and this may be stepped-up to feed the secondary load.

BATTERIES IN PORTABLE EQUIPMENT

Nickel–cadmium (Ni–Cd) rechargeable cells and batteries are used commonly as the power source in a wide variety of portable equipment, including calibration instruments, gas-detection instruments, distance-measuring devices, portable computers, data-logging instruments, electrical instruments and bar-code readers.

Essentially Ni–Cd cells comprise positive and negative plates, separator and electrolyte. In the discharged state, nickel hydroxide is the positive active material and cadmium hydroxide the negative active material. The electrolyte which is normally an aqueous solution of potassium hydroxide does not show any significant change in specific gravity during charge and discharge, i.e. it does not participate in the overall electrochemical reactions but permits ion transfer.

Ni–Cd cells have a nominal voltage of 1·2V but the actual basic e.m.f. is always between 1·25V and 1·3V. The Ni–Cd cells and batteries used in portable equipment are normally of the **sealed** type; some sealed types are fitted with a self-resealing safety valve. These cells require no maintenance and are designed to operate in normal conditions without the release of gas external to the container. Sealed cells and batteries are available with capacities of 100mAh to 10Ah and voltages from 1·2V (single cell) to 12V (ten cells).

Cell Capacity

The capacity (C) of a cell or battery is given in ampere hours (Ah) and is the product of the discharge current and time. The **rated capacity** is specified generally for discharge times of 5 hours (C_5), 10 hours (C_{10}) or 20 hours (C_{20}). For example, a 1·2V Ni–Cd cell of rated capacity C_5 4·5Ah will discharge for 5 hours at 0·9A. The same cell for a discharge time of 10 hours (C_{10}) will discharge for 10 hours at 450mA. The curves of Fig. 23.13 show typical discharge characteristics.

The rated capacity is used also to express a charge or discharge current. For example, if a battery of rated capacity 4Ah is charged at $0·1C_5$A, the charging current will be

$$0·1 \times \frac{4}{5} \text{ A} = 0·08\text{A}.$$

The same battery charged at $2C_5$A will have a charging current of

$$2 \times \frac{4}{5} \text{ A} = 1·6\text{A}.$$

Battery Charging

In selecting the correct charging method for sealed Ni–Cd cells and batteries it is important to consider the characteristics of cell voltage, temperature and pressure (Fig. 23.14). In the interest of safety and reliability it is recommended that Ni–Cd sealed cells are charged from a **constant-current** source. The maximum charging current to be applied to a cell is determined by its ability to accept this current on overcharge. Maximum charge currents

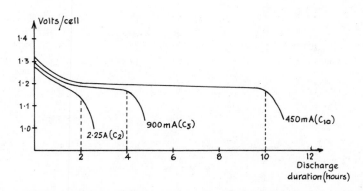

Fig. 23.13 Discharge characteristics of 1·2V Ni-Cd cell with capacity of 4·5Ah.

differ from one type of cell to another and may be different for various sizes of the same type.

The cell voltage characteristic of Fig. 23.14(a) shows how the cell voltage varies during charge and overcharge for normal charge ($0 \cdot 1 C_5 A$ for 16 hours) and rapid charge ($2 C_5 A$ for less than 1 hour). As full charge is reached the cell voltage rises, then the rise of temperature on overcharge has the effect of reducing it. The fall in voltage on overcharge is important since if the applied charger voltage is too high thermal runaway may occur – a cummulative condition in which temperature rise can cause the charging current to increase. It is therefore recommended that **the voltage applied to each cell is limited to 1·55V**, a voltage that will avoid risk of over-pressure.

The internal pressure of a cell on charge is very low during the greater part of the charge (Fig. 23.14(b)) and then rises as full charge is reached. The pressure then comes to a state of equilibrium (normal-charge curve) when the rates of production and consumption of oxygen are equal. The pressure also increases as the charge rate increases (rapid-charge curve) and falls when the temperature increases and is different for each type of Ni–Cd cell. The equilibrium pressure which is settled by the charge rate and the maximum period of charge must be lower than that which will deform the cell container or less than the release pressure of the safety valve (when fitted).

Temperature is practically constant during the greater part of the charge (Fig. 23.14(c)). It rises when the fully charged state is reached and when overcharge commences. The temperature stabilises at a level which depends upon the rate of charge and the thermal exchange characteristics of the cell. In general this temperature should not exceed +50°C. When the temperature of a battery is less than

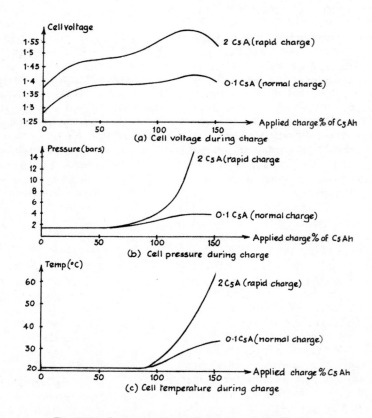

Fig. 23.14 Charging characteristics of sealed cells.

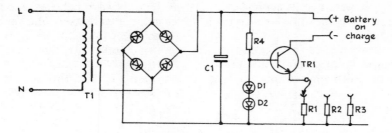

Fig. 23.15 Basic constant current charger.

+5°C it is necessary to limit the charge and overcharge current as the rate of oxygen recombination within the cell lessens and the cell internal pressure rises.

In summary the recommended method for the charging of Ni–Cd sealed cells is:

(a) Charge at a constant current using the manufacturer's recommended normal charge rate.
(b) Ensure that the voltage applied to each cell is limited to 1·55V which will avoid all risk of internal over-pressure at low temperature.

Constant-Current Charger

A basic constant-current charger circuit is given in Fig. 23.15. The mains supply is stepped-down by T1, full-wave rectified and smoothed by C1. For a nominal 6V Ni–Cd battery the d.c. voltage across C1 should be 9·35V. Diodes D1 and D2 provide a constant forward bias for TR1 of 1·2V, thus at TR1 emitter there will be 0·6V. The value of the emitter resistor $R1$ will determine the constant current in TR1; for example, with $R1 = 10\Omega$ the value of the emitter current will be 60mA. If the h_{FE} of the transistor is large the collector current will be practically equal to this value. By varying the value of the emitter resistor, the magnitude of the charging current may be altered.

A 6V Ni–Cd battery will have five cells (1·2V each), thus the maximum voltage across the battery must be limited to $5 \times 1·55V = 7·75V$. There will be about 1V across the transistor as the battery approaches full charge and 0·6V across the emitter resistor giving a total of $7·75 + 1 + 0·6 = 9·35V$ (the supply voltage). Any number of Ni–Cd cells may be connected in series for charging in a

circuit using the above principle. Parallel connection of cells during charge (or discharge) is not recommended. Sealed types may be paralleled only under specific circumstances and normally require diode isolation.

Note: Ni–Cd cells have a very low internal resistance (milli-ohms) thus, if they are accidently short-circuited the high current flowing presents a fire hazard, or a burn risk if the wires are touched.

QUESTIONS ON CHAPTER TWENTY THREE

(1) Refer to Fig. 23.5.
   If the trigger pulses occur later in each half-cycle, the result will be:
   (a) The mean value of current in the load will be less
   (b) The mean value of current in the load will be greater
   (c) The pulsation frequency will increase
   (d) The SCR will be unable to switch 'off'.

(2) Refer to Fig. 23.7.
   When a trigger pulse is applied to SCR2, the essential action is:
   (a) SCR1 passes a larger current into the load
   (b) SCR1 switches 'off'
   (c) D1 conducts
   (d) SCR2 switches 'off'.

(3) The output of an inverter power supply is commonly:
   (a) A sine-wave at a frequency of 400Hz
   (b) 12V d.c.

Electronics Servicing Volume 2

(c) A square wave at a frequency of about 5Hz

(d) 100V d.c.

(4) The maximum voltage applied to a Ni–Cd cell should be limited to:
(a) 2·5V
(b) 20mV
(c) 1·55V
(d) 12V.

(5) If a Ni–Cd battery rated at 4Ah is charged at $0·2C_5A$, the charging current will be:
(a) 0·16A
(b) 0·8A
(c) 8A
(d) 16A.

(Answers on page 370)

CHAPTER TWENTY FOUR

TRANSDUCERS

Objectives
1 To state the purpose of transducers in electronic circuits.
2 To describe typical transducer components.

TRANSDUCERS ARE USED in electronic systems such as industrial process control, audio equipment and scientific and engineering experiments to collect or present physical information in suitable form. In the strict sense of the word a **transducer** is defined as a device that converts variations of one quantity into those of another quantity. **In electronic terms, however, a transducer is usually taken to be a device that converts a non-electrical physical quantity such as flow rate, temperature, pressure, speed or acceleration etc (known as the measurand) into an electrical signal or vice versa**, but there are exceptions to this rule.

Thus, for example, a microphone is a transducer that is used to convert variations in sound wave pressure into an electrical signal (**input transducer**) which may be supplied to the input of an audio amplifier. After amplification, the electrical output of the amplifier may be fed to a loudspeaker to convert the electrical signal back into variations of air pressure to set up a sound wave (**output transducer**). Some typical transducers will now be described.

Photocell, L.E.D. and Optocoupler

A phototransistor, see Fig. 24.1(a), is an **input transducer** which converts variations in light intensity into an electrical signal at its output. When light with sufficient energy falls on the base region of the transistor through its

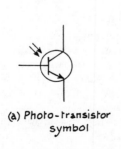

(a) Photo-transistor symbol

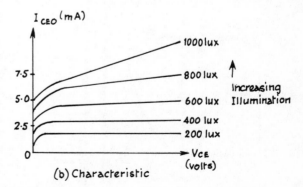

(b) Characteristic

Fig. 24.1 Phototransistor.

'window', electron-hole pairs are generated due to the breaking of covalent links. Under the application of collector-to-emitter voltage, the electron-hole pairs will produce a flow of current in the transistor.

The characteristics of a typical phototransistor are shown in Fig. 24.1(b). It will be seen that they are similar to an ordinary transistor but with the base current replaced by the parameter of illumination; increases in illumination causing corresponding increases in collector current which forms the output signal of the device.

Phototransistors which find applications in flame detectors, alarms, optocouplers and shaft encoders are available in a large variety of forms. In addition to the window through which the incident light passes, some types are fitted with an integral lens to focus the light and improve the sensitivity.

A light emitting diode has already been described in Chapter 6, but its symbol and V/I characteristics are repeated in Fig. 24.2. The l.e.d. is an **output transducer** converting variations of electrical signal voltage into variations in light output. Under forward bias conditions, an l.e.d. will commence to emit light when the forward voltage drop is about 1·5V. L.E.Ds. are made from crystalline gallium arsenide phosphide which can be manufactured to emit light in the red, green, yellow or infra-red parts of the e.m. spectrum.

Light emitting diodes are normally used under pulsed conditions and find applications in seven segment displays, tuning indicators and as light transmitters in remote control transmitters and in fibre optic cable systems for data transmission.

An optocoupler consists of a light emitting diode and a phototransistor placed close together and facing each other in a single package so that they have good optical coupling as in Fig. 24.3. Between them is placed a thin layer of plastic which provides electrical isolation between the input and output of the whole device.

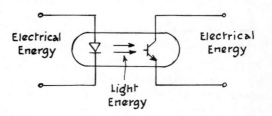

Fig. 24.3 Optocoupler.

Optocouplers are not transducers in the ordinary sense since both input and output are electrical signals. However, they do 'transduce', in this case electrical energy-light energy-electrical energy. Their main use is in providing coupling between electrical circuits on either side of the device which may be at quite different circuit potentials, using light as the coupling medium. They offer a high degree of electrical insulation, typically 3kV. Only a small direct capacitance exists between input and output, typically 0·5 pF.

The light source may be modulated by varying the forward voltage applied to the l.e.d. A variation of the optocoupler package is to use a separate light source and detector connected by fibre-optic cable, allowing large separation up to several kilometres, which may form the basis of a communication link which is not susceptible to electrical interference.

Their main use lies in interfacing applications particularly in logic circuit interfacing and the blocking of mains voltages from thyristor trigger circuits.

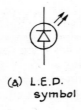

(a) L.E.D. symbol

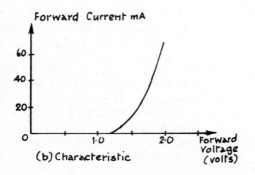

(b) Characteristic

Fig. 24.2 L.E.D.

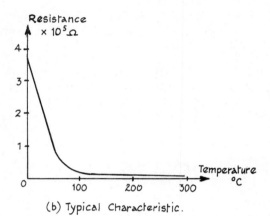

(a) Symbol

(b) Typical Characteristic.

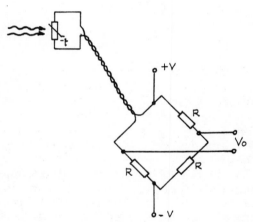

(c) Transistor included in Bridge Circuit

Fig. 24.4 Thermistor.

Thermistor and Thermocouple

Thermistors and thermocouples are **input transducers** that are used to convert temperature variations into an electrical quantity.

Thermistors are **thermally sensitive resistors** formed from semiconductor oxides. They are made in the form of small beads, discs or flakes and are usually encapsulated in vitreous enamel, plastic or glass. They are characte-

rised by a resistance that falls in a non-linear manner with an increase in temperature, see Fig. 24.4(b). Thermistors are of low cost and have the highest sensitivity of the common thermal sensors; over a particular temperature range the resistance falls rapidly with temperature. They are manufactured in a range of values from tens of ohms to hundreds of kilohms at 25°C and can provide a usable output over a wide temperature range of about −100°C to +450°C.

The main application for thermistor sensors is in temperature measurement. They are usually operated in bridge circuits where the changes in resistance with temperature produces a detectable output voltage as the bridge circuit is taken out of balance. An example is given in Fig. 24.4(c) where the thermistor is included in one arm of the bridge with ordinary resistors placed in the other three arms. The bridge is supplied with a constant voltage supply that may be either d.c. or a.c. If the values of the resistors(R) is made the same as the thermistor resistance at, say, 20°C, the bridge will be balanced at this temperature and there will be zero output from the bridge. As the temperature of thermistor sensor is caused to rise, the resistance of the thermistor will fall taking the bridge out of balance thereby producing an output voltage V_o. To improve the sensitivity, the bridge output may be fed to an OP-AMP the output of which may be used to operate a voltmeter that may be calibrated in temperature units.

A thermocouple uses a different principle which is illustrated in Fig. 24.5. In a length of metal the free electrons are uniformly distributed and move at random, see Fig. 24.5(a). If one end of the length of metal is heated as in Fig. 24.5(b) the electron movement at that end will be more energetic resulting in a net difference in the number of electrons at each end. The reduction in electron density at the heated end produces a potential difference between it and the cooler region, i.e. the thermal gradient across the metal gives rise to a potential gradient. The magnitude of the p.d. is proportional to the temperature difference and a coefficient (Thomson coefficient) of value depending upon the metal used.

As different metals have different coefficients, a current can be made to flow in a closed loop of dissimilar metals as in

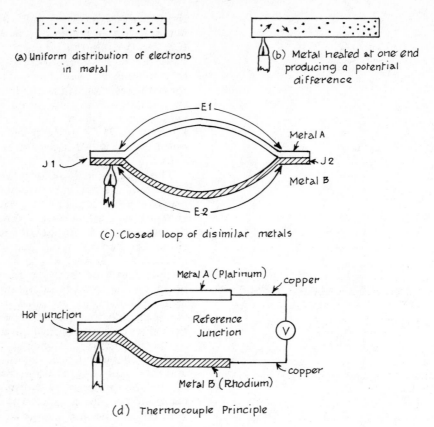

(a) Uniform distribution of electrons in metal

(b) Metal heated at one end producing a potential difference

(c) Closed loop of disimilar metals

(d) Thermocouple Principle

Fig. 24.5 Thermocouple principle.

Fig. 24.5(c) if the two junctions are at **different temperatures**. When J1 is heated there will be a p.d. E1 in metal A and a p.d. E2 in metal B but with different coefficients for the two metals, the p.ds. will be unequal, resulting in a net p.d. which will support current flow in the closed loop.

A thermocouple consists of the arrangement given in Fig. 24.5(d) and if a high resistance voltmeter is introduced as shown, it will indicate a voltage which depends upon the type of metals used and the difference in temperature between the actual junction and the junction(s) formed by the voltmeter connections. The introduction of a third metal (copper leads of the voltmeter) does not alter the voltage provided both junctions of the third metal are at the same temperature. The junctions formed by the voltmeter connections are referred to as the 'cold' junction and these should be maintained at a constant

temperature, e.g. 0°C. For less accurate measurements they may be left at room temperature.

Thermocouples are mainly used for temperature measurements and find numerous applications in the measurement of oven, furnace, soil, frozen food and liquid temperatures. A thermocouple has a very low internal resistance and a sensitivity typically of the order of $10 \mu V/°C$. Common thermocouple metals include platinum-rhodium, tungsten-rhenium and chromel-alumel.

Microphone and Loudspeaker

A microphone is an **input transducer** used to convert variations of sound air pressure into a varying electrical voltage. There are several different types of microphone available depending upon their method of operation, e.g. carbon, ribbon, crystal, moving-coil and capa-

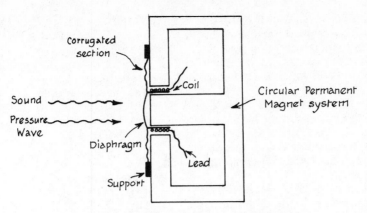

Fig. 24.6 *Principle of moving-coil microphone.*

citor but only the moving-coil type will be described here.

A cross-sectional view of a moving-coil (or 'dynamic') microphone is given in Fig. 24.6. It consists of a circular magnet system with a circular air gap across which is set up a radial magnetic field by the permanent magnet. Into the air gap is fitted a moving coil consisting of a number of turns of wire wound on a light former of parchment type material. Attached to the moving-coil is a diaphragm which may be of aluminium foil or plastic. The diaphragm is held in place by a corrugated section (fitted to suitable supports) which prevents the diaphragm moving radially but allows free movement in the axial direction. A perforated cover is usually placed over the diaphragm to protect against mechanical damage to the diaphragm.

When a sound wave impinges on the diaphragm it causes the coil to move forwards and backwards within the magnetic field of the air gap. In doing so, the coil cuts the magnetic field inducing an e.m.f. into the coil; this is the **generator principle**. During forward movement an e.m.f. of one polarity is obtained but for backward movement the e.m.f. is reversed. Hence an alternating e.m.f. is induced in the coil at the frequency of the sound wave motivating the diaphragm.

The number of turns that can be used in the moving coil is limited by space and the need to keep the mass of the moving parts small. For these reasons the resistance or impedance of the coil is limited to about 25 ohms. Microphones of higher impedance are available but these have built-in step-up transformers

and values of 600 ohms and 50 kilohms are common.

An e.m.f. of a few millivolts is obtainable from this type of microphone but a larger output is available if a step-up transformer is incorporated.

A loudspeaker is an **output transducer** used to convert audio electrical signal power into sound power.

There are a number of different types of loudspeaker but only the **moving coil** type is of importance in modern equipment, see Fig. 24.7. The moving coil loudspeaker uses

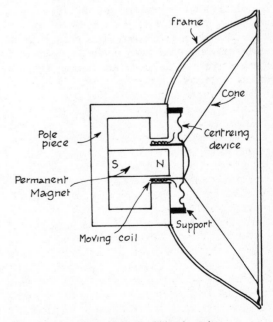

Fig. 24.7 *Moving-coil loudspeaker.*

the **motor principle** in its operation. It consists of a central permanent magnet system with circular pole pieces which set up a radial magnetic field across a narrow air gap. Into the gap is fitted the moving coil which is attached to the cone of the loudspeaker.

When an alternating current is passed through the coil, an alternating force is produced which moves the coil forward and backwards in the air gap (by the motor principle) thus moving the cone and creating sound waves in the air.

The outer edge of the cone is flexibly attached to the frame of the loudspeaker and to ensure that the coil moves in the air gap without touching the pole pieces a centreing device is used. This is corrugated and flexible and allows easy movement in the axial direction only. Flexible connections are made from the moving coil to suitable soldered tags mounted on the loudspeaker frame.

The impedance of the loudspeaker coil is often 4 or 8 ohms but may be higher (25 ohms) in small radio receivers. The d.c. resistance of the coil is rather less than those values. The loudspeaker impedance varies with frequency and the quoted value is about correct at around 1 kHz. In selecting a suitable loudspeaker, not only must its impedance be correct (see Chapter 15) but also its power handling capability. Some small loudspeakers will only handle up to 250 mW of power whereas others can safely deal with 25 W of audio power. Excessive power applied to a loudspeaker can damage the cone or burn out the speech coil.

QUESTIONS ON CHAPTER TWENTY FOUR

(1) Which of the following is an output transducer:
(a) Thermocouple
(b) L.E.D.
(c) Microphone
(d) Solar cell.

(2) Which of the following is an input transducer:
(a) Loudspeaker
(b) L.E.D.
(c) Shaft encoder
(d) Solenoid.

(3) The main use of an Opto-Coupler is in:
(a) Coupling between electrical circuits at different potentials
(b) Changing light of one colour to that of another colour
(c) Converting light energy into electrical energy
(d) Reducing the propagation delay of logic circuits.

(4) The largest e.m.f. will appear across a thermocouple's leads when its 'hot' and 'cold' junctions are at respective temperatures of:
(a) 100°C and 90°C
(b) 100°C and 100°C
(c) 200°C and 100°C
(d) 150°C and 0°C.

(Answers on page 370)

ANSWERS TO QUESTIONS

Chapter 1
No. 1 (d)
    2 (b)
    3 (b)
    4 (b)
    5 (a)
    6 (b)
    7 (a)
    8 (c)

Chapter 2
No. 1 (a)
    2 (d)
    3 (b)
    4 (b)
    5 (d)
    6 (c)
    7 (d)
    8 (c)
    9 (a)
   10 (a)

Chapter 3
No. 1 (b)
    2 (d)
    3 (b)
    4 (a)
    5 (d)
    6 (c)
    7 (b)
    8 (c)
    9 (b)
   10 (d)
   11 (a)
   12 (d)

Chapter 4
No. 1 (a)
    2 (d)
    3 (d)
    4 (c)
    5 (b)
    6 (b)
    7 (c)

Chapter 5
No. 1 (d)
    2 (c)
    3 (c)
    4 (a)
    5 (d)
    6 (a)
    7 (b)
    8 (a)
    9 (b)
   10 (b)

Chapter 6
No. 1 (d)
    2 (a)
    3 (a)
    4 (b)
    5 (b)
    6 (b)
    7 (b)

Chapter 7
No. 1 (d)
    2 (c)
    3 (c)
    4 (b)
    5 (b)
    6 (a)
    7 (a)

Chapter 8
No. 1 (d)
    2 (c)
    3 (a)
    4 (a)
    5 (d)
    6 (b)
    7 (c)
    8 (d)
    9 (b)
   10 (b)
   11 (d)
   12 (b)

Chapter 9
No. 1 (b)
    2 (a)
    3 (b)
    4 (d)
    5 (c)
    6 (b)
    7 (b)
    8 (d)
    9 (c)
   10 (c)
   11 (a)

Chapter 10
No. 1 (b)
    2 (a)
    3 (c)
    4 (d)
    5 (b)

Chapter 11	Chapter 12	Chapter 13	Chapter 14	Chapter 15
No. 1 (c)	No. 1 (a)	No. 1 (c)	No. 1 (c)	No. 1 (b)
2 (a)	2 (d)	2 (b)	2 (a)	2 (d)
3 (d)	3 (c)	3 (a)	3 (a)	3 (c)
4 (c)	4 (a)	4 (d)	4 (b)	4 (d)
5 (a)	5 (b)	5 (a)	5 (c)	5 (d)
6 (b)		6 (b)	6 (a)	6 (b)
7 (d)		7 (c)	7 (c)	7 (d)
8 (d)			8 (c)	8 (d)
9 (d)			9 (a)	9 (b)
10 (a)			10 (c)	10 (c)
11 (a)			11 (c)	11 (c)
12 (d)			12 (a)	12 (d)
			13 (b)	13 (a)
			14 (b)	14 (d)
			15 (c)	15 (b)
				16 (a)

Chapter 16	Chapter 17	Chapter 18	Chapter 19	Chapter 20
No. 1 (d)	No. 1 (d)	No. 1 (d)	No. 1 (d)	No. 1 (d)
2 (a)	2 (b)	2 (b)	2 (b)	2 (b)
3 (d)	3 (a)	3 (a)	3 (a)	3 (c)
4 (b)	4 (c)	4 (c)	4 (c)	4 (b)
5 (c)	5 (d)	5 (c)	5 (a)	5 (b)
6 (b)	6 (a)	6 (c)	6 (d)	6 (c)
7 (a)	7 (b)	7 (c)	7 (b)	7 (a)
8 (b)	8 (b)	8 (a)	8 (a)	8 (d)
9 (a)	9 (d)	9 (d)	9 (d)	9 (d)
10 (c)	10 (a)	10 (b)	10 (c)	10 (a)
	11 (b)			
	12 (c)			

Chapter 21	Chapter 22	Chapter 23	Chapter 24
No. 1 (a)	No. 1 (b)	No. 1 (a)	No. 1 (b)
2 (c)	2 (d)	2 (b)	2 (c)
3 (d)	3 (a)	3 (a)	3 (a)
4 (a)	4 (c)	4 (c)	4 (d)
5 (c)	5 (b)	5 (a)	
	6 (c)		
	7 (a)		
	8 (c)		
	9 (b)		
	10 (d)		

INDEX